# Evolution of Vulne

For uncle Bill

Love,

Dave

**To Yin**

# Evolution of Vulnerability

## Implications for Sex Differences in Health and Development

David C. Geary

AMSTERDAM • BOSTON • HEIDELBERG • LONDON
NEW YORK • OXFORD • PARIS • SAN DIEGO
SAN FRANCISCO • SINGAPORE • SYDNEY • TOKYO
Academic Press is an imprint of Elsevier

Academic Press is an imprint of Elsevier
125 London Wall, London, EC2Y 5AS, UK
525 B Street, Suite 1800, San Diego, CA 92101–4495, USA
225 Wyman Street, Waltham, MA 02451, USA
The Boulevard, Langford Lane, Kidlington, Oxford OX5 1GB, UK

**Notices**

Knowledge and best practice in this field are constantly changing. As new research and experience broaden our understanding, changes in research methods, professional practices, or medical treatment may become necessary.

Practitioners and researchers must always rely on their own experience and knowledge in evaluating and using any information, methods, compounds, or experiments described herein. In using such information or methods they should be mindful of their own safety and the safety of others, including parties for whom they have a professional responsibility.

To the fullest extent of the law, neither the Publisher nor the authors, contributors, or editors, assume any liability for any injury and/or damage to persons or property as a matter of products liability, negligence or otherwise, or from any use or operation of any methods, products, instructions, or ideas contained in the material herein.

**British Library Cataloguing in Publication Data**
A catalogue record for this book is available from the British Library

**Library of Congress Cataloging-in-Publication Data**
A catalog record for this book is available from the Library of Congress

For information on all Academic Press publications
visit our website at http://store.elsevier.com/

Printed in the United Kingdom.
ISBN: 978-0-12-801562-9

# Contents

# Preface

The seeds of this book – that sexual selection can be used to more fully understand sex differences in vulnerability to stressors – were planted during the writing of the first edition of *Male, Female* (Geary, 1998), and fleshed out a bit in the second edition (Geary, 2010). As was the case with *Male, Female* and the other books I have written, I thought about the concept and how to approach this book for several years; of course, I also managed to get a few others things done in the meantime. Although my primary interests are with human vulnerabilities, I decided that it was important to conduct an extensive review of condition-dependent traits in nonhuman species. These reflect an individual's level of exposure to and ability to tolerate various types of stressors, such as poor nutrition or parasites. I spent nearly a year on this review, during which I prepared extensive tables of these traits and the stressors that affect them across a very diverse array of species. These nonhuman studies helped me to better understand condition-dependent traits and the associated reviews and tables are, I believe, useful in and of themselves, whether or not the reader is interested in human vulnerability.

The primary goal however was to address the inevitable objections to my thesis that exposure to stressors will affect boys and girls and men and women differently and in ways that are only understandable when framed in an evolutionary perspective. Whatever objections may arise to my thesis, I believe the extensive reviews of condition-dependent traits in nonhuman species and the simple evolutionary concept that ties them together provides a solid foundation for the study of human vulnerabilities. As the reader will see, I used this foundation to make predictions about when in development, and for which sex, exposure to stressors will be most harmful to the expression of specific physical, behavioral, and brain and cognitive traits. As I did for nonhuman species, I used these predictions to organize reviews of empirical research on how poor nutrition, disease, and exposure to social stressors (e.g., childhood maltreatment) and toxins affected the development and expression of these traits. Conducting these reviews was at times an exercise in frustration, as many of the studies that included the traits of interest did not report sex differences, and many of the studies that did report these differences assessed traits that I suspected won't be particularly vulnerable for either sex. Nevertheless, I found enough extant research to show how exposure to various types of stressors can differentially affect the physical, social, and brain and cognitive health and development of boys and girls and men and women. I hope that the associated reviews will provide a useful foundation for the future study of human vulnerabilities.

During the writing of this book, I contacted various experts to ask questions about one matter or another and asked some of them to read and critique one or all of the chapters. I acknowledge and thank them: Dan Berch, Kingsley Browne, Napoleon Chagnon, Martin Daly, David Epstein, Carl Gerhardt, Jeffrey Gilger, Alex Moore, and Amanda Rose. I want to especially acknowledge and thank my former students, Drew Bailey and Benjamin Winegard, who critiqued the entire book, and Eldin Jašarević, who helped me flesh out these ideas in many thoughtful discussions and during our collaborative work on the topic. I also thank Sarah Becktell for double checking all of the references in the text and tables, and Mary Hoard and Lara Nugent for expertly managing the day-to-day operations of the lab while I was distracted by this project. Most important, my deepest thanks go to my wife Yin Xia, the love of my life. Without her continual support and kindness, I may have never completed this book.

**David C. Geary**
January 16, 2015

Chapter 1

# Vulnerability

## Chapter Outline

The question of whether one sex or the other is more vulnerable to stressors is an intriguing and important one. Historically, the question has focused on the issue of male vulnerability (e.g., Greulich, 1951; Stini, 1969; Stinson, 1985). Even Darwin (1871) noted the excess of premature male mortality in many species, including the higher mortality of boys than girls during infancy. It is indeed the case that boys are more likely to die in infancy than girls, even with the dramatic declines in overall mortality over the past two centuries (Martin, 1949; Read, Troendle, & Klebanoff, 1997), and surviving boys are overrepresented among children with mild to serious medical or physical conditions (Jacobziner, Rich, Bleiberg, & Merchant, 1963). It is also the case that young men die at higher rates than young women – often as a direct result of male-on-male aggression (Wilson & Daly, 1985) or due to status seeking "showing off" (e.g., reckless driving; Evans, 2006) – and that men have a shorter life span than women (Allman, Rosin, Kumar, & Hasenstaub, 1998). These are certainly important vulnerabilities and can be placed in the context of the evolution of life histories (e.g., environmental influences on the timing of reproductive competition), some of which are discussed in Nesse and Williams's (1996) introduction to evolutionary medicine (see also Belsky, Steinberg, & Draper, 1991; Ellis, 2004; Figueredo et al., 2006).

However, they are not my focus. Rather, I am interested in the more nuanced questions of why some traits – specific physical features, behaviors, or cognitive competencies – are more easily disrupted by exposure to stressors than others, and why these trait-specific vulnerabilities can differ between the sexes and across species. For instance, why does poor nutrition during adolescence affect the height and physical fitness of boys more than girls (Prista, Maia, Damasceno, & Beunen, 2003), but the early stage of Alzheimer's disease affects the language competencies of women more than men (Henderson, Watt, & Galen

Evolution of Vulnerability. http://dx.doi.org/10.1016/B978-0-12-801562-9.00001-6
**1**

Buckwalter, 1996)? In broader perspective, why does prenatal exposure to toxins compromise the spatial-navigation abilities of male deer mice (*Peromyscus maniculatus*), but leave unaffected the spatial abilities of same-species females or males of their cousin species, the California mouse (*Peromyscus californicus*; Jašarević et al., 2011; Williams et al., 2013). Vulnerability from a life history perspective, in contrast, is focused on how exposure to stressors influences the timing (not disruption) of reproductive traits, such as age of menarche, or modifies how sexual relationships are formed and maintained (Del Giudice, 2009; Ellis & Del Giudice, 2014). Again, these are important issues, but beyond the scope of what I wish to accomplish in this book.

My goal is to outline and provide evidence for a simple conceptual model – *traits that have been elaborated through sexual or social selection are especially vulnerable to disruption by exposure to environmental and social stressors* – that allows us to understand the vulnerabilities of adolescent boys, women with Alzheimer's disease, and male deer mice, among many others, and places all of them in a unifying evolutionary context. The model enables the identification of sex- and species-specific traits whose development and expression are vulnerable to disruption by disease, poor nutrition, social stressors, and exposure to man-made toxins (e.g., environmental toxins and chemotherapy).

The concept that pulls cross-species vulnerabilities together is found with Darwin's (1871) sexual selection – competition for mates and mate choices – and West-Eberhard's (1983) social selection – competition for reproductively relevant resources (e.g., high-quality food) other than mates. The key is that these social dynamics result in the evolutionary exaggeration of traits that facilitate competition or that make one attractive to mates. These traits are either signaled directly (e.g., through physical size) or indirectly (e.g., through plumage coloration that is correlated with diet quality) and can be physical, behavioral, or involve brain and cognition, as will be illustrated in subsequent chapters. Whatever the trait, they are effective signals because they convey information about the individual's level of exposure to stressors and the ability to cope with them.

Identifying these traits and the conditions that can disrupt their expression is complicated, however, because a trait that signals competitive ability, for instance, in one sex or species may or may not signal competitive ability in the other sex or in other, even closely related species (Andersson, 1994). For either sex or any species, the identification of vulnerable traits requires an understanding of the evolutionary history of the species, in particular the traits that facilitate competition for mates and other resources and that influence mate choices. I provide the background needed to understand competition and choice and the sensitivity of the associated traits to environmental and social stressors in Chapter 2 and illustrate the ubiquity and diversity of these traits in Chapters 3 and 4.

I then apply these same principles to humans and detail the traits that I predict will be more vulnerable to stressors in boys and men, and the traits that

I predict will be more vulnerable in girls and women. The existing literature on human sex differences does not allow for an evaluation of all of these predictions, but I provide proof of concept illustrations of sex differences in physical and behavioral vulnerabilities in Chapter 6 and in brain and cognitive vulnerabilities in Chapter 7. Implications for understanding and studying the nuances of human vulnerabilities are discussed in Chapter 8. I outline some of the key points of subsequent chapters in the second section below. In the first, I provide a few thoughts on why an evolutionary perspective on human vulnerabilities is important.

## THE VALUE ADDED BY AN EVOLUTIONARY PERSPECTIVE

There are many things in the world that can be harmful to people, including premature birth, pre- and postnatal exposure to toxins, poor nutrition, infestation with parasites, poverty, and childhood maltreatment, among others. Indeed, these risks are well recognized and in many cases extensively studied (e.g., Hotez et al., 2008; Kim & Cicchetti, 2003), but they have not been framed in terms of sex differences in risk. The key to fully understanding the consequences of exposure to these potential hazards is to understand the traits that are most likely to be affected by them, and when in development these traits are most likely to be disrupted. Without this knowledge, we may assess traits that are not strongly affected by risk exposure, miss those that are affected, or assess the right traits but at the wrong time or in the wrong sex. The result is an underestimation of the consequences of exposure or even a determination that exposure has no deleterious consequences at all. Moreover, without a conceptual framework for understanding vulnerability, it is also possible that sex differences for one especially vulnerable trait are overgeneralized to all traits, as seemed to have happened historically with boys' early mortality risks and a general belief in "male vulnerability."

As I illustrate in Chapter 2, there is good reason to believe that infection with any number of parasites – viruses, bacteria, worms – will compromise health and development. Indeed, the relation between parasite infestation and many features of children's and adults' physical, behavioral, and cognitive competencies have been assessed for more than a century (Dickson, Awasthi, Williamson, Demellweek, & Garner, 2000; Watkins & Pollitt, 1997), including recent studies in Zaire (Boivin et al., 1993), the Philippines (Ezeamama et al., 2005), Tanzania (Grigorenko et al., 2006), Brazil (Parraga et al., 1996), and Indonesia (Sakti et al., 1999), among others (Adams, Stephenson, Latham, & Kinoti, 1994). Whether one uses an evolutionary framework or not, it is clear to most people that many physical traits and their development differ for boys and girls. Thus, most of the studies of physical growth or fitness reported results for both sexes. This allowed me to better situate these findings in the context of sexual selection and thereby test specific predictions about when in development illness will similarly affect boys and girls (childhood) and when (puberty) and which traits will be differentially affected in boys (e.g., height) and girls (e.g., pelvic width), as we will cover in Chapter 6.

At the same time, most of the studies that assessed cognitive or behavioral outcomes collapsed boys and girls or men and women into a single group, included sex as a "nuisance" variable (and did not report any effects of sex), or assessed outcomes that will be less sensitive to parasite exposure than many of the traits I review in Chapter 5. A similar pattern is evident in studies of the long-term consequences of premature birth (e.g., Caravale, Tozzi, Albino, & Vicari, 2005; Crnic, Ragozin, Greenberg, Robinson, & Basham, 1983), the social consequences of childhood maltreatment (Kim & Cicchetti, 2003), and the potential cognitive deficits resulting from chemotherapy (Vardy, Rourke, & Tannock, 2007), to mention just a few. As I argue in Chapter 5, there are good a priori reasons to believe that boys and men and girls and women, as well as children and adults, will respond to these stressors in different ways. Using studies that did report sex differences, I illustrate these sex- and age-specific vulnerabilities in Chapters 6 and 7.

The overall result of ignoring sex has been an underappreciation of how exposure to stressors can affect some traits but not others and an underestimation of the deleterious effects of these stressors. If we want a more complete and nuanced understanding of how exposure to stressors can disrupt human health and development, most of these studies will need to be redone. I outline the traits that are most likely to show sex-specific disruptions to stressors in Chapter 5, and in Chapter 8 I elaborate on implications for better assessing these vulnerabilities in future studies.

## NONHUMAN VULNERABILITIES

To appreciate and fully understand my evolutionary framing of human vulnerabilities, an introduction to how sexual and social selection work over evolutionary time and how they are expressed in nonhuman species is necessary. As noted, I provide these fundamentals in Chapter 2, focusing on the relation between competition and choice and sex differences in physical (e.g., body size), behavioral (e.g., courtship displays), and brain and cognitive (e.g., as related to bird song) traits. In comparison to naturally selected traits – those important for survival (Darwin, 1859) – the development and expression of the traits that have been exaggerated by competition and mate choice are especially sensitive to environmental and social conditions. Stated differently, the full expression of these traits requires not only the right combination of genes, but also good environmental (e.g., low parasite levels) and social (e.g., parental provisioning) conditions during development and in adulthood. Individuals with this mix of genes and experiences are more likely to fully develop these traits than are other individuals and as a result have competitive advantages and are preferred as mates.

In this circumstance, the benefits of cheating are high, as are the costs of being cheated. Unfit males (e.g., poor immune system) may cheat by diverting resources to the development of these traits (e.g., larger horns, colorful plumage) and thus bluffing other males from directly competing with them or enticing females to mate with them; I provide an example of the latter with the three-spined stickleback (*Gasterosteus aculeatus*) in Chapter 3 (Candolin, 1999). Cheating can be avoided, or at least reduced, if the development and expression of these traits are costly to less fit individuals (Getty, 2006; Zahavi & Zahavi, 1997). The question then becomes what determines who is fit or not and why, and this is where sensitivity to environmental and social conditions becomes important. As an example, parasites are ubiquitous and can significantly compromise health and behavior. Some males, however, are better able to tolerate parasites than others, and those that tolerate parasites generally sire offspring that tolerate them as well (Hale, Verduijn, Møller, Wolff, & Petrie, 2009; Welch, Semlitsch, & Gerhardt, 1998). It is in females' best interest to choose mates that tolerate parasites, and it is in these males' best interest to signal parasite resistance (Hamilton & Zuk, 1982). For a reliable signal of parasite resistance to evolve, the expression of the trait must be modifiable by level of parasite infestation and must be elaborated to the extent that unfit males cannot express the trait and simultaneously cope with parasites (Folstad & Karter, 1992).

The result is the evolution of traits whose expression is dependent on environmental and social conditions. Some of these traits, such as the peacock's (*Pavo cristatus*) tail or the songs of male songbirds, are indirect signals of condition; they are correlated with unseen traits, such as immunocompetence or the integrity of specific brain regions underlying trait expression (Nowicki, Peters, & Podos, 1998). Other traits, such as the spatial-navigational abilities of male deer mice, are directly related to competition and are functional. Both direct and indirect signals are found in a spectacular variety of living organisms, from stalked-eyed flies (*Diasemopsis meigenni*; Bellamy, Chapman, Fowler, & Pomiankowski, 2013) to African elephants (*Loxodonta africana*; Hollister-Smith, Alberts, & Rasmussen, 2008). I was not able to review and catalog these traits and the stressors that can disrupt them for all of these species, but do review and illustrate them for about 125 species in Chapters 3 and 4.

I begin Chapter 3 with birds, because competition and choice have been extensively studied in numerous species since Darwin (1871), and as a result, much is known about the associated traits and their condition-dependent expression. Birds also illustrate the many different types of condition-dependent traits, ranging from the plumage color of the American goldfinch (*Spinus tristis*; McGraw & Hill, 2000) to the comb size of the red jungle fowl (*Gallus gallus*; Zuk, Thornhill, & Ligon, 1990), to the courtship displays of the magnificent frigate bird (*Fregata magnificens*; Chastel et al., 2005), and to the brain regions supporting song production of the male zebra finch (*Taeniopygia guttata*; Buchanan, Leitner, Spencer, Goldsmith, & Catchpole, 2004). I illustrate how the expression of these and similar traits can be disrupted by poor nutrition during development or in adulthood by disease, the stress of social competition, and exposure to toxins. I close Chapter 3 with a brief overview of condition-dependent traits in two well-studied species of fish, the guppy (*Poecilia reticulata*) and the three-spined stickleback. As vertebrates, some of the color traits that signal condition in these species are the same as those described for birds (Price, Weadick, Shim, & Rodd, 2008), illustrating the evolutionary conservation of some of these mechanisms. The review of these species and those in Chapter 4 also helps the reader to appreciate the ubiquity of condition-dependent traits.

I open Chapter 4 with a discussion and review of condition-dependent traits in arthropods (animals with exoskeletons), focusing on insects and a few spiders; no disrespect for crustaceans. The rapid growth of these species facilitates the study of how exposure to developmental stressors can affect the expression of traits related to competition and choice in adulthood. For instance, poor early nutrition affects the adult expression of dominance-related facial markings of the female paper wasp (*Polistes dominulus*; Tibbetts, 2010) and the eye span of the male stalk-eyed fly (Bellamy et al., 2013), among others. These reviews also confirm more general patterns found with birds, fish, and mammals; specifically, that some traits are more strongly affected by developmental stressors and others by current stressors. Whereas poor developmental nutrition affects the physical traits of female paper wasps and male stalk-eyed flies, poor nutrition in adulthood affects the expression of vigorous behavioral displays, such as the courtship song of the field cricket (*Gryllus campestris*; Holzer, Jacot, & Brinkhof, 2003) and the courtship display of the wolf spider (*Hygrolycosa rubrofasciata*; Mappes, Alatalo, Kotiaho, & Parri, 1996).

The shift to mammals in Chapter 4 expands the realm of condition-dependent traits (e.g., including scent) and brings us one step closer to humans. For instance, the study of developmental stressors in birds, fish, and insects nicely illustrates how early difficulties can disrupt the sex-specific expression of traits in adulthood. However, a better understanding of the consequences of human exposure to developmental stressors can be achieved with the study of other mammals, because of the commonalities in prenatal development and across many condition-dependent traits. As an example, prenatal exposure to man-made toxins disrupts the competitive play behavior of male rats (*Rattus norvegicus*; Casto, Ward, & Bartke, 2003), just as it does in boys (below). Poor postnatal nutrition affects the physical development of the male Alpine ibex (*Capra ibex*) but has an especially pronounced effect on the development of sexually selected horns (Toïgo, Gaillard, & Michallet, 1999), just as it does for boys' growth in height during puberty (Jardim-Botelho et al., 2008) and potentially girls' pelvic growth (Hautvast, 1971). Among other things, the study of mammals also broadens our understanding of vulnerable brain and cognitive traits and identifies the hippocampus as a brain region with sex-specific vulnerabilities (Hwang et al., 2010; Xu, Zhang, Wang, Ye, & Luo, 2010).

# HUMAN VULNERABILITIES

As noted earlier, identifying sex-specific vulnerabilities and the ages of heightened vulnerability requires an understanding of the natural history of the species and in particular the dynamics of sexual and social selection. I provide an overview of these dynamics in Chapter 5, using general patterns that emerge across species – for instance physical male-male competition in mammals results in the evolution of larger males than females (Plavcan & van Schaik, 1997) – and across human cultures (Murdock, 1981); a more thorough discussion can be found in Geary (2010). Following the reviews of other species, I identify physical, behavioral, cognitive, and brain traits that I predict will show sex-specific vulnerabilities, with some of these traits being more vulnerable in boys and men and others in girls and women. The *a priori* predictions laid out in Chapter 5 – most of which remain to be evaluated – helped to organize the literature searches and traits covered in Chapters 6 and 7, at least for traits in which there was sufficient research to conduct a review.

Physical vulnerabilities are the easiest to address, because the relation between physical competition and the evolution and expression of physical traits is well understood for primates (Leigh, 1996; McHenry & Coffing, 2000; Plavcan & van Schaik, 1997) and because anthropologists and pediatricians have been studying these same traits in people for many decades (Greulich, 1951; Hewitt, Westropp, & Acheson, 1955; Stinson, 1985), albeit not typically from an evolutionary perspective. In addition to the just mentioned relation between nutritional deficits and disruptions in boys' height and girls' pelvic development, Chapter 6 provides discussion of the relation between exposure to stressors and sex- and age-specific vulnerabilities for muscle mass, fat distribution, physical fitness, and skin condition, among others. For instance, nutritional deficits appear to compromise the fat reserves of boys more than girls just prior to pubertal development (Hagen, Hames, Craig, Lauer, & Price, 2001), and that of girls more than boys during pubertal development (Tanner, Leonard, & Reyes-García, 2014).

The behavioral traits covered in Chapter 6 include children's sex-typical play and social relationships, as well as adults' voice pitch and perceived attractiveness. Among other insights, the associated research reveals that boys' sex-typical play is consistently disrupted by prenatal exposure to toxins, but these have no or subtle effects on girls' play (Swan et al., 2010; Winneke et al., 2014). In contrast, maltreatment can undermine the social skills and development of girls and boys, but potentially in different ways (Parker & Herrera, 1996). I then argue that men's risk taking and emotional composure under stress are behavioral features of male-male competition and as such should be vulnerable traits. A corollary prediction is that relative to same-sex norms, exposure to stressors should have relatively stronger effects on men's anxiety and depression than women's anxiety and depression, despite a higher rate of affective disorders in women than men (Caspi et al., 2014). There is some evidence to this effect, but it is subtle and varies with type of stressor and age of exposure. Maternal stress or malnutrition during prenatal development increases the odds of these disorders more in men than women (de Rooij et al., 2011; Watson, Mednick, Huttunen, & Wang, 1999). Prenatal exposure to toxins, however, does not appear to elevate this risk more in men than women (Bennett, Bendersky, & Lewis, 2002), but toxin exposure in adulthood can (Morrow, Ryan, Goldstein, & Hodgson, 1989). In any case, I argue the social consequence is, or at least have been, more severe for men than women.

I devote the first part of Chapter 7 to assessments of my proposal (Chapter 5) that social-cognitive competencies – for instance, language, sensitivity to facial expressions, and theory of mind – are vulnerable traits in girls and women, whereas spatial-navigation competencies are vulnerable traits in boys and men. Girls' and women's natural language development and related verbal skills (e.g., retrieving words from memory) can indeed be disrupted by premature birth (Largo, Molinari, Pinto, Weber, & Due, 1986), Alzheimer's disease (Henderson & Buckwalter, 1994), and potentially by chemotherapy (Bender et al., 2006); typically, the magnitude of these disruptions is larger for girls and women than for boys and men. The research literature on exposure to stressors and other social-cognitive competencies is sparse, but there is evidence that the malnutrition associated with anorexia nervosa can compromise women's sensitivity to the emotion cues signaled through facial expressions, body language, and vocal intonation (Oldershaw, Hambrook, Tchanturia, Treasure, & Schmidt, 2010).

In contrast, there is evidence that prenatal and postnatal exposures to toxins (Guo, Lai, Chen, & Hsu, 1995; Nilson, Sällsten, Hagberg, Bäckman, & Barregård, 2002), poverty (Levine, Vasilyeva, Lourenco, Newcombe, & Huttenlocher, 2005), and infestation with parasites (Venkataramani, 2012) can compromise some aspects of boys' and men's spatial-navigation abilities and often more so than similarly affected girls and women. I close the chapter with a return to men's emotional composure and review the literature on the relation between two brain regions, the amygdala and hippocampus, and risk of trauma-related post-traumatic stress disorder (PTSD). There do appear to be differences in the reactivity of the amygdala (among other things) to threat – functionally resulting in stronger fear responses – comparing individuals who develop posttrauma PTSD to individuals who experienced the same level of trauma but did not develop PTSD, but boys and girls and men and women are more similar than different in this respect (Felmingham et al., 2010). There is, however, evidence that disruption of the development and functioning of several subregions of the hippocampus may result in higher risk of PTSD in men than women (Felmingham et al., 2010; Gilbertson et al., 2002), and thus may be part of the brain system related to men's condition-dependent emotional composure.

## CONCLUSION

The evolved function of condition-dependent traits is to allow competitors and would-be mates to identify individuals that have been exposed to environmental or social stressors and are unable to cope effectively with them; the functioning of most individuals will be compromised by exposure to stressors but some individuals are more resilient than others. My point is that we can reframe condition dependence and use the associated traits to more fully understand and assess how people respond to stressors, and specifically how sensitivity to them varies across sex, age, and trait. I outline the implications of this perspective in Chapter 8, but note one important limitation here: Exposure to extreme stressors will affect both sexes and naturally selected as well as condition-dependent traits. Exposure to small amounts of arsenic (e.g., through contaminated ground water) may largely disrupt condition-dependent traits – I provide an example in Chapter 7 – but larger doses will have wider effects or even kill you regardless of sex. Similarly, being born a month or so premature may compromise condition-dependent traits, as noted, but being born many months premature will have wider effects (Marlow, Wolke, Bracewell, & Samara, 2005). In other words, these traits are useful for identifying and better understanding vulnerability to mild-to-moderate levels of stressor (this covers most stressors in modern contexts), but with extreme stressors many more traits will be compromised.

Chapter 2

# Sexual Selection and the Evolution of Vulnerability

## Chapter Outline

Charles Darwin and Alfred Wallace independently discovered natural selection; that is, the processes that result in cross-generational changes within each species, as well as the origin of new species (Darwin, 1859; Darwin & Wallace, 1858). Darwin (1859, 1871) also discovered a set of social dynamics that operate within species and are the principle evolutionary drivers of sex differences. These processes do not involve the struggle for existence as with natural selection, but rather struggles with members of ones' own sex and species for control of the dynamics of reproduction. These dynamics are called *sexual selection* and are expressed as competition with members of the same sex over mates (*intrasexual competition*) and discriminative choice of mating partners (*intersexual choice*). Although Darwin's sexual selection languished for nearly a century in the backwaters of scientific obscurity, it began to move to the forefront of evolutionary biology in the 1970s (Campbell, 1971) and is now a thriving area of inquiry. These principles have been successfully used to understand the evolution and the here-and-now, proximate expression of sex differences across hundreds of species (Andersson, 1994; Adkins-Regan, 2005), including our own (Geary, 2010).

Evolution of Vulnerability. http://dx.doi.org/10.1016/B978-0-12-801562-9.00002-8
**11**

My goals for this chapter are to first explain and illustrate how sexual selection works and then explore why the expression of many of the associated traits – those that provide competitive advantage over members of the same sex or that make one attractive to members of the opposite sex – are so easily disrupted. The basic idea is that evolution pushes traits that facilitate competition or choice toward greater and greater elaboration. The building and maintenance of elaborated traits in turn requires the right combination of genes, as well as good nutrition and health during development and in adulthood. Without the right mix of genes, early experiences, and current conditions, many individuals are unable to fully express these traits. As I noted in the previous chapter, the associated vulnerability serves important evolutionary functions; specifically, these traits are social signals that convey information on the individual's competitiveness and the benefits he or she can offer as a mate and thus reduce the likelihood of costly escalation of aggression and poor mate choices (Getty, 2006; Zahavi & Zahavi, 1997). Many of the same developmental and current conditions, such as poor nutrition or exposure to parasites or man-made toxins that disrupt the expression of these traits in nonhuman animals also disrupt them in humans, as we will learn in Chapters 6 and 7. But to fully understand and appreciate the implications for identifying and understanding human vulnerabilities, grounding in sexual selection (this chapter) and condition-dependent trait expression in other species (Chapters 3 and 4) is needed.

## SEXUAL SELECTION

In his extensive descriptions and illustrations of sexual selection, Darwin (1871) focused on male-male competition and female choice, and for good reason. These are very common patterns in nature, and as I describe in the next section emerge from sex differences in parenting (Trivers, 1972; Williams, 1966). At the same time, the success of this traditional approach resulted in a relative neglect of female-female competition and male choice, with the exception of "sex-role reversed" species, which are discussed later in the chapter. It is now clear that males can be choosey if females differ in fertility or quality of parental behavior, even when these males provide little or no investment in their offspring (Kraaijeveld, Kraaijeveld-Smit, & Komdeur, 2007). Likewise, in many species in which females do not compete intensely for access to mates, they are nevertheless highly competitive with one another over access to other resources (Clutton-Brock, 2009; Lyon & Montgomerie, 2012; Stockley & Bro-Jørgensen, 2011). We will discuss female-female competition and male choice at the end of this section.

Finally, I note that the existence of sex differences in and of themselves does not necessarily mean they are the result of sexual selection. As Darwin stated, "the male and female sometimes differ in structures connected with different habits of life, and not at all, or only indirectly, related to the reproductive functions" (Darwin, 1871, Vol. 1, p. 254). Different habits of life include differences

**FIGURE 2.1**    The male (front) and female (back) huia (*Heteralocha acutirostris*) from Buller and Keulemans (1888, Vol. 1, p. Plate II). The differences in bill shape were (the species is now extinct) thought to reflect differences in foraging strategy (Wilson, 2004). (See the color plate section.)

in the types of foods they forage, as illustrated by sex differences in the beak structure of the New Zealand huia (*Heteralocha acutirostris*; Figure 2.1). At the same time, most sex differences are correlated with success at competing for mates or attracting them and very likely evolved by means of sexual selection or, if not related to competition for mates or mate choice, social selection (below) if the trait affects reproductive success (West-Eberhard, 1983).

## Compete for or Choose Among Mates?

Although Darwin (1871) correctly argued that male-male competition over access to mates and female choice of mating partners is more common than female-female competition and male choice, he did not identify why these patterns emerge. Nearly 100 years later, Williams (1966) and Trivers (1972) put the pieces together and proposed that the bias to compete directly for mates or choose among them is tightly linked to parenting. Choosiness increases with increases in investment in offspring, and competitiveness increases with decreases in investment in offspring. In other words, sex differences in the tendency to compete or choose are strongly influenced by the degree to which females and males invest in parenting. The sex that provides more than his or her share of parental investment is an important reproductive resource for members of the opposite sex. The result is competition among members of the lower-investing sex (typically males) over the parental investment of members of the higher-investing sex (typically females). Competition for parental investment creates demand for the higher-investing sex that in turn allows them to be choosey when it comes to mates.

Williams's (1966) and Trivers's (1972) insight into the relation between parenting and competition and choice was a seminal contribution to our understanding of the dynamics of sexual selection but left unanswered the question of why one sex invests more in parenting than the other in the first place. Clutton-Brock and Vincent (1991) provided at least part of the answer: Sex differences in the potential rate of reproduction create biases in the reproductive benefits of competing for mates or investing in parenting and is thus a critical contributor to the male bias to compete and the female bias to invest in offspring. I will briefly describe the reproductive rate argument and how social conditions, in particular the operational sex ratio (OSR) can influence the here-and-now dynamics of competing and choosing. Before beginning, I want to note that the dynamics you are about to read are simplified, as the full picture is currently debated; other factors that can influence the male and female bias to compete or parent (or vice versa) include the costs of competing or parenting, the potential for the lower-investing sex to actually improve the quality of offspring (lower potential limits them to only competing, whereas higher potential gives the option of a mix of competing and parenting), and the expected reproductive benefits of seeking additional mates (Kokko & Jennions, 2008; Kokko, Klug, & Jennions, 2012; Queller, 1997).

## Rate of Reproduction

Across species, the sex with the higher potential rate of reproduction tends to invest more in competing for mates than in parenting, and the sex with the lower rate of reproduction tends to invest more in parenting than in competing (Clutton-Brock & Vincent, 1991). The pattern emerges because members of the sex with the higher potential rate of reproduction can rejoin the mating pool more quickly than can members of the opposite sex and it is often in their reproductive best interest to do so (Parker & Simmons, 1996). Individuals of the lower-investing sex typically have more offspring if they compete for mates than if they parent, whereas members of the higher-investing sex show the opposite pattern, and benefit more from being choosey than do members of the lower-investing sex.

For mammals, internal gestation and obligatory postpartum female care, as with suckling, create a very large sex difference in the potential rate of reproduction (Clutton-Brock, 1991). Once pregnant, females leave the reproductive pool and males have the option of attending to the female during her pregnancy or leaving to compete for additional mates. In short, at this point males can benefit from seeking and obtaining additional mates, whereas females cannot.

These biological factors result in a strong female bias toward parental invest-ment, and an important sex difference in the benefits of seeking additional mates (Trivers, 1972). Thus, the sex difference in reproductive rate, combined with offspring that can be effectively raised by the female, creates the poten-tial for large female-male differences in the mix of parenting and competing, and this difference is found in 95-97% of mammalian species (Clutton-Brock, 1989). Basically, female care of offspring frees males to compete for mates, and successful males have many offspring each breeding season and many other males never reproduce.

## Operational Sex Ratio

Mating dynamics are not simply the result of evolved biases, but are also influ-enced by current conditions, in particular the OSR (Emlen & Oring, 1977). The OSR is the ratio of sexually active males to sexually active females in a given breeding population at a given point in time, and is related to the rate of repro-duction. Because pregnant and nursing female mammals, for instance, leave the mating pool, there are typically many more sexually *receptive* males than sexually *receptive* females in most mammalian populations. This imbalance in the number of males and females seeking mates creates the conditions that lead to intense male-male competition and enable female choosiness.

Conditions that tip the balance toward a more equal OSR or that reverse it can have dramatic effects on mating dynamics and thus on the importance (or not) of sexually selected traits. In species that live in multimale, multifemale groups, the number of females that are in estrous at the same time can have striking effects on the intensity of male-male competition. My point is illustrated by Takahashi's (2004) studies of the Japanese macaque (*Macaca fuscata*). Female macaques do not go into estrous every mating season, which results in considerable varia-tion across seasons in the number of sexually receptive females. During seasons when there were more males than estrous females, dominant males monopolized mating access to them. The result was low-ranking males mated with estrous females less than 20% of the time. In seasons in which there were more estrous females than males, dominant males could not control mating dynamics as ef-fectively. In these seasons, low-ranking males mated almost 50% of the time.

Dramatic changes in the OSR can even occur within a single breeding sea-son, as documented for the two-spotted goby (*Gobiusculus flavescens*; Forsgren, Amundsen, Borg, & Bjelvenmark, 2004). At the beginning of the breeding sea-son, males of this species of fish compete intensely for nesting sites, court fe-males, and then fan and protect eggs. These are very demanding activities and result in high male mortality; by the middle of the breeding season, there are many more females than males. When the OSR reaches about a 4:1 ratio of females to males, females start adopting male-typical behaviors. They begin to court males – "individual males were often surrounded by up to 20 round females courting them at close range" (Forsgren et al., 2004, p. 553) – and they chase other females away from the males in order to get access to mating opportunities with them. In this situation, females are competing for the parental effort (i.e., fanning and protecting eggs) of a small number of males, and these males in turn become choosey about which females they will allow to deposit eggs into their nest.

## Male-Male Competition

As described by Darwin (1871), evolution has produced many and varied ways in which males compete for access to females or for control of the resources females need to reproduce (e.g., nesting sites). The most obvious and richly illustrated by Darwin are traits involved in physical combat. These types of traits are found in species as diverse as the mandibles of Darwin's beetle (*Chiasognathus grantii*; Figure 2.2) to the horns of the kudu (*Tragelaphus strepsiceros*;

**FIGURE 2.2**   The male and female beetle *Chiasognathus grantii*, sometimes called Darwin's beetle, from Darwin (1871, Vol. I, p. 377). Males typically search for mates in trees and compete by attempting to hook their mandibles under the wings of competitors and throw them from the tree.

**FIGURE 2.3**   The male kudu (*Tragelaphus strepsiceros*) from Darwin (1871, Vol. II, p. 255). Males compete by locking horns and pulling and pushing each other as a display of physical strength. In contrast, females are hornless.

Figure 2.3). Competition can also involve complex behavioral displays of endurance and fitness without physical combat as well as the construction of delicate bowers (below). In the same way that physical and behavioral competition elaborates the traits that provide males with advantage, brain and cognitive traits, if they provide competitive advantage, will also become elaborated over evolutionary time. I illustrate each of these different forms of competition – physical, behavioral, and brain and cognitive – below and use them to organize reviews of vulnerable, condition-dependent traits in subsequent chapters.

## Physical Competition

The differences between the males and females of Darwin's beetle and the horns of the male kudu and the hornless female kudu illustrate the basic, evolutionary effect of physical competition; specifically, evolutionary exaggeration of traits in one sex and, through this, sex differences in the size of these traits. In fact, the best indicator of physical intrasexual competition is a sex difference in body size (Andersson, 1994; Leigh, 1995; Plavcan & van Schaik, 1997). An excellent example is the northern elephant seal (*Mirounga angustirostris*) where males weigh between 3000 and 8000 pounds (1360-3629 kg) and females between 400 and 900 pounds (181-409 kg). Males of this species and their cousins, the southern elephant seal (*M. leonina*), have evolved to such large sizes because

**PHOTO 2.1**  Two male northern elephant seals (*Mirounga angustirostris*) fighting for control of a harem. *Photo credit: Dawn Endio, 2004. Creative Commons License. http://commons.wikimedia.org/ wiki/File:Elephant_seal_fight_Part-1.jpg.* (See the color plate section.)

the primary factor that influences which males reproduce and which do not is differential access to females, access that is primarily determined by one-on-one physical fights (Clutton-Brock, 1988; Le Boeuf & Reiter, 1988). These fights occur during the breeding season (see Photo 2.1, inset), when females aggregate on relatively confined beaches and males compete physically with one another for sexual access to them.

> *These encounters consist of two males rearing up on their foreflippers and trumpeting individually distinct calls...at one another. In most cases, one of the males retreats at this stage; if neither male submits, a fight ensues. The two males approach one another and push against each other chest to chest, while delivering open mouth blows and bites at each other's neck, flippers, and head.*
>
> Haley, Deutsch, and Le Boeuf (1994, p. 1250)

Success in such fights is related to physical size, age, and duration of residency (i.e., established males as opposed to newcomers) and determines social dominance that in turn influences reproductive outcomes (Haley et al., 1994; Le Boeuf, 1974; Le Boeuf & Peterson, 1969). To become socially dominant, males must first survive long enough to compete for mates, and only about 10% of them make it to this point. Of males that survive this long, only about ½ secure access to females; even among these males most of the pairings are achieved by a few dominant individuals (Le Boeuf & Peterson, 1969; Le Boeuf & Reiter, 1988).

Size, however, is not the only route to reproduction, as smaller males sometimes sire offspring by "sneaking" into harems and mating with females. This can occur because these "sneaker" males resemble females and thus do not incur the wrath of dominant males when they approach harems (Le Boeuf, 1974). Using DNA fingerprinting to determine paternity, Hoelzel, Le Boeuf, Reiter, and Campagna (1999) confirmed that alpha males tended to monopolize mating access. Among the northern elephant seal, the typical alpha male achieves about five times the expected number of copulations relative to the number that would occur in an egalitarian or monogamous mating system. Nevertheless, paternity tests revealed these males only sired 40% of the pups; some of the remaining pups were sired by a recently displaced alpha male or an alpha male from an adjacent harem, but others were sired by subordinate or "sneaker" males. Despite the alternative strategy of sneaking, the most successful reproductive route for male elephant seals is the achievement of social dominance through physical one-on-one fights, and here size matters – the bigger the better and thus the evolution of large sex differences in physical size.

## Behavioral Competition

Physical fights and aggressive posturing are of course forms of behavioral competition, but there are other forms that do not involve inflicting injury on competitors. These include various types of calls or songs that signal status and vigor to competitors and potential mates, as well as courtship displays. The latter are particularly common in lekking species, where males gather together and strut or display their physical health and vigor to other males (which determines location in the lek) and to would-be mates (Höglund & Alatalo, 1995). An example is provided by field studies of the black grouse (*Tetrao tetrix*) shown in Photo 2.2 (inset) (Höglund, Johansson, & Pelabon, 1997; Siitari, Alatalo, Halme, Buchanan, & Kilpimaa, 2007). Males of this species gather in an arena during breeding season and fight for position at the center of the corresponding lek. Females visit multiple males in the lek and choose a mate or mates (Alatalo, Höglund, Lundberg, & Sutherland, 1992). When visited by a female,

**PHOTO 2.2**    Lekking black grouse (*Tetrao tetrix*) males during mating season. Males compete for location at the center of the lek. Females visit multiple males, especially central males, and choose a mate based on plumage and red comb color as well as the vigor of the courtship display. (See the color plate section.)

males engage in an almost continuous vocalization and present their erect lyre (back tail feathers) and inflated red eye combs to this would-be mate. Males that maintain this courtship display are chosen as mates more often than their lower-stamina peers (Höglund et al., 1997).

There is more on the black grouse in the next chapter, but for now let's turn to the most complex form of behavioral competition offered by nature, outside of humans. I am referring to the bowers built by male bowerbirds (Gilliard, 1969). These structures are constructed from twigs and leaves and are decorated with colorful feathers, shells, and oftentimes man-made debris (e.g., bottle caps), as illustrated in Photo 2.3 (inset) for the satin bowerbird (*Ptilonorhynchus violaceus*). The bowers are not nests or refuge from the weather; their only function is to attract females. Females in turn prefer bowers that are symmetrically built, nicely decorated (e.g., with colorful feathers), and painted. The latter involves males chewing on vegetation and painting the inside of their bower with the plant-saliva mixture. Females nibble on the paint when visiting the bower. Once enticed to visit, males engage in courtship calls and behaviors that, in combination with plumage color, influence female choice (Borgia, 1985a, 2006; Borgia & Coleman, 2000; Coleman, Patricelli, & Borgia, 2004).

Males with the largest and best built and decorated bowers tend to be healthier and more dominant than males without bowers and males with less elaborate bowers (Borgia, 1985b, 1995a, 1995b) and, importantly, sire the vast majority of offspring (Reynolds et al., 2007). Skill at building the type of bower that will attract females is related to social learning – copying bower building of successful males – during a long 10-year development period and social dominance in adulthood (Borgia, 1985a; Borgia & Wingfield, 1991; Collis & Borgia, 1992; Pruett-Jones & Pruett-Jones, 1994). The latter is determined by male fights and threat displays at communal feeding sites and this in turn influences the

**PHOTO 2.3**    Male satin bowerbirds (*Ptilonorhynchus violaceus*) build bowers to attract females. *Photo credit: Gary Curtis, 2005. Creative commons license. http://commons.wikimedia.org/wiki/File:BowerOfSatinBowerbird.jpg.* (See the color plate section.)

dynamics of bower destruction and the stealing of colorful objects from others' bowers (Borgia, 1985a; Wojcieszek, Nicholls, Marshall, & Goldizen, 2006). Socially dominant males do more of both than do other males (Borgia, 1985a), contributing to their success at attracting mates. The result of competition and choice has been the evolution of complex behavioral differences between male and female bowerbirds in the same way that physical competition resulted in the evolution of large sex differences in the size of male and female elephant seals.

## Brain and Cognitive Competition

Just as there is no fine line between physical and behavioral competition, there is often no fine line between behavioral and cognitive competition. The complexity of the male bowerbirds' behavioral competition and their dependence on social observation and learning to develop bower building skills must be dependent to some extent on specialized brain and cognitive systems. Indeed, males of the bower building species have larger brains than do males of related species that live in the same habitat but do not build bowers (Madden, 2001); in the latter species, males clear a patch of forest floor to attract females. Within the family of bowerbirds and especially for males, species with more complex bowers have a larger cerebellum than their less sophisticated cousins (Day, Westcott, & Olster, 2005). The larger size of the cerebellum is potentially important and interesting, because this brain region is critical for procedural learning (a behavioral sequence that reliably produces a specific outcome) through social observation (Leggio et al., 2000), as is found in bower building males.

Vocal communication is another area in which the line between behavioral and cognitive traits is fuzzy; experience-based learning per se is not critical, as many species produce vocalizations without learning but even in these cases the line between behavior and cognition is fuzzy (Gerhardt & Huber, 2002). Birdsong is a well-studied example, whereby males often have two distinct features embedded in their song, one that influences female choice and one that signals dominance and territorial control to other males (Ball & Hulse, 1998). In the next chapter, I classify the social-signal components of these songs; that is, the complexity, specific features, and duration of the produced song as behavioral traits. Studies that focus on learning and the underlying brain regions are classified as brain and cognitive traits. The distinction might be arbitrary but it is useful; it illustrates that sexual selection operates on brain and cognition in the same way it operates on more thoroughly studied physical and behavioral traits.

Song learning in particular is ideal for illustrating how sexual selection can result in sex differences in brain and cognition, because the neural systems underlying this learning have been studied for decades and are well understood (DeVoogd, 1991; DeVoogd, Krebs, Healy, & Purvis, 1993; Nottebohm, 1970, 1971, 1972, 2005). A schematic of the basic organization of the brain systems involved in song learning and production is shown in Figure 2.4. Birds learn songs, either during a developmental window or the current breeding season, by generating songs themselves and comparing these against previously

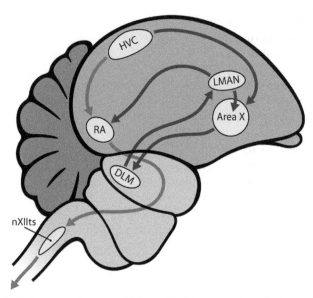

**FIGURE 2.4**   Brain systems that support bird song. HVC is not an acronym but is sometimes termed higher (or high) vocal center; RA, robust nucleus of the arcopallium; nXIIts, tracheosyringeal half of the hypoglossal nucleus; LMAN, lateral magnocellular nucleus of the nidopallium; DLM, dorsolateral anterior thalamic nucleus; area X, portion of the basal ganglia. *From Nottebohm (2005). Creative commons license.  http://www.plosbiology.org/article/info%3Adoi%2F10.1371%2Fjournal.pbio.0030164.* (See the color plate section.)

heard songs (e.g., from their fathers) stored in memory. Through trial-and-error adjustments, they eventually generate songs that match the previously heard ones. Of the areas shown in the schematic, the HVC (sometimes called the higher or high vocal center) is central to the production of these learned songs, acting in concert to with the RA (robustus arcopallium). The projections from the LMAN (lateral magnocellular nucleus of the nidopallium) to the RA create variation in the produced songs. This variation is critical for generating and modifying song patterns that will come to match, through trail-and-error learning, those stored in memory (Kao, Doupe, & Brainard, 2005; Ölveczky, Andalman, & Fee, 2005).

Sex differences in the size of the HVC, RA, and Area X (part of the basal ganglia involved in learning routines) are well documented and are quite large (Nottebohm, 2005; Nottebohm & Arnold, 1976). For instance, the size of the HVC can be three to eight times larger in males than in females, depending on the species. For seasonally breeding species, the magnitude of these differences becomes most pronounced in the breeding season (Nottebohm, 1981). For the canary (*Serinus canarius*), Nottebohm (1980) demonstrated that testosterone implants greatly increase the size of the HVC and RA in females and induces male-like song, whereas male castration reduces the size of these areas and impairs song production. In some species, sex hormones also influence the ways in which these sex-dimorphic areas respond to early environmental cues (e.g., father's song) and song expression in adulthood (Ball & Hulse, 1998; DeVoogd, 1991; Marler, 1991). In other words, the learning and later expression of sexually selected songs typically requires early exposure to song (Petrinovich & Baptista, 1987) and exposure to male hormones (DeVoogd, 1991).

Another example of how sexual selection can produce sex differences in brain and cognition is provided by studies of scramble competition, whereby males expand their territory during the breeding season to search for potential mates (Andersson, 1994). The outcomes are illustrated by comparisons of cousin species of vole (Gaulin, 1992). Males of the polygynous meadow vole (*Microtus pennsylvanicus*) engage in scramble competition during the breeding season, but the males of monogamous prairie (*M. ochrogaster*) and woodland voles (*M. pinetorum*; previously called pine voles) do not. During the breeding season, male meadow voles expand their territory to four to five times the area of females' territory whereas male and female prairie and woodland voles share overlapping territories of about the same size. Territorial expansion and the search for mates that could be situated anywhere in the territory should favor males with enhanced spatial and navigational abilities, and this is the case. Laboratory and field studies show that male meadow voles have better spatial learning and memory than female meadow voles or male prairie and woodland voles (Gaulin & Fitzgerald, 1986). Follow-up studies have shown that male meadow voles with above average spatial abilities visit more females and generally have higher reproductive success than their lower-ability peers (Spritzer, Solomon, & Meikle, 2005). Moreover, the same pattern of species- and sex-differences has now been demonstrated with other mammals (Jašarević, Williams, Roberts, Geary, & Rosenfeld, 2012; Perdue, Snyder, Zhihe, Marr, & Maple, 2011).

Spatial navigation in turn is highly dependent on an area of the brain called the hippocampus (O'Keefe & Nadel, 1978). It is not that the entire volume of the hippocampus is necessarily larger in males that engage in scramble competition; in fact, the evidence on this is mixed (Galea, Perrot-Sinal, Kavaliers, & Ossenkopp, 1999; Jacobs, Gaulin, Sherry, & Hoffman, 1990). Rather, some aspects of the functioning of this region of the brain that are related to spatial learning and memory appear to differ for these males relative to same-species females (Galea, 2008; Kee, Teixeira, Wang, & Frankland, 2007; Ormerod & Galea, 2003; Ormerod, Lee, & Galea, 2004). Of particular importance are the hormone-dependent generation, survival, and incorporation of new cells into the spatial memory networks of a subregion of the hippocampus, the dentate gyrus. Kee et al., for instance, found that male engagement in spatial learning tasks enhanced integration of these cells into spatial memory networks, and Ormerod and Galea found greater cell survival (but not new cell generation) in this region for male meadow voles during the breeding season as compared to males outside of the breeding season.

There are also hormonal influences on the hippocampus of the female meadow vole, but importantly in ways that differ from those found in males. These females reduce their territory size during the breeding season and this in turn reduces predation and increases their reproductive success (Sheridan & Tamarin, 1988). Galea and McEwen (1999) found that sexually active female meadow voles had a smaller hippocampus and less cell generation in the dentate gyrus than did sexually inactive females (see also Ormerod & Galea, 2001), consistent with a breeding season reduction in territory size. None of this should be taken to mean that females of all species have less elaborated spatial abilities than males. As noted, there are no sex differences in spatial abilities when males do not engage in scramble competition, and males and females share an overlapping territory (Gaulin & Fitzgerald, 1986; Jašarević et al., 2012; Perdue et al., 2011).

In fact, when females have larger territories than males or use these territories in more complex ways, females should have better developed spatial abilities. This is exactly what has been found for the brown-headed cowbird (*Molothrus ater*), a brood parasite. Females of this species lay their eggs in the nests of host species, and need to remember the location of these nests so they can deposit their eggs at times when the unwitting host will accept them. Females of this species have a better spatial memory than males (Guigueno, Snow, MacDougall-Shackleton, & Sherry, 2014) and a larger hippocampus (Sherry, Forbes, Khurgel, & Ivy, 1993).

## Female Choice

Female choice of mating partners was one of the sticking points in the acceptance of Darwin's (1871) sexual selection. Many male naturalists did not believe (or did not want to believe) that females had some control over reproductive dynamics (Cronin, 1991). Even those who accepted females' influence debated the importance of the male traits that drove these choices. It was clear that males of many species of bird, for instance, were more colorful or had more elaborate plumage than females. The issue was whether these traits signaled anything important about the male (e.g., health) or whether these "good looks" traits and the females' preference for them evolved for nonpractical reasons. For Darwin and, later, Fisher (1930), the evolution of aesthetically pleasing traits could occur if females simply preferred more colorful or more elaborate males to their less flamboyant peers. Any such preference might initially result from a female sensory bias for certain colors that "may serve as a charm for the female" (Darwin, 1871, Vol. II, p. 92) but that evolved for other reasons, such as detection of fruit (Ryan & Keddy-Hector, 1992).

Darwin's contemporary, Wallace, vacillated on the potential function of these traits but showed considerable foresight in an 1892 article. Here, he argued that these traits signaled the underlying qualities of the male; "We are, therefore, forced to conclude that the two qualities – general vigor and

ornament – *are* not independent of each other, but are developed *pari passu*"
(Wallace, 1892, p. 749; italics in original). The gist of Wallace's position cap-
tures what is now known as good genes models of sexual selection; specifically, that the traits that females use when choosing mates are indicators of the
genetic benefits provided by males to offspring or the males' ability to directly
provision her and her offspring (Borgia, 2006; Sheldon, Merilä, Qvarnström,
Gustafsson, & Ellegren, 1997). In other words, females cannot directly assess
the genetic quality (e.g., genes that will confer resistance to local parasites) or
the future provisioning of males, but they can assess observable traits that are
correlated with them (Hamilton & Zuk, 1982; Zahavi, 1975).

The peacock (*Pavo cristatus*) provides an excellent example of traits that
influence female choice and signal something about male quality. As with the
black grouse, peafowl are a lekking species and peacocks fight for central position on the lek (Höglund & Alatalo, 1995; Petrie, 1994; Petrie, Halliday, &
Sanders, 1991). Achievement of this coveted position is related to the males'
size vis-à-vis that of other males (Loyau, Saint Jalme, & Sorci, 2005). As shown
in Photo 2.4 (inset), males display their tails to females visiting the lek, and females choose mates based on the number, density, and blue-green coloration of
males' eyespots (Dakin & Montgomerie, 2013; Loyau, Saint Jalme, Cagniant, &
Sorci, 2005; Loyau, Saint Jalme, & Sorci, 2005; Petrie et al., 1991). Males who
frequently display and that have more eyespots are healthier, with better immune
systems than other males (Loyau, Saint Jalme, Cagniant et al., 2005). Females
that choose these males as mates are less likely to be infected during copulations
and, more importantly, are likely to receive genes that confer better disease resistance for their offspring (Hale, Verduijn, Møller, Wolff, & Petrie, 2009); for an
additional and well-documented example see Gerhardt and colleagues' studies

**PHOTO 2.4**   The male peafowl (*Pavo cristatus*) displays feathers to would-be mates, and females
choose mates based on the number, density, and blue-green color of the males' eyespots. (See the
color plate section.)

of call duration and good genes in the gray tree frog (*Hyla versicolor*; Welch, Semlitsch, & Gerhardt, 1998; Welch, Smith, & Gerhardt, 2014).

## Female-Female Competition and Male Choice

As noted, Darwin (1871) focused on male-male competition because it is more common or at least more obvious than female-female competition, but this does not mean that females do not compete with one another. Indeed, one of the more elegant features of the parental investment and reproductive rate hypothesis is that females will be more competitive than males when they can reproduce more quickly than males. Although not common, this does occur in so-called "sex-role reversed" species. Competition for mates, however, is not the only factor that can result in the evolution of competitive females (West-Eberhard, 1983). When the resources needed to support their investment in offspring, such as high-quality foods and nesting sites, are in short supply, females are predicted to compete intensely for priority access to them (Heinsohn, 2008; Tobias, Montgomerie, & Lyon, 2012). The result is female status hierarchies and the evolutionary elaboration of the traits that signal relative status and that enable its establishment and maintenance. These socially selected traits are, technically, not the same as sexually selected traits that have been elaborated through male-male competition as defined by Darwin (1871), but nonetheless show some of the same features.

The take home message is that female-female competition, whether it is over mates or other resources that influence reproductive outcomes, results in the evolutionary elaboration of traits that provide females with competitive advantage. The competition will not only result in a sex difference for these traits, but also (presumably to the extent that these are social signals) a condition-dependent expression of them.

### Reversed Sex Roles

These are species in which males invest more in parenting than females, which often includes male incubation and more rarely internal gestation of fertilized eggs (Andersson, 2004; Berglund, Rosenqvist, & Bernet, 1997; Eens & Pinxten, 2000). The latter are species in which males are the pregnant sex. These males are found in pipefish (e.g., broadnosed pipefish, *Syngnathus typhle*), seahorses (e.g., big belly seahorse, *Hippocampus abdominalis*), and seadragons (e.g., leafy seadragon, *Phycodurus eques*). These species are all related to one another and in most of them females transfer eggs into a front pouch on the male for the male to then fertilize (Jones, Moore, Kvarnemo, Walker, & Avise, 2003). The male benefits by ensuring he is the sire of all of the offspring and the female benefits by lower parental investment. Females also have the option of attempting to "impregnate" a second male and most of them attempt to do so. But now, nonpregnant males are a limited resource and under these conditions females are predicted to compete intensely with one another for access to these males, and they do. As in species in which males compete intensely for mates, females of pipefish and seahorse species are often larger, more colorful, and more aggressive than same-species males (Wilson, Ahnesjö, Vincent, & Meyer, 2003).

Although male pregnancy is not found in other species (to the best of my knowledge), the same pattern of more aggressive females than males is also found in bird species in which males incubate eggs but females do not (e.g., red-necked phalarope, *Phalaropus lobatus*; Reynolds, 1987). In these species, once the first clutch is laid and the male securely in place, the female absconds to search and compete for another mate to incubate a second clutch of her eggs.

## Female-Female Competition and Social Selection

West Eberhard (1979, 1983) proposed that competition for resources other than mates is a form of social selection – evolutionary pressures deriving from cooperation and competition with members of the same species (called conspecifics) – and that sexual selection is a subset of these selection pressures; both of which are subsets of natural selection. More precisely, both refer to competition (sometimes aided by others) for control of important resources, but, in sexual selection, the resource at stake is mates and in social selection the resources at stake include access to food and nesting sites, among others, in addition to mates. In this view, and staying focused on reproductive outcomes, we can broaden our search for vulnerable traits to include those that facilitate competition for access to reproduction-related resources, whether or not those resources are mates. This broader perspective provides considerable opportunity for female-female competition and the evolutionary exaggeration of the traits that facilitate this competition, as is now recognized (Clutton-Brock, 2009; Lyon & Montgomerie, 2012; Stockley & Bro-Jørgensen, 2011). These traits are often less conspicuous than those of males – which contributed to their relative neglect – but many of them, perhaps most, are likely to be condition-dependent signals and thus vulnerable to disruption.

At one time, female dominance signals were thought to be the result of genetic correlations; that is, the traits are expressed in females not because females use them to compete but rather because of the expression of genes inherited from their fathers (Lande, 1980). This may be the case for some species, but is not the case for others (West-Eberhard, 1983). It is now known that these traits are often used in status-related competition with other females, in territorial defense against predators or conspecifics of both sexes, or as indicators of fertility or parental behavior in species with male choice (Clutton-Brock, 2007; Kraaijeveld et al., 2007).

To illustrate the point, consider that in most species of beetle, horns are only expressed by males and used in conflict over mates, as described by Darwin (1871). In the genus *Onthophagus*, however, many females develop horns that are physically different than those developed by males and thus cannot be due to genetic correlation (Emlen, Marangelo, Ball, & Cunningham, 2005).

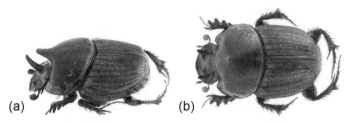

**PHOTO 2.5**   Female (a) and male (b) dung beetle (*Onthophagus sagittarius*). Females with larger horns outcompete females with smaller horns for control of burrows and dung. *Photo credit: Schmidt (2009). Creative commons license. http://commons.wikimedia.org/wiki/File:Onthophagus_sagittarius_Fabricius,_1775_female_(4140682509).jpg.* (See the color plate section.)

Photo 2.5 (inset) shows that females of the dung beetle species *Onthophagus sagittarius* (hereafter dung beetles) possess horns that are qualitatively different in both size and shape from the male's horns; the male develops two relatively small cephalic horns, and the female one large cephalic horn and, above this, a pronotal horn. Males compete with each other for access to mates using their cephalic horns, but females do not use their horns for mating competition and males do not prefer females with larger horns (Watson & Simmons, 2010a). Thus, sexual selection, as traditionally defined, is unlikely to account for horn evolution in female dung beetles.

Social selection, however, may provide the explanation. Females of this species, alone or in cooperation with a male, locate fresh dung that they drag into an excavated tunnel where they construct a brood chamber. The collected dung is then rolled into a brood ball where the female will lay an egg. Upon egg release, the female seals the brood ball with dung and fills the tunnel. The amount of dung in a brood ball is related to offspring fitness, with larger brood balls producing more fecund and competitive offspring. Thus, females that successfully compete with other females for dung and control of brood tunnels will have higher reproductive success than other females. Indeed, when resources are scarce, both females with larger bodies and females with larger horns produced more offspring than did their smaller competitors (Watson & Simmons, 2010b). Critically, competitive success among females was related specifically to horn size, controlling for body size. These studies provide strong evidence that female horns in this species evolved as a result of female-female competition over ecological resources, the control of which results in the production of higher-quality offspring.

The Soay sheep (*Ovis Aries*) provides another example of social competition among females (Clutton-Brock & Pemberton, 2004). As with the dung beetle, the horns differ for males and females of this species. Males grow either large horns that are used in male-male competition for mates or smaller horns; the latter males do not compete directly for females and attempt to mate opportunistically (Clutton-Brock, Wilson, & Stevenson, 1997). Females can grow smaller and larger horns as well, although some are hornless. For males, horn length, body size, and testes size (related to sperm competition) all independently predict male reproductive success (Preston, Stevenson, Pemberton, Coltman, & Wilson, 2003). However, the horns appear to serve a different purpose for females, as they do not have to compete for mating opportunities.

Robinson and Kruuk (2007) demonstrated that females with larger horns had an advantage over their smaller-horned peers during aggressive interactions. These interactions – and, concomitantly, female aggressiveness in general – are facultatively expressed; that is, depending on conditions. When population densities are high, competition for food becomes especially intense and influences offspring survival. During these times, horned females are better able to procure food and protect their offspring by intimidating or fending off other females and as a result enjoy higher reproductive success (Clutton-Brock et al., 1997). These results show that female horns are socially selected weapons that allow females to compete better, not for mates, but for access to limited ecological resources.

## Male Choice

Although Darwin focused on female choice of mating partners, he did not overlook male choice: "it is almost certain that they [high-status males] would select vigorous as well as attractive females" (Darwin, 1871, Vol. 1, p. 263). Indeed, male choice – although less common or exacting than female choice – has been found in dozens of species of insect (Bonduriansky, 2001; LeBas, Hockham, & Ritchie, 2003), many species of fish (Amundsen & Forsgren, 2001; Berglund & Rosenqvist, 2001) and bird (Amundsen & Pärn, 2006), and in some mammals (Muller, Thompson, & Wrangham, 2006; Szykman et al., 2001). Male choice makes sense when males invest more in offspring than females, as with pipefish (Paczolt & Jones, 2010), but it can also occur when males don't invest in offspring and females vary in quality (Edward & Chapman, 2011).

The important question here is whether some of these traits are signals of the quantity or quality of eggs the females carry or the quality of care they will provide to the males' offspring. In other words, are they condition-dependent signals and thus potentially vulnerable to disruption? We do not yet know the extent to which these traits are condition dependent but we do know that many of them are (Pizzari, Cornwallis, Løvlie, Jakobsson, & Birkhead, 2003; Roulin, Ducrest, Balloux, Dijkstra, & Riols, 2003; Roulin, Jungi, Pfister, & Dijkstra, 2000). For instance, Pizzari et al. (2003) found evidence for condition-dependent female ornaments in red jungle fowl (*Gallus gallus*), as well as male choice. Female jungle fowl sport red combs, although smaller and less colorful than those of males. Females with relatively large combs produce larger eggs with more yoke than their peers, and male mate choices indicate they prefer these females to females with smaller combs. Cryptic (after explicit choice of mating partner) male choice was demonstrated by the finding that males transfer more sperm when copulating with females with larger combs; this effect is particularly pronounced for high-status males, as implied by Darwin (1871).

## EXPRESSION OF CONDITION-DEPENDENT TRAITS

As Darwin (1859, 1871) noted, sexually selected traits tend to be more variable in their expression than naturally selected traits. He proposed that the reason for this was less-exacting pressures for sexually selected traits such that male peacocks that have somewhat fewer and less colorful eyespots than the most attractive male in the lek, for instance, will still survive and potentially sire a few offspring in the current season or at least have the potential of siring offspring the following season. However, the pattern is found even in species with intense sexual competition and high reproductive skew – a few males sire most offspring and most never reproduce – where, theoretically, variability in sexually selected traits should be significantly reduced (Fisher, 1930). The maintenance of excess variability in these traits created a conundrum that occupied evolutionary biologists for decades (e.g., Cotton, Fowler, & Pomiankowski, 2004a; Delhey & Peters, 2008; Pomiankowski & Møller, 1995).

As I noted in the introduction to this chapter, the solution to the riddle, or at least part of it, is that sexually and many socially selected traits have evolved to be physical, behavioral, or brain and cognitive signals of the bearer's condition (Zahavi, 1975; Zahavi & Zahavi, 1997). The expression of these traits more so than naturally selected traits is dependent on current health and nutritional status, genetic variability, and the ability to withstand the rigors of social competition or parental provisioning (Hamilton & Zuk, 1982; Rowe & Houle, 1996; Jennions, Kahn, Kelly, & Kokko, 2012; Jennions, Møller, & Petrie, 2001; Johnstone, 1995; McLean, Bishop, & Nakagawa, 2012; Møller & Alatalo, 1999). Zahavi argued that these traits are handicaps in that their expression can be costly. Costly signals are important because they cannot be easily faked by less fit individuals. Stated otherwise, costly signals are honest signals. These "handicaps," however, are not necessarily handicaps – requiring excess, wasteful expenditure above and beyond that needed to produce an honest signal – for honest signalers (Getty, 2002, 2006; Számadó, 2011). The honesty of the signal is maintained by the high costs paid by would-be cheaters.

Mate choices and competition for mates are dependent on multiple traits and thus individuals sport multiple signals (Andersson, 1994; Johnstone, 1995). Each of these might be redundant signals of the same underlying condition (e.g., genetic variability), or a more interesting possibility is that different constellations of traits signal different conditions, such as disease resistance versus nutritional status during development (Borgia & Coleman, 2000; Loyau, Saint Jalme, Cagniant, & Sorci, 2005; Loyau, Saint Jalme, & Sorci, 2005; McGraw & Hill, 2000; Nowicki, Peters, & Podos, 1998; Nowicki, Searcy, & Peters, 2002; Sullivan, 1994) or even susceptibility to different types of parasites (Wedekind, 1992). The color, size, vigor, and so on of different signals can then be used to make inferences about different aspects of the individuals' current condition and different aspects of their condition during development.

Behavioral traits, such as vigor and persistence of courtship displays, are necessarily dependent on the individual's current health, whereas many (but not all) physical signals will be fixed at the time they develop. As we will cover in the next chapter, some aspects of plumage coloration are dependent on the structure of feathers and, as a result, the individuals' condition at the time of molt and during development of new feathers will be reflected (literally) in plumage color (Prum, 2006). Individual birds in poor health due to illness or poor nutrition over winter will not have the physical stamina to cope with the rigors of competition for nesting sites and provisioning of offspring and this will be signaled by plumage color.

Some sexually selected traits may also be indicators of critical brain functions and cognitive competencies. Boogert, Giraldeau, and Lefebvre (2008) found that male zebra finches (*Taeniopygia guttata*) with more complex songs performed better on foraging tasks than did males with less complex songs; zebra finches are socially monogamous and both parents forage and provision offspring. Farrell, Weaver, An, and MacDougall-Shackleton (2012) found a similar pattern with the European starling (*Sturnus vulgaris*; but see Sewall, Soha, Peters, & Nowicki, 2013). As with song system nuclei (next chapter), early nutritional or social stressors can disrupt development of the brain systems that support foraging ability, especially the hippocampus (Pravosudov, Lavenex, & Omanska, 2005). The brain regions that support birdsong and foraging develop at the same time and thus will be affected by the same early conditions. Poor conditions during development would then compromise the male's ability to provision later in life, which in turn is signaled by song features even though these features do not directly contribute to foraging ability (see Spencer & MacDougall-Shackleton, 2011).

Many examples of condition-dependent traits are provided in Chapter 3 (birds and fish) and Chapter 4 (arthropods and mammals) for nonhuman species and in Chapter 6 (physical and behavioral traits) and Chapter 7 (brain and cognitive traits) for humans. For now, we need to briefly review the different types of conditions that can affect the expression of these traits; specifically, genetic variability, parasites, and social and nutritional stressors. Hill (2014) has recently proposed that these different stressors may have a single unifying underlying mechanism; specifically, cellular respiration. The proposal is that the core that ties these together is the efficiency of mitochondrial energy capture, utilization, and the associated generation and control of free radicals that can result in cell-damaging oxidative stress (von Schantz, Bensch, Grahn, Hasselquist, & Wittzell, 1999). It is not that specific stressors are not critical, it's that an individuals' ability to cope with each of them will be limited by the efficiency of cellular respiration. In any case, I close with a few words on the effects of toxin exposure on trait expression. Toxins are not part of the evolutionary history of sexually selected traits – they may now be a selective pressure – but many of them disproportionately affect sexually selected traits, and are relevant to our understanding of human vulnerability.

## Genetic Variance and Inbreeding Depression

Pomiankowski and Møller (1995) proposed that one factor that contributes to variation in sexually selected traits is more additive genetic variance relative to naturally selected traits. Any mutation that by chance results in enhancement of a sexually selected trait will provide the owner with reproductive advantage that in turn will incorporate this gene into the suite of genes underlying the trait and ensure its spread in the population. With many genes underlying sexually selected traits, sexual reproduction will ensure that offspring differ in the absolute number of these genes that they inherit. The accumulation of many genes underlying these traits – with each gene having small effects on trait expression – has the downside of many more potential targets for deleterious mutations, further increasing variation in the trait.

Rowe and Houle (1996) concur that there is considerable variation in sexually selected traits but argue the maintenance of this variation is due to genetic variation in overall condition; that is, health and vigor. Individuals in good condition – due to many processes that differ in efficiency across individuals – can invest more in the expression of sexually selected traits and thus these traits are signals of not only condition but also the many genes that underlie it. If sexually selected traits are potential indicators of an individuals' underlying condition – potentially Hill's (2014) cellular respiration – then anything that compromises the genes that affect health and vigor (e.g., as would be related to foraging efficiency) should also result in poor expression of these traits. A corresponding prediction is that increases in mutational load will result in decrements in condition and fewer resources to devote to the construction and maintenance of sexually selected traits (Tomkins, Radwan, Kotiaho, & Tregenza, 2004).

Inbreeding is one way to evaluate this proposal: Poor health can result from inbreeding because offspring of related parents are more likely to inherit the same copy (one from each parent) of deleterious variants of any particular gene. These deleterious effects – called inbreeding depression – are eliminated or reduced when unrelated parents produce offspring, because combining the deleterious variant with another variant of the same gene reduces the effects of the former (Cavalli-Sforza & Bodmer, 1999). If the individual inherits recessive and highly deleterious mutations from both parents, the result can be lethal, but most mutations will have more subtle effects (Charlesworth & Charlesworth, 1987; Muller, 1950). Ralls, Ballou, and Templeton's (1988) review indicated that, across a wide range of mammalian species, one generation of inbreeding increases, on average, the odds of premature morality by 33%. Fox and Reed's (2011) meta-analysis of mortality risks across plants, insects, and birds showed inbreeding depression is often exaggerated by exposure to environmental (e.g., temperature), nutritional, and social stressors. In a similar analysis, Armbruster and Reed (2005) came to the same conclusion, but also noted that susceptibility to stressors can vary considerably from one inbred lineage within a species to the next.

Clearly, there is much that remains to be learned but these studies indicate that inbreeding will typically have some effect on overall health and, in theory, compromise the expression of sexually selected traits. In fact, the theory means that anything that increases deleterious mutation rates (e.g., exposure to radiation) will undermine overall condition and increase mortality risks (Almbro & Simmons, 2014; Tomkins et al., 2004). Increased mortality risks in turn should be signaled through sexually selected traits and this is indeed the case (Jennions et al., 2001). In fact, these traits are also good signals of offspring survival, likely reflecting a combination of good genes provided by the male and skill at provisioning offspring for parental species (Møller & Alatalo, 1999).

## Parasites and Immunocompetence

In an influential theory, Hamilton and Zuk (1982) proposed that at least some sexually selected traits are indicators of one ubiquitous environmental stressor, parasites. The focus on parasites followed from an earlier proposal that sexual reproduction evolved in the first place as a way to cope with parasites; specifically, by creating variability in the immune system of offspring that then provides more defenses against local parasites (Hamilton, 1980, 1990; Hamilton, Axelrod, & Tanese, 1990; Jaenike, 1978). The proposal is similar to that of Rowe and Houle (1996), but narrows the condition to parasite resistance and the large suite of genes that construct parasite defenses. A decade later, Folstad and Karter's (1992) immunocompetence handicap hypothesis provided a more direct way to link the expression of sexually selected traits, at least in males, and parasite resistance; a pared down version of their model is shown in Figure 2.5. The key factor is the reciprocal relation between sex hormone levels, especially testosterone, and overall competence of the immune system.

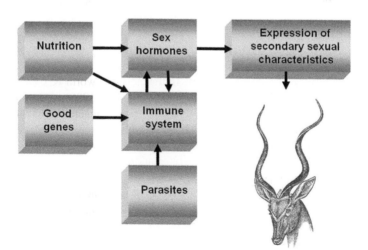

**FIGURE 2.5**  Hypothesized relations among sex hormones, immune functioning, parasites, and the expression of secondary sexual characteristics. From Geary (2010, p. 99). Male kudu (*Strepsiceros kudu*) from Darwin (1871, p. 255). (See the color plate section.)

Infestation with parasites will lead to an increase in immune system activity that can suppress the secretion of testosterone (e.g., Zuk, Johnsen, & Maclarty, 1995). The decline in testosterone will result in poorly developed secondary sexual characteristics, which will then signal parasite infestation to would-be mates and competitors. The model is also appealing in that it incorporates Zahavi's (1975) handicap hypothesis; specifically, immunosuppression is predicted to be more evident in males in generally poor health than in males in better physical condition. The relation between testosterone, the expression of sexually selected traits, and disease resistance is, however, nuanced and can vary across species, traits, and different features of the immune system (Roberts, Buchanan, & Evans, 2004). Across species, the relation between parasite load and testosterone is small, suggesting that high testosterone levels do not necessarily compromise immune functions. These patterns do not necessarily mean that the immunosuppression model is wrong and, in fact, the prediction is that males in good health can tolerate both high testosterone levels – leading to full expression of sexually selected traits – and high parasite loads (Jacobs & Zuk, 2012). It is males that are in marginal health that will pay the immunity price of trait expression.

The best evidence for this comes from field studies that experimentally increase testosterone levels in males and then follow their mating success and health for an extended period of time. In one such study, Deviche and Cortez (2005) implanted male house finches (*Carpodacus mexicanus*) with testosterone and monitored change in different immune functions across 2 months. When initially exposed to parasites, the immune responses of these males did not differ from that of untreated males. Critically, in the days following parasite exposure the immune functions of males with high testosterone levels dropped relative to that of other males. Even longer-term effects have been demonstrated in studies of the male red grouse (*Lagopus lagopus scoticus*; Mougeot, Redpath, & Piertney, 2006; Mougeot, Redpath, Piertney, & Hudson, 2005). Males were captured just before the breeding season and half received testosterone implants (Mougeot et al., 2006). Within a month, the testosterone-treated males had a larger comb – a sexually selected trait similar to the red comb above the eyes of the black grouse (Photo 2.2, inset) – but weighed less, possibly due to increased male-male aggression for nesting territories. Testosterone-treated males were more likely to attract mates than other males and had more offspring, but within a few months paid the price in terms of higher (12%) mortality, compromised immune functions, and infestation with more intestinal worms (*Trichostrongylus tenuis*).

Other studies are in keeping with the prediction that socially dominant males, those preferred by females as mates, are the ones that can tolerate parasite exposure while sporting attractive sexually selected traits (Zuk & Johnsen, 1998). Further nuance is provided by Boonekamp, Ros, and Verhulst's (2008) finding that across various species of mammal and bird, immune challenges were consistently related to subsequent drops in testosterone, as contrasted with a much weaker suppression of the immune system with increases in testosterone

(Roberts et al., 2004). Folstad and Karter's (1992) model would seem to leave females and hormones other than testosterone out in the cold, but this is not the case. The complex relations between sex hormones, including estrogens and progesterone, and the varied immune functions leave abundant opportunity for similar processes to occur in females and in relation to other hormones (Grossman, 1985; Sakiani, Olsen, & Kovacs, 2013).

Wedekind (1992) suggested that different hormones or combinations of them may interact with immune functions in ways that result in parasite-specific suppression of sexually selected traits, with one trait signaling infestation with one type of parasite and other traits signaling other parasites. Females generally have stronger immune responses than males (Sakiani et al., 2013), but some combinations of hormones (e.g., estradiol and progesterone) can result in the suppression of components of females' immune system. Whatever the specific mechanisms, there is now evidence that female ornaments signal immune system functions in species ranging from the Spanish pond turtle (*Mauremys leprosa*; Ibáñez, Marzal, López, & Martín, 2013) to the American goldfinch (*Spinus tristis*; Kelly, Murphy, Tarvin, & Burness, 2012) to the striped plateau lizard (*Sceloporus virgatus*; Weiss, Mulligan, Wilson, & Kabelik, 2013), among others (e.g., Henderson, Heidinger, Evans, & Arnold, 2013; Zanollo, Griggio, Robertson, & Kleindorfer, 2012).

## Nutritional and Social Stressors

Obviously, any individual chronically deprived of food will be in poor health, lack vigor, and unable to fully express sexually selected traits. A more typical situation is fluctuations in food availability and the ability to cope with these. Deprivation during critical developmental periods, as during the development of the brain systems underlying birdsong, may reveal itself in adulthood, as noted earlier (Spencer & MacDougall-Shackleton, 2011). A related issue is whether individuals differ in their ability to secure access to certain types of high-quality food and their ability to efficiently convert it into energy or molecules that support physiological functions. Carotenoids, such as β-carotene, are one such food that has been well studied in the context of sexual selection. These biological molecules cannot be synthesized de novo and thus must be obtained through diet (e.g., seeds, fruits, and vegetables). Once they are ingested, carotenoids or their metabolites contribute to multiple physiological functions, including reduction of oxidative stress and modulation of several types of immune response (Bendich, 1991; Burton & Ingold, 1984; Fitze, Tschirren, Gasparini, & Richner, 2007; McGraw, 2006a; Simons, Cohen, & Verhulst, 2012; Svensson & Wong, 2011). Hill (2014) suggested that carotenoids might also be a direct signal – not simply reserves to be used for immune functions or to cope with social stressors – of the efficiency of cellular respiration, because the pathway from foods to the molecules that produce color is dependent on the mitochondrial processes central to cellular respiration.

**PHOTO 2.6**   The red beak of the male zebra finch (*Taeniopygia guttata*) is an indicator of the quantity of carotenoids in the diet and the ability to efficiently process them. When exposed to stressors or pathogens carotenoids are diverted to the associated physiological reactions, resulting in a bleaching of beak color. (See the color plate section.)

As will be illustrated more fully in the next two chapters, carotenoids contribute to the development of yellow to red coloration in the displays of many species of bird, fish, and insect; the color expressed in some of these traits, particularly fleshy ornaments such as combs (Photo 2.2, inset), are also dependent on testosterone levels (Owens & Short, 1995). The red beak of the male zebra finch is an example of one such trait (Photo 2.6, inset). The color of these displays is a good signal of the individuals' current fitness, because when stressed during mating competition, foraging, or by parasites, the carotenoids in the trait will be diverted to immune or other core physiological functions. The result for the zebra finch is a rapid bleaching of beak color and thereby rapid feedback to competitors and would-be mates that the individual is unable to effectively cope with the stressor. These colorful traits also provide information on the individuals' behavioral vigor and stamina, as carotenoids can only be obtained through foraging. The bottom line is that individuals with richly colored carotenoid-based traits are physiologically and immunologically healthy and behaviorally vigorous.

Social competition and attendant stresses are by definition integral features of sexual selection and, as mentioned, the ability to cope with the rigors of competition is signaled in carotenoid-based and many other sexually selected traits. These rigors will trigger the release of stress hormones, such as corticosterone, that will mobilize the resources needed to cope with the stressor (Adkins-Regan, 2005) and, at a more basic level, engage the mechanisms in cellular respiration described by Hill (2014). "Stress" hormone is a bit of a misnomer, however, because moderate levels can enhance performance, for instance by increasing vigor of courtship displays, but high or chronically elevated levels will generally impair performance (Leary & Knapp, 2014). As reviewed in Leary and Knapp, high or chronic exposure to stress hormones may directly affect the expression of a sexually selected trait, or indirectly affect it through suppression of sex hormones or by compromising immune functions (Padgett & Glaser, 2003).

As an example, San-Jose and Fitze (2013) experimentally increased corticosterone levels in male common lizards (*Zootoca vivipara*) to the maximum level that can occur in natural contexts. Males of this species signal their physical condition to competitors and potential mates by raising-up on their forelimbs to expose a bright orange throat and underbelly. Corticosterone significantly dulled this signal but did not affect coloration of stripes on their sides, which are not sexually selected. Although much remains to be learned about how stress hormones interact with sex hormones and the immune system, it is likely that they are an important part of the processes that affect the expression of sexually selected traits (Leary & Knapp, 2014). Given this, it is not surprising that in some species chronic low-level harassment of competitors and subordinates is a common feature of day-to-day life (Sapolsky, 2005) and may be an evolved behavioral strategy to increase physiological stressors that in turn undermine the victims' ability to compete.

## Toxins

Toxins are so named because of their potential to do harm. Given the sensitivity of sexually selected traits to many different types of stressors, they may be more easily disrupted by toxin exposure than naturally selected traits. Many of these toxins are in fact endocrine disrupting compounds (EDCs) that can interfere with the normal functioning of many different hormones, resulting in the disruption of the immune system and traits and behaviors regulated by sex hormones (Carere, Costantini, Sorace, Santucci, & Alleva, 2010; Palanza, Gioiosa, vom Saal, & Parmigiani, 2008; Palanza, Morellini, Parmigiani, & vom Saal, 1999), among other effects (Milnes et al., 2006). Exposure to EDCs should then readily disrupt the development and expression of sexually selected traits, and this has in fact been found in many species, including American kestrels (*Falco sparverius*; Bortolotti, Fernie, & Smits, 2003), deer mice (*Peromyscus maniculatus*; Jašarević et al., 2011), zebra fish (*Danio rerio*; Coe et al., 2008), and mosquito fish (*Gambusia holbrooki*; Doyle & Lim, 2002), among others noted in Chapters 3 and 4. Moreover, Crews et al. (2007) found that the great grandsons of male rats (*Rattus norvegicus*) exposed to an EDC were less attractive to females (likely influenced by pheromones) than the great grandsons of unexposed males. The implication is that toxin exposure resulted in epigenetic changes (change in gene expression without affecting the underlying DNA) that were transmitted across generations.

EDCs are not the only toxins that can influence the expression of sexually selected traits. Eens and colleagues, for example, found that great tits (*Parus major*) residing in areas with high concentrations of heavy metals had less colorful plumage and less complex mating songs than did birds living in areas with lower concentrations (Dauwe & Eens, 2008; Gorissen, Snoeijs, Van Duyse, & Eens, 2005), although it is unclear whether the effect is due to physiological changes in the great tits or higher mortality of prey species and thus poor nutrition (Geens, Dauwe, & Eens, 2009). I also note that the effects of toxins are often dose dependent and thus not always observed (Peluso, Munnia, & Ceppi, 2014). Toxins that affect natural hormonal systems can also have variable effects, sometimes exaggerating trait expression and sometimes diminishing it. As described above for the red grouse (Mougeot et al., 2005), exaggerated traits may sometimes result in a short-term advantage but with longer-term costs, and this should always be considered when toxins are found to exaggerate the expression of sexually or socially selected traits.

Finally, the potency of many of toxins to disrupt the normal development and expression of sexually selected traits has led to the suggestion that these traits may serve as barometers of ecological contamination (Carere et al., 2010; Hill, 1995), although they are not typically included in toxicology research (Beronius, Johansson, Rudén, & Hanberg, 2013). In any case, my point is that the nearly ubiquitous exposure of humans to a wide array of potential toxins means they need to be included among the factors that can influence sex differences in vulnerability, as discussed in Chapters 6 and 7.

## CONCLUSION

Sexual and social selection can take many forms, from direct physical fights to behavioral displays of stamina to complex songs that are dependent on specialized brain and cognitive systems that support learning and memory. These varied traits are unified by their signaling function; physical, behavioral, and cognitive traits convey information about the senders' condition to competitors and to would-be mates (Zahavi, 1975). Condition in turn can also take many forms, from mutation load to functioning of the immune system and health to the ability to withstand a host of nutritional and social stressors (Hamilton & Zuk, 1982; Rowe & Houle, 1996; Spencer & MacDougall-Shackleton, 2011). These different varieties of condition are often interrelated, such that indicators of compromised functions in one area (e.g., immune functions) are often indicative of compromised functions in other areas (e.g., foraging ability). Hill's (2014) proposal that cellular respiration – efficiency of energy capture and use, as well as control of oxidative stress – is the ultimate mechanism underlying variation in the condition of all sexually selected traits across all species is insightful and potentially very important. The efficiency of cellular respiration provides the limit of an individual's ability to express one trait or another or to cope with the stressors that modulate trait expression. Whether or not an individual is pushed to this limit, however, will varying on multiple other conditions, including all of those described in this chapter (e.g., exposure to parasites, nutrition, and social competition).

In other words, even with individual differences in the efficiency of cellular respiration or any other general physiological mechanism that may underlie condition, variation in these limits will be most apparent in the system that is currently stressed and most apparent in the sexually or socially selected traits that signal integrity of the system. The important point for us is that we can move beyond the evolved functions of sexually and socially selected traits – to signal competitiveness and benefits conferred to mates – to identify sex-specific vulnerabilities to social and nutritional stressors during development and, currently, compromised health (e.g., these traits may be sensitive early indicators of illness), and exposure to environmental toxins. Many examples of the utility of this approach for identifying vulnerability and risk in humans are provided in Chapters 6 and 7. In the next two chapters, I provide reviews and illustrations of the condition-dependent expression of sexually selected traits across a wide range of species and conditions. These reviews provide the scientific foundation for the reviews of condition-dependent trait expression in humans.

# Chapter 3

# Condition-Dependent Traits in Birds and Fish

## Chapter Outline

In this chapter and the next, I provide many examples of condition-dependent traits across a wide variety of nonhuman species. I wanted the reviews to be useful themselves and thus some of the discussion is a bit dry and technical, so I provide a few "takeaway message" subsections for readers who just want the gist. More critically, the reviews illustrate how competition and choice have resulted in condition dependence for traits similar to those we will cover for humans in later chapters. The focus is on sexually rather than socially selected traits, because more is known about the former than the latter. This does not mean I have abandoned social selection, and in fact examples of traits associated with female-female competition over resources other than mates are provided: My working assumption is that the same processes that affect sexually selected traits will operate with socially selected traits and thus the use of sexual selection should be interpreted broadly (e.g., Murphy, Rosenthal, Montgomerie, & Tarvin, 2009). In any case, the reviews to follow illustrate the widespread occurrence of condition-dependent traits and show that for any single species one or more of them can be found in males, females, and often in both sexes.

As was touched upon in the last chapter, condition-dependent traits can be very different from one species to the next, ranging from the red comb of the jungle fowl (*Gallus gallus*; Ligon, Thornhill, Zuk, & Johnson, 1990) to the courtship displays of the stickleback (*Gasterosteus aculeatus*; Sebire, Allen, Bersuder, & Katsiadaki, 2008) to the scent of the golden hamster

Evolution of Vulnerability. http://dx.doi.org/10.1016/B978-0-12-801562-9.00003-X

(*Mesocricetus auratus*; White, Fischer, & Meunier, 1984). To the untrained eye, this collage of traits might seem random and not particularly useful for identifying vulnerability, and this would in fact be the case without an understanding of the evolutionary history of the species. The key unifying concept, as outlined in the last chapter, is that these are traits involved in competition for mates and other resources needed for successful reproduction, or for identifying the best mating partners. These traits can differ from one species to the next, because the nature of the competition or the criteria for mate choice often differs across species (Andersson, 1994). Once the specifics of competition and choice are understood, predictions can be made about which traits are most vulnerable for males and which traits are most vulnerable for females.

Before moving to the reviews of condition-dependent traits in birds and fish, we need to consider Svensson and Wong's (2011) caveats about the difficulty of experimentally detecting changes in these traits; conspecifics can detect subtle variation in these traits better than scientists can. This is because individuals in good condition should be relatively insensitive to many common stressors, such as a moderate change in dietary quality or parasite load that in turn will make contrasts of manipulated (e.g., food restriction) and unmanipulated groups relatively weak (Jacobs & Zuk, 2012). In other words, manipulating stressors may substantially affect some individuals and only have minor effects on others; thus, combining them together in one treated group will underestimate the influence of the stressor for less healthy individuals. As I noted in the last chapter, different sexually selected traits may be sensitive to different forms of stressor (e.g., Wedekind, 1992), and as a result detection of condition dependence might depend on correctly matching the stressor (e.g., early nutrition vs. current parasite load) with the trait that is most sensitive to it (e.g., plumage color vs. courtship display). Matching the right stressor with the wrong trait or vice versa will underestimate the condition dependence of the trait. Finally, the nature of these studies, especially those conducted in the field, often results in small samples of animals that in turn make it difficult to statistically detect subtle effects.

## BIRDS

Birds are a good place to start because the extensive literature on sexual selection in these species provides a wealth of information on the evolution and expression of condition-dependent traits. Several biologists have reviewed aspects of this literature previously, and I started with these reviews and expanded upon them (Andersson, 1994; Cotton, Fowler, & Pomiankowski, 2004a; Griffith, Parker, & Olson, 2006; Johnstone, 1995). I included all of the avian studies reviewed by Cotton et al. (noted in the tables by *) and Griffith et al. (noted in the tables by +), with one exception; Tschirren, Fitze, and Richner (2003) studied nestling coloration in great tits (*Parus major*) and not sexually selected trait expression in adulthood. On the basis of multiple literature searches (e.g., Google Scholar search for condition dependence and courtship display), I included about 100 studies of bird species, 30 of which were included in one or the other of the previously mentioned reviews. Many of the additional studies cover brain and cognitive traits – which were not included in Cotton et al. or Griffith et al. – and many were published after publication of these reviews.

The authors of many of these newer studies took Cotton et al.'s (2004a) critiques of this literature seriously and as a result produced stronger experiments. The best evidence that sexually selected traits are particularly vulnerable to disruption requires demonstration that a similar naturally selected trait (e.g., physical trait vs. physical trait) is less vulnerable or that the effect only occurs in the sex or species in which sexual selection has resulted in trait elaboration. The basic concept is shown in Figure 3.1, where the top shows the sex difference that emerges for a trait that has been elaborated by sexual selection, say made larger, in one sex but not the other. The bottom of Figure 3.1 shows the expected result when both sexes are exposed to the same stressor; that is, the elaborated trait will be more strongly affected by the stressor than will the same trait in the opposite sex. All of the tables indicate whether a contrast trait was included in the assessment or not, and I will point out a few examples of weaker and stronger evidence for condition dependence based on the use of contrasts in each of the reviews. But first, we'll walk through the organization of the reviews.

## Organization of Reviews

Following my descriptions of sexual selection in the last chapter, all of the reviews are organized in terms of physical traits (color and size separately), behavioral traits, and brain and cognitive traits. Tables 3.1–3.4 provide examples

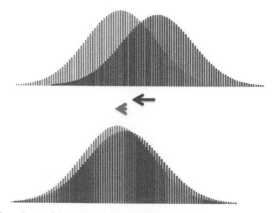

**FIGURE 3.1** Sexual or social selection will result in the elaboration of traits that enhance or signal competitive abilities or influence mate choices. The top distributions show how these processes result in larger traits (darker color) in one sex versus the other; or larger sexually selected than naturally selected traits in the same individual. Exposure to stressors has stronger effects on the elaborated than the contrast trait (bottom). (See the color plate section.)

**TABLE 3.1 Condition-Dependent Color Traits in Birds**

| Species | Scientific Name | ST | Trait | CD | S | Contrast | | Life History | CT | Manipulation | Reference |
|---|---|---|---|---|---|---|---|---|---|---|---|
| | | | | | | Trait | Effect | | | | |
| Black grouse | Tetrao tetrix | F | Comb | Y | M | Body size | C < T | Adult | C | Testosterone | Siitari, Alatalo, Halme, Buchanan, and Kilpimaa (2007) |
| Red jungle fowl | Gallus gallus | N | Comb | Y | M | Body size | C < T | Adult | C | Social dominance | Ligon et al. (1990) |
| | | L | Comb | Y | M | NA | NA | Adult | C | Infection/ parasite | Zuk, Thornhill, and Ligon (1990) |
| Ring-necked pheasant | Phasianus colchicus | L* | Wattle | Y | M | Tarsus length | C < T | Postnatal | C | Diet/ nutrition | Ohlsson, Smith, Råberg, and Hasselquist (2002) |
| | | L | Wattle | N | M | Body size | C = T | Postnatal | C | Infection/ parasite | Orledge, Blount, Hoodless, and Royle (2012) |
| Red-legged partridge | Alectoris rufa | L | Beak | Y | B | Body size | C < T | Postnatal | C | Oxidative stress | Alonso-Alvarez and Galván (2011) |
| | | L | Eye ring | Y | B | Body size | C < T | Postnatal | C | Oxidative stress | Alonso-Alvarez and Galván (2011) |

| Species | Code | Trait | Y/N | B/M | Measure | C vs T | Age | C | Manipulation | Reference |
|---|---|---|---|---|---|---|---|---|---|---|
| Zebra finch *Taeniopygia guttata* | L | Beak | Y | B | Female beak | C<T | Inbreeding | C | Inbreeding | Bolund, Martin, Kempenaers, and Forstmeier (2010) |
| | L+ | Beak | N | M | Body mass | C>T | Postnatal | C | Diet/nutrition | Birkhead, Fletcher, and Pellatt (1999) |
| | L+ | Beak | Y | B | Female beak | C<T | Postnatal | C | Brood size | de Kogel (1997) |
| | L+ | Beak | Y | B | Female beak | C<T | Postnatal | C | Brood size | de Kogel and Prijs (1996) |
| | L* | Beak | Y | M | NA | NA | Adult | C | Diet/nutrition | Blount, Metcalfe, Arnold et al. (2003) |
| | L* | Beak | N | B | Female beak | C=T | Postnatal | C | Diet/nutrition | Blount, Metcalfe, Birkhead, and Surai (2003) |
| | L* | Beak | N[a] | M | Body condition | C>T | Adult | C | Diet/nutrition | Birkhead, Fletcher, and Pellatt (1998) |
| | L* | Beak | Y | B | Female beak | C=T | Adult | C | Multiple breeding cycles | Burley, Price, and Zann (1992) |
| | F* | Beak | Y | B | Female beak | C=T | Adult | C | Diet/nutrition | Burley et al. (1992) |
| | L* | Beak | N | M | NA | NA | Adult | C | Diet/nutrition | Burley et al. (1992) |
| | L* | Beak | Y | M | NA | NA | Adult | C | Social density | Burley et al. (1992) |

*Continued*

**TABLE 3.1** Condition-Dependent Color Traits in Birds—cont'd

| Species | Scientific Name | ST | Trait | CD | S | Contrast Trait | Effect | Life History | CT | Manipulation | Reference |
|---|---|---|---|---|---|---|---|---|---|---|---|
| American goldfinch | Spinus tristis | L | Beak | Y | B | Female beak | C=T | Adult | C | Infection/parasite | Rosenthal, Murphy, Darling, and Tarvin (2012) |
| | | L*+ | Beak | Y | M | Body mass | C<T | Adult | C | Infection/parasite | McGraw and Hill (2000) |
| | | N | Beak | Y[b] | F | Body mass | C<T | Adult | C | Immune functions | Kelly, Murphy, Tarvin, and Burness (2012) |
| | | N | Beak | N | M | Body mass | C=T | Adult | C | Immune functions | Kelly et al. (2012) |
| | | N | Beak | Y | M | Body mass | C<T | Adult | C | Physiological stress | Kelly et al. (2012) |
| | | N | Beak | Y | F | Body mass | C<T | Adult | C | Physiological stress | Kelly et al. (2012) |
| | | N | Plumage | Y[b] | F | Body mass | C<T | Adult | C | Immune functions | Kelly et al. (2012) |
| | | N | Plumage | N | M | Body mass | C=T | Adult | C | Immune functions | Kelly et al. (2012) |
| | | L*+ | Plumage | Y | M | Body mass | C<T | Adult | C | Infection/parasite | McGraw and Hill (2000) |
| | | L+ | Plumage | Y | M | Body mass | C<T | Adult | C | Diet/nutrition | McGraw, Hill, and Parker (2005) |

| | | | | | | | | | | | |
|---|---|---|---|---|---|---|---|---|---|---|---|
| House finch | *Carpodacus mexicanus* | L* | Plumage | Y | M | NA | NA | Adult | C | Diet/nutrition | Hill (1990) |
| | | L* | Plumage | Y | M | Patch size | C < T | Adult | C | Diet/nutrition | Hill (1992) |
| | | L* | Plumage | Y | M | NA | NA | Adult | C | Diet/nutrition | Hill (1993) |
| | | L* | Plumage | Y | M | Melanin tail color | C < T | Postnatal | C | Diet/nutrition | Hill (2000) |
| | | L* | Plumage | Y | M | NA | NA | Postnatal | C | Infection/parasite | Hill and Brawner (1998) |
| | | L*+ | Plumage | Y | M | Body size | C < T | Postnatal | C | Infection/parasite | Brawner, Hill, and Sundermann (2000) |
| | | N | Plumage | Y | M | Feather length | C < T | Adult | C | Social dominance | Hill and Montgomerie (1994) |
| | | N | Plumage | Y | M | NA | NA | Adult | C | Parental investment | Hill (1991) |
| Diamond firetail | *Stagonopleura guttata* | L | Plumage | Y | B | Female plumage | C < T | Adult | C | Immune functions | Zanollo, Griggio, Robertson, and Kleindorfer (2012) |
| Greenfinch | *Carduelis chloris* | L | Tail plumage | Y | M | Other plumage | C < T | Adult | C | Diet/nutrition | Peters, Delhey, Andersson, Van Noordwijk, and Förschler (2008) |
| | | L+ | Plumage | Y | M | Inner feather | C < T | Adult | C | Infection/parasite | Hörak et al. (2004) |

*Continued*

**TABLE 3.1** Condition-Dependent Color Traits in Birds—cont'd

| Species | Scientific Name | ST | Trait | CD | S | Contrast Trait | Contrast Effect | Life History | CT | Manipulation | Reference |
|---|---|---|---|---|---|---|---|---|---|---|---|
| Serin | *Serinus serinus* | N+ | Plumage | Y | M | NA | NA | Adult | C | Infection/parasite | Figuerola, Domenech, and Senar (2003) |
| | | F+ | Plumage | Y | M | NA | NA | Adult | C | Infection/parasite | Figuerola et al. (2003) |
| Great tit | *Parus major* | N/T | Plumage | Y | B | Female color | C=T | Adult | C | Toxin | Dauwe and Eens (2008) |
| | | N/T | Plumage | Y | B | Female color | C=T | Adult | C | Toxin | Geens, Dauwe, and Eens (2009) |
| | | F+ | Plumage | N | B | Female color | C=T | Adult | C | Infection/parasite | Fitze and Richner (2002) |
| Mallard duck | *Anas platyrhynchos* | L | Beak | N[c] | M | Body weight | C=T | Postnatal/adult | C | Diet/nutrition | Butler and McGraw (2012) |
| American kestrels | *Falco sparverius* | L/T | Facial | Y | B | Female facial | C<T | Adult | C | Toxin | Bortolotti, Fernie, and Smits (2003) |
| Yellow-legged gull | *Larus michahellis* | F/T | Beak-spot | N | B | Body mass | C=T | Adult | C | Toxin | Pérez et al. (2010) |
| Blackbirds | *Turdus merula* | L+ | Beak | Y | M | Body mass | C<T | Adult | C | Infection/parasite | Faivre, Grégoire, Préault, Cézilly, and Sorci (2003) |
| Hihi | *Notiomystis cincta* | F | Plumage | Y[d] | M | Melanin plumage | C<T | Postnatal | C | Diet/nutrition | Walker, Stevens, Karadaş, Kilner, and Ewen (2013) |

| Red jungle fowl | *Gallus gallus* | L | Plumage | Y | M | NA | NA | Adult | M | Infection/parasite | Zuk et al. (1990) |
|---|---|---|---|---|---|---|---|---|---|---|---|
| American goldfinch | *Spinus tristis* | L*+ | Black cap | N | M | Body mass | C>T | Adult | M | Infection/parasite | McGraw and Hill (2000) |
| House finch | *Carpodacus mexicanus* | L*+ | Tail | N | M | NA | NA | Postnatal | M | Infection/parasite | Hill and Brawner (1998) |
| House sparrow | *Passer domesticus* | L*+ | Black patch | N | M | Body size | C=T | Adult | M | Diet/nutrition | McGraw, Mackillop, Dale, and Hauber (2002) |
| | | L* | Black patch | N | M | Body size | C>T | Postnatal | M | Diet/nutrition | Gonzalez et al. (1999) |
| Great tit | *Parus major* | F+ | Black stripe | N | B | Female color | C=T | Adult | M | Infection/parasite | Fitze and Richner (2002) |
| Brown-headed cowbirds | *Molothrus ater* | L*+ | Head cap | N | M | Body size | C=T | Adult | M | Diet/nutrition | McGraw et al. (2002) |
| Hihi | *Notiomystis cincta* | F | Plumage | N[d] | M | Carotenoid plumage | NA | Postnatal | M | Diet/nutrition | Walker et al. (2013) |
| Black grouse | *Tetrao tetrix* | F | Plumage | Y | M | Body size | C<T | Adult | S | Testosterone | Siitari et al. (2007) |
| Wild turkeys | *Meleagris gallopavo* | L | Plumage | Y | M | Non-UV color | C<T | Postnatal | S | Infection/parasite | Hill, Doucet, and Buchholz (2005) |

*Continued*

**TABLE 3.1** Condition-Dependent Color Traits in Birds—cont'd

| Species | Scientific Name | ST | Trait | CD | S | Contrast Trait | Contrast Effect | Life History | CT | Manipulation | Reference |
|---|---|---|---|---|---|---|---|---|---|---|---|
| Blue grosbeaks | Guiraca caerulea | N | Plumage | Y | M | NA | NA | Adult | S | Feather growth | Keyser and Hill (1999) |
| | | N | Plumage | Y | M | NA | NA | Adult | S | Body condition | Keyser and Hill (2000) |
| | | N | Plumage | Y | M | NA | NA | Adult | S | Testosterone | Keyser and Hill (2000) |
| | | N | Plumage | Y | M | NA | NA | Adult | S | Parental investment | Keyser and Hill (2000) |
| Blue-black grassquits | Volatinia jacarina | L | Plumage | Y | M | Other plumage | C<T | Adult | S | Social competition | Maia, Brasileiro, Lacava, and Macedo (2012) |
| Blue tit | Parus caeruleus | L | Plumage | N | B | Female color | C=T | Postnatal | S | Diet/nutrition | Peters, Kurvers, Roberts, and Delhey (2011) |
| Hihi | Notiomystis cincta | F | Plumage | N[d] | M | Melanin plumage | C>T | Postnatal | S | Diet/nutrition | Walker et al. (2013) |
| Tree swallows | Tachycineta bicolor | N/T | Plumage | Y | F | Body size | C<T | Adult | S | Toxin | McCarty and Secord (2000) |
| Mallard duck | Anas platyrhynchos | L* | Plumage | N | M | Body weight | C>T | Adult | S | Diet/nutrition | Holmberg, Edsman, and Klint (1989) |

| Blue-black grassquits | Volatinia jacarina | N | Plumage | Y | M | Body size | C<T | Adult | S | Body condition | Doucet (2002) |
|---|---|---|---|---|---|---|---|---|---|---|---|
| Brown-headed cowbirds | Molothrus ater | L*+ | Plumage | Y | M | Body size | C<T | Adult | S | Diet/nutrition | McGraw et al. (2002) |
| Junco | Junco hyemalis | L | Plumage | Y | M | Body size | C<T | Adult | S | Diet/nutrition | McGlothlin, Duffy, Henry-Freeman, and Ketterson (2007) |
| Anna's hummingbird | Calypte anna | L | Plumage | Y | M | Other plumage | C=T | Adult | S | Diet/nutrition | Meadows, Roudybush, and McGraw (2012) |

Note: ST, study type (L, lab experiment; F, field experiment; N, natural variation; T, toxin; *, included in Cotton et al. (2004a) review; +, included in Griffith et al. (2006) meta-analysis); CD, condition dependent (Y, yes; N, no); S, sex of animals included in the study (M, male; F, female; B, both sexes). CT, Color Type (C, carotenoid; M, melanin; S, structural); UV, ultraviolet structural-based color.

[a]There were no group differences, but beak color was correlated with body condition within the experimental group.

[b]Female beak and plumage color were correlated with different aspects of immune functions.

[c]Across groups, higher beak color was associated with stronger responses in some immune functions.

[d]The experiment involved supplementing nestlings nutritionally (without carotenoids), with carotenoids (without nutritional supplement), or both. Carotenoid-, melanin-, and structural-based colors were assessed in adulthood. Structural color (white patch) was affected, but negatively; that is, nutrition supplement was associated with duller color.

**TABLE 3.2** Condition-Dependent Size Traits in Birds

| Species | Scientific Name | ST | Trait | CD | S | Contrast Trait | Contrast Effect | Life History | CT | Manipulation | Reference |
|---|---|---|---|---|---|---|---|---|---|---|---|
| Red grouse | Lagopus lagapus | N | Comb | Y | M | Body size | C<T | Adult | C | Ecological quality | Vergara, Martinez-Padilla, Mougeot, Leckie, and Redpath (2012) |
| | | F | Comb | Y | M | Body size | C<T | Adult | C | Social competition | Vergara, Martinez-Padilla et al. (2012) |
| | | N | Comb | Y | M | Body size | C<T | Adult | C | Infection/parasite | Vergara, Mougeot, Martinez-Padilla, Leckie, and Redpath (2012) |
| | | N | Comb | Y | B | Female comb | C<T | Adult | C | Social density | Vergara, Redpath, Martinez-Padilla, and Mougeot (2012) |
| | | N | Comb | Y | F | Body size | C=T | Adult | C | Infection/parasite | Martinez-Padilla et al. (2011) |
| | | F | Comb | Y | F | Body size | C<T | Adult | C | Antiparasite | Martinez-Padilla et al. (2011) |
| | | F | Comb | Y | M | NA | NA | Adult | C | Parasite/testosterone | Bortolotti, Mougeot, Martinez-Padilla, Webster, and Piertney (2009) |
| | | N | Comb | Y | M | NA | NA | Adult | C | Infection/parasite | Mougeot, Irvine, Seivwright, Redpath, and Piertney (2004) |
| | | F | Comb | Y | M | NA | NA | Adult | C | Testosterone | Mougeot et al. (2004) |

| Red jungle fowl | *Gallus gallus* | L | Comb | Y | M | Tarsus length | C<T | Postnatal | C | Infection/parasite | Zuk et al. (1990) |
|---|---|---|---|---|---|---|---|---|---|---|---|
|  |  | L | Comb | Y | M | Body/feather size | C<T | Adult | C | Testosterone | Zuk, Johnsen, and Maclarty (1995) |
| Domestic fowl | *G. domesticus* | N | Comb | Y | M | Body size | C<T | Adult | C | Social competition | Ligon et al. (1990) |
|  |  | L | Comb | Y^a | M | Body size | C<T | Adult | C | Selective breeding | Verhulst, Dieleman, and Parmentier (1999) |
| Ring-necked pheasants | *Phasianus colchicus* | L* | Wattle | Y | M | Tarsus length | C<T | Postnatal | C | Diet/nutrition | Ohlsson et al. (2002) |
| Wild turkeys | *Meleagris gallopavo* | N | Snood | Y | M | NA | NA | Adult | C | Infection/parasite | Buchholz (1995) |
| Yellow-legged gull | *Larus michahellis* | F/T | Red beak-spot | Y | B | Body mass | C<T | Adult | C | Toxin | Pérez et al. (2010) |
| Zebra finch | *Taeniopygia guttata* | L | Cheek patch | Y | M | Body size | C<T | Postnatal | C | Diet/nutrition | Naguib and Nemitz (2007) |
|  |  | L+ | Cheek patch | N | M | Body condition | C>T | Postnatal | M | Brood size | de Kogel (1997) |
| American goldfinch | *Spinus tristis* | L*+ | Black cap | N | M | Body mass | C>T | Adult | M | Infection/parasite | McGraw and Hill (2000) |

*Continued*

**TABLE 3.2** Condition-Dependent Size Traits in Birds—cont'd

| Species | Scientific Name | ST | Trait | CD | S | Contrast | | Life History | CT | Manipulation | Reference |
|---|---|---|---|---|---|---|---|---|---|---|---|
| | | | | | | Trait | Effect | | | | |
| House sparrow | *Passer domesticus* | L*+ | Black patch | N | M | Body size | C=T | Adult | M | Diet/nutrition | McGraw et al. (2002) |
| | | L* | Black patch | N | M | Body size | C>T | Postnatal | M | Diet/nutrition | Gonzalez et al. (1999) |
| | | F* | Black patch | Y | M | NA | NA | Adult | M | Brood size | Griffith (2000) |
| | | F+ | Black patch | Y | M | Body mass | C<T | Postnatal | M | Cross-foster | Griffith, Owens, and Burke (1999) |
| | | F+ | Black patch | Y | M | NA | NA | Adult | M | Body condition | Veiga and Puerta (1996) |
| | | L+ | Black patch | Y | M | NA | NA | Adult | M | Diet/nutrition | Veiga and Puerta (1996) |
| Great tit | *Parus major* | N/T | Black plumage | Y | M | Body size | C<T | Adult | M | Toxin | Dauwe and Eens (2008) |
| | | F+ | Black stripe | Y | B | Female stripe | C=T | Adult | M | Infection/parasite | Fitze and Richner (2002) |
| Diamond firetail | *Stagonopleura guttata* | L | Plumage spots | Y | B | Male spots | C<T | Adult | S | Immune functions | Zanollo et al. (2012) |

| Common name | Species | ST | Trait | CD | Sex | | C<T | Age | S | | Reference |
|---|---|---|---|---|---|---|---|---|---|---|---|
| Collard flycatchers | Ficedula albicollis | F | Forehead patch | Y | M | NA | NA | Adult | S | Infection/parasite | Garamszegi et al. (2004) |
| | | F* | Forehead patch | Y | M | NA | NA | Adult | S | Brood size | Gustafsson, Qvarnström, and Sheldon (1995) |
| | | N* | Forehead patch | N | M | NA | NA | Postnatal | S | Ecological quality | Qvarnstrom (1999) |
| | | F* | Forehead patch | N | M | NA | NA | Postnatal | S | Brood size | Qvarnstrom (1999) |
| Junco | Junco hyemalis | L | Tail patch | Y | M | Body size | C<T | Adult | S | Diet/nutrition | McGlothlin et al. (2007) |
| Barn swallow | Hirundo rustica | N* | Tail length | Y | B | Female tail | C<T | Adult | NA | Diet/nutrition | Moller (1991) |
| | | N* | Tail length | Y | B | Female tail | C<T | Adult | NA | Infection/parasite | Moller (1991) |
| Jackson's widowbird | Euplectes jacksoni | N | Tail length | Y | M | NA | NA | Adult | NA | Body condition | Andersson (1989) |
| Ring-necked pheasant | Phasianus colchicus | L* | Spur length | N | M | NA | NA | Postnatal | NA | Diet/nutrition | Ohlsson et al. (2002) |
| | | N | Spur length | Y | M | Wing length | C<T | Adult | NA | RS | von Schantz et al. (1989) |
| Black grouse | Tetrao tetrix | F | Tail length | Y | M | Body size | C<T | Adult | NA | Testosterone | Siitari et al. (2007) |

Note: ST, study type [L, lab experiment; F, field experiment; N, natural variation; T, toxin; *, included in Cotton et al. (2004a) review; +, included in Griffith et al. (2006) meta-analysis]; CD, condition dependent (Y, yes; N, no); S, sex of animals included in the study (M, male; F, female; B, both sexes). CT, color type (C, carotenoid; M, melanin; S, structural; NA, not applicable); RS, reproductive success.

[a]Selective breeding was used to produce groups with stronger and weaker immune responses to test for trade-offs between immune system development and development of comb size.

**TABLE 3.3** Condition-Dependent Behavioral Traits in Birds

| Species | Scientific Name | ST | Trait | CD | S | Contrast | | Life History | Manipulation | Reference |
|---|---|---|---|---|---|---|---|---|---|---|
| | | | | | | Trait | Effect | | | |
| Houbara bustard | Chlamydotis undulata | L | Courtship display | Y | M | NA | NA | Adult | Infection/parasite | Chargé, Sorci, Hingrat, Lacroix, and Jalme (2011) |
| Jackson's widowbird | Euplectes jacksoni | N | Courtship display | Y | M | NA | NA | Adult | RS | Andersson (1989) |
| Frigate bird | Fregata magnificens | N | Courtship display | Y | M | Body size | C<T | Adult | T/body condition | Chastel et al. (2005) |
| Rock dove | Columba livia | L | Courtship display | Y | M | Body size | C<T | Adult | Infection/parasite | Clayton (1990) |
| Junco | Junco hyemalis | L | Courtship display | Y[a] | M | Body size | C<T | Adult | Testosterone | Enstrom, Ketterson, and Nolan (1997) |
| Northern harrier | Circus cyaneus | N | Courtship display | Y | M | NA | NA | Adult | RS/provisioning | Simmons (1988) |
| Red jungle fowl | Gallus gallus | L | Courtship display | N[b] | M | Body size | C<T | Adult | Testosterone | Zuk, Popma, and Johnsen (1995) |

| Common name | Species | | Trait | | | | | | Stage | Factor | Reference |
|---|---|---|---|---|---|---|---|---|---|---|---|
| Zebra finch | *Taeniopygia guttata* | L | Song complexity | N | M | NA | NA | | Postnatal | Brood size | Holveck, Vieira de Castro, Lachlan, Carel ten Cate, and Riebel (2008) |
| | | L | Song complexity | Y | M | NA | NA | | Postnatal | Diet/nutrition | Zann and Cash (2008) |
| | | L | Song complexity | Y | M | NA | NA | | Postnatal | Diet/nutrition | Spencer, Buchanan, Goldsmith, and Catchpole (2003) |
| | | L | Song complexity | N | M | NA | NA | | Postnatal | Diet/nutrition | Brumm, Zollinger, and Slater (2009) |
| | | L | Song length | Y | M | NA | NA | | Postnatal | Diet/nutrition | Spencer et al. (2003) |
| | | L | Song length | N | M | NA | NA | | Postnatal | Diet/nutrition | Brumm et al. (2009) |
| | | L | Song length | N | M | NA | NA | | Postnatal | Brood size | Holveck et al. (2008) |
| | | L | Song rate | N | M | NA | NA | | Postnatal | Diet/nutrition | Spencer et al. (2003) |
| | | L | Song rate | N | M | NA | NA | | Postnatal | Corticosterone | Spencer et al. (2003) |
| | | L | Song rate | Y | M | Body condition | C<T | | Inbreeding | Inbreeding | Bolund et al. (2010) |
| | | L+ | Song rate | N | M | Body mass | C>T | | Postnatal | Diet/nutrition | Birkhead et al. (1999) |

*Continued*

**TABLE 3.3** Condition-Dependent Behavioral Traits in Birds—cont'd

| Species | Scientific Name | ST | Trait | CD | S | Contrast Trait | Effect | Life History | Manipulation | Reference |
|---|---|---|---|---|---|---|---|---|---|---|
| | | L* | Song rate | N[c] | M | Body condition | C>T | Adult | Diet/nutrition | Birkhead et al. (1998) |
| | | L | Song rate | N | M | NA | NA | Postnatal | Brood size | Gil, Naguib, Reibel, Rutstein, and Gahr (2006) |
| | | L | Song duration | Y | M | NA | NA | Postnatal | Diet/nutrition | Spencer et al. (2003) |
| | | L | Song duration | Y | M | NA | NA | Postnatal | Corticosterone | Spencer et al. (2003) |
| Collard flycatchers | Ficedula albicollis | F | Song rate | Y | M | NA | NA | Adult | Infection/parasite | Garamszegi et al. (2004) |
| | | F | Song features | N | M | NA | NA | Adult | Infection/parasite | Garamszegi et al. (2004) |
| Pied flycatchers | F. hypoleuca | F | Song rate | Y | M | NA | NA | Adult | Diet/nutrition | Alatalo, Glynn, and Lundberg (1990) |
| Swamp sparrow | Melospiza georgiana | L | Song duration | Y | M | NA | NA | Postnatal | Diet/nutrition | Searcy, Peters, Kipper, and Nowicki (2010) |
| | | L | Song features | N | M | NA | NA | Postnatal | Diet/nutrition | Searcy et al. (2010) |

| | | | | | | | | | | |
|---|---|---|---|---|---|---|---|---|---|---|
| White-crowned sparrow | *Zonotrichia leucophrys* | F | Song rate | Y | M | Body condition | C < T | Adult | Infection/parasite | Gilman, Blumstein, and Foufopoulos (2007) |
| European starling | *Sturnus vulgaris* | L | Song bouts | Y | M | NA | NA | Postnatal | Diet/nutrition | Farrell, Weaver, An, and MacDougall-Shackleton (2012) |
| | | L* | Song bouts | Y | M | Body size | C < T | Postnatal | Diet/nutrition | Buchanan, Spencer, Goldsmith, and Catchpole (2003) |
| | | L* | Song duration | Y | M | Body size | C < T | Postnatal | Diet/nutrition | Buchanan et al. (2003) |
| | | L* | Song latency | Y | M | Body size | C < T | Postnatal | Diet/nutrition | Buchanan et al. (2003) |
| | | L | Song rate | Y | M | Body size | C < T | Adult | Diet/nutrition | Van Hout, Eens, and Pinxten (2011) |
| Atlantic canary | *Serinus canaria* | L | Song complexity | N | M | Body mass | C = T | Postnatal | Diet/nutrition | Müller et al. (2010) |
| | | L | Song length | N | M | Body mass | C = T | Postnatal | Diet/nutrition | Müller et al. (2010) |

*Continued*

**TABLE 3.3** Condition-Dependent Behavioral Traits in Birds—cont'd

| Species | Scientific Name | ST | Trait | CD | S | Contrast | | Life History | Manipulation | Reference |
|---|---|---|---|---|---|---|---|---|---|---|
| | | | | | | Trait | Effect | | | |
| Great tit | Parus major | N/T | Song length | Y | M | NA | NA | Adult | Toxin | Gorissen, Snoeijs, Van Duyse, and Eens (2005) |
| | | F | Song duration | Y | M | Body condition | C<T | Postnatal | Infection/parasite | Bischoff, Tschirren, and Richner (2009) |
| | | F | Song overlap | Y[d] | M | Body condition | C<T | Postnatal | Infection/parasite | Bischoff et al. (2009) |
| | | F | Song latency | N | M | NA | NA | Postnatal | Infection/parasite | Bischoff et al. (2009) |

Note: ST, study type [L, lab experiment; F, field experiment; N, natural variation; T, toxin; *, included in Griffith et al. (2006) meta-analysis]; CD, condition dependent (Y, yes; N, no); S, sex of animals included in the study (M, male; F, female; B, both sexes); T, testosterone; body condition, fat reserves controlling for body size.

[a]The display included song and behavioral components.

[b]Females chose males with more vigorous displays and these males had redder and larger, condition-dependent combs, but testosterone levels were not correlated with the vigor of males' courtship display.

[c]There were no group differences, but song rate was correlated with body condition within the experimental group.

[d]Song overlap occurs when an intruding male sings in a resident male's territory. Degree of overlap is an indicator of social status.

**TABLE 3.4 Condition-Dependent Brain and Cognitive Traits in Birds**

| Species | Scientific Name | ST | Trait | CD | S | Contrast Trait | Contrast Effect | Life History | Manipulation | Reference |
|---|---|---|---|---|---|---|---|---|---|---|
| Zebra finch | *Taeniopygia guttata* | L | HVC volume | N | M | Brain volume | C=T | Postnatal | Brood size | Gil et al. (2006) |
| | | L | RA volume | N | M | Brain volume | C=T | Postnatal | Brood size | Gil et al. (2006) |
| | | L | HVC volume | N[a] | M | Brain Volume | C>T | Postnatal | Diet/nutrition | Woodgate et al. (2014) |
| | | L | RA volume | N[a] | M | Brain volume | C>T | Postnatal | Diet/nutrition | Woodgate et al. (2014) |
| | | L | HVC Volume | Y | M | Brain weight | C<T | Postnatal | Diet/nutrition | Buchanan, Leitner, Spencer, Goldsmith, and Catchpole (2004) |
| | | L | HVC androgen rec | Y | M | Brain weight | C<T | Postnatal | Diet/nutrition | Buchanan et al. (2004) |
| | | L | RA volume | N | M | Brain weight | C=T | Postnatal | Diet/nutrition | Buchanan et al. (2004) |
| | | L | HVC volume | Y | M | Brain weight | C<T | Postnatal | Corticosterone | Buchanan et al. (2004) |
| | | L | HVC androgen rec | Y | M | Brain weight | C<T | Postnatal | Corticosterone | Buchanan et al. (2004) |

*Continued*

**TABLE 3.4** Condition-Dependent Brain and Cognitive Traits in Birds—cont'd

| Species | Scientific Name | ST | Trait | CD | S | Contrast Trait | Contrast Effect | Life History | Manipulation | Reference |
|---|---|---|---|---|---|---|---|---|---|---|
| | | L | RA volume | N | M | Brain weight | C=T | Postnatal | Corticosterone | Buchanan et al. (2004) |
| | | L | Song learning | Y | M | NA | NA | Postnatal | Diet/nutrition | Brumm et al. (2009) |
| | | L | Song learning | Y | M | NA | NA | Postnatal | Brood size | Holveck et al. (2008) |
| | | L | Song learning | N | M | NA | NA | Postnatal | Diet/nutrition | Zann and Cash (2008) |
| | | L | Song learning | N | M | NA | NA | Postnatal | Brood size | Gil et al. (2006) |
| | | L | Song repertoire | N | M | NA | NA | Postnatal | Brood size | Gil et al. (2006) |
| Swamp sparrow | *Melospiza georgiana* | L | HVC volume | Y | M | Brain volume | C=T | Postnatal | Diet/nutrition | Nowicki, Searcy, and Peters (2002) |
| | | L | RA volume | Y | M | Brain volume | C<T | Postnatal | Diet/nutrition | Nowicki et al. (2002) |
| | | L | Song learning | Y | M | NA | NA | Postnatal | Diet/nutrition | Nowicki et al. (2002) |
| | | L | Song repertoire | N | M | NA | NA | Postnatal | Diet/nutrition | Nowicki et al. (2002) |

| Song sparrow | M. melodi | L | HVC volume | Y | B | Brain volume | C<T | Postnatal | Diet/nutrition | MacDonald, Kempster, Zanette, and MacDougall-Shackleton (2006) |
|---|---|---|---|---|---|---|---|---|---|---|
| | | L | RA volume | N | B | Brain volume | C=T | Postnatal | Diet/nutrition | MacDonald et al. (2006) |
| | | L | HVC volume | N | M | Brain volume | C=T | Postnatal | Diet/nutrition | Schmidt, Moore, MacDougall-Shackleton, and MacDougall-Shackleton (2013) |
| | | L | HVC volume | N | M | Brain volume | C=T | Postnatal | Corticosterone | Schmidt et al. (2013) |
| | | L | RA volume | Y | M | Brain volume | C<T | Postnatal | Diet/nutrition | Schmidt et al. (2013) |
| | | L | RA volume | N | M | Brain volume | C=T | Postnatal | Corticosterone | Schmidt et al. (2013) |
| | | N | Song repertoire | Y | M | NA | NA | Inbreeding | Inbreeding | Reid et al. (2005) |
| | | L | Song repertoire | Y | M | NA | NA | Postnatal | Diet/nutrition | Schmidt et al. (2013) |
| | | L | Song repertoire | Y | M | NA | NA | Postnatal | Corticosterone | Schmidt et al. (2013) |
| | | L | Song learning | Y | M | NA | NA | Postnatal | Diet/nutrition | Schmidt et al. (2013) |
| | | L | Song learning | N | M | NA | NA | Postnatal | Corticosterone | Schmidt et al. (2013) |

*Continued*

**TABLE 3.4** Condition-Dependent Brain and Cognitive Traits in Birds—cont'd

| Species | Scientific Name | ST | Trait | CD | S | Contrast Trait | Contrast Effect | Life History | Manipulation | Reference |
|---|---|---|---|---|---|---|---|---|---|---|
| European starlings | *Sturnus vulgaris* | L | Song repertoire | Y | M | Body size | C<T | Postnatal | Diet/nutrition | Spencer, Buchanan, Goldsmith, and Catchpole (2004) |
| Atlantic canary | *Serinus canaria* | L | HVC volume | Y | M | Brain volume | C<T | Postnatal | Infection/parasite | Spencer, Buchanan, Leitner, Goldsmith, and Catchpole (2005) |
| | | L | RA volume | N | M | Brain volume | C=T | Postnatal | Infection/parasite | Spencer et al. (2005) |
| | | L | Song repertoire | Y | M | NA | NA | Postnatal | Infection/parasite | Spencer et al. (2005) |
| | | L | Song repertoire | N | M | Body mass | C=T | Postnatal | Diet/nutrition | Müller et al. (2010) |
| Sedge warbler | *Acrocephalus schoeno-baenus* | N | Song repertoire | Y | M | NA | NA | Adult | Infection/parasite | Buchanan, Catchpole, Lewis, and Lodge (1999) |
| Great tit | *Parus major* | N/T | Song repertoire | Y | M | NA | NA | Adult | Toxin | Gorissen et al. (2005) |
| | | F | Song repertoire | N | M | NA | NA | Postnatal | Infection/parasite | Bischoff et al. (2009) |

Note: ST, study type [L, lab experiment; F, field experiment; N, natural variation; T, toxin; *, included in Cotton et al. (2004a) review; +, included in Griffith et al. (2006) meta-analysis]; CD, condition dependent (Y, yes; N, no); S, sex of animals included in the study (M, male; F, female; B, both sexes). HVC is not an acronym but is sometimes termed higher vocal center. RA, robust nucleus of the arcopallium. Rec, receptor.
*This was a weak nutritional manipulation in comparison to related studies; the primary focus was determining the genetic and environmental contributions to variation in HVC and RA. Variation in both brain structures, especially the HVC, is related to postnatal environment.*

of all of these different types of traits for 41 species of bird across the reviewed studies (see Species Index). The studies cataloged in these tables and all subsequent ones are characterized as field experiments (F), laboratory experiments (L), natural variation in a field setting (N), and studies that involved measurement or experimental administration of a toxin (T). The field experiments involve some type of manipulation, such as providing food or inoculating birds against disease in the animals' natural habitat. The natural variation studies also involved assessment of animals in the field but there is no experimental manipulation. The trait of interest is then indicated and whether (yes, Y) or not (no, N) there is evidence that the trait is condition dependent.

Contrast traits are those that were measured along with the trait of interest and often include some measure of body size or body condition; the latter is often defined as fat reserves, controlling for body size. These are potentially useful contrasts, especially if the sexually selected trait involves an elaboration of size or the males engage in physical competition (Kodric Brown, Sibly, & Brown, 2006). As noted by Cotton et al. (2004a), however, more appropriate contrasts are the same trait in the opposite sex, the same trait in the same sex of a related species, or a similar trait within the same individual. In all cases, the contrast trait cannot be subject to sexual selection or social selection more broadly to ensure that the contrast is not itself a condition-dependent signal. If some type of potential contrast was available it is noted in the table, along with whether or not the manipulation affected the contrast trait less than the sexually selected trait ($C < T$), more than the trait ($C > T$), or both were equally affected ($C = T$). For the latter, both the contrast and focal trait either changed in the same direction and either the degree of change was not assessed or it was assessed and the trait and contrast changed to the same degree (e.g., trait change was no longer significant when the contrast was statistically covaried).

Life history is the age in which the manipulation occurred, which includes inbreeding, postnatal (before adulthood), or adult in the tables associated with in birds, and prenatal (e.g., through maternal diet) in some subsequent tables. Color type refers to whether the trait involved a carotenoid- or melanin-based pigment or structural color, as I describe in the next section. If the color features (e.g., hue, saturation) were directly assessed, the associated traits are included in Table 3.1 (Color), and in Table 3.2 (Size) if only the size of a color-based signal was assessed. Finally, the primary manipulations include restriction or supplementation of diet (diet), increase or decrease of brood size that changed overall parental investment and investment in individual offspring (brood size), and either experimental or natural infection with some type of parasite (e.g., intestinal worms or feather mites; infection/parasite). Less frequent manipulations included inbreeding, implantation of testosterone or the stress hormone corticosterone, administration of chemicals that increased oxidative stress (recall, this can damage cells or cell functioning), social stressors (either density overall or number of same-sex competitors), toxin exposure, or natural variation in either the trait (T) or various indicators of condition described in the notes for each table.

## Physical Traits

As we now know, to be useful and honest signals, condition-dependent traits have to be conveyed to and easily assessed by others (Zahavi, 1975). Recall, the traits themselves are not always functional but they have to be correlated with other traits that are functional, such as disease resistance, fighting ability, or genetic variation, to name a few examples. For birds, plumage coloration or size of plumage badges are common social signals to potential competitors and to would-be mates.

### Color

I begin with description of different types of color signals. The distinction between these different signals is important because it illustrates that some traits tend to signal current condition whereas others tend to signal condition in the near past (e.g., during feather molt). From there, I move to reviews of these different types of signals. The reader who is not interested in all of the technical details can skip ahead to the *Takeaway message* subsection below.

### Types of Color Signals

There are three primary forms of plumage coloration – carotenoid and melanin pigments and structural colors – that create the potential for different types of signals, although they can interact in the production of some colors (Prum, 2006). As we touched upon, carotenoids are found throughout invertebrate and vertebrate species and are critical to the development of yellow to red coloration of plumage, beak, and other traits of arthropods, fish, and birds (McGraw, 2006a), as well as skin health in humans (Chapter 6). The yellow plumage of the American goldfinch (*Spinus tristis*; Photo 3.1, inset) and the red comb of the red jungle fowl

**PHOTO 3.1**   The yellow plumage of the male American goldfinch (*Spinus tristis*) is dependent on adequate dietary carotenoids and signals health of their immune system. (See the color plate section.)

**PHOTO 3.2**    The red color of the comb on the top of the head of the male red jungle fowl (*Gallus gallus*) is dependent in part on adequate dietary carotenoids and exposure to male hormones. Females prefer males with larger and brighter combs as mates. (See the color plate section.)

(*G. gallus*; Photo 3.2, inset) illustrate the color range that can result from carotenoids. As we've discussed, these molecules are critical to several types of immune responses and should be correlated with current disease burden or future risk of poor health (Bendich, 1991; Burton & Ingold, 1984; Fitze, Tschirren, Gasparini, & Richner, 2007; Hill, 2014; Simons, Cohen, & Verhulst, 2012; Svensson & Wong, 2011). Carotenoids are also heavily deposited in yolk (McGraw, 2006a) and may enhance some components of the immune system in nestlings (Biard, Surai, & Møller, 2005; De Neve et al., 2008) and nestlings' sensitivity to carotenoids later in development (Koutsos, Clifford, Calvert, & Klasing, 2003).

Melanin pigments result in gray to reddish-brown to black coloration, as illustrated by the plumage of the red jungle fowl (Photo 3.2, inset)—the red jungle fowl thus illustrates different types of traits (e.g., red comb, plumage color) that may signal different aspects of their condition. Unlike carotenoids, for vertebrates melanin is synthesized in peripheral tissue and thus does not need to be obtained through diet. These pigments serve multiple functions ranging from protection from the harmful effects of exposure to sunlight to strengthening of tissues to protection from bacterial degradation of feathers (e.g., Goldstein et al., 2004; McGraw, 2006b). Previous reviews suggest that for darker colors (e.g., black), the size of the trait rather than the coloration itself influences female choice and male-male aggression in some species, whereas variation in color may be important for gray and reddish-brown traits (Hill, 2006; Rohwer, 1977). Although the status-signaling function of these traits is established (Senar, 2006), the extent to which their expression is condition-dependent remains to be resolved (Griffith et al., 2006; Hill & Brawner, 1998; McGraw & Hill, 2000). The basic issue is that melanin may be too easy to produce and thus not costly enough to serve as a reliable indicator of condition, at least for vertebrates. The story is different for invertebrates, as we will discuss in the next chapter, and may in fact be different for some species of bird.

Structural colors result from the scattering of light by the nanoscale organization of feathers or skin and produce blue to green colors, as well as ultraviolet hues (which are perceived by birds) and white (Prum, 2006). An example is shown by blue plumage color of the male grosbeak (*Guiraca caerulea*) in Photo 3.3 (inset). These colors can influence female mate choice and often serve as male-male status signals (Hill, 2006; Senar, 2006), although Prum suggested their development was not sufficiently costly to serve as condition-dependent traits. Nevertheless, structural colors may be a good indicator of condition during the prior mating season or outside of the mating season. This is because structural colors will be influenced by the quality of the feathers that are generated following the animals' most recent molt, and the quality of these features may be dependent on condition at that time.

**PHOTO 3.3**  The blue plumage of the male grosbeak (*Guiraca caerulea*) illustrates a structural color that signals male condition during the time when new feathers are developing. (See the color plate section.)

## Conditional Dependent Signals

The colorful plumage and distinct badges that are common across species of bird not only catch the attention of other birds they have also captured the attention of avian biologists (Hill & McGraw, 2006). Thus, it is not surprising that these are frequently studied as potential condition-dependent traits, as shown by the dozens of assessments of color-based traits across 25 species in Table 3.1.

In keeping with the discussion in the previous chapter, the majority of studies (39 of the 49 assessments) confirm that carotenoid-based colors are reliable indicators of the individual's condition. Among these are the previously noted beak of the male zebra finch (Photo 2.6, inset), the yellow plumage of the male American goldfinch (Photo 3.1, inset), and the comb of the male red jungle fowl (Photo 3.2, inset). The majority of assessments involved manipulations during adulthood, as would be expected if these traits are reliable indicators of current condition, but the pattern did not differ significantly from that found for postnatal manipulations. The latter suggests that early stressors or inbreeding depression can compromise the individual's trait coloration in adulthood, possibly by undermining the ability to efficiently process carotenoids or disrupting the functioning of the physiological systems that are signaled by carotenoid-based traits (Hill, 2014).

In any case, to illustrate the information conveyed by carotenoid signals let's return to the black grouse (*Tetrao tetrix*). Recall, males gather together in an arena and compete for position in the associated lek that is then visited by females during their search for a mate (Alatalo, Höglund, Lundberg, & Sutherland, 1992; Höglund et al., 1997; Kokko et al., 1999; Siitari et al., 2007). As we learned in Chapter 2, males fight one another for position on the lek and engage in a courtship display when visited by females. The males do not provide food to the females or her offspring and thus genes are the only benefit obtained by females. Females that are sensitive to signals of male genetic quality (e.g., immune system competence) will obtain good genes for their offspring. The male black grouse displays several such signals. In addition to courtship displays, they sport a bright red comb (carotenoid color), blue plumage (structural color), and lyre-shaped tail feathers.

In Siitari et al.'s (2007) study of the condition dependence of these traits, young male black grouse were captured just prior to the onset of the mating season, half of them were administered testosterone, and then they were all released. Young adult males are not typically competitive in this species (Alatalo, Höglund, Lundberg, Rintamaki, & Silverin, 1996), and thus testosterone could be costly not only in terms of risk of immunosuppression, but because premature competition may compromise the young males' physical condition in other ways. About 2 months later, the red eye combs (Photo 2.2, inset) of testosterone-enhanced young males were larger than those of same-age untreated males, but there was no difference in the redness of the combs. The eye comb size and redness of the enhanced males were lower than those of dominant older males, but the enhanced males still achieved spots close to the center of the arena, suggesting they engaged in frequent male-male aggression. The critical test was whether there were long-term costs associated with testosterone enhancement and premature engagement in male-male competition, and indeed these costs were found and were dramatic the next breeding season. Sixty-three percent of the enhanced males survived the first season and 37% the second season, as compared to 95% and 74% of the untreated males, respectively. By the second season, the combs and plumage of enhanced males were duller than those of untreated males, and their tail feathers were shorter. In contrast, there were no differences in body mass: Thus, while size did not predict increased mortality risks, the sexually selected traits did.

As noted, control of body size is sometimes useful, but stronger evidence for condition dependence comes from studies that use comparisons across males and females or within males for similar traits (e.g., carotenoid color vs. color that is not sexually selected). Nearly all (eight out of every nine) of the assessments indicated that carotenoid-based color traits were compromised by exposure to stressors. However, only about half of these assessments provided the strongest evidence for condition dependence; that is, the effect was larger for the trait of interest than the contrast trait. All of the studies that showed the contrast trait was also compromised by exposure to stressors involved comparisons of males and females. In other words, male color traits that signal social dominance or that influence mate choice were contrasted with the same traits in females, assuming these traits are unrelated to competition or choice in females.

For many species, it is now recognized that these traits may in fact be dominance signals to other females, meaning they should also be condition dependent and thus not a good choice for a contrast trait. For instance, male beak color influences female choice in American goldfinches (Johnson, Rosetta, & Burley, 1993) and was the target trait in the Rosenthal et al. (2012) study, with female beak color as the contrast trait. The manipulation involved injection of field-caught birds with a compound that will stimulate an immune reaction without making the bird sick. Following the injection, the beak color of both sexes became pale, especially for individuals that had richly colored beaks before the injection. The results are consistent with diversion of carotenoids from the signal trait to immune functions (Simons et al., 2012), but not entirely consistent with the hypothesis that this trait is a particularly potent signal of males' condition.

However, Murphy et al. (2009) found that female American goldfinches avoid feeding near females with richly colored beaks, suggesting it is a dominance signal related to female-female feeding competition; that is, it is a socially selected status signal, as female beak color did not influence male choice. Kelly et al. (2012) confirmed that beak color is a condition-dependent trait in female American goldfinches and further complicated the matter by showing that plumage color is as well, and that beak color and plumage color signaled activity of different components of the immune system. In this species and probably others, beak color appears to be a condition-dependent signal in *both* sexes and thus use of female beak color as a contrast trait likely underestimated the condition dependence of male beak color.

Unlike carotenoid-based colors, melanin-based colors do not appear to be reliable signals of condition dependence in birds; the story is different for the size of these traits (below) and for arthropods (Chapter 4). It could be that my conclusion is premature, but it is consistent with other reviews (Cotton et al., 2004a; but see Griffith et al., 2006). These traits have not been as frequently assessed as carotenoid-based traits and thus there are only eight direct assessments of melanin-based colors reviewed in Table 3.1; seven of them found no evidence for condition dependence.

As noted earlier, the blue plumage of the male black grouse (Photo 2.2, inset) is a structural color and was found by Siitari et al. (2007) to be condition dependent. Most of the other assessments (11 of 14) of structural-based plumage colors were also consistent with condition dependence, but only 5 of them included strong contrast traits; specifically, contrast with other colors or plumage features or female color. The one of the two assessments that revealed plumage color was more strongly compromised by stressors than the contrast trait involved an adult manipulation (Maia et al., 2012) and the other a manipulation during postnatal development (Hill et al., 2005). Meadows et al. (2012) found that a high-quality diet during feather growth resulted in sharper magenta crown and neck colors of males of the species Anna's hummingbird (*Calypte anna*; Photo 3.4, inset); males of this species erect these features and display them in contests with other males and to attract females. However, the strength

**PHOTO 3.4**  Anna's hummingbird (*Calypte anna*) males erect the magenta throat and crown feathers in dominance displays to other males and to attract females. (See the color plate section.)

of this result was muted but the finding that the high-quality diet also resulted in brighter green tail feathers, which are not sexually selected. Both of the other studies with a strong contrast trait involved a diet manipulation during development and neither found evidence for condition dependence of the assessed plumage colors (Peters et al., 2011; Walker et al., 2013).

## Takeaway Message

Keeping in mind that the demonstration of condition dependence may be difficult (Svensson & Wong, 2011), the results for the carotenoid-based traits are impressive and consistent with previous conclusions that the associated colors do indeed signal condition in many bird species (McGraw, 2006a). As covered in the last chapter, carotenoid-based traits should be particularly sensitive to current condition in vertebrates. This is because only healthy individuals can accumulate (through foraging) the carotenoids needed to maintain these attractive colors, because illness and other stressors will result in the diversion of these molecules from these traits to immune and other basic functions (e.g., Simons et al., 2012), and because the efficiency of core physiological systems may place limits on ability to convert foods into carotenoid pigments (Hill, 2014). At the same time, there is also some evidence that developmental stressors, such as poor diet, might be reflected in the intensity of these colors in adulthood. Whether this reflects early influences on the ability to physiologically process carotenoids in adulthood or is secondary to deficits in foraging remains to be determined; in the latter case, poor early conditions, such as exposure to parasites, compromise the animals' later ability to forage that in turn affects the expression of these colors. Unfortunately, much less is known about female social signals and thus the utility of these traits as a contrast to male sexually selected traits is often unclear, and may result in the underestimation of the condition dependence of male carotenoid-based traits and the underestimation of the importance of these same traits as a status signal among females.

McGraw (2006b) suggested that melanin-based colors are not typically condition-dependent traits in birds whereas Griffith et al. (2006) concluded the evidence was just as strong for the condition dependence of melanin-based traits as carotenoid-based traits. The Griffith et al. meta-analysis, however, combined melanin-based colors and size (below). Five of the six studies used in the Griffith et al. analysis found that melanin-based colors were not condition dependent, consistent with McGraw's conclusion. Three of the studies of melanin-based traits shown in Table 3.1 were not included in Griffith et al., and one found evidence for condition dependence (Zuk et al., 1990) and the other two did not (Gonzalez et al., 1999; Walker et al., 2013). Zuk et al. assessed the reddish-brown hackle feather color of male red jungle fowl (Photo 3.2, inset), whereas Gonzalez et al. assessed the color of the black bib patch of male house sparrows (*Passer domesticus*) and Walker et al. the black head patch of the hihi (*Notiomystis cincta*). The pattern is consistent with variation in reddish-brown color serving as a potential condition-dependent signal (Hill, 2006), but not variation in darker colors (McGraw, 2006b).

Finally, structural colors are not as well studied as carotenoid-based colors, but in theory these two types of signals may provide different types of information about condition. Because the former are based on the physical structure of feathers, they have the potential to capture the individual's condition over a longer span of time than many carotenoid-based traits; specifically, condition over the weeks or months of feather growth. The studies summarized in Table 3.1 suggest that many different types of stressors during this time, ranging from infection (Hill et al., 2005) to intense social competition (Maia et al., 2012), will be reflected in the quality of structural colors during the breeding season. The three negative findings were all for diet manipulations, although three other diet manipulations did find effects on structural colors. It may be that feather development per se is not particularly costly in terms of nutritional requirements (Prum, 2006), but subtle variation in feather structure may be influenced by other factors.

## Size

For many species, including the black grouse (Photo 2.2, inset), condition-dependent traits not only have to be more colorful than those of competitors, but larger; the red comb in the case of the black grouse (Siitari et al., 2007). As was mentioned in the last chapter, for other species, size and color may be expressed in different traits, with each of these potentially signalling different aspects of condition or perhaps condition at different points in development (Nowicki, Peters, & Podos, 1998; Nowicki et al., 2002).

Table 3.2 shows assessments of trait size across 16 species. One-third of these studies involved comb length or similar traits (i.e., wattle, snood) and they all found that exposure to one form of stressor or another – infestation with parasites, poor nutrition, social competition – compromises trait size; 11 involved a variety of different types of manipulations in adulthood and 2 during postnatal development. Most of these studies included reasonable contrast traits (e.g., body size, female comb size) and most of them – all focused on male trait size – found that the trait of interest was more strongly affected by the manipulation than the contrast trait. Martinez-Padilla et al. (2011) focused on the comb size and body size of the female red grouse (*Lagopus lagopus*) and found that both were equally affected by natural variation in parasite load. A follow-up field experiment, however, found that a treatment that killed parasites resulted in growth of female combs, as would be expected if comb size signals parasite load. In any case, comb size may be a condition-dependent trait in females of this species, perhaps related to male choice; this is a socially monogamous species in which both parents invest in offspring.

Relative to fleshy carotenoid-based traits (e.g., comb), there are fewer studies of the size of other types of carotenoid-based traits, but there are a few interesting examples. Naguib and Nemitz (2007) found that the size of the orange cheek patch of male zebra finches (*Taeniopygia guttata*) varied with the adequacy of their postnatal diet, and Pérez, Lores, and Velando (2010) found that toxin exposure reduced the red beak-spot size of yellow-legged gulls (*Larus michahellis*) of both sexes.

In contrast to the quality of melanin-based colors, there is evidence that the size of these traits fluctuates with exposure to various types of stressor; of the 10 studies that assessed melanin-patch size, 6 found evidence of condition dependence. All of the latter were included in Griffith et al.'s (2006) meta-analysis, and two of the three that were not included also provided evidence for the condition dependence of these traits. For example, the size of both the black cap (Dauwe & Eens, 2008) and the breast stripe (Fitze & Richner, 2002) of the great tit (*P. major*; Photo 3.5, inset) are smaller for males exposed to toxins or parasites. The Fitze and Richner study of the great tit included females' breast stripe as the contrast trait and found that it, too, was affected by infestation with parasites, providing yet another example of a condition-dependent trait in females.

The sizes of structural-based plumage signals have also been relatively overlooked, possibly based on an assumption that they are not costly enough to

**PHOTO 3.5**   The size of the black head cap and the breast stripe of the great tit (*Parus major*) signal the males' ability to withstand infections and exposure to man-made toxins. (See the color plate section.)

**PHOTO 3.6**   The size of the white spots of the female diamond firetail (*Stagonopleura guttata*) indicates the health of their immune system. (See the color plate section.)

serve as condition-dependent traits (Prum, 2006); the white plumage spots of the diamond firetail (*Stagonopleura guttata*) illustrate a size-based structural signal (Photo 3.6, inset). Nevertheless, four of the five assessments done in adulthood provided evidence for condition dependence, for male collard fly-catchers (*Ficedula albicollis*; e.g., Gustafsson et al., 1995) and juncos (*Junco hyemalis*; McGlothlin et al., 2007), as well as female (but not male) firetails (Zanollo et al., 2012). The two postnatal manipulations, both with the collard flycatcher, did not find evidence for condition dependence of these traits, suggesting structural signals in this species indicate condition in the near past but not the distant past.

### Takeaway Message

In many species of bird, there are traits that indicate the individual's current ability to tolerate stressors and other traits that signal resilience in the near or distant past. There is strong evidence that comb size and similar traits are reliable signals of males' and females', in at least some species, ability to tolerate parasites, nutritional stressors, and the rigors of social competition, with exposure to these stressors resulting in a reduction in trait size. These are particularly reliable signals of current condition or condition in the near past; there are not enough studies to determine whether they are also sensitive to developmental stressors. On the basis of Griffith et al.'s (2006) meta-analysis and the additional studies included in Table 3.2, the size of melanin-based traits appear to be a reflection of male condition following molt and the many weeks of feather growth (McGraw, 2006b); that is, condition in the near past. The condition dependence of these traits in females is not well studied, but there is suggestive evidence at least for the great tit. Likewise, the condition dependence of the size of carotenoid- and structural-based feather signals has not been thoroughly assessed, but the studies to date suggest they may in fact be condition-dependent signals in both sexes, at least in some species.

## Behavioral Traits

As I noted in the last chapter, behavioral traits will involve engagement of some combination of perceptual, cognitive, or brain systems and thus separating them from traits covered in the brain and cognitive section is somewhat arbitrary (Boogert, Fawcett, & Lefebvre, 2011; Keagy, Savard, & Borgia, 2012). Most of the traits included in this section and in Table 3.3 have a vigor, endurance, or complexity component to them, as in courtship display, song rate, or song complexity, respectively. Song features and complexity are included here, because these often involve the repetition or integration of multiple components into a song during its expression. These may reflect memory and song learning but the complexity of their expression also requires endurance. In any case, the behavioral traits in the brain and cognitive section are restricted to direct measures of learning, typically through exposure to paternal or another male's song, or are an indicator of such learning, specifically, repertoire.

As with the black grouse (Chapter 2), repetitive and vigorous behavioral displays are common when males are courting females (Andersson, 1994; Höglund & Alatalo, 1995). The magnificent frigate bird (*Fregata magnificens*) shown in Photo 3.7 (inset) illustrates one such display. Males of this species gather together and display to females by inflating their red gular pouch, spreading their wings, and pointing their beak upwards. Males that frequently display are in better physical condition and have higher testosterone levels than their less flamboyant peers (Chastel et al., 2005). There are six other examples of courtship display shown in Table 3.3, and all but one of them provided evidence for condition dependence. Even the one failure to show condition dependence was a nuanced result (Zuk et al., 1995). The courtship displays of male red jungle fowl were not related to their testosterone levels but the more

**PHOTO 3.7**    To attract mates, males of the magnificent frigatebird (*Fregata magnificens*) inflate their red gular pouch, spread their wings, and point their beak upwards. Males with higher testosterone levels and in better physical condition engage in this courtship display more frequently than do other males. *Photo credit: Andrew Turner, 2011. Creative Commons license: http://commons.wikimedia. org/wiki/File:Fregata_magnificens_-Galapagos,_Ecuador_-male-8.jpg.* (See the color plate section.)

vigorous males had brighter and larger combs than less vigorous males. Zuk and colleagues suggested that although the courtship displays might not be a direct signal (in isolation) of male condition, it is an integral part of the suite of signaling traits used by females to make mate choices.

All of the other behavioral traits shown in Table 3.3 are components of bird-song. In contrast to the above described color and size traits that largely, but not exclusively, focused on current condition or condition in the near past, the majority of the behavioral studies focused on birdsong as an indicator of sensitivity to developmental stressors (Nowicki et al., 1998). This follows from the fact that most birds learn their song during the developmental period. Nevertheless, because some aspects of song production include an endurance component, they might be indicators of current condition.

Of the 22 assessments that involved some aspect of song duration (i.e., duration, length, rate, and bouts), only 6 assessed adults but 5 of them indicated condition dependence. Poor current diet or infestation with parasites resulted in a slower rate of singing in male collard flycatchers (Garamszegi et al., 2004), pied flycatchers (*F. hypoleuca*; Alatalo et al., 1990), white-crowned sparrows (*Zonotrichia leucophrys*; Gilman et al., 2007), European starlings (*Sturnus vulgaris*; Farrell et al., 2012), and great tits (Gorissen et al., 2005). The one negative finding was for zebra finches (Birkhead et al., 1998). Here, Birkhead and colleagues did not find differences in song rate across a group of adult zebra finch males with unrestricted access to food as compared to their brothers with restricted food access and forced exercise. Within this latter group, however, males in better physical condition sang more than their peers.

The remaining assessments focused on developmental conditions and the results were mixed; sometimes, poor early conditions were related to later deficits in song duration and sometimes they were not. The same mixed pattern is found with assessments of song complexity or song features. The two significant effects were found for the well-studied zebra finch and both involved developmental conditions (Zann & Cash, 2008; Spencer et al., 2003). Two other studies found no evidence that developmental conditions are reflected in adults' song complexity in the zebra finch (Brumm et al., 2009; Holveck et al., 2008). However, many other assessments found that exposure to nutritional stressors, infection, and elevated stress hormones during development influenced either song duration or number of song bouts in adulthood; this is found for zebra finch (Spencer et al., 2003), swamp sparrow (*Melospiza georgiana*; Searcy et al., 2010), European starling (e.g., Farrell et al., 2012), and great tit (Bischoff et al., 2009).

### Takeaway Message

The persistence and vigor of behavioral courtship displays are good indicators of males' current condition; that is, their level of exposure to and tolerance of parasites, poor nutrition, social stressors, and potentially toxins. For songbirds, the rate with which a song is produced appears to be a good indicator of current condition, whereas the duration of the singing episode (during which the song may be repeated many times) or the frequency of song bouts are good indicators of the males' condition during development. It may be that other components of song, such as complexity, are signals of current or developmental conditions, but the evidence to date is less consistent. One possibility is that these song features are only disrupted with more severe stressors than assessed in these studies. A fuller understanding of the factors that influence individual differences in song complexity is an important goal for future studies, given the relation between complexity and volume of some song system brain nuclei (below).

## Brain and Cognitive Traits

To illustrate the condition dependence of brain and cognitive traits, we'll return to the brain systems underlying the learning and production of birdsong introduced in Chapter 2. As we just reviewed, components of birdsong may signal current condition or the ability to tolerate developmental stressors. And, as I noted in Chapter 2, song features may signal other competencies that support the male's ability to provide direct benefits to the female and her offspring (Boogert et al., 2011; Nowicki et al., 1998; Spencer & MacDougall-Shackleton, 2011). Recall, the complexity of the male zebra finches' songs may be a good indicator of their foraging ability (Boogert, Giraldeau, & Lefebvre, 2008) and likely a good indicator of the integrity of the brain systems (e.g., hippocampus) that support this ability (Pravosudov, Lavenex, & Omanska, 2005). The basic idea is that the integrity of any brain system that develops at the same time as the song system will be signaled by song quality (Peters, Searcy, & Nowicki, 2014).

The usefulness of these signals, however, may depend on whether the male's song is fixed during development or modifiable in adulthood. For many species – including the zebra finch (Price, 1979), swamp sparrow (Marler & Peters, 1988), and song sparrow (*M. melodi*; Marler & Peters, 1987) – song learning primarily occurs during a critical developmental period such that illness, nutritional stress, or other poor conditions during this time can disrupt development of the song system nuclei and thus potentially have lifelong effects on song production and mating success (Nowicki et al., 1998). For these species song learning is age limited, meaning that song repertoire is set during development and therefore may provide an honest indicator of the male's resilience to stressors early in life. Song learning in other species – including the European starling (Mountjoy & Lemon, 1995), Atlantic canary (*Serinus canaria*; Nottebohm, Nottebohm, Crane, & Wingfield, 1987), sedge warbler (*Acrocephalus schoenobaenus*; Nicholson, Buchanan, Marshall, & Catchpole, 2007), and great tit (McGregor & Krebs, 1989) – is open-ended; that is, songs often change in adulthood. The plasticity of song learning in these species may enable compensation for exposure to early stressors (Beecher & Brenowitz, 2005), or result in song being a more sensitive indicator of current than developmental condition.

The two most commonly used indicators of the integrity of the song system are song learning – the extent to which the produced song matches the tutor's song – and repertoire – the number of song syllables or songs the male can produce. As we covered in the last chapter, there are multiple song system nuclei that support these song components, but the HVC and RA are the best studied in this context (see Figure 2.4). Garamszegi and Eens's (2004) cross-species meta-analysis revealed a robust relation between the size of these regions and the quality of male song. Importantly, these relations remained significant with control of overall brain volume, especially for the HVC (see also DeVoogd, Krebs, Healy, & Purvis, 1993). We would then expect the HVC to be particularly sensitive to developmental stressors, especially for age-limited song learners (Nowicki et al., 1998).

The assessments listed in Table 3.4 show that for species with age-limited song learning (zebra finch, swamp sparrow, song sparrow), postnatal stressors are sometimes found to influence song learning and repertoire and sometimes not. For each of these three species, there is at least one study showing that song learning is compromised by poor early diet, whereas diet effects on song repertoire have only been found for the song sparrow (Schmidt et al., 2013); increasing brood size should also compromise diet, as there are more mouths to feed, but parents can compensate for this by working harder to provision nestlings and thus this is probably a weaker manipulation than directly changing the diet. There are many fewer studies of the relation between postnatal stressors and song learning and repertoire for species with open-ended song learning (European starling, Atlantic canary, sedge warbler, great tit), and the findings here are also mixed. Both studies of adulthood stressors, however, are consistent with condition dependence of song repertoire for the open-ended sedge warbler (Buchanan et al., 1999) and great tit (Gorissen et al., 2005).

For age-limited song learners, the findings for RA volume are generally consistent, with most (six of eight) of the assessments showing no relation to early conditions. In contrast, poor postnatal diet and elevated stress hormone (corticosterone) levels during development were found to reduce HVC volume, above and beyond reductions in overall brain volume, in two studies of the zebra finch (Buchanan et al., 2004; MacDonald et al., 2006); two other studies of this species found no relation between early diet or brood size and HVC volume (Gil et al., 2006; Woodgate et al., 2011), but these studies had weaker manipulations than the studies that found an effect. A third study found a diet-related reduction in HVC volume in the swamp sparrow, but the extent of this reduction did not differ from reduction in overall brain volume (Nowicki et al., 2002). The results are also mixed for the song sparrow, with MacDonald et al. finding a relation between early diet and HVC volume but Schmidt et al. (2013) finding no such relation.

As I mentioned in Chapter 2 for the hippocampus, it may be the organization or functioning of the HVC rather than volume per se that it critical for song learning (e.g., Dittrich et al., 2013). This has not been well studied to date, but Buchanan et al.'s (2004) finding that early dietary stress and exposure to stress hormones resulted in fewer androgen receptors in the HVC is suggestive. The result would be lower sensitivity of this brain region to testosterone when the male matures and as a result less song production, independent of the overall size of the HVC. We will discuss similar effects for the hippocampus of male rodents in Chapter 4 and men in Chapter 7.

### Takeaway Message

In comparison to color, size, and behavioral traits, much less is known about the condition dependence of brain and cognitive traits. What is known indicates that a poor early diet or exposure to social stressors can compromise the ability to learn songs and thus undermine the males' social dominance in adulthood and their attractiveness as a mate. The most interesting and potentially important point is that exposure to stressors during development can alter brain development in sex-specific ways; that is, in ways that affect cognition in adulthood. With respect to birdsong, HVC development should be particularly sensitive to developmental stressors (see Figure 2.4; DeVoogd et al., 1993; Garamszegi & Eens, 2004), especially in species where song is learned early in life and is not modifiable in adulthood (Nowicki et al., 1998). Although not conclusive, evidence consistent with this hypothesis is found in all three age-limited song learners reviewed here. The broad implication is that competition and choice can result in the evolution of brain and cognitive traits that have a heightened vulnerability to stressors, in the same way that some color, size, or behavioral traits are vulnerable. The implications for identifying sex-specific human vulnerabilities are addressed in Chapters 5 and 7.

### FISH

I presented many examples of different types of vulnerable traits in the discussion of birds with more to follow in the next chapter, and thus kept this section short and focused on two of the most thoroughly studied species of fish, guppies (*Poecilia reticulata*) and three-spined sticklebacks (*G. aculeatus*): The interested reader can find further discussion of sexual selection in fish in Andersson (1994) and how exposure to endocrine disrupting compounds affects sexually selected traits in these species in Söffker and Tyler's (2012) review. In addition to being thoroughly studied, both species are interesting in their own right, as they help to illustrate potential nuance in the evolution and expression of condition-dependent signals.

Trinidadian guppies evolved in streams that differ in water clarity and predation risk, both of which can alter the cost-benefit trade-offs of colorful signals (Reznick, Shaw, Rodd, & Shaw, 1997). It is therefore possible that color traits may be more important signals of condition for males from some locations and less important for males from different locations (Grether, 2000; Houde & Endler, 1990; Sheridan & Pomiankowski, 1997). It is also possible, given the heritability of these traits and the female preference for them, that the traits that signal condition are robust across locations (Kodric-Brown, 1985). I examined these possibilities and found that the males' home stream does not seem to be important for the traits assessed here, but because there are location differences in coloration and other some other traits and for the record, I provide the stream information in the scientific name column of Tables 3.5 and 3.6.

Stickleback males are not as colorful as guppy males, but their inclusion here provides a nice illustration of males deceiving females. Actually, it provides an illustration of how this appears to be the case when condition-dependent traits are studied in contexts that differ from the contexts in which they have evolved. As with many other species of fish (Clutton-Brock, 1991), stickleback males build nests and provide all of the parental investment, once the eggs are laid and fertilized (Van Iersel, 1953). The combination of competing for nest sites, building a nest, and then fanning and protecting the eggs and fry is physically demanding and thus female choice should be influenced by traits that signal the males' ability to make this investment (Candolin, 2000a, 2000b, 2000c; Clutton-Brock, 1991). As covered below, the size and red coloration of the males' jaw signals this potential, but with an important caveat (Tables 3.5 and 3.6).

For the penultimate reproductive cycle, many males in poor condition express this signal (Candolin, 1999). These are males that do not have the energy reserves to successfully invest in a clutch, but signal this ability nonetheless. This in turn can result in females depositing eggs in the nests of these males that then consume some proportion of the eggs. The consumed eggs improve male condition and thus allow for one last successful reproductive cycle with the eggs of another female. The result is that males in poor condition can potentially deceive females, contra the basic assumption that condition-dependent traits are honest signals (Zahavi, 1975). However, when challenged by other males, as would happen in natural contexts (as opposed to a controlled laboratory situation with only one male and one female), the jaw signal of these males fades (Candolin, 2000a, 2000b). This point reinforces my argument that signals are best understood in the context of the natural history of the species; in this case, male-male competition will suppress deceptive signaling by males in poor condition.

For the reader who wishes to skip the details, the other takeaway messages for this section are that carotenoid-based color traits are good indicators of developmental and adult condition, and that the size of these traits are less consistently condition dependent than are the color of the traits. These studies also show that females can be sensitive to one type of trait (e.g., courtship display as a signal of later parenting ability) and males to another trait (e.g., trait size as a signal of fighting ability).

**TABLE 3.5** Condition-Dependent Color Traits in Fish

| Species | Scientific Name | ST | Trait | CD | S | Contrast Trait | Effect | Life History | CT | Manipulation | Reference |
|---|---|---|---|---|---|---|---|---|---|---|---|
| Guppy | *Poecilia reticulata*: Paria | L* | Spot color | Y | M | NA | NA | Adult | C | Infection/parasite | Houde and Torio (1992) |
| | Paria/Aripo | L* | Spot color (red) | Y | M | Body size | C<T | Postnatal | C | Diet/nutrition | Kodric–Brown (1989) |
| | Paria/Aripo | L* | Spot color (orange) | Y | M | Body size | C<T | Postnatal | C | Diet/nutrition | Kodric–Brown (1989) |
| | Paria/Marianne/Quare | L* | Spot color | Y | M | Three morph traits | C<T | Postnatal | C | Diet/nutrition | Grether (2000) |
| | New Mexico | L | Spot color | Y | M | Dorsal fin size | C<T | Adult | C | Body condition | Nicoletto (1991) |
| | Columbia | L/T | Spot color | Y[a] | M | Body size | C<T | Adult | C | Toxin | Baatrup and Junge (2001) |
| | Columbia | L/T | Spot color | Y | M | Body size | C<T | Adult | C | Toxin | Toft and Baatrup (2001) |
| | Columbia | L/T | Spot color | Y[b] | M | Body size | C=T | Postnatal/adult | C | Toxin | Bayley, Junge, and Baatrup (2002) |

| Common name | Species | ST | Trait | CD | S | | C=T | Age | CT | Factor | Reference |
|---|---|---|---|---|---|---|---|---|---|---|---|
| Stickleback | Gasterosteus aculeatus | L | Jaw color | N | M | Blue eyes | C=T | Inbreeding | C | Inbreeding | Frommen, Luz, Mazzi, and Bakker (2008) |
| | | L* | Jaw color | Y | M | Body condition | C<T | Adult | C | Infection/parasite | Milinski and Bakker (1990) |
| | | L* | Jaw color | Y[c] | M | Body length | C=T | Adult | C | Diet/nutrition | Frischknecht (1993) |
| | | N | Jaw color | Y[d] | M | NA | NA | Adult | C | RS | Bakker and Mundwiler (1994) |
| | | L | Jaw color | N | M | Body condition | C=T | Adult | C | Social dominance | Baube (1997) |

Note: ST, study type [L, lab experiment; F, field experiment; N, natural variation; T, toxin; *, included in Cotton et al. (2004a) review]; CD, condition dependent (Y, yes; N, no); S, sex of animals included in the study (M, male). Morph, morphological; CT, color type (C, carotenoid); RS, reproductive success.
[a] The degraded color was found for one dose level of vinclozolin (1 µg/mg); the same pattern was found for a high dose of vinclozolin (10 µg/mg) and both doses of flutamide and the DDT metabolite p,p'-DDE, but the differences were not statistically significant relative to a control group.
[b] Effects found for vinclozolin at 0.1 or 10.0 µg/mg; DDE at 0.1 µg/mg but not 0.01 µg/mg; and flutamide at 1.0 µg/mg, but not 0.01 µg/mg.
[c] Diet was related to short-term improvement in jaw color, but not absolute color.
[d] Natural variation in coloration was associated with better body condition in one site, but not a second site.

**TABLE 3.6 Condition-Dependent Size or Number Traits in Fish**

| Species | Scientific Name | ST | Trait | CD | S | Contrast Trait | Contrast Effect | Life History | CT | Manipulation | Reference |
|---|---|---|---|---|---|---|---|---|---|---|---|
| Guppies | *Poecilia reticulata:* Paria | L* | Spot area | Y | M | Nine morph traits | C<T | Inbreeding | C | Inbreeding | Sheridan and Pomiankowski (1997) |
| | Aripo | L* | Spot area | N | M | Nine morph traits | C=T | Inbreeding | C | Inbreeding | Sheridan and Pomiankowski (1997) |
| | Aripo | L | Spot area | Y | M | Sperm size | C<T | Adult | C | Sperm motility | Locatello, Rasotto, Evans, and Pilastro (2006) |
| | Tacarigua | L* | Spot area | Y | M | Body size | C<T | Inbreeding | C | Inbreeding | Van Oosterhout et al. (2003) |
| | Paria/Aripo | L* | Spot area | N | M | Body size | C=T | Postnatal | C | Diet/nutrition | Kodric-Brown (1989) |
| | Paria/ Marianne/ Quare | L* | Spot area | Y | M | Body size | C<T | Postnatal | C | Diet/nutrition | Grether (2000) |
| | Four sites | N | Spot area | N | M | Body size | C=T | Adult | C | Body condition | Nicoletto and Kodric-Brown (1999) |
| | New Mexico | N | Spot area | Y | M | Body size | C<T | Adult | C | Body condition | Nicoletto (1993) |
| | New Mexico | N | Spot area | N | M | Body size | C=T | Adult | C | Body condition | Nicoletto (1995) |
| | Australia | L | Spot area | Na | M | Length | C<T | Inbreeding | C | Inbreeding | Mariette et al. (2006) |

| Columbia | L/T | Spot area | Y | M | Body size | C<T | Adult | C | Toxin | Baatrup and Junge (2001) |
|---|---|---|---|---|---|---|---|---|---|---|
| Columbia | L/T | Spot area | Y | M | Body size | C<T | Adult | C | Toxin | Toft and Baatrup (2001) |
| Columbia | L/T | Spot area | N | M | Body size | C=T | Postnatal/adult | C | Toxin | Bayley et al. (2002) |
| Nigeria | L/T | Spot area | Y[b] | M | Body size | C<T | Postnatal/adult | C | Toxin | Kristensen et al. (2005) |
| Tacarigua | L* | Spot area | Y | M | Body size | C<T | Inbreeding | M | Inbreeding | Van Oosterhout et al. (2003) |
| Paria | L* | Spot area | N | M | Nine morph traits | C=T | Inbreeding | M | Inbreeding | Sheridan and Pomiankowski (1997) |
| Aripo | L* | Spot area | Y | M | Nine morph traits | C<T | Inbreeding | M | Inbreeding | Sheridan and Pomiankowski (1997) |
| New Mexico | N | Spot area | N | M | Body size | C=T | Adult | M | Body condition | Nicoletto (1993) |
| New Mexico | N | Spot area | Y | M | Body size | C<T | Adult | M | Body condition | Nicoletto (1995) |
| Australia | L | Spot area | N | M | Length | C=T | Inbreeding | M | Inbreeding | Mariette et al. (2006) |
| Paria | L* | Spot area | N | M | Nine morph traits | C=T | Inbreeding | S | Inbreeding | Sheridan and Pomiankowski (1997) |

*Continued*

**TABLE 3.6** Condition-Dependent Size or Number Traits in Fish—cont'd

| Species | Scientific Name | ST | Trait | CD | S | Contrast Trait | Contrast Effect | Life History | CT | Manipulation | Reference |
|---|---|---|---|---|---|---|---|---|---|---|---|
| | Aripo | L* | Spot area | N | M | Nine morph traits | C=T | Inbreeding | S | Inbreeding | Sheridan and Pomiankowski (1997) |
| | New Mexico | N | Spot area | N | M | Body size | C=T | Adult | S | Body condition | Nicoletto (1993) |
| Stickleback | Gasterosteus aculeatus | N | Jaw area | N[c] | M | Body size | C>T | Adult | C | Body condition | Candolin (1999) |
| | | L | Jaw area | N[c] | M | Body size | C>T | Adult | C | Diet/nutrition | Candolin (1999) |
| | | L* | Jaw area | N[c] | M | Body size | C>T | Adult | C | Diet/nutrition | Candolin (2000a) |
| | | L* | Jaw area | Y | M | Body size | C<T | Adult | C | Diet/competition | Candolin (2000a) |
| | | L | Jaw area | Y | M | Body size | C<T | Adult | C | Social competition | Candolin (2000b) |
| | | L | Jaw area | N[c] | M | Body size | C>T | Adult | C | Diet/nutrition | Candolin (2000c) |
| | | L | Jaw area | Y | M | Body size | C<T | Adult | C | Body condition | Candolin (2000c) |
| Guppies | Poecilia reticulata: Paria | L* | FA | N | M | Nine morph traits | C=T | Inbreeding | C | Inbreeding | Sheridan and Pomiankowski (1997) |
| | Aripo | L* | FA | N | M | Nine morph traits | C=T | Inbreeding | C | Inbreeding | Sheridan and Pomiankowski (1997) |
| | Paria | L* | Spot number | N | M | Nine morph traits | C=T | Inbreeding | C | Inbreeding | Sheridan and Pomiankowski (1997) |

| Aripo | L* | Spot number | N | M | Nine morph traits | C<T | Inbreeding | C | Inbreeding | Sheridan and Pomiankowski (1997) |
|---|---|---|---|---|---|---|---|---|---|---|
| Paria/Aripo | L* | Spot number | N | M | Body size | C=T | Postnatal | C | Diet/nutrition | Kodric-Brown (1989) |
| Four sites | N | Spot number | Y^a | M | Body size | C<T | Adult | C | Body condition | Nicoletto and Kodric-Brown (1999) |
| New Mexico | N | Spot number | Y | M | Body size | C<T | Adult | C | Body condition | Nicoletto (1993) |
| New Mexico | N | Spot number | Y | M | Body size | C=T | Adult | C | Body condition | Nicoletto (1995) |
| Paria | L* | FA | N | M | Nine morph traits | C=T | Inbreeding | M | Inbreeding | Sheridan and Pomiankowski (1997) |
| Aripo | L* | FA | N | M | Nine morph traits | C=T | Inbreeding | M | Inbreeding | Sheridan and Pomiankowski (1997) |
| Aripo | L* | Spot number | Y | M | Nine morph traits | C<T | Inbreeding | M | Inbreeding | Sheridan and Pomiankowski (1997) |
| Paria | L* | Spot number | N | M | Nine morph traits | C=T | Inbreeding | M | Inbreeding | Sheridan and Pomiankowski (1997) |
| New Mexico | N | Spot number | N | M | Body size | C=T | Adult | M | Body condition | Nicoletto (1993) |

*Continued*

**TABLE 3.6** Condition-Dependent Size or Number Traits in Fish—cont'd

| Species | Scientific Name | ST | Trait | CD | S | Contrast Trait | Effect | Life History | CT | Manipulation | Reference |
|---|---|---|---|---|---|---|---|---|---|---|---|
| | New Mexico | N | Spot number | N | M | Body size | C<T | Adult | M | Body condition | Nicoletto (1995) |
| | Paria | L* | FA | N | M | Nine morph traits | C=T | Inbreeding | S | Inbreeding | Sheridan and Pomiankowski (1997) |
| | Aripo | L* | FA | N | M | Nine morph traits | C=T | Inbreeding | S | Inbreeding | Sheridan and Pomiankowski (1997) |
| | Paria | L* | Spot number | N | M | Nine morph traits | C=T | Inbreeding | S | Inbreeding | Sheridan and Pomiankowski (1997) |
| | Aripo | L* | Spot number | Y[e] | M | Nine morph traits | C<T | Inbreeding | S | Inbreeding | Sheridan and Pomiankowski (1997) |

Note: ST, study type (L, lab experiment; F, field experiment; N, natural variation; T, toxin; *, included in Cotton et al. (2004a) review); CD, condition dependent (Y, yes; N, no); S, sex of animals included in the study (M, male). Morph, morphological; FA, fluctuating asymmetry (differences comparing the two lateral sides of the body); CT, color type (C, carotenoid; M, melanin; S, structural).

[a] Inbreeding was associated with a reduction in spot area, but this was not statistically significant possibly due to low power.

[b] Significant effects at 200 ng/L of 17α-ethinylestradiol, but not 10 and 50 ng/L.

[c] The red area of the jaw was higher for males in good condition and males in poor condition; the latter were at their penultimate reproductive cycle (see text).

[d] A relation between condition (swim speed) and spot number was found for two of the four locations.

[e] The effect was significant for number of subspots, but not larger spots.

## Physical Traits

### Color

As with birds, sexually selected color signals in fish are primarily based on ca-rotenoid, melanin, and structural colors (Price, Weadick, Shim, & Rodd, 2008). Male guppies express each of these color types, but carotenoid colors (especially orange) appear to be the most important with respect to female choice (Kodric-Brown, 1985), as shown in Photo 3.8 (inset). Similarly, the red carotenoid-based jaw coloration of male sticklebacks is a particularly important driver of female mate choices (Milinski & Bakker, 1990).

All of the assessments listed in Table 3.5 involved carotenoid-based color; six of these were reported in the Cotton et al. (2004a) review and none of them in Griffith et al. (2006). All but two of the assessments suggested the expression of carotenoid colors is indeed condition-dependent in these species. Carotenoid coloration (e.g., chroma) faded when males were exposed to parasites, poor nu-trition, and toxins; the effects on the expression of these colors were larger than the effects on various morphological traits (e.g., body size). These morphologi-cal traits are less rigorous than some of the contrast traits used in many of the bird studies, such as female beak or plumage color (e.g., de Kogel, 1997; Dauwe & Eens, 2008), but are nonetheless useful. All of the guppy studies indicated ca-rotenoid color was condition dependent, regardless of the stream from which the males were obtained and whether the manipulation occurred during postna-tal development or in adulthood.

One null result was found for one or two generations of inbreeding, which did not affect the jaw coloration of male sticklebacks but did reduce the survival rates and hatching success of clutches (Frommen et al., 2008). Given the dif-ferential survival of inbred and outbred males, it is possible that only the most

**PHOTO 3.8** For the male guppy (*Poecilia reticulata*), color of the fins, especially the orange, makes them attractive to females and is a good indicator of their ability to cope with dietary stress-ors, infections, and exposure to man-made toxins. (See the color plate section.)

robust inbred males survived to adulthood, which makes this null finding difficult to interpret. The second null result was also for stickleback males. Here, Baube (1997) found that in laboratory-based contests, natural variation in jaw color was unrelated to actual fighting ability, although it did serve as a threat signal; that is, when coloration was clearly visible, the male with the redder jaw initiated and won more fights.

## Size

The size of the color area has been extensively studied in both guppies (e.g., Kodric-Brown, 1989) and sticklebacks (e.g., Candolin, 1999), as has the number of color spots and less frequently the symmetry of these spots on the two lateral sides of guppy males' bodies (Nicoletto, 1993; Sheridan & Pomiankowski, 1997); the latter is called fluctuating asymmetry (FA). The overall pattern is less consistent than that found for color features (e.g., brightness, chroma).

The results for about half of the assessments are consistent with spot area and spot number being condition-dependent traits in male guppies, with no discernable pattern across inbreeding, postnatal, or adult manipulations. Nearly all of the positive effects included an appropriate contrast trait (e.g., body size), consistent with condition dependence. Some of the null findings may have resulted from low statistical power and manipulations that were too weak. For instance, Mariette, Kelley, Brooks, and Evans (2006) found that the area of carotenoid spots was 20% lower for inbred relative to outbred guppy males, but the difference was not statistically significant. The comparison was, however, based on only 11 males in each group, and on only one generation of inbreeding. A larger sample or additional generations of inbreeding may have produced a significant effect for spot area as found by Van Oosterhout et al. (2003) after three generations of inbreeding. In any case, many of the studies finding no condition-dependent effects for color area or spot number do find such effects for color features (Bayley et al., 2003; Kodric-Brown, 1989) or behavioral traits (Mariette et al., 2006; Nicoletto & Kodric-Brown, 1999). The implication is that spot area and number may be condition-dependent traits in male guppies, but they are not as sensitive to conditions as other traits. Or stated otherwise, males in very poor condition may be detectable based on spot area or number but other traits are needed to detect subtle variation in condition among less severely compromised males.

The interpretation of the signaling value of jaw area for male sticklebacks is complicated by the above noted tendency of males in poor condition to signal the ability to invest in offspring toward the end of their reproductive life span (Candolin, 1999). One result is that under nutritional stress the males in the best condition have a large red jaw area, but so do males in the poorest condition (Candolin, 1999, 2000a); males in fair condition have the smallest red jaw area. As noted, males in good condition will keep the deceptive males in check through male-male competition (Candolin, 2000a, 2000b). The result is that red jaw area is not as useful a signal for females as it is for males. For males it is a threat signal and can trigger male-male aggression that would then reveal males that are falsely signaling their condition.

## Behavioral Traits

The majority of studies revealed that behavioral displays, especially courtship displays, are compromised by exposure to stressors and, as with birds, appear to most strongly signal current condition. Of the 12 such courtship assessments in guppies, the only one that did not suggest condition dependence involved courtship intensity as related to a diet manipulation during development (Kodric-Brown, 1989). About half of the remaining assessments included strong contrast traits, specifically, copulation attempts (e.g., Shenoy, 2012) or overall movement (e.g., Bayley et al., 1999), and all of them revealed that courtship displays were more strongly affected by toxin exposure or inbreeding than these contrasts. All of the assessments of stickleback behavior involved toxin exposure in adulthood and three of these four suggested condition dependence. The only study with a strong contrast trait was that of Sebire et al. (2008) who showed that exposure to the antiandrogen flutamide reduced male sticklebacks' frequency of courtship displays but not their feeding rate (Table 3.7).

## CONCLUSION

The research reviewed in this chapter illustrates that the color and size of physical traits, behavioral displays, as well as aspects of brain development and functioning can all serve as signals of current condition, condition in the near past, or condition during development. Different traits may also signal sensitivity to different types of stressors. Courtship and dominance displays, including aspects of birdsong, are consistently found to be good indicators of current condition (Cotton et al., 2004a). Of the different types of color displays, the size and the richness of the yellow-to-red carotenoid-based traits are good indicators of the current condition of birds and fish (McGraw, 2006a). The melanin-based colors, in contrast, do not emerge as consistently as indicators of condition, but the sizes of melanin-based badges often are indicators in some species of bird, but not in the well-studied guppy. The structural colors of birds' feathers are potentially useful indicators of their condition in the near past; that is, during the weeks or months following molt and the development of new breeding-season feathers. Although structural-based colors have not been as been as thoroughly assessed as carotenoid-based colors, the existing research suggests that they are indeed reflective of the individual's condition during feather development.

The most consistently assessed brain and cognitive traits focused on how resiliency in the face of developmental stressors will be signaled by aspects of song learning and later production of song (Nowicki et al., 1998; Peters et al., 2014). More broadly, the implications are that stressors during the time frame when the brain is developing will be detectable by deficits in the later expression of sexually or social selected traits, and that these deficits will directly or

**TABLE 3.7** Condition-Dependent Behavioral Traits in Fish

| Species | Scientific Name | ST | Trait | CD | S | Contrast | | Life History | Manipulation | Reference |
|---|---|---|---|---|---|---|---|---|---|---|
| | | | | | | Trait | Effect | | | |
| Guppies | *Poecilia reticulata*: Paria | L* | Courtship display | Y | M | NA | NA | Adult | Infection/parasite | Houde and Torio (1992) |
| | Aripo/Guanapo | L/T | Courtship display | Y | M | Cop attempt | C<T | Adult | Toxin | Shenoy (2012) |
| | Aripo/Guanapo | L/T | Male competition | Y | M | Body size | C<T | Adult | Toxin | Shenoy (2012) |
| | Tacarigua | L* | Courtship display | Y | M | Cop attempt | C<T | Inbreeding | Inbreeding | Van Oosterhout et al. (2003) |
| | Paria/Aripo | L* | Courtship intensity | N | M | Body size | C=T | Postnatal | Diet/nutrition | Kodric-Brown (1989) |
| | Four sites | N | Courtship display | Y | M | Body size | C<T | Adult | Body condition | Nicoletto and Kodric-Brown (1999) |
| | New Mexico | N | Courtship display | Y | M | NA | NA | Adult | Body condition | Nicoletto (1993) |
| | Australia | L | Courtship display | Y | M | Cop attempt | C<T | Inbreeding | Inbreeding | Mariette et al. (2006) |
| | Columbia | L/T | Courtship display | Y | M | Body size | C<T | Adult | Toxin | Baatrup and Junge (2001) |

| | ST | | CD | S | | C<T | | | Reference |
|---|---|---|---|---|---|---|---|---|---|
| Columbia | L/T | Courtship display | Y[a] | M | Body size | C<T | Adult | Toxin | Bayley, Larsen, Baekgaard, and Baatrup (2003) |
| Columbia | L/T | Courtship display | Y | M | Overall movement | C<T | Adult | Toxin | Bayley, Nielsen, and Baatrup (1999) |
| Columbia | L/T | Courtship display | Y[b] | M | Posturing | C<T | Postnatal/adult | Toxin | Bayley et al. (2002) |
| Australia | L | Copulations | Y | M | NA | NA | Inbreeding | Inbreeding | Mariette et al. (2006) |
| Nigeria | L/T | Courtship display | Y[c] | M | Cop attempt | C<T | Postnatal/adult | Toxin | Kristensen, Baatrup, and Bayley (2005) |
| Stickleback *Gasterosteus aculeatus* | L/T | Courtship display | N | M | Body size | C=T | Adult | Toxin | Bell (2001) |
| | L/T | Male competition | Y | M | Body size | C=T | Adult | Toxin | Bell (2001) |
| | L/T | Courtship display | Y | M | NA | NA | Adult | Toxin | Sebire et al. (2008) |
| | L/T | Courtship display | Y | M | Feeding rate | C<T | Adult | Toxin | Sebire et al. (2008) |

Note: ST, study type [L, lab experiment; F, field experiment; N, natural variation; T, toxin; *, included in Cotton et al. (2004a) review; CD, condition dependent (Y, yes; N, no); S, sex of animals included in the study (M, male). Cop, copulation.
[a] Courtship was affected by vinclozolin at 0.1, 1.0, and 10 μg/mg of dry food, but significant only at 10 μg/mg.
[b] Effects found for vinclozolin at 0.1 or 10.0 μg/mg; flutamide at 1.0 μg/mg, but not 0.01 μg/mg, but not for DDE at 0.01 or 0.1 μg/mg.
[c] Significant effects at 200 ng/L of 17a-ethinylestradiol, but not 10 and 50 ng/L.

indirectly signal the competitiveness, disease resistance, or provisioning ability of the individual. The existing research is in its infancy but suggestive that the volume or functioning of at least some brain areas are sensitive to developmental stressors in a sex-specific way and may not manifest cognitively and behaviorally until adulthood. We revisit this issue in the next chapter, with studies of how exposure to stressors disrupts the spatial abilities and the development and functioning of the hippocampus of male rodents.

Finally, as was discussed in the last chapter, Darwin's (1871) focus on male-male competition and female choice has resulted in a relative neglect of females' condition-dependent signals. Recall, these could emerge as a result of male choice or female-female competition over mates or other reproductively relevant resources (West-Eberhard, 1983). Male choice of mates based on any such signal, for instance, makes a lot of sense for most species of bird and many species of fish (include the stickleback) because males often provision and protect offspring (Clutton-Brock, 1991). Female signals have in fact captured the attention of many biologists in recent years (e.g., Pizzari, Cornwallis, Løvlie, Jakobsson, & Birkhead, 2003). The research reviewed in this chapter, whether the female trait was the focus of the study (Kelly et al., 2012) or a contrast trait (Burley et al., 1992), is consistent with this expectation. Female condition-dependent signals are often less conspicuous than those of conspecific males, but there are now multiple examples of the existence of these signals, some of which were noted for birds in this chapter and more examples are provided for arthropods and mammals in the next chapter and for girls and women in subsequent chapters.

# Chapter 4

# Condition-Dependent Traits in Arthropods and Mammals

## Chapter Outline

With this chapter, we continue the overview of condition-dependent traits and the factors that influence their expression, but turn our attention to arthropods (recall, animals with exoskeletons) and mammals. In addition to providing further documentation and illustration of how exposure to stressors can compromise the expression of specific traits in one sex or the other, the studies reviewed in this chapter make it clear that condition dependence is found in myriad of species, ranging from the well-known fruit fly (*Drosophila simulans*) to the mandrill (*Mandrillus sphinx*). The traits considered are richly diverse as well, from the length of the eye spans of stalk-eyed flies (e.g., *Cyrtodiopsis whitei*) to the roaring of red deer (*Cervus elaphus*) to the hippocampus of the laboratory mouse (*Mus musculus*). When combined with the reviews of the last chapter, the research reviewed herein shows that condition-dependent social signals have evolved many times and that the type of trait or ability that is signaled varies with the nature of the intrasexual competition or intersexual choice, as we covered in Chapter 2. As a result of their rapid development, studies of arthropods provide a more thorough assessment of the importance of developmental conditions for the later expression of traits related to competition or choice than is provided by the studies of birds, fish, and mammals. The study of mammals of course brings us one step closer to our own species and provides a more direct link to the studies of human vulnerability covered in Chapters 6 and 7.

Evolution of Vulnerability. http://dx.doi.org/10.1016/B978-0-12-801562-9.00004-1

## ARTHROPODS

To keep the review tractable, I focused on insects and a few studies of spiders and do not include crustaceans. This should not be taken to mean condition-dependent traits are not found in crustaceans, as they are and are easily illustrated by studies of various species of fiddler crab (*Uca*; Backwell, Jennions, Christy, & Schober, 1995; Jennions & Backwell, 1998; Kim & Choe, 2003). Males of these species construct burrows and sometimes courtship ornaments (e.g., sand pillars) outside of them that serve to attract females and in which mating and egg incubation occur. Males also attract females by waving their enlarged claw (Photo 4.1, inset) and fight one another for control of burrows in the best locations (e.g., Christy, 1983). In an experimental study of the milky fiddler crab (*U. lacteal*), Kim and Choe found that food-supplemented males built more courtship ornaments and engaged in more frequent claw waving than their unsupplemented peers. Similar results have been found for Beebe's fiddler crab (*U. beebei*; Backwell et al., 1995), and the red-winged fiddler crab (*U. annulipes*; Jennions & Backwell, 1998).

In any case, the reviews follow the same format as in the previous chapter but only cover physical and behavioral traits due to a lack of studies on the condition dependence of brain and cognitive traits in these species. The latter will be covered in the reviews of mammals.

### Physical Traits

Insects have the same three basic forms of color as birds and fish; carotenoid, melanin, and structural. Unlike birds and fish, melanin-based colors are likely to be particularly important signals in insects (Stoehr, 2006). This is because melanin appears to be more costly to produce for insects than for vertebrates and,

**PHOTO 4.1**   Males of the thick-legged fiddler crab (*Uca crassipes*) attempt to attract females by waving their enlarged claw, and fight for possession of burrows in which mating occurs and females lay and incubate their eggs. *Photo credit: Thomas Brown, 2011. Creative Commons license: http://commons.wikimedia.org/wiki/File:Fiddler_Crab_(Uca_crassipes%3F)_(6262758647).jpg.* (See the color plate section.)

critically, is an important component of insects' immune response (e.g., Carton & Nappi, 1997), just as carotenoids are for vertebrates. One aspect of insects' immune response involves the encapsulation of parasites or other pathogens in a melanin-based sheath. Thus, individuals with poor melanin signals – either color quality or trait size – may have low overall melanin reserves and thus unable to mount an effective immune response; other nonmelanin traits can also signal the strength of the encapsulation response in some species (Rantala, Koskimïki, Taskinen, Tynkkynen, & Suhonen, 2000).

## Color

The size of color-based traits is more thoroughly assessed in arthropods than color quality, but there are a few studies of the latter (Table 4.1). At least for the one well-studied species of damselfly, the American rubyspot (*Hetaerina americana*), the color of carotenoid-based traits is not consistently related to condition (e.g., Contreras-Garduño, Buzatto, Abundis, Nájera-Cordero, & Córdoba-Aguilar, 2007; Contreras Garduño, Buzatto, Serrano Meneses, Nájera Cordero, & Córdoba Aguilar, 2008). These findings are preliminary but stand in sharp contrast to the general pattern for birds and fish described in the last chapter.

In contrast, the quality of melanin-based colors do reflect condition for the males of two related species of damselfly, *Mnais costalis* (Photo 4.2, inset; Hooper, Tsubaki, & Siva Jothy, 1999) and *Calopteryx splendens* (Photo 4.3, inset; Siva Jothy, 2000), as well as the male ambush bug (*Phymata americana*; Punzalan, Cooray, Helen Rodd, & Rowe, 2008); however, only one of these studies included a rigorous contrast trait (Punzalan et al., 2008). The quality of structural-based colors has been assessed in a few species, and these too suggest that color is a good signal of current condition and condition during development. For instance, in a laboratory study of the grass butterfly (*Eurema hecabe*), Kemp (2008) showed that male larva that were fed high-quality food had better developed wing color than poorly fed males and that early diet compromised males' wing color more strongly than females' wing color. Moreover, in natural settings, male butterflies with well-developed structural-based colors were in better physical condition than males with duller colors, and these same colors were stronger indicators of males' than females' condition.

## Size

The effect of exposure to stressors on trait size is well-studied in arthropods, and Table 4.2 provides dozens of examples across 23 species; 9 of which were previously reviewed (Cotton, Fowler, & Pomiankowski, 2004a). The size of the red wing spot of the American rubyspot is well represented among these (six assessments). The critical trait is a red spot at the base of each wing that is displayed to courted females and to other males during territorial disputes

**TABLE 4.1  Condition-Dependent Color Traits in Arthropods**

| Species | Scientific Name | ST | Trait | CD | S | Contrast Trait | Effect | Life History | CT | Manipulation | References |
|---|---|---|---|---|---|---|---|---|---|---|---|
| Damselfly | Hetaerina americana | N | Wing spot | N | M | Thorax color | C=T | Adult | C | Territory holder | Contreras-Garduño et al. (2007) |
| | | L | Wing spot | N | M | Thorax color | C=T | Adult | C | Infection/parasite | Contreras-Garduño et al. (2007) |
| | | L | Wing spot | N | M | NA | NA | Adult | C | Diet/nutrition | Contreras-Garduño et al. (2007) |
| | | N | Wing spot | N | M | Thorax color | C=T | Adult | C | FA | Contreras Garduño et al. (2008) |
| | | L | Wing spot | Y[a] | M | Head size | C<T | Adult | C | Infection/parasite | Contreras Garduño et al. (2008) |
| | Mnais costalis | L* | Wing | Y | M | NA | NA | Adult | M | Diet/nutrition | Hooper et al. (1999) |
| | Calopteryx splendens | F | Wing spot | Y | M | NA | NA | Adult | M | Infection/parasite | Siva Jothy (2000) |
| | | L | Wing spot | Y | M | NA | NA | Adult | M | Infection/parasite | Siva Jothy (2000) |
| | | N | Wing spot | N | M | Body size | C=T | Adult | M | Infection/parasite | Rantala, Honkavaara, Dunn, and Suhonen (2011) |

| Common name | Species | ST | Trait | CD | S | Trait | C<T | Age | CT | Factor | Reference |
|---|---|---|---|---|---|---|---|---|---|---|---|
| Ambush bug | *Phymata americana* | L | Lateral color | Y | B | Dorsal color | C<T | Adult | M | Diet/nutrition | Punzalan et al. (2008) |
| Damselfly | *C. maculata* | L | Abdominal | Y | M | NA | NA | Adult | S | Diet/nutrition | Fitzstephens and Getty (2000) |
| Orange butterfly | *Colias eurytheme* | L | Wing | Y | M | Orange color | C<T | Postnatal | S | Diet/nutrition | Kemp and Rutowski (2007) |
| | | L | Wing | Y | M | Orange color | C<T | Postnatal | S | Heat shock | Kemp and Rutowski (2007) |
| Grass butterfly | *Eurema hecabe* | L | Wing | Y | B | Female color | C<T | Postnatal | S | Diet/nutrition | Kemp (2008) |
| | | N | Wing | Y | B | Female color | C<T | Adult | S | Body condition/ LS | Kemp (2008) |
| Jumping spider | *Cosmophasis umbratica* | L | Carapace | Y | M | Body size | C<T | Adult | S | Social competition | Lim and Li (2013) |

*Note:* ST, study type [L, lab experiment; F, field experiment; N, natural variation; *, included in Cotton et al. (2004a) review]; CD, condition dependent (Y, yes; N, no); S, sex of animals included in the study (M, male; B, both sexes); CT, color type (C, carotenoid; M, melanin; S, structural); LS, lifespan; FA, fluctuating asymmetry.
aBrightness was affected but not chroma.

**PHOTO 4.2** The dark, melanin-based color of the male wings of the damselfly species *Mnais costalis* is a good indicator of physical condition. *Photo credit: Alpsdake, 2012. Creative Commons license: http://commons.wikimedia.org/wiki/File:Mnais_costalis_male_on_Iris_japonica. JPG#filelinks.* (See the color plate section.)

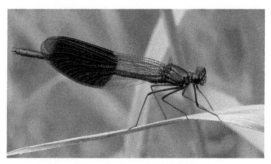

**PHOTO 4.3**    The dark, melanin-based color of the male wings of the damselfly species *Calopteryx splendens* is a good indicator of immune system health. *Photo credit: Andreas Eichler, 2013. Creative Commons license: http://commons.wikimedia.org/wiki/File:2013.08.04.-12-Ladenburg-Gebaenderte_Prachtlibelle-Maennchen.jpg.* (See the color plate section.)

(Photo 4.4, inset). Unlike quality of the red coloration, the size of the color area reflects males' disease resistance and social and reproductive success in adulthood (Contreras Garduño et al., 2008; Grether, 1996), as well as quality of their developmental diet (Álvarez, Serrano-Meneses, Reyes-Márquez, Jiménez-Cortés, & Córdoba-Aguilar, 2013).

Similar studies have been conducted with a related species, the smoky rubyspot (*Hetaerina titia*). The wings of these males include both carotenoid- and melanin-based color areas, although the latter are larger and signals to other males during territorial disputes (e.g., Cordoba-Aguilar, Lesher-Trevino, & Anderson, 2007). Given the size differences, it is not too surprising that the carotenoid-based trait is not sensitive to exposure to stressors but four of the five

**TABLE 4.2** Condition-Dependent Size or Pattern-Based Traits in Arthropods

| Species | Scientific Name | ST | Trait | CD | S | Contrast Trait | Effect | Life History | CT | Manipulation | References |
|---|---|---|---|---|---|---|---|---|---|---|---|
| Damselfly | Hetaerina americana | L | Wing spot | Y | M | NA | NA | Adult | C | Infection/parasite | Contreras-Garduño et al. (2007) |
| | | N | Wing spot | Y | M | Wing size | C<T | Adult | C | RS | Grether (1996) |
| | | N | Wing spot | Y | M | Wing length | C<T | Adult | C | Social dominance | Contreras Garduño et al. (2008) |
| | | L | Wing spot | Y | M | Head size | C<T | Adult | C | Infection/parasite | Contreras Garduño et al. (2008) |
| | | L | Wing spot | Y | M | Body size | C<T | Postnatal | C | Diet/nutrition | Álvarez et al. (2013) |
| | | N | Wing spot | Y[a] | M | Wing size | C<T | Adult | C | RS | Serrano-Meneses, Córdoba-Aguilar, Méndez, Layen, and Székely (2007) |
| | H. titia | N | Wing area | N | M | Wing size | C=T | Adult | C | Territory holder | Cordoba-Aguilar et al. (2007) |
| | | N | Wing area | N | M | Wing size | C=T | Adult | C | Survival | Cordoba-Aguilar et al. (2007) |

*Continued*

**TABLE 4.2** Condition-Dependent Size or Pattern-Based Traits in Arthropods—cont'd

| Species | Scientific Name | ST | Trait | CD | S | Contrast Trait | Contrast Effect | Life History | CT | Manipulation | References |
|---|---|---|---|---|---|---|---|---|---|---|---|
| | | N | Wing area | N[b] | M | Wing size | C=T | Adult | C | Infection/parasite | Cordoba-Aguilar et al. (2007) |
| | | L | Wing area | N | M | Wing size | C=T | Adult | C | Infection/parasite | Cordoba-Aguilar et al. (2007) |
| | | L | Wing area | N[c] | M | Wing size | C=T | Adult | C | Infection/parasite | González-Tokman and Córdoba-Aguilar (2010) |
| | | N | Wing area | Y | M | Wing size | C<T | Adult | M | Territory holder | Cordoba-Aguilar et al. (2007) |
| | | N | Wing area | Y | M | Wing size | C<T | Adult | M | Survival | Cordoba-Aguilar et al. (2007) |
| | | N | Wing area | Y | M | Wing size | C<T | Adult | M | Infection/parasite | Cordoba-Aguilar et al. (2007) |
| | | L | Wing area | Y | M | Wing size | C<T | Adult | M | Infection/parasite | Cordoba-Aguilar et al. (2007) |
| | | L | Wing area | N[c] | M | Wing size | C=T | Adult | M | Infection/parasite | González-Tokman and Córdoba-Aguilar (2010) |
| | *Calopteryx haemorrhoidalis* | F | Wing area | Y | M | Wing size | C<T | Adult | M | RS | Córdoba-Aguilar (2002) |

| | | | | | | | | | | | |
|---|---|---|---|---|---|---|---|---|---|---|---|
| Paper wasp | Polistes dominulus | F | Wing area | Y | M | Wing size | C<T | Adult | M | Survival | Córdoba-Aguilar (2002) |
| | | N | Wing area | Y | M | Age | C<T | Adult | M | Infection/parasite | Córdoba-Aguilar (2002) |
| | | L | Face pattern | Y | F | Face quant | C<T | Postnatal | M | Diet/nutrition | Tibbetts (2010) |
| | | L | Face pattern | Y | F | Weight | C<T | Adult | M | Diet/nutrition | Tibbetts and Banan (2010) |
| Damselfly | C. splendens | L | Wing area | Y | M | Wing size | C<T | Adult | S | Infection/parasite | Rantala et al. (2000) |
| | | F | Wing area | N[d] | M | Wing size | C=T | Adult | S | Infection/parasite | Rantala et al. (2011) |
| Decorated cricket | Gryllodes sigillatus | L | CHC | Y | M | Female CHC | C<T | Postnatal | NA | Diet/nutrition | Weddle et al. (2012) |
| Fruit fly | Drosophila simulans | L | CHC | Y | B | Female CHC | C=T | Adult | NA | Diet/nutrition | Ingleby et al. (2013) |
| | | L | CHC | Y[e] | B | Female CHC | C<T | Postnatal | NA | Diet/nutrition | Ingleby et al. (2013) |
| | | L | CHC | Y | B | Female CHC | C<T | Adult | NA | Temperature | Ingleby et al. (2013) |
| | D. serrata | L | CHC | Y | M | Non-SS CHC | C<T | Adult | NA | Diet/nutrition | Gosden and Chenoweth (2011) |
| | | L | CHC | Y | M | Non-SS CHC | C<T | Postnatal | NA | Diet/nutrition | Delcourt and Rundle (2011) |

*Continued*

TABLE 4.2 Condition-Dependent Size or Pattern-Based Traits in Arthropods—cont'd

| Species | Scientific Name | ST | Trait | CD | S | Contrast Trait | Effect | Life History | CT | Manipulation | References |
|---|---|---|---|---|---|---|---|---|---|---|---|
| Stalk-eyed fly | D. bunnanda | L | Wing shape | Y$^f$ | M | Non-SS wing trait | C<T | Postnatal | NA | Diet/nutrition | McGuigan (2009) |
| | Diasemopsis meigenii | L | Eye span | Y | M | Male thorax size | C<T | Inbreeding | NA | Inbreeding | Bellamy et al. (2013) |
| | | L | Eye span | Y | B | Female eye span | C<T | Inbreeding | NA | Inbreeding | Bellamy et al. (2013) |
| | | L | Eye span | Y | M | Male thorax size | C<T | Postnatal | NA | Diet/nutrition | Bellamy et al. (2013) |
| | | L | Eye span | Y | B | Female eye span | C<T | Postnatal | NA | Diet/nutrition | Bellamy et al. (2013) |
| | D. aethiopica | L* | Eye span | Y | B | Female eye span | C<T | Postnatal | NA | Diet/nutrition | Knell et al. (1999) |
| | D. dubia | N | Eye span | Y$^g$ | B | Female eye span | C<T | Adult | NA | Body condition/LS | Wilkinson and Taper (1999) |
| | | N | Eye span | Y$^g$ | M | Thorax | C<T | Adult | NA | Body condition/LS | Wilkinson and Taper (1999) |
| | Teleopsis dalmanni | L | Eye span | Y | B | Female eye span | C<T | Inbreeding | NA | Inbreeding | Prokop, Leś, Banaś, Koteja, and Radwan (2010) |
| | | L | Eye span | Y | M | Thorax | C=T | Inbreeding | NA | Inbreeding | Prokop et al. (2010) |

| | | | | | | | | | | | |
|---|---|---|---|---|---|---|---|---|---|---|---|
| Cyrtodiopsis whitei | | N$^g$ | Eye span | Y | B | Female eye span | C<T | Adult | NA | Body condition/LS | Wilkinson and Taper (1999) |
| | | N$^g$ | Eye span | Y | M | Thorax | C<T | Adult | NA | Body condition/LS | Wilkinson and Taper (1999) |
| C. dalmanni | | N$^g$ | Eye span | Y | B | Female eye span | C<T | Adult | NA | Body condition/LS | Wilkinson and Taper (1999) |
| | | N$^g$ | Eye span | Y | M | Thorax | C<T | Adult | NA | Body condition/LS | Wilkinson and Taper (1999) |
| | | L* | Eye span | Y | B | Female eye span | C<T | Postnatal | NA | Diet/nutrition | David et al. (1998) |
| | | L* | Eye span | Y | M | Wing size | C<T | Postnatal | NA | Diet/nutrition | David et al. (1998) |
| | | L* | Eye span | Y | M | Wing size | C<T | Postnatal | NA | Diet/nutrition | David, Bjorksten, Fowler, and Pomiankowski (2000) |
| | | L* | Eye span | Y | B | Female eye span | C<T | Postnatal | NA | Diet/nutrition | David et al. (2000) |
| | | L | Eye span | Y | M | Wing size | C<T | Postnatal | NA | Diet/nutrition | Cotton et al. (2004b) |
| | | L | Eye span | Y | B | Female eye span | C<T | Postnatal | NA | Diet/nutrition | Cotton et al. (2004b) |
| Prochyliza xanthostoma | Waltzing fly | L | Head length | Y | B | Female head length | C<T | Postnatal | NA | Diet/nutrition | Bonduriansky and Rowe (2005) |
| | | L | Head width | Y | B | Female head width | C<T | Postnatal | NA | Diet/nutrition | Bonduriansky and Rowe (2005) |

*Continued*

TABLE 4.2 Condition-Dependent Size or Pattern-Based Traits in Arthropods—cont'd

| Species | Scientific Name | ST | Trait | CD | S | Contrast Trait | Contrast Effect | Life History | CT | Manipulation | References |
|---|---|---|---|---|---|---|---|---|---|---|---|
| | | L | Antenna length | N | B | Female antenna | C=T | Postnatal | NA | Diet/nutrition | Bonduriansky and Rowe (2005) |
| | | L | Foretibia length | N | B | Female foretibia | C=T | Postnatal | NA | Diet/nutrition | Bonduriansky and Rowe (2005) |
| | | L | Head length | Y | M | Thorax | C<T | Postnatal | NA | Diet/nutrition | Bonduriansky and Rowe (2005) |
| | | L | Head width | N | M | Thorax | C=T | Postnatal | NA | Diet/nutrition | Bonduriansky and Rowe (2005) |
| | | L | Antenna length | N | M | Thorax | C=T | Postnatal | NA | Diet/nutrition | Bonduriansky and Rowe (2005) |
| | | L | Foretibia length | N | M | Thorax | C=T | Postnatal | NA | Diet/nutrition | Bonduriansky and Rowe (2005) |
| Water strider | Gerris incognitus | L* | Genitalia | Y | M | Morph trait | C>T | Postnatal | NA | Diet/nutrition | Arnqvist and Thornhill (1998) |
| Seed beetle | Callosobruchus maculatus | L | Body size | Yʰ | B | Abdominal segment | C<T | Postnatal | NA | Diet/nutrition | Hallsson, Chenoweth, and Bonduriansky (2012) |
| Armed beetle | Gnatocerus cornutus | L | Mandible size | Y | M | Body size | C<T | Postnatal | NA | Diet/nutrition | Katsuki, Okada, and Okada (2012) |

| Common name | Species | | Trait | | | | | | | | Reference |
|---|---|---|---|---|---|---|---|---|---|---|---|
| Dung beetle | *Onthophagus taurus* | L | Testis size | N | M | Body size | C=T | Postnatal | NA | Diet/nutrition | Katsuki et al. (2012) |
| | | L | Horn size | Y | M | Body size | C<T | Postnatal | NA | Infection/parasite | Demuth, Naidu, and Mydlarz (2012) |
| | | L* | Horn size | Y | M | Body size | C=T | Postnatal | NA | Diet/nutrition | Hunt and Simmons (1997) |
| | *O. ascuminatus* | L* | Horn size | Y | M | Body size | C=T | Postnatal | NA | Diet/nutrition | Emlen (1994) |
| | | L | Horn size | Y | M | Body size | C=T | Postnatal | NA | Diet/nutrition | Emlen (1997) |
| | | L | Horn size | Y | M | Body size | C>T | Postnatal | NA | Diet/nutrition | Emlen (1997) |
| Grain beetle | *Tenebrio molitor* | L* | Pheromone | Y | M | Body size | C=T | Adult | NA | Diet/nutrition | Rantala, Kortet, Kotiaho, Vainikka, and Suhonen (2003) |
| | | L | Pheromone | Y | M | Body size | C<T | Adult | NA | Infection/parasite | Rantala, Jokinen, Kortet, Vainikka, and Suhonen (2002) |
| | | L | Pheromone | Y | M | NA | NA | Adult | NA | Infection/parasite | Worden, Parker, and Pappas (2000) |
| | | L | Pheromone | Y | M | NA | NA | Adult | NA | Infection/parasite | Worden and Parker (2005) |
| | | L | Pheromone | Y | B | Female pheromone | C<T | Adult | NA | Inbreeding | Pölkki et al. (2012) |

*Continued*

TABLE 4.2 Condition-Dependent Size or Pattern-Based Traits in Arthropods—cont'd

| Species | Scientific Name | ST | Trait | CD | S | Contrast | | Life History | CT | Manipulation | References |
|---|---|---|---|---|---|---|---|---|---|---|---|
| | | | | | | Trait | Effect | | | | |
| African butterfly | Bicyclus anynana | L | Pheromone | Y | M | Flight performance | C<T | Inbreeding | NA | Inbreeding | van Bergen, Brakefield, Heuskin, Zwaan, and Nieberding (2013) |

Note: ST, study type [L, lab experiment; F, field experiment; N, natural variation; *, included in Cotton et al. (2004a) review]; CD, condition dependent (Y, yes; N, no); S, sex of animals included in the study (M, male; F, female; B, both sexes); SS, sexually selected; CHC, cuticular hydrocarbon; Morph, morphological; CT, color type (C, carotenoid; M, melanin; S, structural; NA, not applicable); LS, lifespan; body condition/LS, manipulation involved assessment of body condition or LS; RS, reproductive success; Quant, quantity of melanin; SS, sexually selected.

a Wing spot size related to body length that in turn predicted fighting ability and copulation frequency.
b Red pigmented area was associated with a weaker immune response and negatively correlated with melanin area.
c The study included only territorial males that are typically in better condition than nonterritorial males, resulting in low power.
d Males with more structural color area did not have a stronger immune response, but were better at avoiding predators.
e Diet manipulation continued into adulthood and there was some indication of a gene by environment interaction.
f Nutritional quantity was manipulated through changes in social density at larval stage. The manipulation affected only sexually unsuccessful males.
g Field-caught to capture natural genetic variation in stalk, thorax, and body condition. Eye stalk was not condition dependent in three related species for which eye stalk length is not a sexually selected trait; specifically, Teleopsis quadriguttata; Sphyracephala beccarri; Cyrtodiopsis quinqueguttata.
h The dietary manipulation affected both sexes, with no sex by diet interaction. Savalli and Fox (1999) indicate that male size influences female choice and female size influences fecundity, and thus there is selection for large body sizes in both sexes.

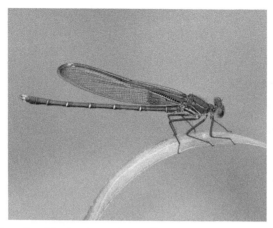

**PHOTO 4.4**   For males of the American rubyspot (*Hetaerina americana*), the size of the red wing spot signals social dominance to other males and to females, and is an indicator of the males' current resistance to parasites and quality of their developmental diet. (See the color plate section.)

assessments revealed that the size of the melanin-based trait is sensitive. The one null result only included territorial males that are typically in better condition than nonterritorial males, and as a consequence of not including the latter provided a less sensitive test of condition dependence than did the other studies (González-Tokman & Córdoba-Aguilar, 2010). Evidence for the condition dependence of the size of the melanin-based wing area is also found for the copper damselfly (*Calopteryx haemorrhoidalis*; Córdoba-Aguilar, 2002).

There are also several studies of a socially selected melanin-based trait in females; specifically, the pattern of melanin stripes (black patch within the yellow) on the face of paper wasps (Photo 4.5, inset; e.g., *Polistes dominulus*;

**PHOTO 4.5**   The pattern of the melanin patch (within the yellow) on the face of the female paper wasp (*Polistes dominulus*) is an indicator of social dominance and is influenced by quality of the developmental diet. *Photo by Zurab Tabatadze (© MzePhotos.com), used with permission.* (See the color plate section.)

Tibbetts, 2010). Females of these species cooperate in nest construction but compete fiercely for social dominance that in turn influences relative reproductive opportunities, work at nest construction, and access to food (Tibbetts & Izzo, 2010; Tibbetts & Sheehan, 2011). The facial pattern reflects fighting ability, and two laboratory experiments demonstrated that the facial stripes are influenced by diet quality in adulthood (Tibbetts & Banan, 2010) and during development (Tibbetts, 2010).

Most of the remaining assessments of physical traits do not involve color and range from cuticular hydrocarbons (CHCs; Gosden & Chenoweth, 2011) to eye span length (Knell, Fruhauf, & Norris, 1999); nine of these assessments were reported in Cotton et al. (2004a). The majority of assessments (~90%) are consistent with condition dependence and the majority of these include strong contrast traits. An example is provided by CHC; these are chains of hydrocarbons found on the outer surface of terrestrial arthropods (Howard & Blomquist, 2005). These help to prevent desiccation (drying out) and serve multiple social functions, including pheromonal (e.g., through contact) recognition of species, nest mates, and castes for eusocial (colony living) insects. In many species, a subset of CHC is sex-specific and signals social dominance and physical condition. Gosden and Chenoweth (2011) provided an example for the Australian fruit fly (*D. simulans*). Here, half-sibling adult males were randomly assigned to high-quality (with live yeast) or low-quality (no yeast) diets and CHC production was assessed. CHCs that are known to influence female choice were more strongly affected by the diet manipulation than CHCs that are unrelated to female choice. Delcourt and Rundle (2011) replicated this finding with a manipulation of diet quality during development, and other adult and developmental manipulations have found the same pattern for several other species of fruit fly (Table 4.2).

Stalk-eyed flies (*Diopsidae*) are another commonly studied group of insects that allows for strong tests of condition dependence (Photo 4.6, inset). In some but not all species, the length of males' eye span influences female choice and male-male dominance contests (Panhuis & Wilkinson, 1999; Wilkinson, Kahler, & Baker, 1998). Wilkinson and Taper (1999) provided an important and especially robust demonstration of the sensitivity of eye span as a signal of male resilience to stressors, but critically only in species where eye span is sexually selected. They studied natural variation in male eye span across three species in which this trait is sexually selected (*C. whitei*: *C. dalmanni*; *Diasemopsis dubia*) and three related species in which it is not (*Teleopsis quadriguttata*; *Sphyracephala beccarri*; *C. quinqueguttata*). Field-collected animals were reared in the lab and half-sibling comparisons enabled estimation of genetic variance in eye span length, as well as the relation between this length and body condition. Eye span length predicted condition more strongly for males than females in the three species in which this trait influences female choice and male-male competition, but did not differentially predict condition of males and females in the three other species. Moreover, there was significantly more genetic variance in eye span length for males of the three former species compared to the three latter

**PHOTO 4.6**  The length of males' eye span in most species of stalk-eyed fly (*Diopsidae*) varies with their physical condition, quality of their developmental diet, and inbreeding. *Photo credit: Hauke Koch, 2006. Creative Commons license: http://commons.wikimedia.org/wiki/File:Diopsid2.jpg.* (See the color plate section.)

species, consistent with the prediction of more genetic variance in sexually than naturally selected traits (Pomiankowski & Møller, 1995; Rowe & Houle, 1996). Studies of related species show that eye span length in adulthood is particularly sensitive to inbreeding (e.g., Bellamy, Chapman, Fowler, & Pomiankowski, 2013) and developmental diet (e.g., Cotton, Fowler, & Pomiankowski, 2004b).

The assessments of color properties and size of color-based traits largely involved natural variation or experimental manipulation of adults. The life history assessment of other sexually selected physical traits is more varied and included inbreeding ($n = 5$), postnatal manipulations ($n = 30$), and adult manipulations ($n = 14$). As noted, the postnatal manipulations of insects provide a more thorough assessment of how early developmental conditions affect the later expression of sexually selected traits than do studies of the other types of animals. This is due in part to the rapid growth of insects and thus the ease of studying the relation between early conditions and later functioning in adulthood. Poor early diet has been shown to influence the adult expression of sexually selected traits in the decorated cricket (*Gryllodes sigillatus*; Weddle, Mitchell, Bay, Sakaluk, & Hunt, 2012) and water strider (*Gerris incognitus*; Arnqvist & Thornhill, 1998), as well as in multiple species of fruit fly (e.g., *D. simulans*; Ingleby et al., 2013), stalk-eyed fly (e.g., *Diasemopsis meigenii*; Bellamy et al., 2013), and beetle (e.g., *Onthophagus acuminatus*; Emlen, 1997).

Five of the six failures to find a relation between early diet and later condition shown in Table 4.2 were from Bonduriansky and Rowe's (2005) study of the waltzing fly (*Prochyliza xanthostoma*). Bonduriansky and Rowe provided larvae with high- and low-quality diets and compared full-sibling males and females on four traits involved in competition and mate choice and four other traits when they reached adulthood. Unsurprisingly, both sexes were larger when fed the high-quality diet, and in terms of absolute size, two of the four sexually selected traits were more strongly affected by diet in males than in females; however, three of the four nonsexually selected traits were also affected more in males than in females. Control of body size provides the most conservative and robust assessment of condition dependence and these results are reported in Table 4.2. Here, only head length, which influences female choice (Bonduriansky & Rowe, 2003), showed evidence of condition dependence; diet affected this trait in males, but not females. The implication is that the quality of early diet may substantially affect the later expression of some sexually selected traits but have little or no effect on the expression of others.

*Takeaway message.* The quality of melanin-based colors and the size of associated traits tell us more about the resiliency of arthropods than do these same traits in birds and fish, but at the same time carotenoid-based color traits are less important for arthropods than they are for birds and fish. These are not arbitrary differences but rather follow from the importance of carotenoid molecules for vertebrate immune functions and melanin for arthropod immune functions. In other words, these differences illustrate that traits directly linked to health are more likely to evolve as condition-dependent signals than are other, seemingly similar traits. As we learned for birds, the color quality of the arthropods' traits is a good indicator of current condition, although a few studies suggest difficulties during development can compromise the expression of structural colors in adulthood. Exposure to developmental stressors appears to compromise the size of these traits more than the color *per se*, although size can also be compromised by stressors in adulthood (e.g., reduction in size of melanin traits as melanin is used to mount an immune response).

## Behavioral Traits

The takeaway message here is that the expression of behavioral traits related to competition and choice are often compromised by exposure to stressors in adulthood and can be compromised by inbreeding and exposure to developmental stressors. As with birds and fish, these traits are largely courtship or dominance displays (Table 4.3). Included among these are call rate, call frequency, or call parameters, similar to the components of birdsong described in the last chapter. Many of the studies did not find these traits to be condition dependent, but considering only the studies with strong contrast traits, such as call components that are not sexually selected, there is consistent evidence for the condition dependence. The expression of courtship or dominance calls can be compromised by inbreeding and by poor diet during development and in adulthood, as illustrated by studies of two species of cricket (*Gryllus lineaticeps*; *G. campestris*: Holzer, Jacot, & Brinkhof, 2003; Scheuber, Jacot, & Brinkhof, 2003a, 2003b; Wagner & Hoback, 1999) and one species of fruit fly (*D. montana*; Aspi, 2000).

**TABLE 4.3** Condition-Dependent Behavioral Traits in Arthropods

| Species | Scientific Name | ST | Trait | CD | S | Contrast Trait | Contrast Effect | Life History | Manipulation | References |
|---|---|---|---|---|---|---|---|---|---|---|
| Black field cricket | Teleogryllus commodus | L | Call rate | N | M | Body size | C=T | Inbreeding | Inbreeding | Drayton, Hunt, Brooks, and Jennions (2007) |
| | | L | Call parameters | Y | M | Body size | C<T | Inbreeding | Inbreeding | Drayton et al. (2007) |
| | | L | Call rate | Y | M | NA | NA | Inbreeding | Inbreeding | Drayton, Milner, Hunt, and Jennions (2010) |
| | | L | Call parameters | N | M | NA | NA | Inbreeding | Inbreeding | Drayton et al. (2010) |
| | | L | Call rate | N[a] | M | NA | NA | Adult | Infection/parasite | Drayton, Hall, Hunt, and Jennions (2012) |
| | | L | Call parameters | N[a] | M | NA | NA | Adult | Infection/parasite | Drayton et al. (2012) |
| | | N | Call parameters | Y | M | NA | NA | Adult | Infection/parasite | Simmons, Zuk, and Rotenberry (2005) |
| Field cricket | Gryllus lineaticeps | L | Call rate | N[b] | M | NA | NA | Postnatal | Diet/nutrition | Tolle and Wagner (2011) |

Continued

**TABLE 4.3** Condition-Dependent Behavioral Traits in Arthropods—cont'd

| Species | Scientific Name | ST | Trait | CD | S | Contrast Trait | Contrast Effect | Life History | Manipulation | References |
|---|---|---|---|---|---|---|---|---|---|---|
| | | L* | Call rate | Y | M | Call components | C<T | Adult | Diet/nutrition | Wagner and Hoback (1999) |
| | | L* | Call rate | N | M | NA | NA | Adult | Diet/nutrition | Wagner and Reiser (2000) |
| | G. campestris | F* | Call rate | Y | M | Call components | C<T | Adult | Diet/nutrition | Holzer et al. (2003) |
| | | L* | Call rate | Y | M | Call components | C<T | Adult | Diet/nutrition | Scheuber et al. (2003a) |
| | | L* | Call sound frequency | Y | M | Call components | C<T | Postnatal | Diet/nutrition | Scheuber et al. (2003b) |
| | G. texensis | L* | Courtship chirp rate | N | M | NA | NA | Adult | Diet/nutrition | Gray and Eckhardt (2001) |
| | | L* | Courtship chirp rate | N | M | NA | NA | Postnatal | Diet/nutrition | Gray and Eckhardt (2001) |
| | G. pennsylvanicus | N | Call parameters | Y | M | NA | NA | Adult | Body condition | Harrison, Thomson, Grant, and Bertram (2013) |
| | | N | Call rate | N^c | M | NA | NA | Adult | Body condition | Harrison et al. (2013) |

| | | | | | | | | | | |
|---|---|---|---|---|---|---|---|---|---|---|
| House cricket | *Acheta domesticus* | L | Call parameters | Y | M | Body size | C<T | Adult | Infection/parasite | Ryder (2000) |
| Fruit fly | *Drosophila montana* | L | Song frequency | Y | M | Other song features | C<T | Inbreeding | Inbreeding | Aspi (2000) |
| | *D. grimshawi* | L* | Courtship display | Y | M | Physical condition | C=T | Adult | Diet/nutrition | Droney (1996) |
| Dung beetle | *Onthophagus taurus* | L* | Courtship rate | Y | M | Body size | C=T | Adult | Diet/nutrition | Kotiaho, Simmons, and Tomkins (2001) |
| | | L* | Courtship rate | Y | M | Body size | C=T | Adult | Diet/nutrition | Kotiaho (2002) |
| | *O. binodis* | L* | Courtship rate | Y | M | Body size | C=T | Adult | Diet/nutrition | Kotiaho (2002) |
| | *O. australis* | L* | Courtship rate | Y | M | Body size | C=T | Adult | Diet/nutrition | Kotiaho (2002) |
| African butterfly | *Bicyclus anynana* | L | Mating success | Yᵈ | M | NA | NA | Inbreeding | Inbreeding | Joron and Brakefield (2003) |
| | | L | Courtship display | Yᵈ | M | NA | NA | Inbreeding | Inbreeding | Joron and Brakefield (2003) |
| Wolf spider | *Hygrolycosa rubrofasciata* | L* | Signal rate | Y | M | Body weight | C=T | Adult | Diet/nutrition | Mappes et al. (1996) |
| | | L* | Signal rate with female | Y | M | Signal rate no female | C<T | Adult | Diet/nutrition | Mappes et al. (1996) |

*Continued*

**TABLE 4.3** Condition-Dependent Behavioral Traits in Arthropods—cont'd

| Species | Scientific Name | ST | Trait | CD | S | Contrast | | Life History | Manipulation | References |
|---|---|---|---|---|---|---|---|---|---|---|
| | | | | | | Trait | Effect | | | |
| | | N | Signal rate with female | Y | M | Body weight | C<T | Adult | Body condition | Kotiaho et al. (1996) |
| | | N | Signal rate | Y[e] | M | Body weight | C<T | Adult | Infection/parasite | Ahtiainen, Alatalo, Kortet, and Rantala (2004) |
| Damselfly | *Calopteryx virgo* | F | Social dominance | Y | M | Body weight | C<T | Adult | Infection/parasite | Koskimäki, Rantala, Taskinen, Tynkkynen, and Suhonen (2004) |

*Note:* ST, study type [L, lab experiment; F, field experiment; N, natural variation; *, included in Cotton et al. (2004a) review]; CD, condition dependent (Y, yes; N, no); S, sex of animals included in the study (M, male).

[a]*In both studies, natural variation in capsulation response was assessed, not parasite load per se.*

[b]*There was a family by nutrition interaction whereby call rate increased with high nut diet in some families but decreased in others.*

[c]*The largest and smallest males had the highest call rate, suggesting a terminal reproductive effort for the latter.*

[d]*Assessed in laboratory condition and in a seminatural setting.*

[e]*Signal rate was related to the encapsulation component of the immune response but not a second component; the latter was related to mobility, which is important for males' search for females.*

The remaining assessments involved some type of courtship display, behavioral male-male competition, or actual mating. As with studies of birds and fish, all of these assessments suggested these displays are reliable indicators of current condition, but only three of these included rigorous contrast traits. Two of them involved the study of courtship displays in male wolf spiders (*Hygrolycosa rubrofasciata*; Kotiaho, Alatalo, Mappes, & Parri, 1996; Mappes, Alatalo, Kotiaho, & Parri, 1996). Males of this species drum dry leaves with their abdomen and females prefer males with high drum rates. Kotiaho et al. found that males with high drum rates were not only chosen by females more frequently than their peers, but also survived longer. In one manipulation, Mappes et al. induced high drumming rates in males by having a female continually present. These males did indeed drum more than males that were not in the presence of a female, but also suffered higher mortality. Despite higher overall mortality, males that had the highest drum rates in the female-present condition suffered lower mortality than their slower peers. Drumming is clearly a costly signal in this species, and one that can only be maintained by the most-fit males.

## MAMMALS

As with arthropods, I keep the review of condition-dependent traits in mammals brief, but as noted, begin to more explicitly set the foundation for the upcoming reviews of human vulnerability. At the same time, I ask the reader to also reflect on the previous reviews; that is, to consider how the same basic principle – traits exaggerated through sexual or social selection are vulnerable to disruption by a variety of stressors – that links the effects of stressors in nonhuman mammals to the effects of stressors in humans also links all of these species to vulnerabilities in birds, fish, and arthropods.

### Physical Traits

The takeaway message of this section is that skin and fur color are often reliable signals of males' social dominance and may be indicators of female reproductive status. The extent to which these colors fluctuate with exposure to stressors (e.g., poor nutrition) and their relation to female-female social competition is not yet well understood. Horns and antlers are used in male-male competition over access to females, and possibly female-female competition over access to food. These are generally good indictors of social dominance, above and beyond the influence of body size, and their growth is disrupted by exposure to parasites and poor nutrition.

### *Color*

With the exception of primates and marsupials, most mammals have poor color vision and thus it is not surprising that we do not find as many colorful displays as those found in birds and fish (Caro, 2013; Prum & Torres, 2004; Sumner & Mollon, 2003; Surridge, Osorio, & Mundy, 2003). There are a few important exceptions that include structural blue coloration of the skin of a few primates and marsupials (Prum & Torres, 2004); the color is due to the organization of collagen in the skin and often an underlying layer of melanin. The blue facial color of the mature male mandrill (*M. sphinx*) shown in Photo 4.7 (inset) provides an example. The color of mammalian fur is due to the relative distribution of two different forms of melanin and can produce reddish-brown, orange, white, gray, and black colors (Sumner & Mollon, 2003), although color expression is also influenced by sex hormones (Clough, Heistermann, & Kappeler, 2009). Carotenoids are not found in mammalian fur but can accumulate in the skin, although they do not produce the bright yellow to red coloration found in birds, fish, and arthropods. Nevertheless, carotenoids contribute to skin health and influence people's rated attractiveness of skin (Stephen, Coetzee, & Perrett, 2011), as we will cover in Chapter 6 for humans. Although not carotenoid dependent, many primates have bright red skin patches that can signal social dominance in males or fertility status in females. The physiological processes that create these colors are not as well understood as those that create similar color in birds, but they are related to circulating levels of sex hormones that in turn appear to increase oxygenated blood flow to these skin patches (Bradley & Mundy, 2008).

Multiple examples of color traits in mammals are shown in Table 4.4. The most thoroughly studied of these traits is the blue and red coloration of the face of the male mandrill (their hind quarters are similarly colored). The male mandrill's red facial color is a reliable signal of social dominance or prior social dominance above and beyond the influence of body size (e.g., Setchell & Dixson, 2001a; Wickings & Dixson, 1992). The blue facial coloration has not emerged as an indicator of dominance in the semifree-ranging groups studied by Setchell, Dixson,

**PHOTO 4.7**   Mature and socially dominant male mandrills (*Mandrillus sphinx*) sport blue (structural color) and red (likely related to oxygenated blood) facial signals. The red coloration is related to testosterone levels and social dominance; the blue may also correlate with dominance in some groups. (See the color plate section.)

**TABLE 4.4** Condition-Dependent Color Traits in Mammals

| Species | Scientific Name | ST | Trait | CD | S | Contrast Trait | Contrast Effect | Life History | CT | Manipulation | References |
|---|---|---|---|---|---|---|---|---|---|---|---|
| Brown lemur | Eulemur fulvus | N | Facial hair color | N[a] | M | NA | NA | Adult | M | Social dominance | Clough et al. (2009) |
| | | N | Facial hair color | N[b] | M | NA | NA | Adult | M | Reproductive success | Clough et al. (2009) |
| Lion | Panthera leo | N | Mane color | Y | M | NA | NA | Adult | M | Social dominance | West and Packer (2002) |
| Gelada baboon | Theropithecus gelada | N | Chest patch color | Y[c] | M | NA | NA | Adult | OH | Social dominance | Bergman et al. (2009) |
| Vervet | Cercopithecus aethiops | N | Scrotal color | Y | M | NA | NA | Adult | S | Social dominance | Isbell (1995) |
| | | N | Scrotal color | Y | M | NA | NA | Adult | S | Social dominance | Henzi (1985) |
| | | N | Scrotal color | Y | M | Body size | C<T | Adult | S | Social dominance | Gerald (2001) |
| Macaque | Macaca mulatta | N | Facial color | Y | M | NA | NA | Adult | OH | Reproductive success | Dubuc et al. (2014) |

Continued

**TABLE 4.4** Condition-Dependent Color Traits in Mammals—cont'd

| Species | Scientific Name | ST | Trait | CD | S | Contrast Trait | Contrast Effect | Life History | CT | Manipulation | References |
|---|---|---|---|---|---|---|---|---|---|---|---|
| Mandrill | *Mandrillus sphinx* | N | Facial color | Y | F | NA | NA | Adult | OH | Reproductive success | Dubuc et al. (2014) |
| | | N | Facial color | N[d] | F | Body size | C=T | Adult | S/OH | Social dominance | Setchell et al. (2006) |
| | | N | Facial color | N | F | Body size | C=T | Adult | S/OH | Body condition | Setchell et al. (2006) |
| | | N | Facial color | Y[e] | F | Body size | C<T | Adult | S/OH | Reproductive condition | Setchell et al. (2006) |
| | | N | Facial color | N | F | NA | NA | Adult | S/OH | Infection/parasite | Setchell et al. (2009) |
| | | N | Facial color | Y | M | Body size | C<T | Adult | S/OH | Social dominance | Wickings and Dixson (1992) |
| | | N | Facial color | Y | M | NA | NA | Adult | S/OH | Social dominance | Setchell and Wickings (2005) |
| | | N | Facial color | Y | M | Body size | C<T | Adult | S/OH | Social dominance | Setchell and Dixson (2001a) |
| | | N | Facial color | Y[f] | M | Body size | C<T | Adult | S/OH | Social dominance | Setchell and Dixson (2001b) |

| Species | | | | | | | | | | Reference |
|---|---|---|---|---|---|---|---|---|---|---|
| | N | Facial color | Y | M | NA | NA | Adult | S/OH | Social dominance | Setchell, Smith, Wickings, and Knapp (2008) |
| | N | Facial color | N[g] | M | NA | NA | Adult | S/OH | Infection/parasite | Setchell et al. (2009) |
| | N | Facial color | N | M | NA | NA | Adult | S/OH | Cortisol | Setchell, Smith, Wickings, and Knapp (2010) |
| Drill *M. leucophaeus* | N | Groin color | Y[h] | M | Body size | C<T | Adult | S/OH | Social dominance | Marty et al. (2009) |

Note: ST, study type (L, lab experiment; F, field experiment; N, natural variation); CD, condition dependent (Y, yes; N, no); S, sex of animals included in the study (M, male; F, female). CT, color type (M, melanin; S, structural; OH, oxygenated hemoglobin).

[a] Facial hair color was not related to social dominance but was related to testosterone levels.

[b] Facial hair color was not related to reproductive success but was related to testosterone levels.

[c] The mechanisms underlying these red patches are not well understood but may involve changes in oxygenated hemoglobin, perhaps with contributions from distribution of underlying melanin (Bradley & Mundy, 2008).

[d] Facial color is composed of blue structural color and red color that is related to testosterone levels and likely related to oxygenated hemoglobin levels.

[e] Females with brighter red faces had more offspring and face color varies over ovulatory cycle, but it was not correlated with other reproductive variables (e.g., age of first birth), although it may be related to male choice.

[f] Movement to alpha status increases testosterone levels, testes size, and red (not blue) facial and genital color; loss of alpha status results in less dramatic changes in red facial color.

[g] Males' red facial color was unrelated to parasite load, but was related to diversity of several major histocompatibility genes (immune system genes).

[h] For male drills, groin and lip color (the latter is red) are correlated and thus the latter also signals dominance but was not directly assessed in this study.

and their colleagues, but Prum and Torres (2004) suggest that it may still convey such information in some groups. In any case, because the red signal is dependent on sex hormone levels and blood flow, it will be a much more dynamic signal than the blue structural color.

The associated studies of mandrills, however, have found no relation between facial color and stress hormone levels and parasite load in either sex, but these results are difficult to interpret because the group is provisioned, which will lessen the health impact of stress and illness (Setchell, Charpentier, Abbott, Wickings, & Knapp, 2009). Indeed, males with bright red facial colors had more variable immune systems than their duller peers, suggesting color may signal immunocompetence in more natural conditions. It is not just about males, as the faces of female mandrills can also be colorful, albeit not as conspicuous as that of males. There is some evidence that the red facial color of female mandrills is an honest signal of their current reproductive condition (Setchell, Wickings, & Knapp, 2006), but it is not known if this is a dominance signal to other females.

There are also multiple studies showing that the structural (Photo 4.8, inset) blue scrotal color of male vervet monkeys (*Cercopithecus aethiops*) is a signal of social dominance, although only one of these studies controlled for body size

**PHOTO 4.8**    The blue scrotal color of the male vervet (*Cercopithecus aethiop*) signals social dominance. *Photo credit: Stig Nygaard, 2007. Creative Commons license: http://commons.wikimedia.org/ wiki/File:Black_faced_vervet_monkey.* (See the color plate section.)

**PHOTO 4.9** The red chest patch of the male gelada baboon (*Theropithecus gelada*) is a signal of social dominance. (See the color plate section.)

(Gerald, 2001). Other examples of condition-dependent color signals include the blue and red groin coloration of the male drill (*Mandrillus leucophaeus*; Marty, Higham, Gadsby, & Ross, 2009), the red chest patch of the male gelada baboon (*Theropithecus gelada*; Bergman, Ho, & Beehner, 2009) shown in Photo 4.9 (inset), as well as the lion's mane (*Panthera leo*; West & Packer, 2002). One possible exception to this pattern – that mammalian skin and fur colors signal social dominance and overall physical condition – is the red facial hair of male brown lemurs (*Eulemur fulvus*). Clough et al. (2009) found no relation between the color of this hair, which appears to influence female choice of mates, and male social dominance or reproductive success. Still, redder hair was associated with higher testosterone levels suggesting hair color may predict dominance striving in some contexts. The only other study of females is that of Dubuc et al. (2014), who found that red facial color of female rhesus macaques (*Macaca mulatta*) predicted their reproductive success; specifically, the frequency with which they birthed offspring.

## Size

As with birds, fish, and arthropods, there are many examples of mammalian traits that have increased in size, over evolutionary time, as a result of competition or mate choice. As I illustrated in Chapter 2 using the northern elephant seal (*Mirounga angustirostris*), physical male-male competition typically results in larger males than females (Andersson, 1994). Such competition can also result in the enlargement and elaboration of traits other than body size. Good examples of these are the antlers of the male red deer (*C. elaphus*) in Photo 4.10 (inset) and the horns of the male alpine ibex (*Capra ibex*) in Photo 4.11 (inset). Table 4.5 lists studies of the condition dependence of these traits and many others like them. Most of these studies provide evidence that antlers, horns, and the lions' mane (West & Packer, 2002) do indeed signal social dominance (Bartoš & Losos, 1997), disease resistance (Ditchkoff, Lochmiller, Masters, Hoofer, & Bussche, 2001), and genetic diversity (von Hardenberg et al., 2007).

However, only about half of the studies included contrast traits. The best evidence comes from studies that control for body size, as horns and antlers are often used in physical male-male combat in which body size is important. There is evidence that antlers do indeed signal some aspect of condition, above and beyond the importance of body size, for fallow deer (*Dama dama*; Bartoš & Losos, 1997) and red deer (Kruuk et al., 2002), as do horns for bighorn sheep (*Ovis canadensis*; Coltman et al., 2002), soay sheep (*O. aries*; Preston, Stevenson, Pemberton, & Wilson, 2001), and the alpine ibex (von Hardenberg et al., 2007). Ezenwa and Jolles (2008) found the same pattern for the African

**PHOTO 4.10**    Antler size of the male red deer (*Cervus elaphus*) is an indicator of social dominance and sperm quality. (See the color plate section.)

**PHOTO 4.11**   Horn size of the male alpine ibex (*Capra ibex*) is an indicator of genetic diversity and nutritional condition during development. (See the color plate section.)

buffalo (*Syncerus caffer*), but this held for both males and females. Males use horns in combat with other males over mates, and females will sometimes attack one another using their horns, but it is not known whether this is related to competition over food; that is, social selection.

## Behavioral Traits

I have broken the behavioral studies into scent (pheromones) and behavior. Pheromone communication is widespread in animals (Wyatt, 2009), is well-studied in mammals, and potentially has implications for the assessment of human vulnerability, as discussed in Chapter 6. For the latter reasons, I cover the utility of using scent itself as a measure of condition in the first section below, and include scent marking in the second section with other behavior indicators of condition.

The takeaway message of these sections is that scents conveyed through pheromones and scent-marking behaviors themselves are common dominance signals for males and females of many species of mammal. These scents convey information about illness, genetic variation, and general physical condition, as would be expected for condition-dependent traits. Other mammalian behavioral traits that signal dominance and that can be disrupted by exposure to stressors (e.g., toxins, social competition) include play fighting during development, exploratory behaviors, various types of vocal calls (e.g., roars), as well as courtship or dominance displays.

### Scent

Pheromones are a common form of communication among mammals, with the associated information conveyed through urine, feces, or scent glands (Ralls, 1971). These scents influence social behavior and relationships across a wide range of species, and are important for signaling reproductive status and social

**TABLE 4.5 Condition-Dependent Size Traits in Mammals**

| Species | Scientific Name | ST | Trait | CD | S | Contrast | | Life History | Manipulation | References |
|---|---|---|---|---|---|---|---|---|---|---|
| | | | | | | Trait | Effect | | | |
| Fallow deer | *Dama dama* | N | Antler size | Y | M | NA | NA | Adult | Social dominance | Ciuti and Apollonio (2011) |
| | | N | Antler size | Y | M | Body size | C<T | Adult | Social dominance | Bartoš and Losos (1997) |
| Reindeer | *Rangifer tarandus* | F | Antler size | Y | M | NA | NA | Adult | Social dominance | Espmark (1964) |
| Roe deer | *Capreolus capreolus* | N | Antler size | Y[a] | M | Body size | C>T | Adult | Reproductive success | Vanpé et al. (2010) |
| | | N | Antler size | Y[b] | M | NA | NA | Adult | Body condition | Vanpé et al. (2007) |
| Red deer | *Cervus elaphus* | N | Antler size | Y[c] | M | NA | NA | Adult | Social dominance | Bartoš and Bahbouh (2006) |
| | | N | Antler size | Y | M | Body size | C<T | Adult | Reproductive success | Kruuk et al. (2002) |
| | | N | Antler size | Y | M | NA | NA | Adult | Ecological quality | Kruuk et al. (2002) |
| | | N | Antler size | Y | M | Fat reserve | C<T | Adult | Sperm motility | Malo, Roldan, Garde, Soler, and Gomendio (2005) |

| Common name | Species | | Trait | | | | | | Condition | Reference |
|---|---|---|---|---|---|---|---|---|---|---|
| White-tailed deer | Odocoileus virginianus | N | Antler size | Y[d] | M | NA | NA | Adult | Diet/nutrition | Foley et al. (2012) |
| | | N | Antler size | Y | M | Body size | C=T | Prenatal | Maternal nutrition | Monteith, Schmitz, Jenks, Delger, and Bowyer (2009) |
| | | N | Antler size | Y | M | NA | NA | Adult | Parasite/infection | Ditchkoff et al. (2001) |
| | | N | Antler size | Y | M | NA | NA | Adult | MHC | Ditchkoff et al. (2001) |
| | | N | Antler size | Y | M | Genetic diversity | C<T | Adult | Body condition | Scribner, Smith, and Johns (1989) |
| | | N | Antler size | Y | M | NA | NA | Adult | Genetic diversity | Scribner et al. (1989) |
| Bighorn sheep | Ovis canadensis | N | Horn size | Y | M | Body weight | C<T | Adult | Reproductive success | Coltman et al. (2002) |
| | | N | Horn size | Y[e] | M | Body weight | C=T | Postnatal | Body condition | Festa-Bianchet, Jorgenson, and Réale (2000) |
| Soay sheep | O. aries | N | Horn size | Y | M | Body size | C<T | Adult | Reproductive success | Preston et al. (2001) |
| Alpine ibex | Capra ibex | N | Horn size | Y | B | Female horn | C<T | Postnatal | Diet/nutrition | Toïgo, Gaillard, and Michallet (1999) |

*Continued*

**TABLE 4.5** Condition-Dependent Size Traits in Mammals—cont'd

| Species | Scientific Name | ST | Trait | CD | S | Contrast | | Life History | Manipulation | References |
|---|---|---|---|---|---|---|---|---|---|---|
| | | | | | | Trait | Effect | History | | |
| | | N | Horn size | N | M | NA | NA | Postnatal | Longevity | Bergeron, Festa-Bianchet, Von Hardenberg, and Bassano (2008) |
| African buffalo | | N | Horn size | Y | M | Body size | C<T | Inbreeding | Inbreeding | von Hardenberg et al. (2007) |
| African buffalo | Syncerus caffer | N | Horn size | Y | B | Female horn | C=T | Adult | Parasite/infection | Ezenwa and Jolles (2008) |
| Mandrill | Mandrillus sphinx | N | Body size | N$^f$ | B | Female body size | C>T | Inbreeding | Inbreeding | Charpentier et al. (2006) |
| Lion | Panthera leo | N | Mane length | Y | M | NA | NA | Adult | Social dominance | West and Packer (2002) |

*Note:* ST, study type (L, lab experiment; F, field experiment; N, natural variation); CD, condition dependent (Y, yes; N, no); S, sex of animals included in the study (M, male; B, both sexes); MHC, major histocompatibility complex (immune system genes) variation.

*a In this study antler size was correlated with yearly reproductive success, but was not significant when body size was controlled. Overall body size was more strongly related to reproductive success than antler size.*

*b Larger males had larger antlers, and prime-age males had larger antlers than predicted based on body size alone; this was also true for some older males.*

*c The effect here was particularly large. A one standard deviation increase in antler size resulted in a 7.85-fold increase in the odds of becoming a harem holder.*

*d This was a quasi-experimental study, with some groups supplemented and others not supplemented. There was more variation in antler size with poorer nutritional conditions (e.g., not supplemented groups during a year with low abundance of natural foods).*

*e Weight at 3 weeks (still suckling) and weaning weight predicted horn size in adulthood.*

*f Inbreeding was associated with smaller females but had no effect on male body size. The absence of an effect might be because this is a provisioned colony.*

dominance (Thiessen & Rice, 1976). A common approach to the study of pheromones is to expose a female to the scent of a dominant and subordinate male (or a male infected with a parasite vs. one that is not infected) but not the males themselves, and her preference is determined by the amount of time she spends near the scent of one male versus the other (e.g., Drickamer, 1992).

The influence of scent on the social behavior of conspecifics has been studied for decades, and Table 4.6 provides a review of some of this research, as it relates to the condition of the individual providing the scent (or in some cases, inferred influence of scent based on the behavior of potential mates or would-be competitors; Mills et al., 2010). As noted, studies that assessed the frequency of scent-marking behavior rather than the influence of scent *per se* are shown in Table 4.7; scent or territorial marking is a common dominance behavior and often increases in contexts in which status is challenged and there is high potential for escalation to physical aggression (Ralls, 1971), although these of course are not the only social functions of scent (Lazaro-Perea, Snowdon, & de Fátima Arruda, 1999).

Given the long history of research in the area and the important status-related information provided by pheromones, it is not too surprising that many studies confirm that scent conveys information on social dominance in species as varied as the bank vole (*Myodes glareolus*; Kruczek, 1997) and African elephant (*Loxodonta africana*; Hollister-Smith, Alberts, & Rasmussen, 2008). Although not as thoroughly studied, pheromones have been found to convey information on parasite resistance in the mouse (Kavaliers & Colwell, 1995a) and genetic variation that will influence immunocompetence in the ring-tailed lemur (*Lemur catta*; Charpentier, Boulet, & Drea, 2008). Scent marking and thus use of pheromone cues is generally more common in male than female mammals, but it is common among female mammals that form dominance hierarchies and compete for reproductively valuable resources such as nesting sites or reproductive opportunity in communal breeders (see Thiessen & Rice, 1976).

The common marmoset (*Callithrix jacchus*) shown in Photo 4.12 (inset) is an example of the latter (Abbott, 1993; Epple, 1970). Barrett, Abbott, and George (1990) found that exposure to the scent of dominant females resulted in the reproductive suppression of subordinates, although this can also be achieved through visual cues (Barrett, Abbott, & George, 1993). In addition to the marmoset, pheromones or scent-marking behavior also convey social dominance among females in the Australian rabbit (*Oryctolagus cuniculus*; Mykytowycz, 1965) and golden hamster (*Mesocricetus auratus*; Drickamer & Vandenbergh, 1973; Johnston, 1977), among others (Erlinge, Sandell, & Brinck, 1982; Heistermann, Kleis, Pröve, & Wolters, 1989).

## Behavior

As with birds, fish, and arthropods, condition-dependent behavioral traits in mammals often involve courtship or dominance displays, and the just-described scent marking is one such example. As shown in Table 4.7, scent marking is

**TABLE 4.6** Condition-Dependent Scent Traits in Mammals

| Species | Scientific Name | ST | Trait | CD | S | Contrast Trait | Contrast Effect | Life History | Manipulation | References |
|---|---|---|---|---|---|---|---|---|---|---|
| Mouse | *Mus musculus* | L | Scent | Y | M | NA | NA | Adult | Infection/parasite | Kavaliers and Colwell (1995a) |
| | | L | Scent | Y | M | NA | NA | Adult | Infection/parasite | Kavaliers and Colwell (1995b) |
| | | L | Scent | Y | M | Body weight | C<T | Adult | Social competition | Drickamer (1992) |
| | | L | Scent | Y | M | NA | NA | Adult | Genetic variation | Lenington (1983) |
| | | L | Scent | Y[a] | M | Body weight | C<T | Adult | Infection/parasite | Raveh et al. (2014) |
| | | L | Scent | Y | M | NA | NA | Adult | Infection/parasite | Zala, Potts, and Penn (2004) |
| Bank vole | *Myodes glareolus* | L/F | Scent | Y[b] | M | NA | NA | Adult | Social competition | Mills et al. (2010) |
| | | L | Scent | Y | M | NA | NA | Adult | Social competition | Hoffmeyer (1982) |
| | | L | Scent | Y | M | Body size | C<T | Adult | Social competition | Kruczek (1997) |
| N. American brown lemming | *Lemmus trimucronatus* | L | Scent | Y | M | Body weight | C<T | Adult | Social competition | Huck, Banks, and Wang (1981) |
| | | L | Scent | Y | M | NA | NA | Adult | Social competition | Huck and Banks (1982) |

| Golden hamster | Mesocricetus auratus | L | Scent | Y | M | Body weight | C<T | Adult | Social competition | White, Fischer, and Meunier (1984) |
|---|---|---|---|---|---|---|---|---|---|---|
| | | L | Scent | Y | M | Body weight | C<T | Adult | Social competition | White, Fischer, and Meunier (1986) |
| | | L | Scent | Y | M | Body weight | C<T | Adult | Social dominance | Drickamer, Vandenbergh, and Colby (1973) |
| | | L | Scent | Y | F | Body weight | C<T | Adult | Social dominance | Drickamer and Vandenbergh (1973) |
| Ring-tailed lemur | Lemur catta | N | Scent | Y | F | Scent-nonbreeding | C<T | Adult | Genetic variation | Boulet et al. (2010) |
| | | N | Scent | Y | M | Scent-nonbreeding | C<T | Adult | Genetic variation | Charpentier et al. (2008) |
| Marmoset | Callithrix jacchus | L | Scent | Y | F | NA | NA | Adult | Social dominance | Barrett et al. (1990) |
| | | L | Scent | N | F | NA | NA | Adult | Social dominance | Barrett et al. (1993) |
| African elephant | Loxodonta africana | L | Scent | Y[c] | M | NA | NA | Adult | Social dominance | Hollister-Smith et al. (2008) |
| | | N | Musth | Y | M | Age | NA | Adult | Reproductive success | Hollister-Smith et al. (2007) |
| | | N | Musth | Y | M | NA | NA | Adult | Social dominance | Poole and Moss (1981) |
| | | N | Musth | Y | M | NA | NA | Adult | Social dominance | Poole (1987) |
| | | N | Musth | Y | M | Body size | NA | Adult | Social dominance | Poole (1989) |

*Continued*

**TABLE 4.6** Condition-Dependent Scent Traits in Mammals—cont'd

| Species | Scientific Name | ST | Trait | CD | S | Contrast | | Life History | Manipulation | References |
|---|---|---|---|---|---|---|---|---|---|---|
| | | | | | | Trait | Effect | | | |
| Asian elephant | Elephas maximus | N | Musth | Y | M | Body size | C<T | Adult | Social dominance | Chelliah and Sukumar (2013) |
| | | N | Musth | Y | M | NA | NA | Adult | Testosterone | Jainudeen, Katongole, and Short (1972) |
| | | N | Musth | Y | M | NA | NA | Adult | Body condition | Jainudeen, McKay, and Eisenberg (1972) |

Note: ST, study type (L, lab experiment; F, field experiment; N, natural variation); CD, condition dependent (Y, yes; N, no); S, sex of animals included in the study (M, male; F, female).

[a]In this study, females chose one of two males and were then mated with either the preferred or nonpreferred male. Following infection with a common parasite, offspring sired by preferred males had higher survival rates than those sired by nonpreferred males, but for those offspring that survived immune functions did not differ.

[b]In this study, dominance was first determined through male-male completion for an estrous female. Males and females were placed in a seminatural enclosure and dominant males sired more offspring. It was not clear what determined female choice of these males, but scent is likely. These males had higher testosterone, but lower immune resistance, suggesting a trade-off.

[c]These were zoo elephants exposed to musth urine from other males; subordinate males avoided urine from dominant males.

**TABLE 4.7** Condition-Dependent Behavioral Traits in Mammals

| Species | Scientific Name | ST | Trait | CD | S | Trait | Effect | Life History | Manipulation | References |
|---|---|---|---|---|---|---|---|---|---|---|
| | | | | | | | Contrast | | | |
| Mouse | *Peromyscus maniculatus* | L/T | Explore | Y | B | Female explore | C<T | Prenatal/postnatal | Toxin | Jašarević et al. (2011) |
| | | L/T | Explore | Y | B | Female explore | C<T | Prenatal/postnatal | Toxin | Jašarević et al. (2013) |
| | *P. californicus* | L/T | Explore | N | B | Female explore | C>T | Prenatal/postnatal | Toxin | Williams et al. (2013) |
| | | L/T | Scent marking | Y | B | Male spatial | C<T | Prenatal/postnatal | Toxin | Williams et al. (2013) |
| | *Mus musculus* | L | Scent marking | Y | M | NA | NA | Adult | Social competition | Rich and Hurst (1998) |
| | | L | Scent marking | Y | M | NA | NA | Adult | Social competition | Rich and Hurst (1999) |
| | | L/T | Explore | Y | B | Female explore | C<T | Postnatal | Toxin | Xu et al. (2011) |
| Rat | *Rattus norvegicus* | L | Explore | Y | B | Female explore | C<T | Postnatal | Stress | Shimozuru et al. (2007) |
| | | L | Play fighting | Y | M | Unexposed male | C<T | Prenatal | Toxin | Casto et al. (2003) |
| | | L | Play fighting | Y | M | Other social | C<T | Postnatal | Toxin | Hotchkiss et al. (2003) |

*Continued*

**TABLE 4.7** Condition-Dependent Behavioral Traits in Mammals—cont'd

| Species | Scientific Name | ST | Trait | CD | S | Contrast Trait | Contrast Effect | Life History | Manipulation | References |
|---|---|---|---|---|---|---|---|---|---|---|
| | | L | Play fighting | Y[a] | B | Female play | C<T | Prenatal | Toxin | Colbert et al. (2005) |
| | | L | Play fighting | Y | B | Female play | C=T | Postnatal | Toxin | Holloway and Thor (1987) |
| | | L | Play fighting | N | B | Female play | C=T | Prenatal/postnatal | Toxin | Ferguson, Flynn, Delclos, and Newbold (2000) |
| | | L | Play fighting | Y | M | Unexposed male | C<T | Prenatal | Maternal stress | Morley Fletcher et al. (2003) |
| | | L | Play fighting | Y | B | Female play | C<T | Postnatal | Stress | Arnold and Siviy (2002) |
| | | L | Play fighting | Y | B | Female play | C=T | Postnatal | Stress | Shimozuru et al. (2007) |
| | | L | Play fighting | Y[b] | B | Female play | C=T | Prenatal | Toxin | Meyer and Riley (1986) |
| Meadow vole | Microtus pennsylvanicus | L | Scent marking | Y | M | NA | NA | Adult | Social competition | Johnston, Sorokin, and Ferkin (1997a) |
| | | L | Scent marking | Y | M | NA | NA | Adult | Social competition | Johnston, Sorokin, and Ferkin (1997b) |

| | | | | | | | | | | |
|---|---|---|---|---|---|---|---|---|---|---|
| Long-tailed hamster | Tscherskia triton | L | Scent marking | Y | M | Body weight | C<T | Adult | Testosterone | Zhang, Zhang, and Wang (2001) |
| Golden hamster | Mesocricetus auratus | L | Scent marking | Y | M | NA | NA | Adult | Social competition | Huck, Lisk, and Gore (1985) |
| | | L | Scent marking | Y[c] | F | Other marking | C<T | Adult | Social competition | Johnston (1977) |
| Mongolian gerbil | Meriones unguiculatus | L | Scent marking | Y | M | NA | NA | Adult | Social dominance | Thiessen, Owen, and Lindzey (1971) |
| Australian rabbit | Oryctolagus cuniculus | N | Scent marking | Y | M | NA | NA | Adult | Social dominance | Mykytowycz (1965) |
| | | N | Scent marking | Y | F | NA | NA | Adult | Social dominance | Mykytowycz (1965) |
| Stoat | Mustela erminea | L | Scent marking | Y | F | NA | NA | Adult | Social dominance | Erlinge et al. (1982) |
| | | L | Scent marking | Y | M | NA | NA | Adult | Social dominance | Erlinge et al. (1982) |
| Marmoset | Callithrix jacchus | N | Scent marking | N[d] | F | NA | NA | Adult | Social dominance | Lazaro-Perea et al. (1999) |
| | | L | Scent marking | Y[e] | F | NA | NA | Adult | Social dominance | Epple (1970) |
| | | L | Scent marking | Y | M | NA | NA | Adult | Social dominance | Epple (1970) |

*Continued*

**TABLE 4.7** Condition-Dependent Behavioral Traits in Mammals—cont'd

| Species | Scientific Name | ST | Trait | CD | S | Contrast Trait | Contrast Effect | Life History | Manipulation | References |
|---|---|---|---|---|---|---|---|---|---|---|
| Cotton-top tamarin | Saguinus oedipus | L | Scent marking | Y | F | NA | NA | Adult | Social dominance | Heistermann et al. (1989) |
| Sac-winged bat | Saccopteryx bilineata | N | Flight display | Y | M | NA | NA | Adult | Social dominance | Voigt and von Helversen (1999) |
| | | N | Song activity | Y^f | M | Body size | NA | Adult | Reproductive success | Behr et al. (2006) |
| White-throated bat | Lophostoma silvicolum | N | Nest building | Y | M | NA | NA | Adult | Social dominance | Dechmann, Kalko, König, and Kerth (2005) |
| Northern elephant seal | Mirounga angustirostris | F | Vocal call | Y | M | NA | NA | Adult | Social competition | Insley, Holt, Southall, and Atwood (2011) |
| Southern elephant seal | M. leonina | N | Vocal call | Y | M | NA | NA | Adult | Social competition | Sanvito, Galimberti, and Miller (2007) |
| Fallow deer | Dama dama | N | Vocal call | Y | M | Body size | C<T | Adult | Social dominance | Vannoni and McElligott (2008) |

| | | | | | | | | | | |
|---|---|---|---|---|---|---|---|---|---|---|
| Red deer | *Cervus elaphus* | N | Roaring | Y | M | NA | NA | Adult | Social competition | Clutton-Brock and Albon (1979) |
| | | N | Roaring | Y | M | Body size | C<T | Adult | Reproductive success | Reby and McComb (2003) |
| N. American bison | *Bison bison* | N | Bellow/roar | N[B] | M | NA | NA | Adult | Reproductive success | Wyman, Mooring, McCowan, Penedo, and Hart (2008) |
| | | N | Bellow/roar | Y | M | Body size | C<T | Adult | Copulations | Wyman et al. (2012) |
| | | N | Bellow/roar | N | M | Body size | C=T | Adult | Reproductive success | Wyman et al. (2012) |
| | | N | Bellow/roar | N | M | Body size | C=T | Adult | Social dominance | Wyman et al. (2012) |
| Yellow baboon | *Papio cynocephalus* | N | Vocal call | Y | M | Body size | C<T | Adult | Social dominance | Fischer et al. (2004) |
| Macaque | *Macaca sylvanus* | F | Vocal call | Y | F | NA | NA | Adult | Fertility | Semple and McComb (2000) |
| Black-and-white colobus | *Colobus guereza* | N | Vocal call | Y | M | NA | NA | Adult | Body size | Harris, Fitch, Goldstein, and Fashing (2006) |

*Continued*

**TABLE 4.7** Condition-Dependent Behavioral Traits in Mammals—cont'd

| Species | Scientific Name | ST | Trait | CD | S | Contrast Trait | Contrast Effect | Life History | Manipulation | References |
|---|---|---|---|---|---|---|---|---|---|---|
| Ursine colobus | C. vellerosus | N | Vocal call | Y | M | NA | NA | Adult | Social dominance | Teichroeb and Sicotte (2010) |
|  |  | N | Behavioral display | Y | M | NA | NA | Adult | Social dominance | Teichroeb and Sicotte (2010) |
| Lion | Panthera leo | N | Roaring | N | M | Body size | C=T | Adult | Body condition | Pfefferle, West, Grinnell, Packer, and Fischer (2007) |

Note: ST, study type (L, lab experiment; F, field experiment; N, natural variation; T, toxin); CD, condition dependent (Y, yes; N, no); S, sex of animals included in the study (M, male; F, female; B, both sexes).
[a]Prenatal and early (through postnatal day 3) exposure to the fungicide vinclozolin increased males' social play.
[b]Prenatal exposure to ethanol decreased males' play fighting and increased females' play fighting. Both sexes were affected, relative to unexposed same-sex individuals, but in opposite directions.
[c]Females increased vaginal markings in the presence of male odors and before ovulation, and flanking in the presence of female odors.
[d]Reproductively subordinate females scent marked more than dominant females during intergroup encounters and these may have been related to attracting mates rather than establishing position within the female dominance hierarchy. No status differences in scent marking outside of these encounters.
[e]Male and female marmosets form sex-specific dominance hierarchies and are thus considered separately, rather than one serving as a contrast for the other.
[f]These included frequency of song and some components that were related to male reproductive success but were not correlated with male body size.
[g]These authors predicted that a louder bellow would be a costly signal, but found that dominant males with higher reproductive success have a softer bellow. It is possible that the softer bellow is a condition-dependent signal to other males.

**PHOTO 4.12**   The scent of a dominant female marmoset (*Callithrix jacchus*) can suppress the reproduction of subordinate females. *Photo credit: Leszek Leszczynski, 2012. Creative Commons license: http://commons.wikimedia.org/wiki/File:Common_marmoset_(Callithrix_jacchus).jpg.* (See the color plate section.)

found in a diverse group of species, and in both males and females, ranging from the male California mouse (*Peromyscus californicus*; Williams et al., 2013) to the female cotton-top tamarin (*Saguinus oedipus*; Heistermann et al., 1989). Lazaro-Perea et al.'s (1999) field study of female marmosets was the only assessment reviewed in Table 4.7 that did not support the condition dependence of scent marking. Within the wild groups studied by these scientists, dominant and subordinate females did not differ in the frequency of scent marking and in fact subordinate females scent marked more than dominant females during intergroup encounters. Generally, dominance-related behavioral displays will spike when the alpha individual (male or female) is challenged either from within the group or by an outsider, but once dominance is established these displays are less frequent (e.g., Thiessen & Rice, 1976). There was no indication of any such challenges in the groups studied by Lazaro-Perea et al. (1999), and this may have accounted for the finding that subordinate females scent marked as frequently as the dominant female in their group. These authors also suggested subordinate females scent marked more than dominant females during intergroup encounters as a means of attracting mates rather than establishing position within the female dominance hierarchy.

As with birds and arthropods, courtship or dominance displays often involve some type of vocal call in mammals, although many vocalizations serve other functions, such as predator alarms (Ey, Pfefferle, & Fischer, 2007). Included among the dominance displays are the energetically demanding territorial song of the sac-winged bat (*Saccopteryx bilineata*; Behr et al., 2006) and the equally demanding "wahoo" calls of dominant male yellow baboons (*Papio cynocephalus*; Fischer, Kitchen, Seyfarth, & Cheney, 2004). Not all of the assessments of vocal displays in Table 4.7 were consistent with condition dependence, but the majority of them were (12 of 16). I also included several other traits that were not considered in the studies of birds, fish, and arthropods but are nevertheless sexually selected in many species of mammal (likely other species as well, but not as fully studied), and provide important background for interpretation of some of the human studies described in Chapters 6 and 7; specifically, play and exploratory behavior.

Recall, studies of the polygynous meadow vole (*Microtus pennsylvanicus*) reviewed in Chapter 2 demonstrated that males' home range expansion during the breeding season to search for mates is associated with enhanced spatial abilities relative to conspecific females and relative to males of related species in which males do not expand their home range (Gaulin, 1992; Gaulin & Fitzgerald, 1986). These spatial-navigation abilities are sexually selected in male meadow voles, and other species in which males search for mates (Jašarević et al., 2012; Perdue et al., 2011), and thus their development should be condition dependent, as covered in the next section. The behavioral component of territorial expansion includes an increase in activity and exploration and this too should be condition dependent. Jašarević and colleagues tested this hypothesis in a pair of studies of the deer mouse (*P. maniculatus*), a species in which males have the same mate-search strategy as found in the meadow vole (Jašarević et al., 2011, 2013). In both studies, prenatal exposure to toxins [bisphenol A, an EDC (recall, endocrine disrupting compound)] resulted in dampened exploratory behavior in males but had little effect on that of females; Xu, Tian, Hong, Chen, and Xie (2011) found the same for the laboratory mouse.

The California mouse is a monogamous cousin of the deer mouse, with males and females sharing a territory (Ribble, 1992). In other words, sex differences in exploratory behavior and spatial abilities are not expected in this species and in fact are not found (Jašarević et al., 2011). The critical finding for this discussion is that prenatal exposure to the same toxin that disrupted the exploratory behavior of male deer mice had no effect on the exploratory behavior or spatial abilities of male (or female) California mice (Williams et al., 2013). Territorial or scent marking, in contrast, is a dominance-related behavior in California mice and along with physical fighting is how dominant males keep other males away from their mates (Becker, Petruno, & Marler, 2012; Eisenberg, 1962). To test whether prenatal toxin exposure disrupted this behavior, toxin-exposed and unexposed males were placed in a single cage bisected by a barrier that allowed them to see and smell each other but not physically fight. As shown in Figure 4.1, over the course of a week the scent marking of unexposed males increased while that of exposed males decreased, indicating the latter were subordinate and in natural contexts would be significantly disadvantaged when competing for mates.

Finally, we need to consider whether the expression of sex-typed behaviors during development, especially play, are condition dependent, as these often reflect behavioral sex differences in adulthood and thus at least some of them are components of sexual selection; they are part of the preparation for reproductive competition in adulthood (Bekoff & Byers, 1998; Burghardt, 2005; Power, 2000). If these behaviors are condition dependent, it should be readily observable

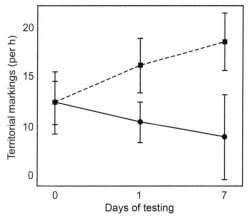

**FIGURE 4.1**    Territorial or scent marking in California mice (*Peromyscus californicus*) males that were prenatally exposed to bisphenol A (●) and unexposed males (■). Males were placed together for 1 h a night for 7 days and across this time scent marking increased in unexposed males and decreased in exposed males. *Figure adapted from Williams et al. (2013).*

in play fighting. As reviewed by Power, males in species with intense male-male competition over mates nearly always engage in more play fighting during development than do females, a pattern found across species of marsupial (e.g., red kangaroos, *Macropus rufus*), pinniped (e.g., northern elephant seal), ungulate (Alpine ibex), rodent (Norway rat, *Rattus norvegicus*), and primate (e.g., chimpanzee, *Pan troglodytes*). Carnivores are an important exception that proves the rule. Intense competition over mates or food is the norm for both sexes, and both sexes tend to engage in play fighting during development. A notable exception among carnivores is the spotted hyena (*Crocuta crocuta*) in which females compete fiercely with other females over food – a form of social selection – and are dominant over males (East, Burke, Wilhelm, Greig, & Hofer, 2003). In this species, females engage in more play fighting than males (Pedersen, Glickman, Frank, & Beach, 1990).

All of the studies of the relation between exposure to stressors and play fighting shown in Table 4.7 involved the laboratory rat. And, all but one of them showed that exposure to toxins (Casto, Ward, & Bartke, 2003; Colbert et al., 2005; Hotchkiss, Ostby, Vandenbergh, & Gray, 2003), prenatal stress (through maternal stress), or postnatal stress (Morley Fletcher, Rea, Maccari, & Laviola, 2003; Shimozuru et al., 2007) disrupted the later play fighting of males. Five of the eight studies found stressors affected males' play more strongly than females' play. Six of the studies found reductions in males' play fighting following exposure to the stressor, often to the level seen in normal females (e.g., Arnold & Siviy, 2002). Colbert et al. found that exposure to small doses of vinclozolin, a fungicide that interferes with male hormone receptors, resulted in an increase in aspects of male play fighting but had no effect on female social play. Much larger doses of the same toxin had the opposite effect; that is, substantial decreases in male play fighting (Hotchkiss et al., 2003), suggesting potentially important dose-response effects. Increases in play fighting might at first glance be interpreted as a potential advantage for these exposed males, but this is not necessarily the case in the long term. Recall from Chapter 2 that artificial exaggeration of sexually selected traits can increase risk of disease and premature mortality (Mougeot et al., 2005). Costs were also evident in the exposed males in the Colbert et al. study. The males exhibited primary sexual dysfunctions (e.g., fewer erections) that were correlated with the increased play fighting.

Finally, there are studies of the relation between malnutrition and social play in primates that demonstrated severe deficits associated with protein and caloric deficiency but they did not report sex differences (Elias & Samonds, 1977; Zimmermann, Geist, & Ackles, 1975; Zimmermann, Steere, Strobel, & Hom, 1972). I was unable to locate studies of the relation between parasite infestation and sex differences in play fighting, although prenatal infestation with at least one type of parasite (*Toxoplasma gondii*) has been shown to increase aggressive behavior in adult mice (Arnott, Cassella, Aitken, & Hay, 1990).

## Brain and Cognitive Traits

The most important takeaway message of this section is that exposure to toxins, poor nutrition, parasites, and maternal stress during prenatal development can result in sex-specific disruptions in cognitive abilities and brain development and functioning. There is much that still remains to be learned, but these studies confirm that competition and choice can result in the elaboration of brain and cognitive traits in mammals, as with birdsong, and these same traits appear to be easily disrupted by exposure to stressors.

As we covered in Chapter 2, two of the best-studied sex differences in brain and cognition related to competition and choice are birdsong and spatial ability (Gaulin & Fitzgerald, 1986; Nottebohm, 1970, 2005). These are by no means the only domains in which brain and cognitive sex differences should be found. As an example, primates that engage in more frequent social play, including play fighting, have a larger hypothalamus – important for basic motivations, including sex and aggression (Raisman & Field, 1973) – and amygdala – important for processing social information (e.g., facial expressions) and emotions (Adolphs et al., 2005) – than do their less social cousins (Lewis & Barton, 2006). Sex differences in these two brain regions as related to exposure to sex hormones and behavioral sex differences have been well documented in mammals (e.g., Collaer & Hines, 1995; Hines, Allen, & Gorski, 1992; Nishizuka & Arai, 1981; Raisman & Field, 1973), including humans (Neufang et al., 2009). Meaney, Dodge, and Beatty (1981) demonstrated that damage to the amygdala reduces the level of male rats' play fighting to that found in female rats; infestation with some parasites can alter amygdala-dependent behaviors as well, such as fear of predators (Klein, 2003); and, prenatal exposure to toxins can change patterns of gene expression in sex-specific ways in the amygdala and hypothalamus (Cao et al., 2013; Cao, Joyner, Mickens, Leyrer, & Patisaul, 2014), although the latter have not been explicitly linked to behavioral sex differences.

For all of these reasons and those described for play fighting above, the development and functioning of the amygdala, hypothalamus, and related brain regions are predicted to be condition dependent, or at least the subregions (nuclei) within them that contribute to behavioral sex differences. Unfortunately, this hypothesis has not been systematically explored and as a result the studies summarized in Table 4.8 focus on spatial learning and memory and one critical supporting brain region, the hippocampus. On the basis of previous research, spatial abilities and the supporting hippocampus should be especially sensitive to stressors during the later prenatal and early postnatal periods, as this is when sexual differentiation of these abilities and underlying brain systems largely occur (Williams & Meck, 1991). If my general vulnerability thesis is correct, this sensitivity will only be found in species in which spatial cognition is a sexually selected trait. Indeed, as noted, prenatal and early postnatal exposure to toxins had no effect on the spatial abilities of male California mice, a species in which male spatial abilities are not sexually selected (Williams et al., 2013).

In contrast, for the two species of mouse and the rat species covered by the studies shown in Table 4.8, spatial abilities are sexually selected. In these species, males are polygynous, expanding their territory during the breeding season to search for mates. Spatial learning and memory, along with the exploratory behavior discussed above, support territory expansion and thus the development of these cognitive abilities should be condition dependent. Most of the associated studies reviewed in Table 4.8 were not informed by sexual selection, but the results support condition dependence. For male mice, spatial learning and memory are disrupted by prenatal and early postnatal exposure to toxins (Jašarević et al., 2011) or poor early nutrition (Boitard et al., 2012), as well as by parasite infestation in adulthood (Kavaliers, Colwell, & Galea, 1995).

The same basic pattern is found for the laboratory rat, although the results are less consistent. The same level of prenatal and early postnatal exposure to the PCB (polychlorinated biphenyl) Aroclor resulted in deficits in male but not female spatial learning and memory in one study (Roegge, Seo, Crofton, & Schantz, 2000), but had no effect on either sex in another study (Gilbert, Mundy, & Crofton, 2000). Similarly, maternal stress during pregnancy has been found to disrupt the later spatial learning or memory of male but not female offspring in some studies (e.g., Zagron & Weinstock, 2006), but not others (Zuena et al., 2008). Still other studies found that maternal stress disrupts spatial learning but not memory (Szuran, Pliška, Pokorny, & Welzl, 2000) or vice versa (Meunier, Gué, Récasens, & Maurice, 2004). The inconsistencies may be due to differences in the number of days (4-11) the stressors were administered and to differences in the intensity of the stressors. Despite this variation and the mixed results, all but one of the

**TABLE 4.8** Condition-Dependent Brain and Cognitive Traits in Mammals

| Species | Scientific Name | ST | Trait | CD | S | Contrast Trait | Effect | Life History | Manipulation | References |
|---|---|---|---|---|---|---|---|---|---|---|
| Mouse | Peromyscus maniculatus | L/T | Spatial learning | Y | B | Female learning | C<T | Prenatal/postnatal | Toxin | Jašarević et al. (2011) |
| | | L/T | Spatial memory | Y | B | Female memory | C<T | Prenatal/postnatal | Toxin | Jašarević et al. (2011) |
| | | L/T | Spatial learning | Y | B | Female learning | C<T | Prenatal/postnatal | Toxin | Jašarević et al. (2013) |
| | | L/T | Spatial memory | Y | B | Female memory | C<T | Prenatal/postnatal | Toxin | Jašarević et al. (2013) |
| | Mus musculus | L/T | Hippocampus | Y | B | Female hippocampus | C<T | Adult | Toxin | Xu et al. (2013) |
| | | L | Hippocampus | Y | M | NA | NA | Prenatal/postnatal | Diet/nutrition | Jašarević et al. (2014) |
| | | L | Hippocampus | Y[a] | M | Adult contrast | C<T | Postnatal | Diet/nutrition | Boitard et al. (2012) |
| | | L | Hippocampus | Y | B | Female hippocampus | C<T | Postnatal | Diet/nutrition | Hwang et al. (2010) |
| | | L | Hippocampus | Y | M | NA | NA | Prenatal/postnatal | Toxin | Xu et al. (2010) |
| | | L | Spatial memory | Y | M | NA | NA | Prenatal/postnatal | Toxin | Xu et al. (2010) |

| | | | | | | | | |
|---|---|---|---|---|---|---|---|---|
| L | Spatial learning | Y | M | NA | NA | Prenatal/postnatal | Toxin | Xu et al. (2010) |
| L/T | Spatial memory | Y | B | Female memory | C<T | Adult | Toxin | Xu et al. (2013) |
| L/T | Spatial learning | Y | B | Female learning | C<T | Adult | Toxin | Xu et al. (2013) |
| L | Spatial learning | Y | M | Vision | C<T | Adult | Infection/parasite | Kavaliers and Colwell (1995c) |
| L | Spatial memory | Y | M | Vision | C<T | Adult | Infection/parasite | Kavaliers and Colwell (1995c) |
| L | Spatial learning | Y | M | Vision | C<T | Adult | Infection/parasite | Kavaliers and Colwell (1995d) |
| L | Spatial memory | Y | M | Vision | C<T | Adult | Infection/parasite | Kavaliers and Colwell (1995d) |
| L | Spatial learning | Y | M | Vision | C<T | Adult | Infection/parasite | Kavaliers et al. (1995) |
| L | Spatial memory | Y | M | Vision | C<T | Adult | Infection/parasite | Kavaliers et al. (1995) |
| L/T | Spatial learning | Y | B | Female learning | C<T | Postnatal | Toxin | Xu et al. (2011) |
| L/T | Spatial memory | N | B | Female memory | C=T | Postnatal | Toxin | Xu et al. (2011) |
| L | Spatial learning | Y | M | Activity level | C<T | Prenatal/postnatal | Diet/nutrition | Jašarević et al. (2014) |

*Continued*

**TABLE 4.8** Condition-Dependent Brain and Cognitive Traits in Mammals—cont'd

| Species | Scientific Name | ST | Trait | CD | S | Trait | Effect | Life History | Manipulation | References |
|---|---|---|---|---|---|---|---|---|---|---|
| | | | | | | **Contrast** | | | | |
| | | L | Spatial memory | N | M | Activity level | C=T | Prenatal/postnatal | Diet/nutrition | Jašarević et al. (2014) |
| | | L | Spatial learning | Y | M | Adult contrast[a] | C<T | Postnatal | Diet/nutrition | Boitard et al. (2012) |
| | | L | Spatial memory | Y | M | Adult contrast[a] | C<T | Postnatal | Diet/nutrition | Boitard et al. (2012) |
| Rat | *Rattus norvegicus* | L/T | Hippocampus | Y | M | NA | NA | Adult | Toxin | Fan et al. (2013) |
| | | L/T | Hippocampus | N[b] | B | Female hippocampus | C>T | Paternal | Paternal toxin | Fan et al. (2013) |
| | | L/T | Hippocampus | Y | B | Female hippocampus | C=T | Prenatal/postnatal | Toxin | Gilbert et al. (2000) |
| | | L | Hippocampus | Y | B | Female hippocampus | C=T | Prenatal | Maternal stress | Feng et al. (2012) |
| | | L | Hippocampus | Y | B | Female hippocampus | C<T | Prenatal | Maternal stress | Mandyam et al. (2008) |
| | | L | Hippocampus | Y[c] | M | NA | NA | Prenatal | Maternal stress | Yang, Han, Cao, Li, and Xu (2006) |

| L | Hippocampus | Y | B | Female hippocampus | C<T | Prenatal | Maternal stress | Zuena et al. (2008) |
|---|---|---|---|---|---|---|---|---|
| L | Hippocampus | Y | M | NA | NA | Prenatal | Maternal stress | Lemaire, Koehl, Le Moal, and Abrous (2000) |
| L | Hippocampus | Y | B | Female hippocampus | C<T | Adult | Diet/nutrition | Lindqvist et al. (2006) |
| L | Hippocampus | Y | B | Female hippocampus | C<T | Prenatal | Maternal stress | Mandyam et al. (2008) |
| L/T | Spatial memory | Y | M | NA | NA | Adult | Toxin | Fan et al. (2013) |
| L/T | Spatial learning | Y | M | NA | NA | Adult | Toxin | Fan et al. (2013) |
| L/T | Spatial learning | Y | B | Female learning | C=T | Paternal exposure | Paternal toxin[b] | Fan et al. (2013) |
| L/T | Spatial memory | N | B | Female memory | C>T | Paternal exposure | Paternal toxin[b] | Fan et al. (2013) |
| LT | Spatial learning | Y | B | Female learning | C<T | Prenatal/postnatal | Toxin | Roegge et al. (2000) |
| L/T | Spatial memory | Y | B | Female memory | C<T | Prenatal/postnatal | Toxin | Roegge et al. (2000) |
| L/T | Spatial learning | N | B | Female learning | C=T | Prenatal/postnatal | Toxin | Gilbert et al. (2000) |
| L/T | Spatial memory | N | B | Female memory | C=T | Prenatal/postnatal | Toxin | Gilbert et al. (2000) |

*Continued*

**TABLE 4.8** Condition-Dependent Brain and Cognitive Traits in Mammals—cont'd

| Species | Scientific Name | ST | Trait | CD | S | Contrast Trait | Contrast Effect | Life History | Manipulation | References |
|---|---|---|---|---|---|---|---|---|---|---|
| | | L | Spatial learning | Y | B | Female learning | C=T | Prenatal | Maternal stress | Feng et al. (2012) |
| | | L | Spatial learning | Y | B | Female learning | C<T | Prenatal | Maternal stress | Zagron and Weinstock (2006) |
| | | L | Spatial learning | N | B | Female learning | C=T | Prenatal | Maternal stress | Meunier et al. (2004) |
| | | L | Spatial memory | Y | B | Female memory | C<T | Prenatal | Maternal stress | Meunier et al. (2004) |
| | | L | Spatial learning | Y[d] | B | Female learning | C<T | Prenatal | Maternal stress | Szuran et al. (2000) |
| | | L | Spatial memory | N | B | Female memory | C=T | Prenatal | Maternal stress | Szuran et al. (2000) |
| | | L | Spatial learning | Y | B | Female learning | C<T | Prenatal | Maternal stress | Nishio, Kasuga, Ushijima, and Harada (2001) |
| | | L | Spatial learning | Y[c] | M | NA | NA | Prenatal | Maternal stress | Yang et al. (2006) |
| | | L | Spatial memory | Y[c] | M | NA | NA | Prenatal | Maternal stress | Yang et al. (2006) |

| ST | Trait | CD | S | Female learning | C>T | | | Reference |
|---|---|---|---|---|---|---|---|---|
| L | Spatial learning | N | B | | | Prenatal | Maternal stress | Zuena et al. (2008) |
| L | Spatial learning | Y | M | NA | NA | Prenatal | Maternal stress | Lemaire et al. (2000) |
| L | Spatial learning | N | M | NA | NA | Prenatal/adult | Diet/nutrition | White et al. (2009) |
| L | Spatial memory | Y[e] | M | NA | NA | Prenatal/adult[e] | Diet/nutrition | White et al. (2009) |

*Note:* ST, study type (L, lab experiment; F, field experiment; N, natural variation; T, toxin); CD, condition dependent (Y, yes; N, no); S, sex of animals included in the study (M, male; B, both sexes).

[a] *The effect was only found for males whose mothers consumed a high fat diet during pregnancy and lactation and the males continued to consume it in adulthood. Prenatal exposure or exposure only during adulthood did not affect spatial memory.*

[b] *In this study, adult males were exposed to 50 mg of bisphenol A (BPA) before mating, and their offspring were assessed when the offspring reached adulthood.*

[c] *The study included cross-fostering of pups to rule out effects due to stress-related changes in maternal behavior.*

[d] *This affected male but not female water maze learning when the water was 10 °C but not 20 °C.*

[e] *The memory deficit was found for males exposed to a high fat diet prenatally and in adulthood, but not for males only exposed prenatally or in adulthood.*

studies found that maternal stressors during the last trimester of pregnancy disrupted male offspring's spatial learning, memory, or both.

The one exception did not find an effect on male spatial learning, but did find that maternal stress during pregnancy disrupted the hippocampal development of male but not female offspring (Zuena et al., 2008). In addition to exposure to maternal stress, the functioning of the male hippocampus is disrupted by poor prenatal and early postnatal diet (Boitard et al., 2012; Jašarević, Hecht, Fritsche, Beversdorf, & Geary, 2014) and by toxin exposure (Xu, Zhang, Wang, Ye, & Luo, 2010). As an example, Xu et al. found that late prenatal and early postnatal exposure to bisphenol A (recall, an EDC) resulted in changes in hippocampal gene expression in adulthood that in turn contributed to the spatial deficits of males. The sensitivity of the male hippocampus and associated spatial abilities to prenatal and early postnatal stressors is not surprising, given this spans the critical window for the sexual differentiation of these abilities (Williams & Meck, 1991). The studies shown in Table 4.8 also indicate that this sensitivity continues into adulthood, possibly because the hippocampus continues to generate new neurons throughout the life span (Cameron & Mckay, 2001). In any case, exposure to toxins (Xu et al., 2013), parasites (Kavaliers & Colwell, 1995c), and poor nutrition (Lindqvist et al., 2006) in adulthood have all been found to undermine the hippocampal functioning or spatial abilities of males, and when both sexes were assessed more so for males than for females.

The mechanisms that result in these sex differences in vulnerability are not fully understood but are related to disruption of the normal postnatal and early prenatal hormonal environment. For instance, exposure to maternal stress hormones can suppress the testosterone levels of male fetuses that in turn will undermine the normal sexual differentiation of spatial abilities (Weinstock, 2007), and as discussed in Chapter 2 many of the toxins used in these studies have the same disruptive effects (Carere et al., 2010; Palanza et al., 2008). These stressors may also result in brain inflammation and increases in oxidative stress (White et al., 2009), both of which damage these brain systems (Hill, 2014; von Schantz et al., 1999). Finally, none of these studies should be taken to mean that exposure to these stressors has no effects on female spatial abilities or hippocampal functions. They can and do (Mandyam, Crawford, Eisch, Rivier, & Richardson, 2008). The critical finding is heightened vulnerability of males relative to females for sexually selected brain and cognitive traits.

## CONCLUSION

The research overviewed in this chapter highlights the ubiquity of condition-dependent traits and reinforces several points made in previous chapters. The first is that a trait that reflects condition in one species may not be condition dependent in other species, even closely related ones. We saw this in the last chapter, and here with the description of how the size of red (carotenoid color) wing spots reflects the condition of male American rubyspots (e.g., Grether, 1996) and the size of brown (melanin color) wing spots reflects the condition of males in a related species, the smokey rubyspot (e.g., Cordoba-Aguilar et al., 2007). The point is even better illustrated with the contrasts of the deer and California mouse, where prenatal exposure to the same toxin had sex-, species-, and trait-specific effects – disrupting the exploratory behavior and spatial abilities in male but not female deer mice and disrupting scent marking in male California mice (Jašarević et al., 2011; Williams et al., 2013). The same caveat can even apply to exactly the same trait in closely related species, as Wilkinson and Taper (1999) demonstrated for related species of stalk-eyed fly. Differences in the importance of the quality of carotenoid colors in birds and fish described in Chapter 3 and melanin colors for arthropods described in this chapter hit on the same issue, and follow from the importance of carotenoids for immune and other physiological functions in vertebrates (Hill, 2014; McGraw, 2006a) and an analogous role of melanin for the immune response of invertebrates (Carton & Nappi, 1997). The takeaway message is that the identification of condition-dependent traits requires an understanding of the natural history of the species and especially the dynamics of sexual and social selection in natural contexts, as well as a consideration of the costs of trait expression.

Second, the research reviewed in this chapter reinforces the point about the evolution of condition-dependent traits in females noted in the previous chapter, and more broadly West-Eberhard's (1979, 1983) points about social selection reviewed in Chapter 2. To be sure, female-female competition remains understudied in comparison to the work on male-male competition, and for most species the latter will be more intense than the former (Andersson, 1994). For most species, we would then expect more condition-dependent traits or more sensitive traits in males than females, but this is not the same as concluding there are no such traits in conspecific females. As is the case with beak color for the American goldfinch (*Spinus tristis*; Kelly et al., 2012; Murphy et al., 2009), many traits that are currently identified as condition dependent in males may also be condition dependent in females. A common, if implicit assumption that these traits are not condition dependent in females not only overlooks female sensitivity to stressors, it results in an underestimation of male sensitivity when the female trait is used as a contrast.

In any case, in addition to the goldfinch and several other bird species (e.g., diamond firetail, *Stagonopleura guttata*; Zanollo et al., 2012) reviewed in Chapter 3, the reviews presented in this chapter are consistent with the evolution of condition-dependent traits in females for the paper wasp (Tibbetts, 2010), golden hamster (Drickamer & Vandenbergh, 1973), Australian rabbit (Mykytowycz, 1965), and stoat (*Mustela ermine*; Erlinge et al., 1982), as well as many species of primate including the ring-tailed lemur

(Boulet et al., 2010), marmoset (Epple, 1970), cotton-top tamarin (Heistermann et al., 1989), and macaque (*Macaca sylvanus*; Semple & McComb, 2000). There is little doubt that this list of species will expand with biologists' current interest in competition among females (Clutton-Brock, 2009; Tobias et al., 2012). As we will cover in the next chapter, our own species needs to be included in this list (Geary, 2010).

# Chapter 5

# Sexual Selection and Human Vulnerability

## Chapter Outline

The implication of Darwin's (1859) origin of species for understanding humanity's place in nature generated an uproar and considerable criticism directed both at Darwin personally and his theory (Browne, 2001). Even Wallace (1869) joined the fray, arguing that the moral and mental development of humans is not explainable by natural selection alone. And, matters only became worse with publication of Darwin's (1871) second masterwork, *The Descent of Man, and Selection in Relation to Sex*. Although Huxley (1863) was the first to discuss humans in the context of natural selection, Darwin's work was more thorough and focused on matters that provoked the ire of his contemporaries, as shown in Figure 5.1. The nature and origin of sex differences was one of these matters, and as noted in Chapter 2 languished with respect to nonhuman species for nearly a century (Cronin, 1991) until resurgence of interest and research over the past four decades (Andersson, 1994). Likewise, for well over a century psychologists and social scientists generally ignored or explicitly rejected sexual selection as a cause of human sex differences (e.g., Woolley, 1914). Even with the emergence of evolutionary psychology over the past several decades, Darwin's insight that competition and choice will result in the evolution of sex differences including those found in humans remains controversial (e.g., Wood & Eagly, 2002).

Despite many valiant efforts to explain nonphysical human sex differences through purely social and social-cognitive processes (e.g., people's beliefs about how boys and girls should play; Hyde, 2005; Wood & Eagly, 2002), the argument

Evolution of Vulnerability. http://dx.doi.org/10.1016/B978-0-12-801562-9.00005-3

**FIGURE 5.1** *The Hornet*'s satirical cartoon of Darwin; "Venerable Orang-Outang: A contribution to Unnatural History."

that humans and our ancestors have somehow eluded the rigors of sexual selection is no longer scientifically tenable. To be sure, the here-and-now expression of evolved biases as related to competition for mates and mate choices can be strongly influenced by the social contexts within which people are embedded, but this is in no way evidence against the importance of sexual selection. As was covered in Chapter 2, the operational sex ratio (recall, ratio of sexually active males to females in the local group) can have dramatic effects on mating dynamics in nonhuman species (Emlen & Oring, 1977), and so too for humans (Guttentag & Secord, 1983). Socially imposed monogamy – legal suppression of male polygyny – is arguably the most significant cultural rule influencing human well-being. This is because socially imposed monogamy is associated with substantial reductions in violence, shifts away from harsh child rearing, increases in men's investment in children, and other widespread social benefits (Barry, Josephson, Lauer, & Marshall, 1976; Flinn & Low, 1986; Geary, 2010; Henrich, Boyd, & Richerson, 2012). Still, the core of all of these benefits pivots on the equalization of the operational sex ratio (i.e., one girl for every boy, more or less).

One unintended consequence of ignoring sexual selection and the continuing controversy it generates is an underestimation of the vulnerability of children and adults to a host of stressors. As I hope is now clear from the reviews of condition-dependent traits in the roughly 125 nonhuman species reviewed in Chapters 3 and 4, there is consistent evidence that the development and expression of sexually selected traits, and socially selected traits more broadly, are indeed especially vulnerable to a wide variety of stressors. Given the breadth of species in which this has been documented, there is every reason to believe this vulnerability extends to humans. The keys to understanding this vulnerability are first the identification of sexually selected traits in our species, and second the identification of studies that have adequately assessed such traits under stressful conditions. As I lamented in Chapter 1, the majority of studies – for instance, of the relation between parasite infestation and children's cognitive abilities (for a review, see Watkins & Pollitt, 1997) – that had the potential to yield insights into these vulnerabilities did not report sex differences or assessed outcomes that would be insensitive to any such vulnerabilities. In this chapter, I set the stage for the reviews of sex differences in human vulnerability presented in Chapters 6 and 7, and lay the groundwork for future studies.

## VULNERABILITY IN BOYS AND MEN

For both boys and men and girls and women, I interleaf the discussion of sexual and social selection with the discussion of the associated vulnerable traits; a more nuanced and thorough assessment of sexual and social selection in humans can be found elsewhere (Geary, 2010; Geary, Winegard, & Winegard, 2014). Table 5.1 presents examples of key human traits that I predict will show sex-specific vulnerabilities to stress exposure – all sexually and socially selected traits should, in theory, exhibit some degree of vulnerability but there are too many to cover all of them here (again, see Geary, 2010). Following previous chapters and the discussion below, the table identifies physical, behavioral, and cognitive traits, the more vulnerable sex, and predictions regarding the magnitude of the effect of stressor exposure during different life history stages.

As an example, developmental exposure to chronic stressors, such as malnutrition or infectious disease, is predicted to affect the height of boys more than girls. Exposure to childhood stressors is predicted to have smaller to modestly larger effects on boys' height than girls' height, whereas exposure during adolescence is predicted to effect boys' growth substantially more than girls' growth. Of course, the effects of stressors during adulthood would not influence height but should influence other physical traits. The magnitudes listed under life history are estimates based on the general principles (e.g., that sex differences tend to be small early in life; Darwin, 1871) and empirical research on human sex differences. They should be interpreted independently for each trait, such that small for height in childhood is relative to large for height in adolescence but small across height and muscle mass are not necessarily directly comparable. Finally, the systems of integrated brain regions underlying

**TABLE 5.1** Predicted Condition-Dependent Traits in Humans

| Trait | Sex | Potential Measures | Life History | | |
|---|---|---|---|---|---|
| | | | Child | Adolescent | Adult |
| **Physical Traits** | | | | | |
| Skeletal growth | M | Height, femur, ulna, radius relative to sex- and age-norms | + | +++ | — |
| Physical fitness | M | Running endurance, heart rate recovery, vital capacity[a] | + | +++ | +++ |
| Physical activity | M | Activity level relative to sex-specific norms | ++ | ++ | ++ |
| Muscle mass | M | Lean muscle mass, upper body strength | + | +++ | +++ |
| Upper body fat | M | Triceps skin fold[b]; abdominal fat | + | ++ | ++ |
| Facial structure | B | Chin, cheek, eye size | — | +++ | — |
| Skin complexion | F | Rated attractiveness; carotenoid levels in dermis | — | +++ | +++ |
| Lower body fat | F | Hip, buttocks fat[c] | — | +++ | +++ |
| Skeletal growth | F | Pelvis width | — | +++ | — |
| Waist-to-hip ratio | F | Abdominal swelling[d] | — | +++ | +++ |
| **Behavioral traits** | | | | | |
| Rough-and-tumble play | M | Frequency relative to sex- and age-norms | +++ | ++ | +[e] |
| Coalitional play | M | Frequency of engagement in group-level competition | ++ | +++ | + |
| Peer network density | M | Group cohesion – mutual friendships within the group[f] | ++ | +++ | +++ |

**TABLE 5.1** Predicted Condition-Dependent Traits in Humans—cont'd

| Trait | Sex | Potential Measures | Life History | | |
|---|---|---|---|---|---|
| | | | Child | Adolescent | Adult |
| Physical aggression | M | Behavioral aggression as related to status striving, threats | + | +++ | +++ |
| Risk taking | M | Engagement in risky behavior related to potential status gains | + | +++ | ++ |
| Exploratory behavior | M | Approach to novelty, exploration of physical space | + | ++ | ++ |
| Throwing | M | Distance, velocity, accuracy | ++ | +++ | +++ |
| Emotional composure | M | Fear expression under threat | + | +++ | +++ |
| Facial displays | M | Anger displays in response to social threat | + | +++ | +++ |
| Vocal features | B | Sex-typical formant frequencies and dispersion | — | +++ | +++ |
| Dyadic friendships | F | Emotional reciprocity and social support | ++ | +++ | +++ |
| Relational aggression | F | Frequency relative to sex- and age-norms | + | ++ | ++ |
| **Cognitive traits** | | | | | |
| Face processing | M | Detection of anger, contempt in men's faces | + | ++ | ++ |
| Voice processing | M | Detection of anger, contempt in men's voices | + | ++ | ++ |
| In-group bias | M | Enhanced in-group cooperation with group conflict | + | ++ | ++ |

*Continued*

**TABLE 5.1** Predicted Condition-Dependent Traits in Humans—cont'd

| Trait | Sex | Potential Measures | Life History | | |
|---|---|---|---|---|---|
| | | | Child | Adolescent | Adult |
| Spatial navigation | M | Way finding, map reading, sensitivity to cardinal direction | + | +++ | +++ |
| Spatial representation | M | Mental generation and manipulation of images | + | +++ | +++ |
| Visuospatial tracking | M | Accuracy in tracking object motion, catching | + | +++ | +++ |
| Visuospatial memory | M | Recall of maps and routes | + | +++ | +++ |
| Object detection | M | Detecting objects embedded other others | + | +++ | +++ |
| Distance vision | M | Visual acuity | + | + | + |
| Nonverbal processing | F | Detecting subtle variation in same-sex nonverbal cues | + | ++ | ++ |
| Face processing | F | Detecting subtle variation in same-sex facial expressions | + | ++ | ++ |
| Natural language | F | Fluency, grammatical structure of utterances, pragmatics | + | ++ | ++ |
| Vocal intonation | F | Detecting subtle change in intonation, especially in other females | + | ++ | ++ |
| Verbal learning | F | Accuracy in learning verbal associations | + | ++ | ++ |

**TABLE 5.1** Predicted Condition-Dependent Traits in Humans—cont'd

| Trait | Sex | Potential Measures | Life History Child | Adolescent | Adult |
|-------|-----|--------------------|--------------------|------------|-------|
| Verbal memory | F | Memory for learned associations, casual conversation | + | ++ | ++ |
| Theory of mind | B | Skill at assessing thoughts and emotions of same-sex competitors[g] | + | ++ | ++ |

Note: Sex, the sex predicted to show relatively greater vulnerability for the trait; B indicates the trait is expected to be condition dependent in both sexes, although with respect to sex-typical development of the trait. When the traits are similar but the specifics differ (e.g., face processing), they are listed separately for males and females. Life history indicates how vulnerability may change with development; + refers to small, sex-dependent vulnerabilities, whereas ++ and +++ refer to moderate to large, sex-dependent vulnerabilities.

[a]Heart rate recovery is rate of drop in heart rate after exercise, with faster drops to baseline indicating higher fitness (e.g., Shetler et al., 2001). Vital capacity is the volume of air that can be expelled from the lungs after a maximum breath, and is another common indicator of fitness and health (Blair, Kannel, Kohl, Goodyear, & Wilson, 1989).

[b]In modern populations, the importance of abdominal fat may be an inverted U shape, with individuals with low and high fat (i.e., obese) levels having the poorest fitness; the latter is unusual in traditional populations. Boys undergo an increase in fat in the triceps that precedes the onset of puberty (Frisancho, 1974). Triceps fat may then indicate condition in childhood for boys but not thereafter.

[c]This refers specifically to the relative distribution of fat; that is, disproportionately in the hips and buttocks relative to the upper body.

[d]Swelling signals infestation with some types of parasitic worm (e.g., Schistosomiasis japonica; Olveda et al., 1996).

[e]Rough-and-tumble play in adulthood would be in the context of parent-child play.

[f]This can be assessed using social network analyses of peer relationship patterns (e.g., Dijkstra, Cillessen, & Borch, 2013).

[g]Overall, this may be more condition dependent in girls and women than boys and men, especially with respect to individual relationships. Men may be better at making predictions in the context of larger-scale conflicts and politics.

the cognitive traits listed in Table 5.1 are not included in the table, but I provide discussion of brain regions that are candidates for sex-specific vulnerability in the associated text.

## Physical Traits

As with the northern elephant seal (*Mirounga angustirostris*) discussed in Chapter 2, intense physical competition and high reproductive skew (i.e., dominant males sire a disproportionate number of offspring) will result in the evolution of larger and physically stronger males than females. Applying this principle to the fossil record and our most likely ancestors produce the estimated

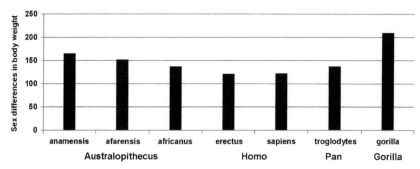

**FIGURE 5.2**    Estimated percent of male body weight to female body weight for various species of *Australopithecus*, *Homo*, and extant chimpanzees (*Pan troglodytes*) and gorillas (*Gorilla gorilla*).

sex differences in weight shown in Figure 5.2. About 4 million years ago, our male predecessors of the species *Australopithecus anamensis* were at least 50% larger than our female predecessors (Leakey, Feibel, McDougall, Ward, & Walker, 1998), a pattern that continued with *Australopithecus afarensis* and that may have lessened slightly with *Australopithecus africanus* (McHenry, 1992, 1994; McHenry & Coffing, 2000). The differences approached those seen in modern humans roughly 1.8 million years ago with the emergence of *Homo erectus* (early appearing specimens of the species are sometimes called *Homo ergaster*; McHenry & Coffing, 2000).

The magnitude of the sex difference in the Australopithecines suggests single male harems similar to those found in modern gorillas (*Gorilla gorilla*), and the decline in this difference could be the result of a lessening of male-male competition or a shift from one-on-one physical to coalitional competition (Duda & Zrzavý, 2013; Geary, Bailey, & Oxford, 2011; Plavcan & van Schaik, 1997; Plavcan, van Schaik, & Kappeler, 1995). The pattern of warfare found in traditional societies and the evolutionary change in brain size – suggesting dramatic changes in the complexity of human social groups (Alexander, 1989; Dunbar, 1998; Flinn, Geary, & Ward, 2005; Geary, 2005) – are consistent with the latter, as described in the next section.

Even the comparatively modest sex difference in the weight of modern humans belies substantial differences for some other physical traits (Tanner, 1990). The higher proportion of body fat in women (stored calories for breast feeding) than men biases the sex difference shown in Figure 5.2 (Kim et al., 2006); these differences were not likely present in Australopithecines, based on the low levels of body fat for primates in natural conditions (Dufour & Sauther, 2002). For healthy young adults, the differences in lean muscle mass and strength, especially in the upper body, are at a level found in modern gorillas; that is, there is little overlap in the distributions of males and females on many of these measures (Lassek & Gaulin, 2009; Pheasant, 1983; Tanner, 1990). There are also skeletal differences resulting in broader shoulders, and longer forearms and legs in men than women (Tanner, 1990); the 13 cm (~5 in.) sex difference in height is quite large, and due in part to the comparatively longer legs of men than women.

The sex differences in adulthood follow from a developmental pattern common to primates with intense male-male competition; the developmental pattern is also common to many other species with intense male-male competition or exacting female choice, as Darwin (1871) noted (see p. 297, vol. 2). In these species, males and females are more similar than different during the juvenile years (i.e., childhood), and males show an extended or exaggerated pubertal growth spurt during which most of the physical differences found in adults emerge (Leigh, 1996). As a telling contrast, for monogamous species with reduced physical competition, such as the common marmoset (*Callithrix jacchus*), males and females show similar patterns of physical development and are about the same size as adults (Leigh, 1995).

For people, the physical changes that emerge during adolescence are dramatic. At 9 years of age, boys have about 8% more muscle than girls (Kim et al., 2006). During the next 6 years, boys' lean muscle mass doubles whereas girls' increases about 50%. At this point (i.e., 15 years), boys have about 70% more muscle tissue than girls, differences that increase over the next several years because muscle growth is complete in girls and continues for at least 3 more years in boys (Tanner, 1990). Nine-year-old girls have about 25% more fat than boys but this increases to 60% more fat over the next 6 years (Kim et al., 2006). The facial features that women find attractive in men (e.g., prominent jaw and cheek bones; Cunningham, Barbee, & Pike, 1990) also emerge during this time, but there are less marked changes in girls' faces; "in some girls scarcely any detectable spurt in face dimensions occurs at all" (Tanner, 1990, p. 68). The minor changes result in the retention of the youthful appearance that men find attractive in women's faces (Cunningham, 1986). Over the course of puberty "boys [also] develop larger hearts ... larger lungs, higher systolic blood pressure, lower resting heart rate, a greater capacity for carrying oxygen in the blood, and a greater power of neutralizing the chemical products of muscular exercise" (Tanner, 1990, p. 74).

Boys' and men's key physical traits that are predicted to be vulnerable to stressors are shown in the upper section of Table 5.1. These are traits related to male-male competition or female choice during our evolutionary history (Geary, 2010), and as such they are predicted to be more vulnerable to stressors in boys and men than girls and women, particularly during pubertal development. During childhood, exposure to chronic stressors (e.g., parasite infestation, poor nutrition) should result in small but more consistent effects on boys' than girls' height, muscle mass, physical fitness, and overall physical condition (fat and muscle reserves relative to height). Upper body fat and lower body fat are listed separately because the former is more readily available than the latter as a fast source of energy during physical exertion (Cashdan, 2008; Ross, Rissanen, Pedwell, Clifford, & Shragge, 1996). Given this and boys' and men's greater physical activity, the modest upper body fat reserves, particularly in the abdomen, may be important components of physical condition. Moreover, toward the end of childhood boys but not girls show an increase in upper arm body fat that precedes the onset of pubertal growth and thus may be more susceptible to stressors in boys than girls during late childhood and early adolescence; girls in contrast show steady increases in arm fat and exceed that of boys during adolescence and adulthood (Frisancho, 1974).

As boys move into puberty, the modest effects of childhood stressors on these traits is expected to become quite large should the stressors continue into adolescence or new ones emerge. During this life history stage the relative effects of stressors on these traits is expected to be much larger for boys than for same-age girls. Vulnerability is expected to continue into adulthood for traits that do not involve physical growth, such as physical fitness, but the consequences of exposure to developmental stressors should remain evident. As adults, these men are likely to be shorter, less muscular, in worse physical condition, and evidence a less masculine skeletal structure than unexposed men, with much smaller differences between exposed and unexposed women. The skeletal traits would include facial features (e.g., cheekbones and chin), narrower shoulder breadth, and shorter bones related to throwing projectiles, such as the ulna and radius (i.e., forearm; Gindhart, 1973).

## Behavioral Traits

Following Irons's (1979) proposal that men's cultural success – their success in achieving control over culturally important resources (e.g., cows, camels, or cash) and social influence – predicts their reproductive success, elsewhere I discuss how male-male competition can be expressed differently in different social contexts (Geary, 2010; see also von Rueden, Gurven, & Kaplan, 2011). To make predictions about condition-dependent traits, however, the focus needs to be on competition in traditional contexts; specifically, contexts in which evolved forms of competition are not influenced by formal laws, policing, and customs (e.g., socially imposed monogamy) that result in the suppression of the associated behaviors. In these societies, successful men are polygynous and unsuccessful men never reproduce (Betzig, 1986, 2012; Murdock, 1981), the same dynamic described for the northern elephant seal and that found for more than 95% of other mammalian species (Clutton-Brock, 1989).

The nature of male-male competition under these conditions is well documented in the ethnological and archeological records (Chagnon, 1988, 1997; Chagnon & Macfarlan, 2015; Ember, 1978; Keeley, 1996; Walker & Bailey, 2013; White & Burton, 1988), and essentially involves one-on-one physical and political competition to achieve dominance within the male social hierarchy and cooperation with in-group members to better compete against coalitions of other males (i.e., out-groups). Chagnon's studies of the Yanomamö, who live in the Amazonian jungle (Venezuela), illustrate men's within-group struggles. These

social dynamics include frequent social displays and physical aggression to resolve disputes, often over sexual infidelity, and to establish or maintain social
dominance. As with other animals, disputes begin with relatively benign displays
of status and strength and escalate only if these displays do not resolve the issue
(Chagnon, 1997; Maynard Smith & Price, 1973). Escalation involves forms of
physical aggression that are consistent with the above-described sex differences
in upper body build and strength; the aggression ranges from chest pounding to
club fights to machete fights (using the flat part of the blade). The goal is not to
kill the opponent – a within-group ally in the context of between-group warfare –
but to cause sufficient injury to make him withdraw from the duel.

Whereas within-group physical aggression is typically regulated by rules
to ensure no one dies, although this does happen at times, there are often no
such restraints when it comes to between-group competition. In fact, the explicit goal is often to kill one or more men from a competing village. In a review of these dynamics, Keeley (1996) found that ambushes and raids occur
near continuously or frequently in about 70% of hunter-gatherer societies and
even more frequently in agricultural and pastoral societies; peaceful societies
tend to be relatively isolated or politically subjugated to larger groups. These
raids often involve ambushing men (sometimes women, although this is usually
incidental) and killing them with the use of projectile weapons, including spears
and bows and arrows. Across these societies and well into the history of Western
civilization, between 15% and 30% of men died at the hands of other men during some form of duel, raid, ambush, or larger-scale conflict (Daly & Wilson,
1988; Keeley, 1996; MacFarlan, Walker, Flinn, & Chagnon, 2014; Pinker, 2011;
Walker & Bailey, 2013). Examples of associated mortality rates in a few traditional societies are shown in Figure 5.3.

In these contexts, success in male-male competition includes not only the
physical competencies noted above, but also the social skills needed to integrate
into a coalition as well as the ability to tolerate pain and remain calm in the face
of grave social threats. As a Yanomamö warrior and headman, Kaobawä related
to Napoleon Chagnon, "Never show fear to your enemy! Be strong and calm.
The moment you reveal that you are afraid, you are in mortal danger! That is
when your enemy will kill you" (Chagnon, 1997, p. 256). There is in fact considerable research showing sex differences in emotional expression that supports Kaobawä's claim. Men generally have more muted emotional responses
than women, and when they do respond they are more likely to mask their feelings than are women (Gross & John, 1998). The one consistent exception is
that men are more likely than women to threaten to (e.g., through facial expressions) or engage in actual behavioral aggression when provoked (Archer, 2004;
Knight, Guthrie, Page, & Fabes, 2002; Reed, DeScioli, & Pinker, 2014). From
this perspective, much of the hazing that occurs within men's groups and as part
of modern military training function to test men's ability to cope with pain and
stress while remaining focused on the task at hand, as well as to promote unity
within the group (Browne, 2007, 2012).

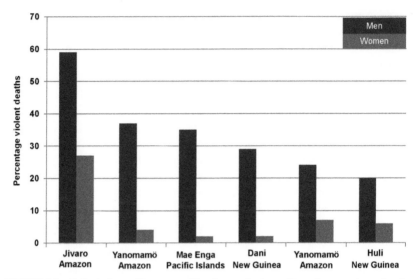

**FIGURE 5.3** Estimated mortality rates resulting from ambushes, raids, or larger-scale warfare for six traditional societies. The two estimates for the Yanomamö are for different groups. *Based on data presented in Keeley (1996).* (See the color plate section.)

These forms of behavioral competition are presaged by well-documented sex differences in play fighting and engagement in coalitional play during childhood; the latter will manifest as self-initiated (e.g., not initiated by parents or teachers) engagement in team sports. By the time they are 3 years old, boys in all societies in which it has been studied begin to enthusiastically engage in rough-and-tumble play, or play fighting (Eibl-Eibesfeldt, 1989; Maccoby, 1988; Whiting & Edwards, 1973, 1988). The sex difference is most evident with groups of three or more children and without adult supervision (Maccoby, 1988; Pellegrini, 1995). In these situations, groups of boys engage in various forms of playful physical assaults and wrestling three to six times more frequently than do groups of same-age girls (DiPietro, 1981; Maccoby, 1988). These activities peak between the ages of 8 and 10 years, at which time boys spend about 10% of their free time in play fighting or related forms of roughhousing (Pellegrini & Smith, 1998). As is common in other species with physical male-male competition, as boys move from juvenility to adolescence, the roughness of the play intensifies and the line between play and outright physical aggression blurs and begins to influence social dominance and attractiveness to adolescent girls (Pellegrini & Bartini, 2001).

In keeping with coalitional competition in traditional societies, boys also show a preference for group-level over dyadic activities as early as 3 years of age (Benenson, 1993, 2014), show a strong bias against members of competing groups by 5 years (Yee & Brown, 1992), and consistently form larger groups than girls by 6 years (Rose & Rudolph, 2006). During this play, boys learn how to coordinate their activities and work as a team, typically in the context of competition against other groups. Boys and men self-organize as coalitions about three times as often as girls and women (Deaner, Geary, et al., 2012, Deaner, Goetz, Shattuck, & Schnotala, 2012; Lever, 1978), and show much more intergroup stability than do the groups of girls and women (Parker & Seal, 1996). Other behavioral differences that emerge during this time and are often expressed in competitive contexts include running, jumping, and throwing projectiles; these differences emerge early in development and become quite large by adulthood (Thomas & French, 1985).

Some of the key behavioral traits that are associated with male-male competition and that also influence female choice are shown in the middle section of Table 5.1. Obviously, men are expected to display physical aggression or competence (e.g., strength, agility) as a means to increase or maintain social status within the male hierarchy; again, this pertains to societies in which overt aggression is not actively suppressed by third parties (e.g., police). These will typically be accompanied by displays of aggression and lack of fear, as conveyed in verbal threats, facial expressions, and vocal intonation (Puts, Apicella, & Cárdenas, 2012; Reed et al., 2014). The tendency to display physical competencies and aggression, as well as facial, vocal, and other signals of social dominance (e.g., body posture) are all predicted to be condition-dependent traits and thus vulnerable to disruption by exposure to stressors. Exposure to chronic stressors should also disrupt boys' and men's ability to form male-typical social networks and goal-oriented relationships, reduce their physical activity levels, and compromise competencies related to the use of projectile weapons, such as throwing distance, velocity, and accuracy.

Developmentally, these would manifest as reductions in rough-and-tumble and group-level competitive play. The psychological literature on social relationships, however, is generally biased toward women (e.g., Taylor, Klein, Lewis, et al., 2000, Taylor, Klein, Minich, & Hack, 2000); specifically, healthy relationships often are defined in terms of the intimacy and disclosure common among girls and women, and boys' and men's relationships are often seen as somehow "deficient." One consequence is a poor understanding of the mechanisms that promote boys' and men's relationships (Geary, Byrd-Craven, Hoard, Vigil, & Numtee, 2003; Geary & Flinn, 2002), and more practically for our purposes insufficient details on how to best assess how stressors might affect the associated social competencies. There are nevertheless studies of the relation between stressors (e.g., childhood abuse) and the overall quality of relationships with peers that are covered in the next chapter. Likewise, there are studies of the relation between overall differences in engagement in sex-typed play – but not specific activities (e.g., frequency of play fighting) – that provide a useful test of the vulnerability hypothesis; specifically, that exposure to stressors (e.g., toxins) will more strongly disrupt boys' than girls' engagement in sex-typical play.

Moving into adolescence and adulthood, exposure to chronic stressors should disrupt men's ability to maintain emotional composure in the face of threats. The result is a counterintuitive prediction given the sex differences in emotional expression, favoring women, and in anxiety and depression. Beginning in adolescence, girls and women experience more frequent and severe forms of anxiety and depression than do same-age boys and men (Caspi et al., 2014; Kessler et al., 2005; Nolen-Hoeksema, 1987), and as elaborated below in many situations react to some stressors more intensely than do boys and men (e.g., Leadbeater, Blatt, & Quinlan, 1995). My prediction here is that exposure to chronic stressors will affect the ability of both sexes to emotionally cope with threats and conflict, but relative to sex-specific norms the effects will be larger for boys and men than for girls and women. Adolescence might be a particularly risky time, as male-male competition begins to intensify (Wilson & Daly, 1985) and the brain regions that enable emotional composure under threat show rapid, sex-specific changes (next section).

## Brain and Cognitive Traits

Psychologists have been studying cognitive sex differences for more than a century (e.g., Burt & Moore, 1912; for summary, see Ellis et al., 2008) and differences in brain anatomy and functions for decades (e.g., Wada, Clark, & Hamm, 1975), but unfortunately very little of this research has been informed by sexual selection (Halpern, 2000; Kimura, 1999). The condition-dependent expression of cognitive abilities and supporting brain systems should be, in theory, most evident for evolved domains, and thus distinguishing evolved from nonevolved, largely school-taught academic abilities is an important consideration (Geary, 1995). For instance, sex differences in evolutionarily recent domains, such as mathematics or reading, are well studied, of practical importance in the modern world, but are at best indirect measures of our evolutionary history (Geary, 1996). For this reason, I did not include school-taught abilities in my reviews of the condition-dependent cognitive competences and associated brain regions in Chapter 7.

Figure 5.4 presents a functional taxonomy of domains of mind that are likely to be evolved and thus provides a framework for identifying human vulnerabilities in brain and cognition (see Geary, 2005, 2010). These are universal cognitive competences that are organized around the domains of folk psychology, folk biology, and folk physics. These competencies represent the basic skills needed to negotiate social relationships, extract resources from the ecology (e.g., through hunting), and navigate in and manipulate (e.g., as in making tools) the physical world (e.g., Baron-Cohen, 1995; Baron-Cohen, Wheelwright, Stone, & Rutherford, 1999; Gallistel, 1990; Gelman, 1990; Medin & Atran, 1999; Pinker, 1994; Spelke, Breinlinger, Macomber, & Jacobson, 1992). Boys and girls and men and women have some level of competence in all of the domains shown in Figure 5.4, but there are several areas in which one sex or the other has well-documented advantages. As with physical and behavioral sex differences, cognitive sex differences are generally modest during childhood and become larger during adolescence (e.g., Matthews, 1992). My focus here is largely on

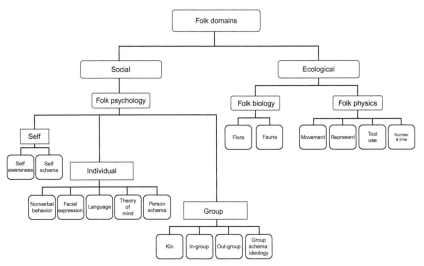

**FIGURE 5.4**   Evolved modular systems in the domains of folk psychology, folk biology, and folk physics.

boys' and men's advantages in many of the folk physics domains, and below on girls' and women's advantages in the individual-level, folk psychological domains. However, before turning to folk physics, I highlight several social-cognitive competencies and biases that should facilitate male-male competition in traditional contexts.

## Folk Psychology

As we cover below, girls and women have an advantage over boys and men in many areas of folk psychology, including detecting subtle variation in nonverbal behavior and facial expressions (Hall, 1984; Hall & Matsumoto, 2004; McClure, 2000; Rosenthal, Hall, DiMatteo, Rogers, & Archer, 1979). One consistently found exception is detection of anger in other males, especially grown men and when the anger is directed toward them, as with direct eye contact (Dimberg & Öhman, 1996; Rotter & Rotter, 1988; Williams & Mattingley, 2006). Boys and men also have more extreme biases that favor their group and disfavor other groups, especially in the context of between-group competition (Sidanius & Ekehammar, 1983; Sidanius, Pratto, & Mitchell, 2001). These biases manifest as a sex difference, favoring boys and men, in sensitivity to the relative dominance of competing groups, pressure on in-group members to adhere to social norms, and in cooperation with and support of other in-group members (Davis, Cheng, & Strube, 1996; Towson, Lerner, & de Carufel, 1981; Van Vugt, De Cremer, & Janssen, 2007; Van Vugt & Spisak, 2008).

These are cognitive competencies and biases that will be important for supporting engagement in one-on-one and coalitional competition, as I have previously outlined (Geary, 2010). The point here is that the expression of these traits should not only be condition dependent in boys and men (Table 5.1), they provide an important contrast to the predicted condition-dependent social-cognitive traits in girls and women (below).

## Folk Physics

There are multiple aspects of male-male competition in traditional societies that depend on enhanced visuospatial abilities (Geary, 2010). In these societies, men's travel ranges as related to hunting and between-village relations (i.e., either politics or warfare) are 2–4 times larger than those of women (MacDonald & Hewlett, 1999); the same is true in the personal travel of men and women in modern metropolitan areas and for the play ranges of boys and girls in traditional and modern societies (Ecuyer-Dab & Robert, 2004; Matthews, 1992; Whiting & Edwards, 1988). In the same way that larger territories are associated with better spatial abilities in meadow vole (*Microtus pennsylvanicus*, Chapter 2) males than females, men's larger range sizes have resulted in the evolution of enhanced navigational and related abilities relative to those of women. As noted in Table 5.1, these differences are found during actual way finding (i.e., real-world navigating) and in experimental measures, such as navigating in a virtual maze or recalling the geometric location of landmarks on a map (Choi & Silverman, 2003; Coluccia, Iosue, & Brandimonte, 2007; Galea & Kimura, 1993; Holding & Holding, 1989; Silverman et al., 2000).

As noted, men's upper body is well designed for the use of projectile weapons. The effective use of such weapons requires the ability to identify targets and accurately track the movement of objects as they travel through space. Tracking is important for both hitting targets, especially moving ones, and to avoid being hit by projectiles launched by others – the latter is a defensive skill that suggests men's use of projectile weapons first evolved in the context of male-male competition and was only later used in hunting (see Geary, 2010). Important supporting skills include the ability to detect moving objects at a distance against background objects, and objects in embedded foliage. Empirical studies confirm boys' and men's predicted advantages over girls and women in the identification of obscured objects, as well as in throwing accuracy, estimating when an object moving toward them will hit them, and for the defensive dodging or blocking of such objects (Cashdan, Marlowe, Crittenden, Porter, & Wood, 2012; Peters, 1997; Peters, Lehmann, Takahira, Takeuchi, & Jordan, 2006; Schiff & Oldak, 1990; Voyer, Voyer, & Bryden, 1995; Watson & Kimura, 1991). I list examples of some associated traits in Table 5.1, most of which are easy to assess with currently available paper-and-pencil and experimental tests (e.g., Peters et al., 1995; Vandenberg & Kuse, 1978).

## Brain

Along with traditional neurobiological and neuropsychological studies, brain imaging research has contributed greatly to our understanding of the neural systems that underlie many cognitive and social competencies (e.g., Cacioppo et al., 2002), including some sex differences (Gur et al., 1999; Ingalhalikar et al., 2014; Leonard et al., 2008; McGlone, 1980). The majority of the latter studies, however, have not been informed by sexual selection and thus our understanding of the brain systems underlying sex differences in folk abilities is in its infancy. Still, enough is known to enable inferences about potential human condition-dependent brain systems that may be analogous to those described for birdsong in Chapter 3 and spatial navigation in Chapter 4.

One such system is shown in Figure 5.5 and includes interconnected portions of the amygdala (e.g., triggers fear in threatening situations), hippocampus (e.g., important for memory of the threat and associated emotions), and the medial prefrontal cortex (regulates amygdala and hippocampal responses) that contribute to people's ability to regulate emotional reactions under stressful conditions (Bremner, 2006; Etkin & Wager, 2007). From an evolutionary perspective, the fear and anxiety that can be produced by this system are critical to the behavioral avoidance of threats, including inherent responses to predators and conspecifics as well as acquired fears (e.g., Öhman, 2002). In the context of male-male competition, avoidance of social threats would undermine status striving and, as Kaobawä stated, expressing fear during confrontations with other males could be very risky and at the very least would result in a loss of status (Winegard, Winegard, & Geary, 2014). The associated selection pressures would favor a dampening of the responsiveness of the amygdala and hippocampus to threats and enhancement of the prefrontal regions involved in inhibiting such responses.

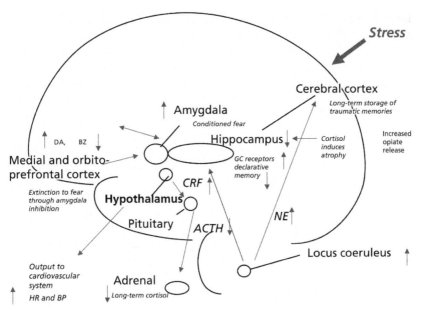

**FIGURE 5.5** The key integrated brain regions involved in stress regulation. *From Traumatic stress: Effects on the brain.* Dialogues in Clinical Neuroscience, *by J. D. Bremner, p. 447, Copyright 2006. Reprinted with permission of the author.* (See the color plate section.)

In fact, there are important sex differences in this system that are consistent with this evolutionary prediction. Stanton, Wirth, Waugh, and Schultheiss (2009) found that testosterone levels in men, but not women, are associated with reduced amygdala activation and increased medial prefrontal activation when processing angry faces, suggesting muted fear and stress responses in men (Rubinow et al., 2005). The hormone changes that occur during puberty result in an increase in the size of boys' hippocampus and amygdala and a decrease in the size of these regions in girls (Bramen et al., 2011; Neufang et al., 2009). These changes are coincident with the emergence of girls' heightened risk for anxiety disorders (or risk avoidance) and an escalation of boys' aggression, risk taking, and status striving (Kessler et al., 2005; Wilson & Daly, 1985).

In other words, this system is a prime candidate for underpinning the prediction that men's emotional composure is a condition-dependent psychological trait (Table 5.1).

The brain regions that support some of the cognitive traits described in Table 5.1 are also reasonably well understood. Whereas some areas of the hippocampus are important for memory formation and in the above example fear conditioning – remembering the threat context and experiencing fear in that context – other areas are important for spatial learning and memory (O'Keefe & Nadel, 1978), as we covered in previous chapters. The right parietal cortex (area 7, Figure 5.6) also contributes to the ability to mentally represent and navigate in large-scale space (Maguire et al., 1998; O'Keefe & Nadel, 1978; Spiers et al., 2001). Locating objects in space engages parts of the parietal cortex as well as parahippocampal areas (areas surrounding the hippocampus; e.g., area 27, Figure 5.6) and part of the fusiform gyrus (area 37, Figure 5.6; Ekstrom et al., 2003); the latter is engaged in object identification and naming. The detection of and behaviorally reacting to objects moving in space involve the coordination of the spatial location and attentional-control regions of the parietal cortex (e.g., areas 7, 40, Figure 5.6) with areas of the visual (e.g., area 19, Figure 5.6) and motor cortices (e.g., area 4, Figure 5.6; Milner & Goodale, 1995; Scott, 2004).

There are subtle sex differences in the architecture of most of these brain regions and in patterns of brain activation when engaged in spatial tasks (Amunts et al., 2007; Goldstein et al., 2001; Sowell et al., 2007). For instance, in a large brain imaging study, Colom et al. (2013) found sex differences in the size of the left and right hippocampus, favoring men, and sex differences in the relation between hippocampal volume and performance on cognitive measures of spatial abilities. Overall, a larger right hippocampus was associated with better spatial abilities in men, and was related to performance on measures of spatial reasoning and working memory. Amunts et al. (2007), as another example, found that men had more volume and surface area in the motion-detection region of the right hemisphere (parts of areas 19, 37, and 39, Figure 5.6) than did women. The right motion-detection region might also have more connections to other brain regions in men than women, including the spatial attention areas of the right parietal cortex (Posner, 1994) and to other regions that support behaviorally

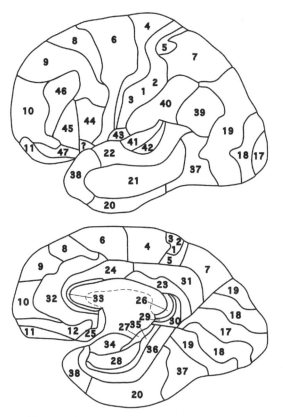

**FIGURE 5.6**    Maps of Brodmann's (1909) areas of the human neocortex. Illustration by Mark Dubin.

responding to and acting on the external world (Jeannerod, 2003; Milner & Goodale, 1995). These are brain regions that would support men's advantages in skill at tracking and reacting to objects moving in space.

All of these regions are candidates for sex differences in condition-dependent neural traits. Indeed, Teicher, Anderson, and Polcari (2012) found that higher childhood stressors were associated with modestly lower hippocampal volumes and weaker connections between the hippocampus and other areas of the brain associated with navigation and spatial working memory, but they did not assess sex differences; analogously, Lemaire et al. (2000) found that exposure to prenatal stress disrupted hippocampal development and spatial learning in male rats (*Rattus norvegicus*). The point here is there are specific brain regions whose development and functioning can be identified a *priori* – those that support the behavioral and cognitive traits listed in Table 5.1 – as being potentially vulnerable to sex-specific disruption by exposure to stressors. Unfortunately, this hypothesis has not been tested for most of these regions, but I provide an example of how this can be done in Chapter 7.

## VULNERABILITY IN GIRLS AND WOMEN

As with boys and men, descriptions of physical, behavioral, and cognitive traits that are sexually or socially selected in women and thus potentially vulnerable to stressors are found in Table 5.1. From a traditional perspective on sexual selection and parenting, as described in Chapter 2, female-female competition and male choice follow from men's investment in children (Geary, 2000). However, given that marriage partners are typically chosen by parents or other kin in traditional societies (Apostolou, 2007; Walker, Hill, Flinn, & Ellsworth, 2011), the opportunity for female-female competition over mates may be diminished – males must still compete to gain status or resource control before parents will consider them attractive partners for their daughters (e.g., Borgerhoff Mulder, 1990). This situation might also lessen the influence of female choice and male choice of mating partners. Nevertheless, there is amble opportunity for competition and choice even with arranged marriages. These can manifest in the context of extramarital relationships, which are more likely with arranged marriages than free choice marriages (Scelza, 2011), and in the context of polygynous marriages (Geary et al., 2014). In the latter, competition among cowives for the resources and attention of their husband is rife and has reproductive consequences (Jankowiak, Sudakov, & Wilreker, 2005; Strassmann, 1997). Of course, female-female competition as well as female choice and male choice blossom in the absence of arranged marriages, as would be expected of evolved biases and preferences (Buss, 1988, 1989; Buss & Shackelford, 1997; Kenrick & Keefe, 1992).

### Physical Traits

Girls and women do not physically assault one another, either playfully or during an actual conflict, anywhere near as often as boys and men, although they do so at times. When it occurs, physical aggression among women is typically seen in contexts with very scarce resources (e.g., a limited number of successful men) and even in these situations the violence is not as harmful as that among men (Campbell, 1995, 2002; Daly & Wilson, 1988). Physical competition among women is more likely to be expressed through the enhancement of traits that influence men's mate choices (Li, 2007), and the derogation of these same traits in competitors (Buss, 1988; Cashdan, 1993; Jonason, 2007). These are traits related to women's facial and body attractiveness, shown in Table 5.1, and are indicators of fertility, especially in populations without modern medical care.

The facial traits that men find attractive include relatively large eyes, prominent cheekbones, and a large smile area (Cunningham, 1986; Puts, Jones, & DeBruine, 2012), features that reflect a combination of youth and sexual maturity. These are cues to a woman's age and thus her fertility, which is low in the teen years, peaks in the middle 20s, and declines to near zero by 45 years (Menken, Trussell, & Larsen, 1986). Women's facial attractiveness and perceived health is also influenced by skin color and carotenoid levels within the skin (Boelsma et al., 2003; Coetzee et al., 2012; Fink, Grammer, & Matts, 2006; Stephen, Coetzee, & Perrett, 2011). In natural populations, parasitic infections are common and often cause noticeable skin lesions on the face or other body areas. For instance, Dreyfuss et al. (2000) found that women infected with hook-worms (e.g., *Ancylostoma duodenale*; *Necator americanus*) were iron deficient and at elevated risk of anemia (see also Brooker, Hotez, & Bundy, 2008). Iron-based anemia increases the odds of premature birth, low birth weight, and poor infant health (Allen, 2000), and results in a pale, unhealthy looking skin tone.

These parasites also affect men's appearance and health, but the social and psychological effects appear to be more costly for women than for men, including lower marriage prospects for women (Amazigo, 1994; Brieger, Oshiname, & Ososanya, 1998). In a review of these consequences in traditional societies, Litt, Baker, and Molyneux (2012) concluded that generally, "[men] become concerned about sexual performance and economic prospects, whereas women express worries about life chances and marriage" (p. 197). Holm, Esmann, and Jemec (2004) found that adolescent girls and women with skin diseases re-ported a lower quality of life than similarly affected boys and men, especially if the disease was in a visible area of the body, specifically, face, neck, or hands.

The body features that men find attractive in women include a waist-to-hip ratio (WHR) of 0.7; that is, relatively large hips and a small abdomen, along with symmetric, youthful looking breasts (Møller et al., 1995; Rilling, Kaufman, Smith, Patel, & Worthman, 2009; Singh, 1993a,b). Men's preference for relative fat levels, however, varies from one culture to the next, with a preference for "plumper" women being common in societies with fluctuations in food availabil-ity (Anderson, Crawford, Nadeau, & Lindberg, 1992). Even in these societies, the preference for the 0.7 WHR is maintained; fat is distributed such that "plumper" but not obese women maintain this ratio. These traits have all been linked to women's fertility (Singh, 1993a; Jasieńska, Ziomkiewicz, Ellison, Lipson, & Thune, 2004; Zaadstra et al., 1993), the health and competence of their children (Pawlowski & Dunbar, 2005; Lassek & Gaulin, 2008), and their own long-term health (Barker, Osmond, Kajantie, & Eriksson, 2009; Yusuf et al., 2005).

Moreover, Kjetland et al. (2010) found that women with schistosomiasis, a common parasitic infection, were 3.5 times more likely to be infertile than uninfected women; treatment improves the chances of becoming pregnant (El-Mahgoub, 1982). Schistosomiasis often results in liver disease and enlarge-ment that in turn will increase the WHR and thereby lower women's attrac-tiveness (e.g., Olveda et al., 1996). Women's WHR can also be affected by vitamin D deficiencies early in life that in turn affect pelvic development and predict their children's later health (Barker et al., 2009).

## Behavioral Traits

Women might not physically beat on one another as often as men do, but they socially and psychologically attack one another at least as often if not more so than men do (Archer & Coyne, 2005; Card, Stucky, Sawalani, & Little, 2008;

Björkqvist, Osterman, & Lagerspetz, 1994; Feshbach, 1969; Grotpeter & Crick, 1996). This is called relational aggression and involves the use of gossip, rumors, and lies to sully the reputation, manipulate the friendships, and socially ostracize potential competitors. Although both sexes can be the target of relational aggression, the effects are more significant for girls and women than for boys and men; for the latter, verbal and social attacks eventually have to be backed up physically. A study of more than 2500 adolescents revealed that girls who are the victims of relational aggression are 2.6 times more likely to suffer from depression or anxiety than are girls who are not victimized or boys who are victimized (Bond, Carlin, Thomas, Rubin, & Patton, 2001). The risk for girls is particularly high if they lack social support from friends or family; this vulnerability continues into adulthood (Kendler, Myers, & Prescott, 2005). In another large study of adolescents, Leenaars, Dane, and Marini (2008) found that physically attractive girls, but not boys, were victimized more often than their less attractive peers; "a one standard deviation increase in physical attractiveness increased the odds of females being indirectly victimized by 35% ... and decreased the odds of males being victimized by 25%" (Leenaars et al., 2008, p. 410). These findings are consistent with women's use of relational aggression to attack sexual competitors and consistent with the importance of the above-described physical traits that influence women's attractiveness.

All of these studies, however, have been conducted in modern settings with socially imposed monogamy and without arranged marriages. In these contexts, female-female competition and male choice are clearly important. As noted, in polygynous cultures with arranged marriages, direct competition among women to find a mate is diminished but competition after they are married is heightened. Women in these contexts do not compete for a mate per se, but rather compete with cowives for access to material resources controlled by their husband, for the emotional and sexual attention of their husband, and for social or material resources (e.g., land) that will be inherited by their children (Jankowiak et al., 2005). The level of competition will vary with whether or not a cowife is a sister, the extent to which cowives must cooperate to produce food, and the relative ages of the wives (Jankowiak et al., 2005; White, 1988). Whatever the specifics, these women often have less healthy offspring and fewer surviving offspring than do monogamously married women, even when the overall level of resources available to children is the same or higher in polygynous than monogamous families (Amey, 2005; Josephson, 2002; Omariba & Boyle, 2007; Strassmann, 1997, 2011; Strassmann & Gillespie, 2002). Moreover, within polygynous marriages, dominant cowives often have more surviving children than subordinate cowives (Gibson & Mace, 2006).

It is not just their children who suffer. As with adolescent girls and young women in modern contexts, female-female competition undermines the well-being of women in polygynous marriages. In a review of the mental health of these women, Shepard (2012) concluded that in comparison to their monogamously married peers. Polygynously married women were at increased risk of heightened anxiety and depression, as well as more serious psychiatric disorders. Although not conclusive, their findings are consistent with Jankowiak et al.'s (2005) finding of nearly ubiquitous hostility and conflict among cowives across hunter-gatherer, agricultural, and other traditional societies. The reproductive effects of these continual stressors are not fully understood for humans, but there is some evidence that the result may be reduced fertility in some women (e.g., Buck Louis et al., 2011; Hjollund et al., 1999).

Friendships provide a critical buffer to the potential harm inflicted through relational aggression (Kendler et al., 2005), as well as a buffer to other stressors, such as child rearing (Taylor, Klein, Lewis, et al., 2000, Taylor, Klein, Minich, et al., 2000). Whereas boys' and men's friendships are typically embedded in the context of a larger group, girls' and women's friendships tend to be dyadic and exclusive; that is, they tend to be focused on one or two core relationships (Benenson, 2014; Eder & Hallinan, 1978; Lever, 1978; Maccoby, 1990, 1998; Rose & Rudolph, 2006). In comparison to boys and men, girls' and women's friendships are characterized by higher levels of emotional support, more frequent intimate exchanges (e.g., talking about their problems), and they are a more central source of help and guidance in solving social and other problems (Maccoby, 1990, 1998; Parker & Asher, 1993; Rose & Asher, 1999; Savin-Williams, 1987). Girls and women are more interpersonally engaged in the relationship and know more personal information about their friends than do boys and men (Markovits, Benenson, & Dolenszky, 2001).

Girls and women are more sensitive to the social-emotional cues of their partner (Buck, Savin, Miller, & Caul, 1972), and work harder to minimize perceived inequalities (Ahlgren & Johnson, 1979; Winstead, 1986). Conflicts of interest are of course common among friends of both sexes, but girls and women invest more in resolving these conflicts and attempt to do so through accommodation, compromise, and other socially constructive means (Parker & Asher, 1993; Rose & Asher, 1999). Despite the more subtle approach to conflict management, girls and women are more sensitive to personal slights on the part of their best friend, exhibit more friendship jealousy, and respond with more initial and lingering negative affect (e.g., sadness, anger) than do boys and men (e.g., Parker, Low, Walker, & Gamm, 2005; Whitesell & Harter, 1996). As a result, their friendships are more fragile; they are much more likely to permanently dissolve as a result of conflict, betrayal, or other stressors on the relationship (Benenson & Christakos, 2003; Lever, 1978). These former friends often engage in relational aggression, using information they gleaned during the relationship to undermine the social standing of their erstwhile friend.

The development of relational aggression and dyadic relationships mirrors that found for boys' play and social development. When boys are play fighting and forming competitive teams, girls are developing close, intimate dyadic friendships and engaging in much more family oriented play (e.g., doll play) than are boys (Eibl-Eibesfeldt, 1989; Pitcher & Schultz, 1983). Relational aggression emerges at about the same age as boys' play fighting, and as girls move into adolescence it increases in intensity and becomes focused on romantic relationships (Bond et al., 2001; Crick, Casas, & Mosher, 1997). As Pellegrini and Bartini (2001) found for physical dominance among boys, LaFontana and Cillessen (2002) found for girls. Dominant girls are those who effectively use relational aggression. These girls are socially visible and influential among other girls, and are considered attractive by boys (Smith, Rose, & Schwartz-Mette, 2010).

As shown in the behavioral section of Table 5.1, the prediction is that girls' and women's ability to effectively use relational aggression and their sensitivity to its use by other women will be condition dependent, as will their ability to maintain same-sex dyadic relationships. As I described for boys, assessment of many specific traits – for instance, skill at creating plausible deniability when aggressing against other girls – is not possible with the existing literature. Nevertheless, exposure to stressors is predicted to more broadly manifest as difficulties in women's use of social skills to negotiate female dominance hierarchies and friendships, and manifest developmentally by disruptions in peer relationships.

## Brain and Cognitive Traits

Girls' and women's use of relational aggression to control social dynamics that are important to them falls under sexual selection when the competition is directly over mates and social selection when cowives compete over control of their husband's resources (Geary et al., 2014). Either way, the associated competition is supported by the individual-level, folk psychological domains shown in Figure 5.4. Girls and women do indeed have advantages over boys and men in these domains, as would be expected for traits that have been elaborated by relational aggression over evolutionary time (Geary, 2010). The key here is that the development and functioning of these same traits should be vulnerable to exposure to stressors, as shown in the cognitive traits section of Table 5.1.

### Decoding Nonverbal Behavior and Facial Expressions

The subtlety of relational aggression, in comparison to men's physical aggression, places a premium on the ability to detect slight variations in nonverbal communication and facial expressions, and indeed girls and women have advantages in these areas over boys and men from infancy forward. These advantages are manifested by skill at reading emotional states conveyed in facial expressions, gesture, and body language and in generating nuance in the social use of these cues (Buck et al., 1972; Hall & Matsumoto, 2004; McClure, 2000; Rosenthal et al., 1979; van Beek & Dubas, 2008; Wagner, Buck, & Winterbotham, 1993). When assessed separately, girls' and women's advantages in these areas are modest, but substantial when all of the cues are presented simultaneously as would happen in a real-world social encounter (Hall, 1978; Rosenthal et al., 1979).

Consistent with trait elaboration through female-female competition, girls and women are more sensitive to the nonverbal cues and facial expressions of other females than to those of boys and men. As an example, Buck et al. (1972) found that dyads of women are more effective in expressing and reading the emotion cues of the other member of the pair, as signaled by changes in facial expression, than are dyads of men (also Rotter & Rotter, 1988). Rehnman and Herlitz (2006) found that 9-year-old girls have a better memory for faces than do boys, and that girls have an especially large advantage for recognizing the faces of other girls and women than the faces of boys and men; this same-sex memory bias is also found in adults (Rehnman & Herlitz, 2007). These findings appear to reflect a combination of girls and women allocating more attention to the processing of same-sex faces than boys and men, the greater sensitivity of girls and women to the emotion cues signaled by facial expressions and other nonverbal behaviors, and a greater expressiveness of the part of women than men (Herlitz & Rehnman, 2008; Hall, 1984). Whatever the cognitive mechanisms, sensitivity to subtle social cues expressed through body language and facial expressions, especially when conveyed by girls and women, is predicted to be condition dependent in girls and women.

## Language

Given the centrality of language to relational aggression, it is not surprising that girls and women have advantages over boys and men in many basic aspects of language production, comprehension, and the pragmatics of language (Anderson & Leaper, 1998; Kimura, 1999; Majeres, 2007; Shaywitz et al., 1995). The latter refers to the use of language in social contexts, and is often used by boys and men to express their desire for status and social dominance, especially if there is an audience (Anderson & Leaper, 1998; Leaper & Smith, 2004; Vigil, 2009); as noted, in the long run however, men's boasts, verbal dominance displays, and so forth have to be backed up by producing culturally important outcomes (e.g., large hunting gains) or physically.

The study of girls' and women's pragmatics has largely been with Western, relatively wealthy samples, and has highlighted their supportive and socially enabling uses of language (Maccoby, 1990). This usage is certainly an important part of girls' and women's ability to develop and maintain reciprocal friendships, but has largely overlooked girls' and women's aggressive use of language (see Campbell, 2002). Jankowiak et al.'s (2005) ethnographic review of the relations among cowives suggests that open verbal and sometimes physical hostility is common when a new cowife joins the family. Over time the open hostility tends to lessen and is replaced by simmering resentment and more subtle forms of aggression. The latter often involves women's use of language to subtly spread rumors, gossip, and lies to undermine their competitors, and often framed so as to enable some degree of plausible deniability should they be confronted by their victim.

The subtlety of women's relational aggression is one reason they often discuss and rehash social episodes with a best friend (Rose, Schwartz-Mette, Glick, Smith, & Luebbe, 2014). They do this to evaluate and decipher any potential hidden messages in what was said and how it was said (e.g., accompanying vocal tone or facial expressions). Of course, women also do this to better understand what their boyfriend or husband "really meant," but their greater sensitivity to the social cues of other women in comparison to those of men suggests that the selective context was female-female relationships not female-male relationships. In any case, the usefulness of rehashing and evaluating these experiences is dependent on a strong episodic memory (i.e., memory for personal experiences) and a strong verbatim recall of language, areas in which girls and women do in fact have advantages over boys and men (Herlitz, Nilsson, & Bäckman, 1997; Lewin, Wolgers, & Herlitz, 2001).

Girls and women also have advantages for other components of language including the length and quality of utterances, the ease and speed of articulating complex words and strings of words, the speed of retrieving individual words from long-term memory, and skill at discriminating basic language sounds from one another (Block, Arnott, Quigley, & Lynch, 1989; Halpern, 2000; Hampson, 1990; Majeres, 2007). There is also evidence that women process the prosody (e.g., emotional tone) of language more quickly and with less allocation of attention than do men (Schirmer, Kotz, & Friederici, 2002, 2005).

## Theory of Mind and Person Schema

Theory of mind represents the critical ability to make inferences about the intentions of other people and their beliefs and to infer whether the emotions or other states signaled by social cues are or are not an accurate reflection of the actual emotional state or intentions of the individual (Baron-Cohen, 1995; Leslie, Friedman, & German, 2004). The person schema is related to theory of mind, but is focused on knowledge about specific significant others, rather than the more general ability to make inferences about the internal states of others. In comparison to the research base on the other individual-level, folk psychological abilities shown in Figure 5.4, much less is known about sex differences in these areas.

Despite the sparse research base, I predict girls and women will have an advantage in some aspects of theory of mind and in the richness of personal information they are motivated to accrue about significant others. On the basis of the dynamics of relational aggression, girls and women should have advantages when it comes to understanding other girls' and women's thoughts, intentions, and feelings about significant relationships, including same-sex friendships. Boys and men, in contrast, should focus on competitors' thoughts and intentions as they relate to larger-scale groups and politics, and the competencies (e.g., physical skills) that would make them reliable and effective members of competitive coalitions or teams (Benenson, 1990; Geary et al., 2003). Rather than a focus on what the competitor is intending with respect to a few specific relationships, the focus is on how a potential competitor intends to organize larger, competitive groups. The theory of mind research that has focused on sex differences does not address these predictions.

At this time, studies that have examined sex differences in theory of mind suggest either no difference (Lucariello, Durand, & Yarnell, 2007), or that girls and women have a small advantage (e.g., Banerjee, 1997; Calero, Salles, Semelman, & Sigman, 2013). The tasks used in these studies are not particularly difficult, however, which will obscure any sex differences. Using relatively difficult and thus more sensitive theory of mind tasks, Bosacki (2000; Bosacki & Astington, 1999) found that three out of four adolescent girls were more skilled than the average same-age boy at making inferences about the thoughts, feelings, and social perspective of their peers (see also Ibanez et al., 2013). Benenson et al. (2013) found that women were more sensitive to social cues that signaled risk of social exclusion, a common goal with relational aggression. In a related study, the same research group found that women had higher heart rate increases when reading scenarios of social exclusion, suggesting higher risks and costs of social exclusion for women than men (Benenson, Markovits, Emery Thompson, & Wrangham, 2011).

Relational aggression is presumably most effective when it targets social and psychological vulnerabilities of the would-be victim and thus girls and women should be motivated to gather more personal information about others in their social sphere than boys and men. This hypothesis has not been broadly assessed, except in the context of friendships. In these relationships, girls and women do know more personal information about their friends than boys and men (Benenson, 1990; Markovits et al., 2001; Mehta & Strough, 2009; Swenson & Rose, 2003). This personal information is a key feature of the support that girls and women provide to one another in their dyadic friendships. At the same time, this is also information that can be used aggressively should the relationship disintegrate, as it often does (Benenson, 2014; Benenson & Christakos, 2003). Once the relationship has turned sour and often even before this, the personal information that was revealed during the friendship can now be used to socially manipulate and undermine the psychological and social well-being of their former friend (Campbell, 2002; Crick & Nelson, 2002). Of course, women can also pretend to develop a friendship as a means to gain this information and then use it aggressively.

## Brain

Girls' and women's folk-psychological abilities that I predict will be vulnerable to disruption by exposure to stressors are shown in Table 5.1. As with men's folk physics, some of the systems of brain regions that support the development and expression of these abilities are understood, but associated studies of sex differences have not been informed by sexual selection. Still, enough is known about of these systems to make several informed predictions, and more critically to reinforce the argument that the sexes not only differ in which brain systems are sensitive to stressors but also that these sex-specific vulnerabilities are predictable.

As described earlier, the amygdala is among the core brain systems involved in the processing of emotion-laden information and is structurally and functionally different in women and men (e.g., Goldstein et al., 2001; Kilpatrick, Zald, Pardo, & Cahill, 2006). The ventral (bottom) and medial (center) areas of the prefrontal cortex are also critical for the processing, evaluating, and responding to social-emotional information, as would be important in the context of relational aggression; these regions include areas 10, 11, 12, and 25 in Figure 5.6 (Adolphs, 2003). After correcting for the sex difference in brain size, the social-emotional processing areas of the prefrontal cortex are larger in women than in men (Goldstein et al., 2001; Gur, Gunning-Dixon, Bilker, & Gur, 2002); area 11 in Figure 5.6 may be especially large in women (Wood, Heitmiller, Andreasen, & Nopoulos, 2008). In addition to the sex differences in size of the amygdala (larger in men) and ventromedial prefrontal cortex (larger in women), these regions are interconnected differently in women and men (Tranel, Damasio, Denburg, & Bechara, 2005). There appears to be greater functional connectivity between these regions in the right hemisphere for men and the left hemisphere for women. The side bias may contribute to the sex difference in memory for the details of personal experiences, as vivid episodic memories are associated with activation of the left amygdala, as compared to memory for overall gist of the episode, which is associated with activation of the right amygdala (Cahill et al., 2001).

In a now classic study, Geschwind and Levitsky (1968) demonstrated that the planum temporale (processes speech sounds) is physically larger in the left temporal cortex than the comparable area in the right cortex for about two out of three people, but this asymmetry (i.e., left larger than right) is less pronounced and sometimes reversed in more women than men (McGlone, 1980; Wada et al., 1975). It appears that many basic language skills are represented in both hemispheres for many women but are largely represented in the left hemisphere for most men (e.g., Jaeger et al., 1998; Shaywitz et al., 1995); this may be one reason there are more white matter connections across the left and right hemisphere for women and more within hemisphere connections in men (Ingalhalikar et al., 2014). Moreover, women have several disproportionally large (after controlling for overall brain size) areas of the brain that support language processing (Good et al., 2001; Leonard et al., 2008; Sowell et al., 2007); some of these areas also support theory of mind.

In particular, areas of enhanced thickness in women correspond to the classic language area; that is, Wernicke's area, including the planum temporale in and around area 22 in Figure 5.6 (Sowell et al., 2007). The corresponding and nearby regions in the right hemisphere are also important for identifying specific people based on their voice (Formisano, De Martino, Bonte, & Goebel, 2008). Witelson, Glezer, and Kigar (1995) conducted a detailed analysis of the neuronal architecture of this area and found that women have a higher density of neurons in the input layers of this region but no sex difference for the output layers. It cannot be known with certainty from this study, but the sex difference in the input layers might provide women with an advantage in discriminating nuances in language sounds. In an unusually large brain imaging study, Leonard et al. (2008) found that the planum temporale was not only disproportionately larger in women than in men, it was large in women independent of overall brain size. For men, larger overall brain size was associated with larger areas throughout the cortex, including the planum temporale, but this was not the case for women. The raw size of this brain region was maintained in women, regardless of their overall brain size, consistent with a selection pressure that acts more strongly on this region in women than in men and that involves the use of language.

When integrated with the individual-level, folk psychological competencies that support relational aggression, several predictions emerge from these neural sex differences. The development and functioning of areas of the prefrontal cortex (e.g., area 11, Figure 5.6) and perhaps some specific nuclei of the amygdala that are important for detecting and responding to nuance in socially conveyed information will be more easily disrupted by exposure to stressors in girls and women than boys and men. The language system – specific brain regions and white matter connections between them – is a prime candidate for condition dependence in girls and women. Moreover, the basic language areas of both hemispheres develop prenatally and thus the nuances of girls' and women's competencies in this area might be particularly vulnerable to prenatal stressors (Kasprian et al., 2011; Wada et al., 1975).

## CONCLUSION

The goals of this chapter were to provide a brief overview of how competition and choice are expressed in our species, at least in traditional contexts, and to simultaneously identify traits that are candidates for condition-dependent expression and thus for heightened vulnerability. The 38 traits shown in Table 5.1 are not the only ones that are likely to show sex-specific vulnerabilities in humans (see Geary, 2010), but they do provide the core for their study. In the following chapters, I describe the results of my literature searches on how exposure to parasites, malnutrition, social stressors, and toxins can have sex-specific effects on the development and expression of many of the traits shown in Table 5.1. I took the same approach for our species as described for the many other species reviewed in the two previous chapters; specifically, once a study that assessed a sexually or socially selected outcome, such as height or language fluency, and some type of stressor (e.g., malnutrition or sexual abuse) was identified, the study was classified in terms of whether or not it provided evidence for condition dependence, whether there was a suitable contrast trait, life history stage when the stressor was experienced, and so forth.

The result is a more nuanced assessment of human vulnerability than that based on the traditional male vulnerability hypothesis (Greulich, 1951; Stini, 1969; Stinson, 1985), as I discussed in Chapter 1. One benefit of this traditional hypothesis has been the accumulation of a considerable literature on the effects of stressors on physical traits, which I cover in Chapter 6. At the same time, this approach has not been applied to the behavioral and cognitive traits listed in Table 5.1, much less a consideration of how girls and women might be vulnerable to stressors. As a consequence, there is little if any literature on the effects of stressors on sex differences in the expression of some of the traits listed in Table 5.1, such as peer network density, an issue that I return to in Chapter 8. There is nonetheless enough research to test the sex-specific vulnerabilities hypothesis for many of these traits, including spatial and language abilities that provides a proof of concept and lays the foundation for the design of more sensitive, theoretically informed assessments for future studies.

Chapter 6

# Human Vulnerability for Physical and Behavioral Traits

## Chapter Outline

To my frustration, there are few, sometime no studies of the relation between exposure to stressors and sex-specific vulnerabilities for many of the physical and behavioral traits listed in Table 5.1. Nevertheless, there are enough studies to demonstrate a number of sex-specific vulnerabilities that are important in and of themselves and that provide a critical proof of concept: Humans are no different than the many other species covered in previous chapters and like these species exposure to stressors can disrupt the development and expression of traits that have been exaggerated through sexual or social selection. I begin with physical traits related to competition and choice, as reviewed in Chapter 5, including height, pelvic development, fitness, fat reserves, facial structure, and skin complexion, among others. As we will see, there is strong evidence for sex-specific vulnerabilities for some of them and suggestive evidence for others. In the second part of the chapter, I move to behavioral traits but was limited to those in which there was at least some information on sex-specific vulnerabilities. These include children's engagement in sex-typical play and their relationships with other children, as well as factors that may compromise men's ability to psychologically cope with the stressors of male-male competition. Again, the evidence for sex-specific vulnerabilities is strong for some of these traits and suggestive for others.

Evolution of Vulnerability. http://dx.doi.org/10.1016/B978-0-12-801562-9.00006-5

## PHYSICAL VULNERABILITIES

Of the predicted condition-dependent physical traits listed in Table 5.1, I found relevant studies for boys' and men's height, muscle mass, physical fitness, fat reserves prior to the pubertal growth spurt and facial features, as well as for girls' and women's pelvic development, facial features, and skin attractiveness. Following the reviews of other species described in Chapters 3 and 4, my focus was on the potential for inbreeding, poor nutrition, parasite infestation, and toxin exposure to disrupt the development and expression of these traits; I also included studies that examined the relation between these traits and evolutionarily significant outcomes, such as reproductive success (e.g., Apicella, 2014) or are indicators of other traits related to competition or choice (e.g., facial features and physical aggressiveness; Carré & McCormick, 2008).

I also considered socioeconomic status (SES) as a potential risk factor, and included studies that provided direct comparisons of children from lower- and higher-status families (Bogin & MacVean, 1978; Garn, Shaw, & McCabe, 1978), as well as studies of children living in poverty and compared to standardized growth norms (McGarvey et al., 1992). The result of growing up in a lower SES family, especially in developing nations, is increased risk of exposure to parasites, inadequate calories, and poor nutrition, along with the stressors that are common to low social status in all nations (Adler et al., 1994). Natural variation in nutritional status includes measurement of well-established indicators of malnutrition, such as triceps skin fold thickness (Frisancho & Garn, 1971b), documented malnutrition (Graham, Adrianzen, Rabold, & Mellits, 1982), and direct measurement of or supplementation with calories or specific nutrients such as vitamin A (West, Djunaedi, Pandji, Tarwotjo, & Sommer, 1988), zinc (Castillo-Durán et al., 1994), or animal protein (Grillenberger et al., 2006).

### Skeletal Development

As we covered in Chapter 5, the sex differences in physical size, including height, are a strong indicator of physical male-male competition in our ancestors (Plavcan & van Schaik, 1997) and thus exposure to developmental stressors should affect boys' developing stature more severely than that of girls, in the same way stressors affect antler size in red deer (*Cervus elaphus*; Kruuk et al., 2002) and horn size in Alpine ibex (*Capra ibex*; Toïgo et al., 1999), among other previously discussed species (Table 4.5). The vulnerability of boys relative to girls, however, should be small prior to adolescence and large during adolescence, as I noted in Chapter 5. This life history prediction is consistent with the similar nutritional needs and growth patterns of boys and girls during childhood, and marked differences during pubertal development (Jacob & Nair, 2012; Tanner, 1990). Within an evolutionary context, the pattern also follows Darwin's (1871) observation that sex differences tend to be small prior to maturation and reproductive competition.

The same basic life history argument applies to bi-iliac width; that is, pelvic width in girls. One difference is that while male height has the clear characteristics of a sexually selected trait, the evolution of female pelvic width was probably influenced by natural (to accommodate increases in fetal head size) and sexual (i.e., male choice) selection. The associated prediction is that male height will be comparatively more sensitive to exposure to stressors than the developmental of female pelvic width, although the latter may be sensitive as well.

## Height

As is evident in Table 6.1, there is a long history of research on the relation between exposure to developmental stressors, such as poor nutrition, and children's growth. Previous reviews of this literature, however, have not taken advantage of evolutionary and comparative insights and as a result conflated stressors during childhood and adolescence. Conflating stressors across these developmental periods will result in an overestimation of boys' vulnerability during childhood and an underestimation during adolescence (e.g., Stinson, 1985). Indeed, the studies of the relation between exposure to stressors during childhood and sex differences in height suggest that boys are only slightly more vulnerable than girls. About a third of the studies indicate that boys' and girls' growth is equally compromised by poor nutrition or low SES (e.g., Frisancho et al., 1970; Martorell et al., 1984), as do four of the seven studies of the relation between parasite infestation or chronic infection and growth (e.g., Martorell, Yarbrough, Lechtig, Habicht, & Klein, 1975). In some cases, the nutritional or SES deficits had larger effects on girls' height than boys' height but in many of these cases girls were fed less than boys (Chen et al., 1981; Dewey, 1980, 1983). The latter indicates differences in parental investment rather than an increased physical vulnerability of girls. Nevertheless, about half of the studies indicate that poor nutrition and parasite infestation affects boys' growth more than girls' growth during childhood (e.g., Stoltzfus et al., 1997; Ulukanligil & Seyrek, 2004), potentially due to the great physical activity and thus caloric needs of boys than girls.

The pattern that emerges from research on adolescent growth, including studies that combined assessments of children and adolescents is clear-cut: Nearly all of these studies show that boys' growth is more vulnerable to disruption during pubertal development than girls' growth. The sex difference in vulnerability is related to SES (Dreizen et al., 1953), poor nutrition (Jardim-Botelho et al., 2008), anemia (Zemel et al., 2007), and infestation with parasites (McGarvey et al., 1992). It is not simply that boys need more calories than girls during pubertal development, there are also differences in their nutritional needs (Jacob & Nair, 2012; Prasad, 1985). As an example, several randomized control studies have found that zinc supplementation – much of zinc is naturally obtained through animal protein – improves the growth of boys more than that of girls in childhood (e.g., Castillo-Durán et al., 1994), but may be especially

**TABLE 6.1** Condition-Dependent Physical Traits in Boys and Men

| Species | Scientific Name | ST | Trait | CD | S | Contrast Trait | Effect | Life History | Manipulation | References |
|---|---|---|---|---|---|---|---|---|---|---|
| Human | *Homo sapiens* | N | Height | Y | B | Female height | C=T | Inbreeding | Inbreeding | Freire-Maia et al. (1983) |
| | | N | Height | Y | B | Female height | C=T | Inbreeding | Inbreeding | Schreider (1967) |
| | | N | Height | Y | M | BMI | C<T | Inbreeding | Inbreeding | Özener (2010) |
| | | N | Height | N | B | Female height | C=T | Inbreeding | Inbreeding | Neel et al. (1970) |
| | | N/T | Height | Y[a] | B | Female height | C<T | Prenatal | Toxin | Gladen, Ragan, and Rogan (2000) |
| | | F | Height | Y | B | Female height | C=T | Prenatal/childhood | Nutrition | Barrett, Radke-Yarrow, and Klein (1982) |
| | | N | Height | Y | B | Female height | C=T | Childhood | Birth length | Barker, Osmond, Forsén, Kajantie, and Eriksson (2005) |
| | | N | Height | Y | B | Female height | C<T | Childhood | Birth length | Barker et al. (2005) |
| | | N | Height | Y[b] | B | Female height | C>T | Childhood | SES | Dewey (1980) |
| | | N | Height | Y | M | Low SES male | C<T | Childhood | SES | Obert et al. (1994) |
| | | N | Height | Y[c] | B | Female height | C<T | Childhood | SES | Garn et al. (1978) |
| | | N | Height | Y | B | Female height | C=T | Childhood | SES | Frisancho, Garn, and Ascoli (1970) |

| Reference | | | | | | | | |
|---|---|---|---|---|---|---|---|---|
| Douglas and Simpson (1964) | SES | Childhood | C>T | Female height | B | N | Height | N |
| Dreizen, Currie, Gilley, and Spies (1953) | SES | Childhood | C=T | Female height | B | Y | Height | N |
| Ulukanligil and Seyrek (2004) | SES | Childhood | C<T | Female height | B | Y | Height | N |
| Bogin and MacVean (1978) | SES | Childhood | C<T | Female height | B | Y | Height | N |
| Cameron (1992) | SES | Childhood | C=T | Female height | B | Y | Height | N |
| Martorell, Leslie, and Moock (1984) | Diet/nutrition | Childhood | C=T | Female height | B | Y | Height | N |
| Chen, Huq, and d'Souza (1981) | Diet/nutrition | Childhood | C>T | Female height | B | Y[b] | Height | N |
| Abaheseen, Harrison, and Pearson (1981) | Diet/nutrition | Childhood | C>T | Female height | B | Y | Height | N |
| Dewey (1983) | Diet/nutrition | Childhood | C>T | Female height | B | Y[b] | Height | N |
| Graham et al. (1981) | Diet/nutrition | Childhood | C<T | Female height | B | Y | Height | N |
| Yarbrough, Habicht, Malina, Lechtig, and Klein (1975) | Diet/nutrition | Childhood | C=T | Female height | B | Y | Height | N |
| Frisancho, Guire, Babler, Borken, and Way (1980) | Diet/nutrition | Childhood | C=T | Female height | B | Y | Height | N |

*Continued*

**TABLE 6.1** Condition-Dependent Physical Traits in Boys and Men—cont'd

| Species | Scientific Name | ST | Trait | CD | S | Contrast Trait | Effect | Life History | Manipulation | References |
|---|---|---|---|---|---|---|---|---|---|---|
| | | N | Height | Y | B | Female height | C=T | Childhood | Diet/nutrition | Frisancho and Garn (1971a) |
| | | N | Height | Y | B | Female height | C<T | Childhood | Diet/nutrition | Graham et al. (1982) |
| | | N | Height | Y | B | Female height | C<T | Childhood | Diet/nutrition | Espinosa, Sigman, Neumann, Bwibo, and McDonald (1992) |
| | | F | Height | Y | B | Female height | C<T | Childhood | Diet/nutrition | Castillo-Durán et al. (1994) |
| | | F | Height | Y | B | Control male | C<T | Childhood | Diet/nutrition | Walravens, Krebs, and Hambidge (1983) |
| | | F | Height | N | B | Female height | C=T | Childhood | Diet/nutrition | West et al. (1988) |
| | | F | Height | Y[d] | B | Female height | C<T | Childhood | Diet/nutrition | Grillenberger et al. (2006) |
| | | F | Height | Y | B | Female height | C<T | Childhood | Diet/nutrition | Donnen et al. (1998) |
| | | N | Height | N | B | Female height | C=T | Childhood | Diet/nutrition | Greulich (1951) |
| | | N | Height | Y | B | Female height | C=T | Childhood | Infection/parasite | Martorell, Yarbrough et al. (1975) |
| | | N | Height | N | M | Unexposed male | C=T | Childhood | Infection/parasite | Nokes, Grantham-McGregor, Sawyer, Cooper, and Bundy (1992) |

| Reference | | | | | | | | |
|---|---|---|---|---|---|---|---|---|
| Stephenson, Latham, Adams, Kinoti, and Pertet (1993) | Infection/parasite | Childhood | C<T | Untreated male | M | Y | Height | F |
| Donnen et al. (1998) | Infection/parasite | Childhood | C=T | Female height | B | N | Height | F |
| Stoltzfus, Albonico, Tielsch, Chwaya, and Savioli (1997) | Infection/parasite | Childhood | C<T | Female height | B | Y | Height | N |
| McGarvey et al. (1992) | Infection/parasite | Childhood | C=T | Female height | B | N | Height | N |
| Hewitt, Westropp, and Acheson (1955) | Infection/parasite | Childhood | C<T | Female height | B | Y | Height | N |
| Parraga et al. (1996) | SES | Childhood/adolescence | C<T | Female height | B | Y | Height | N |
| Malina, Himes, Stepick, Lopez, and Buschang (1981) | SES | Childhood/adolescence | C<T | Female height | M | Y | Height | N |
| Ashcroft, Heneage, and Lovell (1966) | SES | Childhood/adolescence | C<T | Female height | B | Y | Height | N |
| Bharati (1989) | SES | Childhood/adolescence | C<T | Female height | B | Y | Height | N |
| Frisancho and Garn (1971b) | Diet/nutrition | Childhood/adolescence | C<T | Female height | B | Y | Height | N |
| Mupfasoni et al. (2009) | Infection/parasite | Childhood/adolescence | C<T | Female height | B | Y | Height | N |

*Continued*

**TABLE 6.1** Condition-Dependent Physical Traits in Boys and Men—cont'd

| Species | Scientific Name | ST | Trait | CD | S | Contrast Trait | Contrast Effect | Life History | Manipulation | References |
|---|---|---|---|---|---|---|---|---|---|---|
| | | N | Height | N | B | Female height | C>T | Childhood/adolescence | Infection/parasite | Parraga et al. (1996) |
| | | F | Height | Y | B | Female height | C<T | Childhood/adolescence | Infection/parasite | Assis et al. (1998) |
| | | N | Height | Y | B | Female height | C>T | Childhood/adolescence | Infection/parasite | Zhou et al. (2005) |
| | | N | Height | Y | B | Female height | C<T | Adolescence | SES | Dreizen et al. (1953) |
| | | N | Height | Y | B | Female height | C<T | Adolescence | SES | Stini (1969) |
| | | N | Height | N | B | Female height | C>T | Adolescence | SES | Douglas and Simpson (1964) |
| | | N | Height | Y | B | Female height | C<T | Adolescence | SES | Frisancho et al. (1970) |
| | | N | Height | Y | B | Female height | C<T | Adolescence | SES | Cameron (1992) |
| | | N | Height | Y | B | Female height | C<T | Adolescence | Diet/nutrition | Jardim-Botelho et al. (2008) |
| | | N | Height | Y | B | Female height | C<T | Adolescence | Diet/nutrition | Prista, Maia, Damasceno, and Beunen (2003) |
| | | F | Height | Y | B | Female height | C<T | Adolescence | Diet/nutrition | Castillo-Durán et al. (1994) |

| Reference | Factor | Age | Comparison | Vulnerable group | M/B | Y/N | Trait | F/N |
|---|---|---|---|---|---|---|---|---|
| Carter et al. (1969) | Diet/nutrition | Adolescence | C=T | Control male | M | N | Height | F |
| Prasad and Cossack (1984) | Diet/nutrition | Adolescence | C<T | Control male | M | Y | Height | F |
| Halsted et al. (1972) | Diet/nutrition | Adolescence | C<T | Control male | M | Y | Height | F |
| Greulich (1951) | Diet/nutrition | Adolescence | C<T | Female height | B | Y | Height | N |
| Zemel, Kawchak, Ohene-Frempong, Schall, and Stallings (2007) | Sickle cell anemia | Adolescence | C<T | Female height | B | Y | Height | N |
| Rhodes et al. (2009) | Sickle cell anemia | Adolescence | C<T | Female height | B | Y | Height | N |
| Ibrahim et al. (1983) | Infection/parasite | Adolescence | C<T | Control male | M | Y | Height | N |
| McGarvey et al. (1992) | Infection/parasite | Adolescence | C<T | Female height | B | Y | Height | N |
| Deaner, Goetz, Shattuck, & Schnotala (2012) | Physical aggression | Adult | C>T | Male weight | M | N | Height | N |
| Obert et al. (1994) | SES | Childhood | C<T | Low SES male | M | Y | Muscle | N |
| Dewey (1980) | SES | Childhood | C=T | Female muscle | B | N | Muscle | N |
| Malina et al. (1981) | SES | Childhood/adolescence | C<T | Female muscle | B | Y | Muscle | N |
| Dewey (1983) | Diet/nutrition | Childhood | C>T | Female muscle | B | Y[c] | Muscle | N |

*Continued*

**TABLE 6.1** Condition-Dependent Physical Traits in Boys and Men—cont'd

| Species | Scientific Name | ST | Trait | CD | S | Contrast | | Life History | Manipulation | References |
|---|---|---|---|---|---|---|---|---|---|---|
| | | | | | | Trait | Effect | | | |
| | | N | Muscle | Y | B | Female muscle | C=T | Childhood | Diet/nutrition | Martorell et al. (1984) |
| | | F | Muscle | Y | B | Female muscle | C<T | Childhood | Diet/nutrition | West et al. (1988) |
| | | F | Muscle | N | B | Female muscle | C=T | Childhood | Diet/nutrition | Grillenberger et al. (2006) |
| | | F | Muscle | Y | B | Female muscle | C<T | Childhood | Infection/parasite | Adams, Stephenson, Latham, and Kinoti (1994) |
| | | N | Muscle | Y | B | Female muscle | C<T | Childhood/ adolescence | Infection/parasite | Jardim-Botelho et al. (2008) |
| | | F | Muscle | Y | B | Female muscle | C<T | Childhood/ adolescence | Infection/parasite | Assis et al. (1998) |
| | | N | Muscle | Y | B | Female height | C<T | Adolescence | Infection/parasite | McGarvey et al. (1992) |
| | | N | Muscle | N | B | Female muscle | C>T | Adult | Infection/parasite | Lassek and Gaulin (2009) |
| | | N | Muscle | Y | M | Running speed | C<T | Adult | Reproductive success | Apicella (2014) |
| | | N | Fat reserves | Y | B | Female reserves | C<T | Childhood | SES | Kulin, Bwibo, Mutie, and Santner (1982) |

| | | | | | | | | |
|---|---|---|---|---|---|---|---|---|
| N | Fat reserves | Y | B | Female reserves | C=T | Childhood | SES | Cameron (1992) |
| N | Fat reserves | Y | B | Female reserves | C=T | Childhood | Diet/nutrition | Martorell et al. (1984) |
| N | Fat reserves | Y | B | Female reserves | C<T | Childhood | Diet/nutrition | Hagen, Hames, Craig, Lauer, and Price (2001) |
| F | Fat reserves | Y | B | Female reserves | C<T | Childhood | Diet/nutrition | West et al. (1988) |
| N | Fat reserves | Y | B | Female reserves | C=T | Childhood | Diet/nutrition | Tanner, Leonard, and Reyes-García (2014) |
| F | Fat reserves | Y | M | Untreated male | C<T | Childhood | Infection/parasite | Stephenson et al. (1993) |
| F | Fat reserves | Y | B | Female reserves | C<T | Childhood/adolescence | Infection/parasite | Assis et al. (1998) |
| N | Physical fitness | Y | B | Female fitness | C<T | Childhood | Diet/nutrition | Prista et al. (2003) |
| N | Physical fitness | Y | M | Na | NA | Inbreeding | Inbreeding | Schreider (1969) |
| F | Physical fitness | Y | M | Untreated male | C<T | Childhood | Infection/parasite | Stephenson, Latham, Kinoti, Kurz, and Brigham (1990) |
| F | Physical fitness | Y | M | Untreated male | C<T | Childhood | Infection/parasite | Stephenson et al. (1993) |

*Continued*

**TABLE 6.1** Condition-Dependent Physical Traits in Boys and Men—cont'd

| Species | Scientific Name | ST | Trait | CD | S | Contrast Trait | Contrast Effect | Life History | Manipulation | References |
|---|---|---|---|---|---|---|---|---|---|---|
| | | F | Physical fitness | Y | M | Untreated male | C<T | Childhood | Infection/parasite | Latham, Stephenson, Kurz, and Kinoti (1990) |
| | | N | Physical activity | Y | B | Female physical | C<T | Childhood | Diet/nutrition | Wachs et al. (1995) |
| | | F | Physical activity | Y | B | Female physical | C=T | Childhood | Infection/parasite | Adams et al. (1994) |
| | | F | Physical activity | $Y^f$ | B | Female physical | C=T | Childhood | Infection/parasite | Kvalsvig (1986) |
| | | N | Body condition | $Y^g$ | B | Female condition | C<T | Childhood | SES | Ulukanligil and Seyrek (2004) |
| | | F | Body condition | $Y^g$ | M | Untreated male | C<T | Childhood | Infection/parasite | Stephenson et al. (1993) |
| | | N | Physical fitness | Y | B | Female fitness | C<T | Childhood/ adolescence | Diet/nutrition | Bustinduy et al. (2011) |
| | | F | Physical fitness | Y | B | Female fitness | C<T | Childhood/ adolescence | Infection/parasite | Hürlimann et al. (2014) |
| | | N | Physical fitness | $N^h$ | B | Female fitness | C=T | Childhood/ adolescence | Infection/parasite | Bustinduy et al. (2011) |
| | | N | Physical fitness | N | B | Female fitness | C=T | Childhood/ adolescence | Infection/parasite | Müller et al. (2011) |

| | | | | | | | | |
|---|---|---|---|---|---|---|---|---|
| N | Physical fitness | Y | B | Female fitness | C<T | Childhood/adolescence | Infection/parasite | Yap et al. (2012) |
| N | Physical fitness | Y | B | Female fitness | C<T | Adolescence | Diet/nutrition | Prista et al. (2003) |
| N | Physical fitness | N | B | Female fitness | C=T | Adolescence | Infection/parasite | Jarosz et al. (2010) |
| N | Body shape | Y | M | NA | NA | Adult | Physical fitness | Hönekopp et al. (2007) |
| N/T | Sexual maturation | N | B | NA | NA | Prenatal | Toxin | Gladen et al. (2000) |
| N | Sexual maturation | Y | M | NA | NA | Adolescence | Infection/parasite | Cole, Salem, Hafez, Galal, and Massoud (1982) |
| N | Facial features | N | B | Female face | C=T | Adult | Health | Hume and Montgomerie (2001) |
| N | Facial features | Y | M | NA | NA | Adult | MHC | Roberts et al. (2005) |
| N | Facial features | Y | M | NA | NA | Adult | Testosterone reactivity | Lefevre, Lewis, Perrett, and Penke (2013) |
| N | Facial features | Y | M | NA | NA | Adult | Reproductive success | Loehr and O'Hara (2013) |

*Continued*

**TABLE 6.1** Condition-Dependent Physical Traits in Boys and Men—cont'd

| Species | Scientific Name | ST | Trait | CD | S | Contrast | | Life History | Manipulation | References |
|---|---|---|---|---|---|---|---|---|---|---|
| | | | | | | Trait | Effect | | | |
| | | N | Facial features | N | M | NA | NA | Adult | War mortality | Loehr and O'Hara (2013) |
| | | N | Facial features | N | M | NA | NA | Adult | Military rank | Loehr and O'Hara (2013) |
| | | N | Facial features | Y | B | NA | NA | Adult | Physical aggression | Carré and McCormick (2008) |
| | | N | Facial features | N | M | Body size | C>T | Adult | Physical aggression | Deaner et al. (2012) |
| | | N | Facial features | N | M | NA | NA | Adult | Physical aggression | Gómez-Valdés et al. (2013) |
| | | N | Facial features | Y | M | NA | NA | Adult | Reproductive success | Gómez-Valdés et al. (2013) |
| | | N | Facial features | N | M | NA | NA | Adult | Physical fitness | Hönekopp et al. (2007) |
| | | N | Facial features | N | M | NA | NA | Adult | Upper body size | Sell et al. (2009) |
| | | N | Facial features | Y | B | Female face | C<T | Adult | Upper body size | Sell et al. (2009) |
| | | N | Facial features | Y | M | NA | NA | Adult | Upper body size | Sell et al. (2009) |

| ST | Trait | CD | S | | | Age | | Reference |
|---|---|---|---|---|---|---|---|---|
| N | Facial features | Y | M | NA | NA | Adult | Hand grip strength | Fink, Neave, and Seydel (2007) |
| N | Facial features | Y | M | Athletic ability | C<T | Adult | Social competition | Mueller and Mazur (1997) |
| N | Facial features | Y | M | NA | NA | Adult | Testosterone | Penton-Voak and Chen (2004) |
| N | Facial features | Y | B | Female face | C<T | Adult | Social competition | Stirrat, Stulp, and Pollet (2012) |
| L | Facial features | Y | B | Female face | C<T | Adult | Reactive aggression | Carré and McCormick (2008) |
| L | Facial features | Y | M | NA | NA | Adult | Reactive aggression | Carré, McCormick, and Mondloch (2009) |

Note: ST, study type (L, lab experiment; F, field experiment; N, natural variation; T, toxin); CD, condition dependent (Y, yes; N, no); S, sex of participants for trait of interest (M, male; B, both sexes). BMI, body mass index; MHC, major histocompatibility complex (immune system genes) variation; RS, reproductive success; SES, socioeconomic status.

[a]Prenatal exposure to DDT (dichlorodiphenyltrichloroethane) but not PCBs (polychlorinated biphenyl) was associated with taller height in adolescent males but not females.

[b]Boys' height was affected by SES or nutrition but the relative effect was larger in girls, possibly due to the finding that girls were provided with fewer calories than boys.

[c]The effect was found for white but not black children.

[d]Girls grew more in absolute height but boys more in terms of sex-specific norms.

[e]Girls had lower calorie intake than boys and in comparison to norms relatively lower muscle mass, but both sexes were below norms.

[f]Treatment with antiparasite drug increased the physical activity of both sexes. The effect was larger in boys than girls, but it was not statistically significant.

[g]Body condition is weight controlling for height (an estimate of fat and muscle reserves), a common measure of physical condition in biological field studies.

[h]Parasite loads were not directly related to fitness as measured by a run test, but they were related to poor nutrition and stunting, which were related to physical fitness.

[i]The first two of the Sell et al. (2009) studies involved undergraduate students from the United States, whereas the other two included Tsimane men (Bolivia) and Andean pastoralists (Argentina).

important during periods of rapid growth during infancy and pubertal development (Halsted et al., 1972; Prasad & Cossack, 1984). The mechanisms through which these effects work are not fully understood, but contributing factors may be improved appetite for young boys (smaller effect on girls; Krebs, Hambidge, & Walravens, 1984) and improved testicular development and testosterone synthesis during pubertal development (Prasad, 1985).

Short stature will not only undermine men's physical competitiveness and attractiveness to potential mates (Hönekopp et al., 2007; Nettle, 2002); it is also predictive of some aspects of long-term health (Davey Smith et al., 2000; Hebert et al., 1993; McCarron, Okasha, McEwen, & Smith, 2002). In a 40-year prospective study of more than 8000 men, McCarron et al. found that below average stature at 20 years of age was associated with about a 25% increase in the odds of premature death due to cardiovascular or heart disease, but was unrelated to risk for other diseases (e.g., cancer). In a cross-sectional study of more than 22,000 male physicians, Herbert et al. found that for each one-inch increase in height there was a 2-3% decrease in the odds of myocardial infarction (heart attack) in middle and old age. In a study of more than 386,000 Asian men, Song, Smith, and Sung (2003) also found that short stature was associated with increased risk of premature death, but not from heart disease. Rather, risk of premature death due to stroke and respiratory diseases were elevated in shorter men. The differences across studies may in part be due to whether the shorter stature is because of a relatively shorter torso or shorter legs. Davey Smith et al. found that men with shorter torsos had relatively poor lung capacity and health, whereas those with relatively shorter legs had a number of factors, such as insulin resistance, that would increase risk of cardiovascular disease.

## Pelvic Development

The above findings should not be taken to mean that stressor-related reductions in girls' height are without consequences, only that boys' height is more strongly compromised than that of girls. In fact, small stature can also result in health risks for women, including poor pelvic development and through this increased risk of complications during childbirth (Prentice et al., 2013). Unfortunately, most of the studies that assessed compromised height did not simultaneously assess girls' pelvic width. As shown in Table 6.2, girls who are poorly nourished (Banik, 2014) or living in low SES households (Hautvast, 1971) show compromised pelvic development but, at least in childhood, these effects are not above and beyond their compromised height or any more severe than boys' compromised pelvic development (Walker et al., 2006). Banik found that poor nutrition during adolescence was related to smaller pelvic size in girls, but the effect was not statistically significant. However, neither this study nor the childhood studies provided the information needed to assess any nuanced sensitivity of girls' pelvic development to stressors, only that both height and pelvic development were or were not affected.

**TABLE 6.2** Condition-Dependent Physical Traits in Girls and Women

| Species | Scientific Name | ST | Trait | CD | S | Trait | Effect | Life History | Manipulation | References |
|---------|-----------------|----|----|----|----|----|----|----|----|----|
| | | | | | | Contrast | | | | |
| Human | *Homo sapiens* | N | Fat reserves | N | B | Male reserves | C=T | Childhood/adolescence | SES | Malina et al. (1981) |
| | | N | Fat reserves | Y | B | Male reserves | C<T | Childhood/adolescence | Infection/parasite | Parraga et al. (1996) |
| | | F | Fat reserves | Y | B | Male reserves | C>T | Childhood/adolescence | Infection/parasite | Assis et al. (1998) |
| | | N | Fat reserves | Y | B | Male reserves | C=T | Childhood/adolescence | Infection/parasite | Zhou et al. (2005) |
| | | N | Fat reserves | Y | B | Male reserves | C<T | Adolescence | SES | Cameron (1992) |
| | | N | Fat reserves | Y | B | Male reserves | C<T | Adolescence | SES | Kulin et al. (1982) |
| | | N | Fat reserves | Y | F | BMI | C<T | Adolescence | Diet/nutrition | Khan and Ahmed (2005) |
| | | N | Fat reserves | Y | B | Male reserves | C<T | Adolescence | Diet/nutrition | Tanner et al. (2014) |
| | | F | Fat reserves | Y[a] | F | Muscle mass | C<T | Adolescence | Diet/nutrition | Reiches et al. (2013) |

*Continued*

**TABLE 6.2** Condition-Dependent Physical Traits in Girls and Women—cont'd

| Species | Scientific Name | ST | Trait | CD | S | Contrast Trait | Effect | Life History | Manipulation | References |
|---|---|---|---|---|---|---|---|---|---|---|
| | | N | Fat reserves | Y | B | Male reserves | C<T | Adolescence | Infection/parasite | McGarvey et al. (1992) |
| | | N | Pelvic development | N | F | Height | C=T | Childhood | SES | Hautvast (1971) |
| | | N | Pelvic development | Y | F | NA | NA | Childhood | SES | Greulic and Thoms (1938) |
| | | N | Pelvic development | Y | F | Height | C=T | Childhood | Diet/nutrition | Banik (2014) |
| | | N | Pelvic development | Y[b] | B | Male pelvic | C=T | Childhood | Diet/nutrition | Walker, Chang, and Powell (2006) |
| | | N | Pelvic development | Y | F | Height | C=T | Childhood | Diet/nutrition | Bénéfice et al. (2001) |
| | | N | Pelvic development | Y[c] | B | Male pelvic | C=T | Childhood/adolescence | SES | Bharati (1989) |
| | | N | Pelvic development | Y | F | Height | C<T | Adolescence | SES | Hautvast (1971) |
| | | N | Pelvic development | N[d] | F | Height | C=T | Adolescence | Diet/nutrition | Banik (2014) |
| | | N | Face features | Y | F | NA | NA | Adult | Estrogen | Smith et al. (2006) |

| ST | | CD | S | Male face | C=T | Adult | Health | |
|---|---|---|---|---|---|---|---|---|
| N | Face symmetry | N | | NA | NA | Adult | | Hume and Montgomerie (2001) |
| N | Face attractiveness | Y[e] | F | NA | NA | Adult | Testosterone, BMI | Wheatley et al. (2014) |
| F | Skin health | Y[f] | B | NA | NA | Adult | Diet/nutrition | Dayan, Arkins, Sharma, Paterson, and Barnes (2011) |
| F | Skin health | Y | F | NA | NA | Adult | Diet/nutrition | Heinrich, Neukam, Tronnier, Sies, and Stahl (2006) |
| F | Skin health | Y | F | NA | NA | Adult | Diet/nutrition | Segger and Schönlau (2004) |
| F | Skin health | Y | F | NA | NA | Adult | Diet/nutrition | Udompataikul, Sripiroj, and Palungwachira (2009) |
| N | Skin health | Y | F | NA | NA | Adult | Infection/parasite | Amazigo (1994) |

Note: ST, study type (F, field experiment; N, natural variation); CD, condition dependent (Y, yes; N, no); S, sex of participants for trait of interest (f, female, B, both sexes). BMI, body mass index; SES, socioeconomic status.

[a] Changes in fat and muscle mass were examined across high and low food seasons for adolescent girls in Gambia. Younger, still growing girls lost more fat than muscle during the "hungry" season, whereas older girls who were no longer growing lost smaller amounts of fat but more muscle. Overall, the girls were thin (BMI of 20 to 21) but not malnourished.

[b] Poor nutrition and stunting from birth to 2 years of age was associated with smaller hip breadth at age 17 to 18 years.

[c] The study examined adults who grew up in lower- or higher-SES regions. Men and women growing up in lower-SES families were shorter and had narrower pelvic widths. Men's height was more affected than their pelvic width and women's pelvic width was more affected than their height, but the latter differences were small and not tested statistically.

[d] Malnutrition was associated with shorter hip breadth (d=0.54) and more variation in hip breadth for adolescent girls, relative to their better-nourished peers, but the difference was not statistically significant.

[e] Face attractiveness was inversely related to circulating testosterone levels and BMI in college students and age in the Hadza. BMI was unrelated to voice or face attractiveness in the Hadza but showed much less variation than in the college sample

[f] 61 women and 15 men completed the study. The primary result of nutrition supplementation was increase in skin carotenoid levels.

One exception was Hautvast's (1971) study of the physical development of Tanzanian children and adolescents from wealthier and poorer communities. Hautvast reported both height and pelvic width at different ages across these two SES groups, allowing for an assessment of the relative physical costs of growing up in a low SES family. In childhood, there were no significant differences in pelvic width of the girls from the two communities. In fact, as shown in Figure 6.1, 8-year-old girls from lower SES families were modestly taller than their peers from higher SES families, but girls from the latter families had a slightly narrower pelvic width. By 14 years of age, the girls from the poorer community were significantly shorter than their better off peers, but critically the difference in relative pelvic width was double the difference in height. A second exception was Bharati's (1989) study of adults who grew up in lower- or higher-SES regions in India. Men and women growing up in lower-SES families were shorter and had narrower pelvic widths, but men's height was more affected than their pelvic width whereas women's pelvic width was more affected than their height. However, the latter differences were small and not tested statistically. These results suggest that girls' pelvic development may be particularly vulnerable to disruption by exposure to stressors during adolescence, but given the inconclusive results from the other studies, Hautvast's and Bharati's findings are in need of replication and extension to other forms of stressor (e.g., parasite levels).

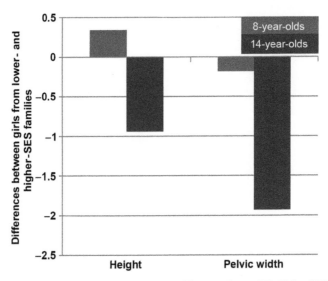

**FIGURE 6.1**    The figure shows standard deviation differences (lower SES–higher SES) in height and pelvic width for 8- and 14-year-olds from lower SES and higher SES families. Eight-year-olds from lower SES families were somewhat taller than their higher-SES peers, but this reversed for 14-year-olds. Critically, the SES gap for pelvic width was larger than that for height and was nearly twice as large in adolescence as in childhood. *Based on data presented in Hautvast (1971).* (See the color plate section.)

## Muscle Mass and Fat Reserves

As I described in Chapter 5, 9-year-old boys have about 8% more muscle tissue than same-age girls (Kim et al., 2006), but this increases to a difference of about 70% by the time they are 15 years old (Tanner, 1990). On the basis of these differences and the developmental issues noted above, it is not surprising that the effects of childhood stressors on sex differences in muscle development are mixed. Just as many studies show that muscle mass is equally compromised by exposure to stressors in boys as in girls (Grillenberger et al., 2006), as show that boys are more vulnerable (West et al., 1988). One study even showed that poor nutrition affected the muscle development of girls more than boys but, as with the height reversals, this was related to a significantly lower calorie intake in girls than boys (Dewey, 1983). The pattern is again different for adolescents, where lower SES and parasite loads consistently have larger effects on male than female muscle development (Malina et al., 1981; McGarvey et al., 1992). The one seeming exception shown in Table 6.1 is Lassek and Gaulin's (2009) finding that men with higher muscle mass had more sexual partners than their less muscular counterparts, but also a weaker natural immune response. The latter, however, is consistent with potential trade-offs between the expression of sexually selected traits and aspects of immune functions, as discussed in Chapter 2.

As I noted in Chapter 5, beginning in childhood girls and women have more body fat than boys and men, but there is a temporary increase in boys' triceps fat prior to the onset of puberty (Frisancho, 1974). The fat increase may provide an important reserve to support the early phases of pubertal growth and as a result may indicate boys' condition in late childhood. The childhood studies shown in Table 6.1 support this prediction: During this developmental window, poor nutrition (Hagen et al., 2001) and infestation with parasites (Stephenson et al., 1993) affects triceps fat levels at least as strongly, if not more so in boys than girls. The pattern differs from that found in adolescence where low SES (Cameron, 1992), poor nutrition (Khan & Ahmed, 2005), and infestation with parasites (McGarvey et al., 1992) compromises the fat reserves of girls more than boys (Table 6.2). The four studies that combined children and adolescents give a more mixed pattern, although three of these are consistent with condition dependence. One study found that the fat reserves of boys and girls are equally affected by parasite infestation (Malina et al., 1981), whereas another found boys were more vulnerable (Assis et al., 1998) and still another found that girls were more vulnerable (Parraga et al., 1996).

The mixed findings likely result from variation in the onset of girls' pubertal growth spurt that in turn will influence age-related estimates of the relative vulnerability of the fat reserves of boys and girls (Kulin et al., 1982). Kulin et al.'s study of the relation between SES and fat reserves in Kenyan children and adolescents illustrates the issue. At 10 years of age boys from higher SES families had more triceps fat reserves than girls from the same background, but thereafter boys' reserves dropped and girls' increased. Girls from lower SES families did not show gains in fat reserves until 3 years after their better-off peers and even then the increases were relatively modest; the fat reserves of boys from these backgrounds were consistently low across age. The overall result was a larger fat reserve deficit for 10-year-old boys than girls, a sex difference that was reversed for 13-year-olds. However, if the study had only included low SES children, the fat reserve deficit of girls would not occur until later in adolescence.

The assessment of relative vulnerability of fat reserves is further complicated by trade-offs between use of fat versus muscle during nutritional shortfalls. Of course, fat is stored energy for any such shortfall, but women need a large fat reserve to become pregnant and to support breast feeding (Frisch, 1984) and thus after pubertal growth, women's fat reserves may be conserved. Reiches et al. (2013) tested this hypothesis for adolescent girls and young women in Gambia across seasons of high versus low food availability. Younger, still growing girls lost more fat than muscle during the "hungry" season whereas older girls and young women who were no longer growing lost smaller amounts of fat but larger amounts of muscle.

Overall, the research in this area suggests that exposure to stressors may compromise boys' muscle development more than that of girls during childhood, but any such sex difference in vulnerability is small. During pubertal development, however, exposure to stressors consistently affects boys' muscle development more than that of girls. Similarly, fat reserves are disrupted by exposure to stressors at different points in development for boys and girls; boys' sensitivity peaks in late childhood and girls' during the pubertal growth spurt.

## Physical Fitness and Activity

Across species with intense physical male-male competition, the associated sex difference in physical size is generally small during juvenile development and emerges rapidly prior to engagement in actual male-male competition (Darwin, 1871; Leigh, 1996). The behavioral differences, however, can emerge much earlier, as illustrated in Chapter 4 for play fighting (Bekoff & Byers, 1998; Burghardt, 2005; Power, 2000). This is also the case with humans: As reviewed in Chapter 5, sex differences in rough-and-tumble and coalitional play (e.g., team sports) emerge early in childhood. Boys' engagement in these activities likely contributes to the development of the social and physical skills needed for one-on-one and coalitional competition in adulthood, at least in traditional societies (Deaner & Smith, 2013; Geary et al., 2003). The prediction that boys' social play is sensitive to stressors is discussed in the Play section below. The focus here is on the prediction that the well-documented sex differences in physical activity and fitness (see Thomas & French, 1985), which I assume have coevolved with the sex differences in play fighting, are vulnerable traits in childhood as well as in adolescence.

Indeed, the studies reviewed in Table 6.1 indicate that growing up in lower SES families (Ulukanligil & Seyrek, 2004), with poor nutrition (Prista et al., 2003), and with heavy parasite loads (Hürlimann et al., 2014) affect boys' physical fitness and activity levels more strongly than those of girls throughout childhood and into adolescence. These sex differences in vulnerability are illustrated by Yap et al.'s (2012) study of the relation between infection with parasitic worms and fitness among children and adolescents of the Bulang of rural China. Cardiorespiratory fitness was assessed using the 20-m shuttle run, a commonly used measure on which boys consistently outperform girls from at least 3 years of age, forward (Thomas & French, 1985). Infection with two types of worms (*Ancylostoma duodenale, Necator americanus*) was common and related to fitness in both sexes. As shown in Figure 6.2, the performance differences across uninfected and infected boys (31% and 25% for *A. duodenale* and *N. americanus*, respectively) were two to three times larger than the differences between uninfected and infected girls' (15% and 8%).

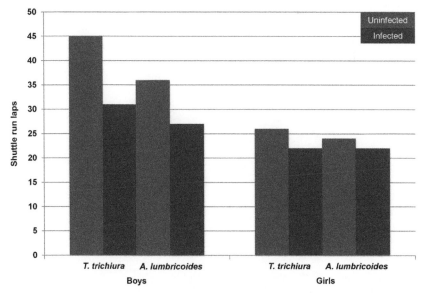

**FIGURE 6.2**    Relative to healthy same-sex peers, boys infected with one or two common parasitic worms showed larger decrements in fitness than did infected girls, based on the commonly used shuttle run measure, whereby fitness is determined by the number of 20-m back-and-forth laps that can be completed in a fixed amount of time. *Based on data (combined across children and adolescents) presented in Yap et al. (2012).* (See the color plate section.)

## Facial Features and Skin Attractiveness

There are many studies of the correlates of men's facial features and reproductively relevant outcomes (Table 6.1). Not surprisingly, most of these studies show that the physical traits that emerge during pubertal development and that women find attractive, such as a prominent jaw (Cunningham, et al.,1990), are predictive of men's reproductive success (Loehr & O'Hara, 2013), testosterone levels and reactivity (Lefevre, Lewis, et al., 2013), upper body size (Sell et al., 2009), and sometimes to proneness to physical aggression (Carré & McCormick, 2008). Similarly, women's facial features that men find attractive are correlated with hormone profiles that could affect fertility (Table 6.2; Smith et al., 2006; Wheatley et al., 2014). None of the studies, however, examined whether the development of these facial traits is vulnerable to disruption by exposure to parasites or other stressors during adolescence, although theoretically they should be vulnerable for both sexes (Gangestad & Buss, 1993).

Aspects of facial and physical attractiveness might also signal current condition. More precisely, skin attractiveness might be particularly sensitive to current condition, for two reasons. First, skin lesions and other changes (e.g., facial paleness) are common in individuals who are infected with one of the many parasitic worms and other diseases that plague humans in developing regions of the world and sometimes in developed regions. An example is provided in Photo 6.1 (inset) that shows an individual infected by a species of hookworm (*Ancylostoma braziliense*) and the cutaneous migration of this species' larva. Second, as described in Chapter 2 and illustrated in Chapter 3, carotenoids (and many other micronutrients) are important for vertebrate immune and stress responses and are signaled by trait color in many species. Likewise, variation in skin carotenoid levels correlates with some aspects of people's health

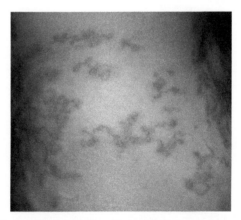

**PHOTO 6.1**    Skin lesions due to infection with parasitic worms are common in the developing world. The photo shows the migration of the larva of one species of hookworm (*Ancylostoma braziliense*). *Photo credit, Weis Sagung, 2009. Creative Commons license: http://commons.wikimedia. org/wiki/File:Larva_Migrans_Cutanea.jpg.* (See the color plate section.)

(Boelsma et al., 2003; Guerin, Huntley, & Olaizola, 2003; Hata et al., 2000), and other people can easily detect this variation (Lefevre, Ewbank, et al., 2013; Stephen et al., 2011).

To be sure, the subtle changes in human skin color that occur with the presence of carotenoids, and other micronutrients is not as conspicuous as the many examples I provided for other species in previous chapters, but it does not have to be: To be an effective signal of current condition, the changes only need to be detectable and influence perceived health and attractiveness. The corresponding prediction that the condition of facial skin and that of other ex-posed parts of the body (e.g., hands) will be vulnerable to exposure to parasites and poor nutrition is well established, as noted in Chapter 5, but the critical link to perceived attractiveness and thus mate choices has not been as system-atically studied. Nevertheless, the studies that have been conducted reveal that variation in skin complexion (Fink et al., 2006) and a yellow tint to skin color (Coetzee et al., 2012; Stephen et al., 2011) influences the perceived health and facial attractiveness of women, as illustrated in Photo 6.2 (inset); presumably it influences the attractiveness of men as well but this has not been systemati-cally assessed. The latter is influenced by dietary carotenoid levels (Coetzee et al., 2012) and thus should be an honest signal of current nutritional status and through this health.

I list a number of controlled clinical studies of the effects of supplemen-tation with carotenoids and other micronutrients on women's skin health in Table 6.2 (Dayan et al., 2011; Heinrich et al., 2006; Segger & Schönlau, 2004; Udompataikul et al., 2009). Heinrich et al. randomly assigned women to low- and high-flavanol – naturally obtained through dietary fruits and

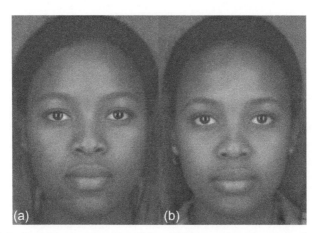

**PHOTO 6.2**  Composite images of low (a) and high attractive (b) women. Several factors influence rated attractiveness, including homogeneity of skin color and a slight yellow color-ation. The latter is correlated with skin carotenoid levels. *From African perceptions of female attractiveness, by Coetzee et al., 2012. Creative commons license, http://www.plosone.org/article/ info%3Adoi%2F10.1371%2Fjournal.pone.0048116.* (See the color plate section.)

vegetables – supplements for 12 weeks and then assessed changes in skin health and appearance. Supplementation resulted in better blood flow and better protection against damage from ultraviolet light, as well as visible changes that would influence rated attractiveness (e.g., scaling and smoothness). Segger and Schönlau (2004) found similar results with supplements that included carotenoids, and Stephen et al. (2011) found that natural variation in the amount of fruits and vegetables in the diet was correlated with skin carotenoid levels and skin coloration in women and men. Stephen et al. also provided two men and eight women with carotenoid supplements, and after 8 weeks found increases in carotenoid levels in the skin of the shoulders, palms, cheeks, and forehead. These diet-related changes in skin appearance will influence perceived attractiveness, and in traditional contexts can have reproductive consequences: Amazigo (1994) found that Nigerian women infected with a parasitic worm (*Onchocerca volvulus*) that results in skin lesions married later than uninfected women and breast fed their children for shorter durations (because suckling is uncomfortable).

In total, these studies are consistent with the proposal that skin color and appearance are condition-dependent signals of current health and can influence mate choices. It is very likely that this is the case for both men and women, but the social consequences appear to be more substantial for women. Generally, women's marriage prospects, including the quality of the mate they can attract, are more strongly influenced by physical attractiveness than are men's prospects (Buss, 1989; Lippa, 2007). As found by Amazigo (1994) and reviewed in Chapter 5, skin quality and perceived attractiveness do indeed influence women's marriage prospects in traditional societies. These traits may be reliable signals of current resistance to common parasites, and aspects of skin color reflect (literally) the nutritional quality of their diet, as with carotenoid- and other nutrition-based signals in many other vertebrate species (Tables 3.1 and 3.5).

## Scent and Health

As was reviewed in the last chapter (Table 4.6), pheromones are reliable signals of social dominance and health in many mammals, and thus it is reasonable to assume these and other types of scent may be condition-dependent signals in humans as well. There is in fact some evidence that natural scents can influence the attractiveness of potential mates and may provide clues about the diversity of the donor's immune-system genes and women's fertility status (Herz & Inzlicht, 2002; Penn et al., 2007; Singh & Bronstad, 2001; Thornhill & Gangestad, 1999; Thornhill et al., 2003; Wedekind, Seebeck, Bettens, & Paepke, 1995), although these findings are not always replicated (Thornhill et al., 2003). There are in other words sex-specific volatile organic compounds (VOCs) or odor cues that signal reproductively relevant traits (Penn et al., 2007), and as such could be indicators of condition in the same way as the other traits reviewed in this and previous chapters.

There is in fact a long history of the use of odors as diagnostic cues for a variety infectious, metabolic, and other diseases (see Shirasu & Touhara, 2011), such as tuberculosis (Syhre, Manning, Phuanukoonnon, Harino, & Chambers, 2009), streptococcal intertrigo (Honig, Frieden, Kim, & Yan, 2003), cholera (Garner, Smith, Bardhan, Ratcliffe, & Probert, 2009), and fungal infections (Shirasu, Nagai, Hayashi, Ochiai, & Touhara, 2009), among many others. Some of the associated VOCs are distinct and yield discriminable order cues for at least some different diseases and disorders, and may even be useful in assessing overall levels of oxidative stress (see Chapter 2; Amann et al., 2014). Olsson et al. (2014) showed that triggering the innate immune response – a response triggered by many different types of parasites – results in the development of a detectable unpleasant body odor within a few hours. Moshkin et al. (2012) found a similar pattern when women were asked to evaluate the odor (collected in underarm cotton pads embedded in T-shirts) of men currently infected with gonorrhea (*Neisseria gonorrhoeae*), successfully treated men, and uninfected men. Women reported the odors of infected men, but not uninfected or cured men, to be unpleasant ("putrid") and the degree of unpleasantness was related to the intensity of the men's immune responses; they did not assess whether infected women produce similar odors.

The evidence is consistent with odor cues providing reliable information about some disease conditions and that the unpleasantness of these odors creates a behavioral defense (avoidance) against infectious disease. However, these studies do not address whether the odors that signal disease and disorder are sex-specific or more easily triggered in one sex or the other. Most of the studies of disease-specific VOCs do not report sex differences, and those that report them suggest more similarities than differences. Syhre et al. (2009) identified VOCs associated with tuberculosis and potentially detectable through breath odor but these were very similar for infected men and infected women (see also Banday et al., 2011). Phillips et al. (1999) identified breath VOCs associated with lung cancer but again these appear to have been largely the same for men and women; Peng et al. (2010) also found considerable overlap in the VOCs of men and women with different forms of cancer. These results suggest that disease-specific VOCs will be very similar in men and women, but these types of studies do not address the critical question of whether any or all of these diseases disrupts sex-specific status or mate value VOCs. In other words, there are sex differences in odor-related VOCs, some of which appear to be status and fertility signals, but whether disease disrupts these VOCs in sex-specific ways has not been systematically studied.

## BEHAVIORAL VULNERABILITIES

In this section, we turn our attention to the behavioral traits listed in Table 5.1. Unfortunately, there is little to no research on the effects of exposure to stressors and sex differences for many of these behaviors, such as engagement in exploratory behavior and relational aggression. There is nonetheless sufficient research to assess the relation between stressor exposure and some of the vulnerability predictions described in Chapter 5. These include children's sextypical play behavior, aspects of children's and adults' social relationships and social signals, as well as men's emotional composure.

## Children's Play

Again, male play fighting during the juvenile years is common in mammals and likely contributes to preparation for male-male competition in adulthood (Bekoff & Byers, 1998; Burghardt, 2005; Power, 2000). Likewise, sex differences in play parenting are common, especially in primates, and appear to contribute to the development or maintenance of parenting behaviors (Pryce, 1993). The same is true for humans, where sex differences in play are well documented and are quite large. During the preschool years and into childhood there is very little overlap in boys' and girls' suites of play behavior (Golombok & Rust, 1993; Golombok et al., 2008), including differences in the frequency of engagement in rough-and-tumble play, team sports, and doll and family play, among others. In addition to developing specific play-related skills, engagement in sex-typical play contributes to children's developing friendships – through engagement in mutually enjoyable activities (Pasterski et al., 2011) – and is related at least in part to prenatal and early postnatal exposure to androgens (male hormones; Berenbaum & Hines, 1992; Lamminmäki et al., 2012).

If boys' engagement in rough-and-tumble and coalitional play is an evolved component of male-male competition, as proposed in Chapter 5, then engagement in these social behaviors should be disrupted by prenatal and early postnatal exposure to stressors. Girls' play parenting and family oriented play may contribute to later competencies in these areas, but are likely driven in large part by natural selection, which is why I did not include them as vulnerable traits in Table 5.1. Some influence of sexual selection is, however, possible because men in traditional societies value these skills when choosing (or keeping) a wife (Betzig, 1989). Thus, girls' sex-typical play may be vulnerable to early disruption, but even so, I would expect these behaviors to be less easily disrupted than boys' sex-typical play.

As shown in Table 6.3, there is now evidence that children's sex-typical play can indeed be disrupted by exposure to toxins (Swan et al., 2010), maternal stress during pregnancy (Barrett et al., 2014), and poor nutrition (Barrett et al., 1982). Most of these studies assessed play behavior using the *Pre-School Activities Inventory* (Golombok & Rust, 1993) or a parallel version for older children (Golombok et al., 2008). These are very useful tests, but report overall engagement in boy-typical or girl-typical play rather than engagement in specific behaviors, such as rough-and-tumble or doll play. As a result, the studies only provide an overall assessment of whether exposure to stressors masculinizes (or demasculinizes) or feminizes (or defeminizes) overall play behavior,

**TABLE 6.3** Condition-Dependent Behavioral Traits in Humans

| Species | Scientific Name | ST | Trait | CD | S | Contrast Trait | Effect | Life History | Manipulation | References |
|---|---|---|---|---|---|---|---|---|---|---|
| **Boys' play behavior** | | | | | | | | | | |
| Human | *Homo sapiens* | N/T | Sex-typical play | Y[a] | M | Level of exposure | C<T | Prenatal | Toxin | Barrett, Redmon, Wang, Sparks, and Swan (2014) |
| | | N/T | Sex-typical play | Y | M | Level of exposure | C<T | Prenatal | Toxin | Swan et al. (2010) |
| | | N/T | Sex-typical play | Y[b] | M | Level of exposure | C<T | Prenatal | Toxin | Winneke et al. (2014) |
| | | N | Sex-typical play | Y | M | Level of exposure | C=T | Prenatal | Toxin | Hines et al. (2002) |
| | | N/T | Sex-typical play | Y | M | Level of exposure | C<T | Prenatal | Toxin | Vreugdenhil, Slijper, Mulder, and Weisglas-Kuperus (2002) |
| | | N/T | Sex-typical play | Y | M | Level of exposure | C<T | Prenatal | Toxin | Winneke et al. (2014) |
| | | N | Sex-typical play | N | M | Level of exposure | C=T | Prenatal | Maternal stress | Hines et al. (2002) |
| | | N | Sex-typical play | N | M | Level of exposure | C=T | Prenatal | Maternal stress | Barrett et al. (2014) |
| | | N/T | Sex-typical play | N | M | Level of exposure | C<T | Breastfeeding | Toxin | Vreugdenhil et al. (2002) |
| | | N/T | Sex-typical play | Y | M | Level of exposure | C<T | Breastfeeding | Toxin | Winneke et al. (2014) |
| | | F | Rough-and-tumble play | Y | B | Female play | C<T | Prenatal/childhood | Diet/nutrition | Barrett et al. (1982) |
| | | F | Assertive play | Y | B | Female play | C<T | Prenatal/childhood | Diet/nutrition | Barrett et al. (1982) |

*Continued*

**TABLE 6.3** Condition-Dependent Behavioral Traits in Humans—cont'd

| Species | Scientific Name | ST | Trait | CD | S | Contrast Trait | Effect | Life History | Manipulation | References |
|---|---|---|---|---|---|---|---|---|---|---|
| | | F | Competitive play | Y[c] | B | Female competitive | C=T | Childhood | Diet/nutrition | Barrett and Radke-Yarrow (1985) |
| | | F | Play exploration | Y[c] | B | Female exploration | C=T | Childhood | Diet/nutrition | Barrett and Radke-Yarrow (1985) |

*Girls' play behavior*

| Species | Scientific Name | ST | Trait | CD | S | Contrast Trait | Effect | Life History | Manipulation | References |
|---|---|---|---|---|---|---|---|---|---|---|
| Human | *Homo sapiens* | N/T | Sex-typical play | N | F | Level of exposure | C=T | Prenatal | Toxin | Barrett et al. (2014) |
| | | N/T | Sex-typical play | N | F | Level of exposure | C=T | Prenatal | Toxin | Swan et al. (2010) |
| | | N/T | Sex-typical play | N | F | Level of exposure | C=T | Prenatal | Toxin | Winneke et al. (2014) |
| | | N | Sex-typical play | Y | F | Level of exposure | C=T | Prenatal | Toxin | Hines et al. (2002) |
| | | N/T | Sex-typical play | N[d] | F | Level of exposure | C<T | Prenatal | Toxin | Vreugdenhil et al. (2002) |
| | | N | Sex-typical play | Y | F | Level of exposure | C<T | Prenatal | Maternal stress | Hines et al. (2002) |
| | | N | Sex-typical play | Y | F | Level of exposure | C<T | Prenatal | Maternal stress | Barrett et al. (2014) |
| | | N/T | Sex-typical play | N[d] | F | Level of exposure | C<T | Breastfeeding | Toxin | Vreugdenhil et al. (2002) |
| | | N/T | Sex-typical play | Y | F | Level of exposure | C<T | Breastfeeding | Toxin | Winneke et al. (2014) |

**Social behavior**

| Human | Homo sapiens | N/T | Social skills | Y | B | Level of exposure | C < T | Prenatal | Toxin | Miodovnik et al. (2011) |
|---|---|---|---|---|---|---|---|---|---|---|
| | | F | Physical aggression | Y^e | B | Female aggression | C < T | Prenatal/childhood | Diet/nutrition | Barrett et al. (1982) |
| | | F | Social assertiveness | Y | B | Female assertiveness | C < T | Prenatal/childhood | Nutrition | Barrett et al. (1982) |
| | | N | Peer status | Y | M | NA | NA | Childhood | Diet/nutrition | Waterflow (1974) |
| | | N | Peer status | Y | B | NA | NA | Childhood | Stress/abuse | Dodge, Pettit, and Bates (1994) |
| | | N | Boy negative social | Y | B | Female negative | C < T | Childhood | Stress/abuse | Parker and Herrera (1996) |
| | | N | Boy negative social | Y | B | Female negative | C < T | Childhood | Stress/abuse | Howe and Parke (2001) |
| | | N | Girl positive social | Y | B | Male positive | C < T | Childhood | Stress/abuse | Parker and Herrera (1996) |
| | | N/T | Male social isolation | Y | M | NA | NA | Adult | Toxin | Morrow, Ryan, Goldstein, and Hodgson (1989) |
| | | N/T | Male social deficits | Y | M | Unexposed Male | C < T | Adult | Toxin | Condray, Morrow, Steinhauer, Hodgson, and Kelley (2000) |

*Continued*

**TABLE 6.3** Condition-Dependent Behavioral Traits in Humans—cont'd

| Species | Scientific Name | ST | Trait | CD | S | Contrast Trait | Contrast Effect | Life History | Manipulation | References |
|---|---|---|---|---|---|---|---|---|---|---|
| **Social signals** | | | | | | | | | | |
| Human | *Homo sapiens* | N | Anger display | Y | B | Female display | C<T | Adult | Upper body size | Price, Dunn, Hopkins, and Kang (2012) |
| | | N | Male voice pitch | Y | B | Female voice | C<T | Adult | Reproductive success | Apicella, Feinberg, and Marlowe (2007) |
| | | N | Male voice pitch | N | M | NA | NA | Adult | Body size | Collins (2000) |
| | | N | Male voice pitch | Y | M | Lung capacity | C<T | Adult | Upper body size | Evans, Neave, and Wakelin (2006) |
| | | N | Male voice pitch | Y | M | NA | C<T | Adult | Testosterone | Evans, Neave, Wakelin, and Hamilton (2008) |
| | | N[i] | Male voice pitch | Y | B | Female voice | C<T | Adult | Testosterone | Dabbs and Mallinger (1999) |
| | | N | Male voice pitch | N | B | Female voice | C<T | Adult | Body size | González (2004) |
| | | N | Male voice pitch | Y | M | NA | NA | Adult | Strength | Puts, Apicella, and Cárdenas (2012) |
| | | N | Male voice pitch | N | M | NA | NA | Adult | Strength | Puts et al. (2012) |
| | | N | Male voice pitch | Y | M | NA | NA | Adult | Body size | Puts et al. (2012) |
| | | N | Male voice pitch | Y | B | Female voice | C<T | Adult | Height | Rendall, Kollias, Ney, and Lloyd (2005) |

| | | | | | | | | | |
|---|---|---|---|---|---|---|---|---|---|
| | | Male voice attractive | N | Y | B | Female voice | C<T | Adult | SHR | Hughes, Dispenza, and Gallup (2004) |
| | | Female voice pitch | N | Y | F | NA | NA | Adult | Body size | Collins and Missing (2003) |
| | | Female voice attractiveness | N | Y | B | Male voice | C<T | Adult | WHR | Hughes et al. (2004) |
| | | Female voice attractiveness | N | Y[f] | F | NA | NA | Adult | Age, BMI | Wheatley et al. (2014) |
| ***Risk taking and emotional composure*** | | | | | | | | | | |
| Human | *Homo sapiens* | Male harm avoidance | N | Y | B | Female harm avoidance | C<T | Adult | Infection/parasite | Flegr, Novotná, Fialová, Kolbeková, and Gašová (2010) |
| | | Male affective disorder | N | Y | B | Female affective disorder | C<T | Prenatal | Diet/nutrition | Brown, Susser, Lin, Neugebauer, and Gorman (1995) |
| | | Male anxiety | N | N | B | Female anxiety | C=T | Prenatal | Diet/nutrition | de Rooij, Veenendaal, Räikkönen, and Roseboom (2012) |
| | | Male anxiety | N | Y | B | Female anxiety | C<T | Prenatal | Diet/nutrition | de Rooij et al. (2011) |
| | | Male anxiety | N/T | N | B | Female anxiety | C>T | Prenatal | Toxin | Braun et al. (2011) |
| | | Male anxiety | N/T | Y[g] | B | Female anxiety | C=T | Prenatal | Toxin | Bennett, Bendersky, and Lewis (2002) |

*Continued*

**TABLE 6.3** Condition-Dependent Behavioral Traits in Humans—cont'd

| Species | Scientific Name | ST | Trait | CD | S | Contrast | | Life History | Manipulation | References |
|---|---|---|---|---|---|---|---|---|---|---|
| | | | | | | Trait | Effect | | | |
| | | N/T | Male anxiety | Y | B | Female anxiety | C<T | Prenatal | Toxin | Harley et al. (2013) |
| | | N/T | Male anxiety | N[b] | B | Female anxiety | C<T | Prenatal | Toxin | Perera et al. (2012) |
| | | N/T | Male anxiety | N | B | Female anxiety | C=T | Prenatal | Toxin | Hong et al. (2013) |
| | | N | Male anxiety | N | B | Female anxiety | C=T | Childhood | Diet/nutrition | Espinosa et al. (1992) |
| | | N/T | Male anxiety | N | B | Female anxiety | C=T | Childhood | Toxin | Braun et al. (2011) |
| | | N/T | Male anxiety | Y | B | Female anxiety | C<T | Childhood | Toxin | Harley et al. (2013) |
| | | N/T | Male anxiety | Y | B | Female anxiety | C=T | Childhood | Toxin | Hong et al. (2013) |
| | | N | Male anxiety | Y | B | Female anxiety | C=T | Childhood | Stress/abuse | Briere and Elliott (2003) |
| | | N | Male anxiety | Y | B | Female anxiety | C<T | Childhood | Stress/abuse | Silverman, Reinherz, and Giaconia (1996) |
| | | N | Male anxiety | Y | B | Female anxiety | C=T | Childhood | Stress/abuse | Nelson et al. (2002) |
| | | N | Male anxiety | N | M | Unexposed male | C=T | Adult | Infection/parasite | Lindová, Příplatová, and Flegr (2012) |
| | | N/T | Male anxiety | N | M | Unexposed male | C=T | Adult | Toxin | Condray et al. (2000) |
| | | N | Male anxiety | Y | M | Sociability | C<T | Adult | Toxin | Haenninen, Hernberg, Mantere, Vesanto, and Jalkanen (1978) |

| | | | | | | | | |
|---|---|---|---|---|---|---|---|---|
| N/T | Male anxiety | Y | | NA | NA | Adult | Toxin | Morrow et al. (1989) |
| N | Male depression | Y | B | Female depression | C<T | Prenatal | Diet/nutrition | de Rooij et al. (2011) |
| N | Male depression | Y | B | Female depression | C<T | Prenatal | Maternal stress | Watson, Mednick, Huttunen, and Wang (1999) |
| N | Male depression | Y | B | Female depression | C<T | Prenatal | Maternal illness | Machón, Mednick, and Huttunen (1997) |
| N/T | Male depression | N | B | Female depression | C>T | Prenatal | Toxin | Braun et al. (2011) |
| N/T | Male depression | Y[g] | B | Female depression | C=T | Prenatal | Toxin | Bennett et al. (2002) |
| N/T | Male depression | Y | B | Female depression | C<T | Prenatal | Toxin | Harley et al. (2013) |
| N/T | Male depression | N[h] | B | Female depression | C<T | Prenatal | Toxin | Perera et al. (2012) |
| N/T | Male depression | Y | B | Female depression | C<T | Prenatal | Toxin | Hong et al. (2013) |
| N/T | Male depression | N | B | Female depression | C=T | Childhood | Toxin | Braun et al. (2011) |
| N/T | Male depression | Y | B | Female depression | C=T | Childhood | Toxin | Hong et al. (2013) |
| N/T | Male depression | N | B | Female depression | C>T | Childhood | Toxin | Harley et al. (2013) |
| N | Male depression | Y | B | Female depression | C=T | Childhood | Stress/abuse | Briere and Elliott (2003) |
| N | Male depression | Y[i] | B | Female depression | C=T | Childhood | Stress/abuse | Silverman et al. (1996) |
| N | Male depression | Y | B | Female depression | C=T | Childhood | Stress/abuse | Nelson et al. (2002) |
| N | Male depression | Y | B | Female depression | C=T | Childhood | Stress/separation | Pesonen et al. (2007) |

*Continued*

**TABLE 6.3** Condition-Dependent Behavioral Traits in Humans—cont'd

| Species | Scientific Name | ST | CD | S | Contrast | | | Manipulation | References |
|---|---|---|---|---|---|---|---|---|---|
| | | | | | Trait | Effect | Life History | | |
| | | N | Y | B | Unexposed male | C<T | Childhood | Stress/abuse | Nelson et al. (2002) |
| | | N/T | Y | M | Unexposed male | C<T | Adult | Toxin | Condray et al. (2000) |
| | | N/T | Y | M | NA | NA | Adult | Toxin | Morrow et al. (1989) |

Note: ST, study type (L, lab experiment; N, natural variation; T, Toxin); CD, condition dependent (Y, yes; N, no); S, sex of participants for trait of interest (M, male; F, female; B, both sexes). BMI, body mass index; SHR, shoulder-to-hips ratio; WHR, waist-to-hip ratio.

[a] Maternal alcohol use during pregnancy was related to increased masculine play in boys, with no effect for girls.

[b] The sex-by-play interaction was not significant for masculine play but was for feminine play. The result was highly feminized boys, and a trend toward defeminization for girls (p < 0.06).

[c] The study involved low- and high-nutritional supplements for children at risk for malnutrition. Competitive play was lower in boys than girls in the low-supplement condition and higher in the high-supplement condition, but the effects were not statistically significant.

[d] For the measure of prenatal toxin exposure there was no effect on female-typical play, but there was an effect (p = 0.059) for one of two measures of male-typical play; girls with high levels of exposure had more masculinized play. Toxin levels in breast milk were not associated with female-typical play but there was a trend (p = 0.065) for an increase in male-typical play.

[e] Better nourished boys were more physically aggressive during play than poorly nourished boys; there was no effect of nutritional status on girls' physical aggression.

[f] Vocal attractiveness was inversely related to BMI, but not testosterone, in college students and showed a nonlinear relation to age in the Hadza (hunter-gatherers, Tanzania), with peak attractiveness at age 26.

[g] Maternal use of marijuana but not alcohol or cocaine during pregnancy was associated with higher internalizing disorders in 4-year-old boys and girls.

[h] Prenatal exposure to bisphenol A, an endocrine disrupting compound, was associated with higher internalizing scores in 3-to-5-year-old boys and lower scores in same-age girls. Both effects and the interaction were marginally significant (p < 0.10).

[i] At age 21, there was elevated risk of major depressive disorder associated with childhood physical abuse in both sexes, although somewhat higher in men. Abused men had higher internalizing disorders than nonabused men, with no difference for abused and nonabused women.

not specific play behaviors. The toxicology studies are also nonspecific; that is, the mixture of toxins assessed across studies often differs. Moreover, some of the studies include endocrine disrupting compounds (EDCs, see Chapter 2) that can – depending on dosage, sex, and EDC – result in disrupted or exaggerated sex-typical traits (e.g., Swan et al., 2010) and others do not include EDCs (e.g., Hines et al., 2002). Despite the imprecision in the assessments of toxin exposure and sex-typical behaviors, the studies allow us to determine if children's play is vulnerable to stressors overall and in a sex-specific way.

In Figure 6.3, I present the relation between level of toxin exposure, including EDCs during prenatal or early postnatal development and engagement in sex-typical play (Swan et al., 2010; Vreugdenhil et al., 2002; Winneke et al., 2014). The figure shows the estimated change in boy-typical or girl-typical play for each doubling of the level of toxin exposure. Doubling the prenatal exposure to the mixture of toxins assessed by Swan et al. resulted in a substantial reduction (demasculinization) in boys' engagement in boy-typical play, but had no effects on boys' engagement in girl-typical play or either type of play in girls. The magnitude of the effect means that 19 out of 20 of these boys engaged in boy-typical play less often than the average unexposed boy. Vreugdenhil et al. also found that prenatal toxin exposure demasculinized boys' play but less dramatically than found by Swan and colleagues. There was also a trend (nearly statistically significant) for girls' play to become slightly masculinized; that is, there was a small increase in engagement in boy-typical activities. The result for Winneke and colleagues is for toxin levels in maternal breast milk and revealed a significant increase (feminization) in boys' engagement in girl-typical play

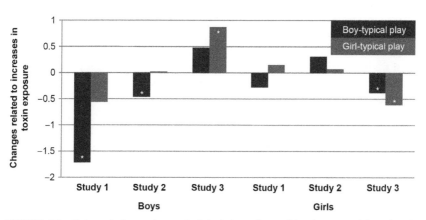

**FIGURE 6.3** Estimated changes in standard deviation units resulting from a doubling of toxin exposure. *Statistically significant effect. Different mixtures of toxins were assessed across studies, and thus general conclusions about toxin exposure and the nature of changes in children's play cannot be drawn. The critical point is exposure to toxins consistently changes sex-typical play in boys and sometimes in girls. *Based on data presented in Swan et al. (2010, Study 1), Vreugdenhil et al. (2002, Study 2), and Winneke et al. (2014, Study 3). (See the color plate section.)*

and a decrease in girl's engagement in this type of play, as well as a modest decline in girls' engagement in boy-typical play; Winneke et al. found the same pattern for prenatal exposure to the same toxins, and thus differences across studies are likely related to differences in the types of toxins assessed, not timing of exposure.

Two studies found that maternal stress during pregnancy was associated with more boy-typical play in girls but was unrelated to the play behavior of boys (Barrett et al., 2014; Hines et al., 2002). Controlling for other factors (e.g., SES, alcohol use), Barrett et al. found that a one standard deviation increase in maternal stress (i.e., mother's in about the top 15-20% of stress levels) was associated with a modest increase in girls' engagement in boy-typical play – about 7 out of 10 of these girls engaged in boy-typical play more frequently than girls exposed to average levels of stress – and no effect on engagement in girl-typical play. Hines et al. found that same pattern, although the effect on girls play was smaller than that found by Barrett et al.

Finally, there are a few studies of the relation between nutritional stressors and sex differences in specific types of play behavior, such as rough-and-tumble play (Barrett et al., 1982). All of the assessed behaviors are more common in boys than in girls and are therefore included in the Boys' Play Behavior section in Table 6.3. Barrett and colleagues observed the social play of 6- to 8-year-old Guatemalan children with same-sex peers. These were children from a larger study of the benefits of prenatal and early postnatal (up to age 4 years) nutritional supplements on physical growth and cognitive development. Girls and boys with higher levels of prenatal and preschool nutritional supplements were more active and socially engaged with their peers. Boys and girls were more similar than different in this respect except that supplemented boys were more aggressive, assertive, and engaged in more rough-and-tumble play than their poorly nourished peers; there was either no effect or a much smaller effect of nutritional supplements on girls' engagement in these behaviors. A related analysis revealed that during participation in a race game, poorly nourished boys were the least engaged and competitive and well-nourished boys were the most engaged and competitive (Barrett & Radke-Yarrow, 1985). The engagement and competitiveness of the poorly and better-nourished girls was in-between that of the two boys' groups. The pattern is consistent with a sex-specific vulnerability for engagement in competitive physical play, but the interaction between sex and nutritional status was not statistically significant in this study.

Overall, prenatal exposure to toxins is consistently related to boys' engagement in sex-typical play, although the nature of the effects can range from substantial demasculinization to the modest feminization depending on the toxin mixture. In contrast, prenatal toxin exposure has less consistent effects, including many null effects, on girls' engagement in sex-typical play. The results for the two assessments of exposure to toxins through breastfeeding are mixed for both sexes; exposure in the first few months of life may influence later play behavior but this requires additional research to determine with any certainty.

Sex-specific effects also emerged for prenatal exposure to maternal stress, with available studies suggesting small to modest increases in girls' engagement in boy-typical play, but no effects on boys' play. The only studies that examined specific play behaviors suggested poor nutrition compromises boys' engagement in sex-typical play more than girls' engagement, but the results are in need of replication before strong conclusions can be drawn.

## Social Behavior

The vulnerability of children's play, especially that of boys, has important implications for their broader social development. To illustrate how play influences social development, let us return to the coalitional or between-group male-male competition that is common among men in traditional societies (Chapter 5). Just as rough-and-tumble play emerges long before men's engagement in one-on-one physical aggression in adulthood their between-group competition is preceded by years of coalitional play during childhood and adolescence (Lever, 1978; Parker & Seal, 1996; Savin-Williams, 1987; Sherif, Harvey, White, Hood, & Sherif, 1961). Boys' organize themselves into groups that compete with other groups of boys, and over time the boys within these groups develop a hierarchy, generally positive relationships with all other group members, and become very skilled at coordinating their behaviors in competitive contexts (Savin-Williams, 1987). Engagement in this form of play – team sports in modern societies – fosters the development and maintenance of cooperative relationships that in turn allow boys and later men to better compete with other organized groups of boys and men. Girls' social play also fosters their skill at forming cooperative relationships that allow them to better cope with competitive relationships before reaching adulthood, but these relationships – cooperative and competitive – are dyadic rather than coalitional (Benenson, 2014; Savin-Williams, 1987), as described in Chapter 5.

In other words, the differences in how men and women in traditional societies cooperate and compete with same-sex individuals (Chapter 5) means that boys and girls have to learn different types of social skills for the development and maintenance of cooperative relationships and to prepare them for male-male or female-female competition in adulthood (Geary, 2010; Geary et al., 2003). From this perspective and assuming developmental activities are in part evolved components of sexual and social selection, it is not surprising that by early childhood boys and girls strongly segregate into same-sex groups and develop different types of cooperative and competitive relationships within these groups (Maccoby, 1988; Martin & Fabes, 2001; Rose & Rudolph, 2006). Stressors that disrupt children's ability to form same-sex relationships and integrate into and understand boys' and girls' and later men's and women's "cultures," that is, the implicit rules for how relationships are developed and maintained has, in theory, potential long-term consequences for their well-being (Egan & Perry, 2001; Geary & Flinn, 2002; Martin et al., 2012; Taylor, Klein, Lewis, et al., 2000).

It is indeed the case that engagement in sex-typical activities contributes to acceptance by peers and is related to some indicators of social adjustment, especially for boys (Boivin, Dodge, & Coie, 1995; Crick, 1997; Egan & Perry, 2001; Fagot, 1977; Green, 1976; Young & Sweeting, 2004; Zucker, 2005). Relative to children who engage in sex-typical play, boys who engage in sex-atypical behaviors, such as doll play, are treated more negatively by same-sex peers and often by adults than are girls who engage in sex-atypical play, such as rough-and-tumble play (e.g., Fagot, 1977, 1984). Young and Sweeting found that adolescent boys who did not engage in sex-typical behaviors were more victimized, socially isolated, and had more depressive symptoms than did girls who did not engage in sex-typical behaviors; in fact, the sex-atypical and sex-typical girls did not differ socially or psychologically from one another (see also Berenbaum, Korman Bryk, Duck, & Resnick, 2004). The relation between children's sex-typical behaviors and their social development speaks to the importance of the stressor-related disruptions of sex-typical play reviewed above.

There is also research on the relation between exposure to psychological and social stressors and children's developing social competencies. In particular, various types of maltreatment (e.g., physical or sexual abuse) have been shown to disrupt the development of peer relationships in children, but most of these studies did not report whether the magnitude of the disruptions varied for boys and girls (e.g., Blanchard-Dallaire & Hébert, 2014; Bolger, Patterson, & Kupersmidt, 1998; Salzinger, Feldman, Hammer, & Rosario, 1993). Given that boys and girls form different types of social relationships, it is likely that maltreatment disrupts different aspects of the social behaviors and competencies in boys and girls, but only a few studies reported sex differences for specific social behaviors or relationships across maltreated children and their better-treated peers.

As an example, peer network density – the degree to which all members of a coalition like one another – is one of the specific behaviors that I predicted to be more vulnerable to stressors for boys than for girls (Table 5.1). Salzinger et al. (1993) found that physically abused children had smaller social networks and less integration within them than did their peers, consistent with social stressors disrupting peer network density and social competencies more generally. Seventy-one percent of the abused children in this study were boys, indicating the social competences of abused boys' would influence the overall results more strongly than the competencies of abused girls, but firm conclusions cannot be drawn because results were not reported separately for boys and girls. As shown in the Boys' Play Behavior section of Table 6.3, a few studies did report specific behavioral or social differences for maltreated girls and boys or only assessed one sex (Dodge et al., 1994; Howe & Parke, 2001; Parker & Herrera, 1996). The results suggest differences in the social behaviors of maltreated girls and boys and that these differences can influence the quality of same-sex social relationships.

Parker and Herrera (1996), for instance, found that maltreated girls but not maltreated boys were less socially positive and supportive in their interactions with peers. Positive and supportive language is more common among girls and women than boys and men when first interacting with another same-sex individual and in the context of dyadic friendships (Maccoby, 1990; Parker & Asher, 1993; Rose & Asher, 1999). As a result, I suggested that positive, supportive social behaviors in the context of same-sex friendships would be more vulnerable to disruption in girls and women than boys and men (Table 5.1). The Parker and Herrera results suggest this may indeed be the case. At this time, however, the research literature on the relation between exposure to stressors and sex-specific social behaviors and competencies is too sparse to draw definitive conclusions, but there is enough to warrant follow up studies, preferably focusing on social behaviors listed in Table 5.1.

## Social Signals

We covered many different types of dynamic condition-dependent social signals across a wide range of nonhuman species in previous chapters, such as the many different forms of vocal (e.g., Table 3.3) and courtship (e.g., Table 3.7 and 4.7) display discussed in Chapters 3 and 4. It is thus not surprising that analogous traits have been hypothesized and studied in humans, including one study of anger displays (Price et al., 2012) and multiple studies of vocal pitch and rated attractiveness (e.g., Puts et al., 2012; Wheatley et al., 2014) shown in the Social Signals section of Table 6.3. I separated these from the facial features described above and shown in Table 6.1, because the facial traits are static and the traits listed in Table 6.3 are dynamic. For humans and many other species, vocal characteristics will be influenced in part by the absolute size of the vocal tract and this in turn creates differences in the fundamental frequency or pitch of the associated signal (e.g., Puts et al., 2012; Rendall et al., 2005). As with many other species in which males are larger than females, men have a lower pitch than females and as a result vocal calls provide reliable cues to the callers' sex.

A more relevant issue for us is whether a man's voice characteristics signal dominance, health, and other traits that would influence male-male competition or female choice, as it does for many of the nonhuman species covered in previous chapters. As shown in the Social Signals section of Table 6.3, men's vocal characteristics do seem to be reliable indicators of traits related to competition and choice, such as physical size, relative to other men (e.g., Apicella et al., 2007; Evans et al., 2006). For instance, in a study of the Hadza, a traditional society in Tanzania, Apicella et al. found that men with a lower vocal pitch sired more children than did other men, but women's vocal characteristics were unrelated to their reproductive success. Although it has not been as well studied as men's vocal traits and despite Apicella et al.'s null results, there is some indication that women's vocal attractiveness is a reliable cue to traits that influence men's mate choices, such as waist-to-hip ratio (Hughes et al., 2004; Wheatley et al., 2014).

However, none of these studies examined how these traits are affected by exposure to parasites, nutrition, social stressors, or toxins. As described above, exposure to these forms of stressor during adolescence compromises boys' physical development and it very likely does the same for their vocal characteristics, given the relation between voice pitch and height (Rendall et al., 2005). Framed somewhat differently, vocal traits may be useful indicators of exposure to stressors during pubertal development. And, these traits may also be an indicator of current condition, because voice pitch will often (but not always) increase for individuals under stress (Giddens, Barron, Byrd-Craven, Clark, & Winter, 2013), but whether this happens in the context of male dominance disputes remains to be determined.

## Risk Taking and Emotional Composure

We now return to Kaobawä's admonition (Chapter 5): "Never show fear to your enemy! Be strong and calm. The moment you reveal that you are afraid, you are in mortal danger! That is when your enemy will kill you" (Chagnon, 1997, p. 256). Emotional composure in the face of physical, often life-endangering threats as well as engagement in other forms of physically risky behaviors can enhance one's status in the male hierarchy and is critical in traditional contexts in which male-male competition is fierce and common (e.g., Chagnon, 1988; Keeley, 1996; Walker & Bailey, 2013). The finding that boys' engagement in both risky physical aggression and other forms of status-motivated risky behaviors (e.g., reckless driving) increases dramatically during pubertal development, remains high throughout young adulthood – at least until they are married – and is modulated by testosterone are all consistent with components of male-male competition (Archer, 2006; Daly & Wilson, 1988; Wilson & Daly, 1985; Zuckerman & Kuhlman, 2000). The associated traits listed in Table 5.1 include behavioral risk taking and emotional composure in threatening circumstances.

Now, we know that lower-status men in modern contexts are more prone to physical aggression and physical risk taking than are higher-status men (Argyle, 1994; Wilson & Daly, 1985); higher-status men take financial and occupational, not physical risks. However, in more traditional contexts, engagement in physical aggression and risk taking will often result in increases in status and reproductive success (Chagnon, 1988). This of course is consistent with the physical sex differences described earlier for humans and in previous chapters for many other species – this is how sexually selected traits become exaggerated. Still, engagement in highly risky aggression and other behaviors in modern contexts might be interpreted as a form of vulnerability and potentially inconsistent with my proposal that social stressors can compromise the expression of sexually selected traits. Or stated differently, stressors that reduce physical risk taking may yield benefits, such as fewer accidental injuries, in many modern contexts. This may be the case, but even so it may also compromise risk taking or emotional composure in other status-related endeavors that are costly (e.g., occupationally) in these contexts.

Either way, the immediate issue for us is whether exposure to social stressors and parasites and poor nutrition undermines men's psychological ability to cope with the risky and intense competition they would experience during male-male competition in natural contexts. Most men in the modern world never experience this level of stress, and we will consider those that do with discussion of combat-related post-traumatic stress disorder in the next chapter. Unfortunately, I was not able to find direct studies of exposure to stressors and engagement in risk taking behaviors and composure under stress, but was able to find some studies of personality and affective proxies of these, including extraversion and neuroticism. Components of the personality trait of extraversion include social assertiveness and engagement in risky activities (Costa, Terracciano, & McCrae, 2001), and across traditional and modern societies extraverted men consistently have more children than their more reserved peers (Alvergne, Jokela, & Lummaa, 2010; Bailey et al., 2013; Berg, Lummaa, Lahdenperä, Rotkirch, & Jokela, 2014; Gurven, von Rueden, Stieglitz, Kaplan, & Rodriguez, 2014). Neuroticism, in contrast, is associated with a proneness to anxiety, depression, and mood swings and with lower levels of extraversion (van der Linden, te Nijenhuis, & Bakker, 2010).

I proposed in Chapter 5 that stressor-related increases in anxiety and depression might be useful indexes of men's ability to cope with male-male competition. Again, I am not arguing that men are more prone to anxiety and depression than are women, as they are not (Caspi et al., 2014; Kessler et al., 2005; Nolen-Hoeksema, 1987; Tolin & Foa, 2006). Nor am I proposing that exposure to stressors will not increase women's anxiety, it does; including in the context of female-female relational aggression (Kendler et al., 2000; Kendler et al., 2005). The point is that anxiety is an affective mechanism that reduces behavioral engagement in risky and potentially harmful activities (Maner et al., 2007). The associated sex difference can be viewed as an enhanced risk-avoidance mechanism in women – they do not need to risk as much as men to reproduce in natural contexts (Betzig, 2012) – or conversely the suppression of the sensitivity of this system enables males to better compete in risky contexts. Framed differently, anxiety is the obverse of the emotional composure that enables men to be successful in highly threatening, competitive contexts. Relatedly, depression is typically associated with social withdrawal and self-assessment as being of low status and thus has the potential to compromise status striving (Price, Sloman, Gardner, Gilbert, & Rohde, 1994). Both anxiety and depression can nevertheless manifest at times as impulsive behavioral aggression in some men (Caspi et al., 2014), but not as the calm use of strategic aggression.

As a result, the reproductive consequences for anxious, depressed, or generally neurotic men are predicted to be more severe than for equally or more strongly affected women. Results from associated studies are mixed but generally consistent with the prediction that anxiety and depression negatively influence men's reproductive prospects and either do not affect or more weakly affect those of women (Berg et al., 2014; Gurven et al., 2014; Jokela, Alvergne,

Pollet, & Lummaa, 2011; Reis, Dörnte, & von der Lippe, 2011). In a longitudinal study of more than 15,000 adults, Jokela and colleagues (2011) found that men who were in the top 15-20% on a measure of neuroticism were 10% less likely to marry than were typical men, and extremely neurotic men (top 2%) were 20% less likely to marry. In contrast, there was no relation between neuroticism and women's chances of marriage. In a large-scale study of the Tsimane (Amazonian horticulturalists), Gurven and colleagues (2014) found that neurotic men had fewer children than other men, especially extraverted and conscientious men. Alvergne and colleagues (2010) found that neurotic Senegalese men were of lower social status than their emotionally stable peers but did not have fewer children; conversely, moderately neurotic women tended to have more children than emotionally stable women. These reproductive consequences mean that anxiety and depression are useful proxies for men's ability to cope with the psychological stressors of male-male competition.

Studies that enabled an assessment of the corresponding prediction that anxiety and depression will be condition dependent in men are shown in the Risk Taking and Emotional Composure section of Table 6.3. Before considering these studies, I mention one conceptually similar study that assessed the relation between parasite (*Toxoplasma gondii*) exposure and performance on a measure of harm avoidance (Flegr et al., 2010); this is an assessment of the tendency to avoid risky behaviors and decisions and one in which men score lower (less harm avoidance) than women (Miettunen, Veijola, Lauronen, Kantojärvi, & Joukamaa, 2007). Unexposed men had lower harm avoidance scores than did unexposed women, as expected, and exposed and unexposed women did not differ significantly. Parasitized men, in contrast, were more harm avoidant than unexposed men and even more harm avoidant than exposed and unexposed women; men's risk however varied with blood Rh factor, and thus some men might be genetically buffered from this particular parasite.

Prenatal exposure to natural stressors, especially during the second trimester, might place men at greater risk than women for later difficulties with anxiety and depression. Maternal malnutrition, severe illness, and severe stress during pregnancy have been shown to increase risk of depression and anxiety for men but not women in adulthood (Brown et al., 1995; de Rooij et al., 2011; Machón et al., 1997; Watson et al., 1999), as well as increase risk of later schizophrenia (Khandaker, Zimbron, Lewis, & Jones, 2013). An example is provided by Watson and colleagues' long-term study of the aftermath of the 1976 Tangshan earthquake in China that killed 240,000 people. Eighteen years later, about 600 people who were in utero when their mothers' lived through the earthquake were assessed for major depression, and compared to demographically matched peers. Rates of depression were elevated for prenatally exposed men and women, but the result was not statistically significant for women. In contrast, men exposed to prenatal stress in the second trimester were nearly three times more likely to suffer from severe depression than their unexposed peers, as compared to a twofold elevation of risk for men exposed in the first or third trimesters. A few studies of maltreatment (e.g., physical abuse) suggest that these stressors may also elevate boys' risk of anxiety and depression more than that of girls (e.g., Pesonen et al., 2007), but most of the studies suggest that both sexes are harmed equally (Briere & Elliott, 2003; Nelson et al., 2002).

In contrast to the results for exposure to natural – parasites, nutrition, and social – stressors and for children's sex-typical play, the relation between exposure to toxins and children's anxiety and depression is more mixed. For prenatal toxin exposure, only about half of the studies suggest elevated risk for later anxiety or depression. Of those consistent with elevated risk, some show boys are more vulnerable than girls (Harley et al., 2013), others show girls are more vulnerable than boys (Braun et al., 2011), and still others show similar levels of vulnerability for boys and girls (Bennett et al., 2002). Some of the variation is likely because the mix of potential toxins assessed in these studies often differs, as noted earlier, but even when the same compound is assessed, the results can be contradictory. Braun et al., for instance, found that prenatal exposure to bisphenol A (BPA) was associated with more externalizing behaviors (e.g., rule breaking) and depressive symptoms in girls but not boys, whereas Perera et al. (2012) found that BPA exposure was associated with fewer than average externalizing behaviors and depressive symptoms in girls but elevated levels in boys. The differences may be related, in part, to differences in the timing of toxin exposure and to differences in the other chemicals to which the children were exposed but not assessed in these studies. In any case, the results for toxin exposure during childhood are also mixed.

However, there are several studies that suggest exposure to some types of toxins in adulthood can compromise men's psychological and social functioning; the focus of these studies is typically on men because they suffer more job-related toxin exposures than do women. The studies do not include strong contrast traits and involve exposure to different types of industrial chemicals and across a wide range of doses but in total should be considered suggestive of heightened risk of psychological disturbance for men (Condray et al., 2000; Morrow et al., 1989). Condray et al. conducted psychiatric interviews of journeymen painters with chronic exposure to solvents (e.g., acetone) and elevated blood lead levels and demographically matched peers. Forty-one percent of the painters were clinically diagnosed with major depression or a related mood disorder, as compared to 16% of their unexposed peers. There was not an elevated risk of anxiety disorders, but using a less stringent criterion Morrow et al. found elevated levels of anxiety, depression, and social isolation among men chronically exposed to solvents.

In all, the studies covered in this section are not ideal for assessing my prediction that risk taking and emotional composure are condition-dependent traits in men. The studies of stressor-related risk of anxiety and depression are suggestive, however, and point to early prenatal development as a potentially critical window for development of the stress-response system in males (Räikkönen et al., 2012). As I described in Chapter 5, this system – including the amygdala, hippocampus, and parts of the prefrontal cortex – also undergoes sex-specific changes during pubertal development (Bramen et al., 2011; Neufang et al., 2009), creating a second developmental window for sex-specific vulnerabilities. The prediction for males is that exposure to stressors that suppress testosterone will disrupt the maturation of this system and compromise the ability to later cope with competitive stressors vis-à-vis the coping abilities of other males, but this remains to be determined.

## CONCLUSION

On the basis of the extensive coverage of sex-specific vulnerabilities described for nonhuman species in Chapters 3 and 4, evidence for similar vulnerabilities in humans should not be surprising. In fact, as I mentioned in Chapter 1 there is a history of the study of sex-specific vulnerabilities in humans, but the focus has been on the physical vulnerability of boys and men (e.g., Greulich, 1951; Stini, 1969; Stinson, 1985). Boys and men are in fact physically vulnerable but in a much more nuanced way than previously assumed. The vulnerability varies across traits, across development, and most critically in ways that are consistent with the condition dependence of sexually selected traits, especially those related to male-male competition. In keeping with Darwin's (1871) insight that physical sex differences are generally small early in development, exposure to stressors during childhood appears to have somewhat but not substantially larger effects on boys' physical development than on that of girls, but these relative risks become larger and more differentiated during pubertal development; specifically, boys' height and muscular development become more vulnerable, and girls' pelvic development and fat reserves may become more vulnerable.

The sex differences in vulnerability for physical fitness and social behavior, however, emerge early in development, a pattern seemingly inconsistent with Darwin's (1871) insight. However, these early sex differences are consistent with his insight if they involve a preparation for competition and choice in adolescence and adulthood, as I have suggested (e.g., Geary, 2010; Geary et al., 2003). Among these telling early vulnerabilities are boys' physical fitness, activity levels, engagement in sex-typical play, and their peer relationships. It is not just boys who are at risk; girls' sex-typical play and potentially their peer relationships may also be disrupted by exposure to stressors. An interesting and potentially important pattern to emerge from these studies is that different stressors may affect boys' and girls' activities and relationships. Peer relationships are disrupted by exposure to social stressors in both sexes, but prenatal exposure to toxins, especially EDCs, may be more harmful to boys' early development. Elevated maternal stress during pregnancy, in contrast, is associated with some changes in girls' sex-typed activities, but not that of boys, whereas these same stressors may affect men's later emotional composure more strongly than that of women. The implication is there may be important sex-by-trait-by-stressor effects that have not been systematically explored.

Finally, although I argued that men's emotional composure is critical to male-male competition in adulthood, and thus a condition-dependent trait, we cannot lose sight of the fact that girls' anxiety and their depressive symptoms increase substantially during adolescence, and that female-female competition in the form of relational aggression may contribute to this increase (Bond et al., 2001). The reader may wonder why coping with relational aggression did not heighten girls' and women's emotional composure to the same extent I propose male-male competition heighted that of boys' and men. I suspect this is because of different cost-benefit trade-offs for men and women in competitive contexts. As noted earlier, in traditional societies women do not need to take as many risks as men to marry and reproduce and this will favor psychological mechanisms, such as anxiety and harm avoidance that will reduce women's risk taking. Moreover, women's heightened sensitivity to subtle social cues and emotional reactions to these cues will improve the ability to detect and react to the subtleties of relational aggression. The cost, however, is an increase in false alarms; that is, emotionally "overreacting." As I stated, the benefit of men's composure and lower levels of anxiety and depression is in terms of facilitating engagement in risky status striving. The costs are lower sensitivity to social nuance, and engagement in activities that can lead to premature death (Wilson & Daly, 1985).

Chapter 7

# Human Vulnerability for Brain and Cognitive Traits

## Chapter Outline

My search for cognitive vulnerabilities centered on the individual-level folk psychological and folk physics domains shown in Figure 5.4. Recall, I proposed that the former is particularly important for the use of relational aggression during female-female competition (Geary et al., 2014), and thus should be more vulnerable in women than in men. Men's coalitional competition should and does result in sex differences ease of forming groups and biases regarding the characteristics of in-groups and out-groups, especially during times of conflict (Benenson, 2014; Sidanius, Pratto, & Bobo, 1994). However, there were no studies of how exposure to stressors (e.g., parasites) other than the competition itself influenced group dynamics and thus I was unable to include discussion of any potential vulnerability. The folk physics competencies that are related to aspects of male-male competition include travel to unfamiliar territory (e.g., raids of other villages), tracking the movement of projectiles in space, and construction of tools (Geary, 2010). The available literature was limited here, too, but there were enough studies on some components of these abilities to gauge whether these competencies are indeed more easily compromised in boys and men than in girls and women.

I returned once again to Kaobawä's admonition regarding fear and men's emotional composure under stress to illustrate how my proposal about sex differences in evolved, vulnerable traits can be applied to the brain; specifically,

Evolution of Vulnerability. http://dx.doi.org/10.1016/B978-0-12-801562-9.00007-7

whether one or several components of the brain system involved in threat detection and regulation of associated emotions is more vulnerable to disruption by exposure to stressors in men than women. The approach is analogous to that described for the system of brain regions that support the song learning and production of male songbirds described in Chapters 2 and 3 (Nowicki et al., 2002).

## COGNITIVE VULNERABILITIES

Given the historical focus on male vulnerability (e.g., Greulich, 1951; Stini, 1969; Stinson, 1985), it seemed prudent to start with examples of female vulnerabilities and therefore the section opens with folk psychology. We then move to folk physics and consideration of male vulnerabilities in aspects of visuospatial abilities.

## Folk Psychology

We begin with consideration of nutritional stressors and women's theory of mind and sensitivity to the emotional states of other people. We then move to consideration of how various types of stressors influence language development and specific language competencies (e.g., word retrieval).

### Theory of Mind and Emotion Recognition

All but one of the studies reviewed in this section and shown in the Theory of Mind and Emotion Recognition portion of Table 7.1 are based on studies of women suffering from anorexia nervosa – a disturbance of body image that results in highly restricted food intake (American Psychiatric Association, 2013). The result is chronic malnutrition, which is why I classified these studies as diet/nutrition in the manipulation column of the table. The theory of mind tests used in these studies included presenting the women with a sequence of events and asking them to make inferences about a person's mental state (e.g., a person's beliefs) or a physical state (e.g., the location of misplaced car keys) depicted in the sequence (Happé, Brownell, & Winner, 1999). The emotion recognition tests required the women to identify positive or negative emotions signaled by others through facial expressions, vocal intonation, or filmed sequences of body posture and motion (e.g., Baron-Cohen et al., 1999; Golan, Baron-Cohen, Hill, & Golan, 2006; Golan, Baron-Cohen, Hill, & Rutherford, 2007; Oldershaw et al., 2010).

Although the number of available studies is too small to draw definitive conclusions, there is evidence that women with anorexia have theory of mind deficits that are unrelated to intelligence (Tapajóz Pereira de Sampaio et al., 2013) or the ability to make physical-state inferences (Russell et al., 2009). Russell et al., for instance, found that healthy women were better at making inferences

**TABLE 7.1** Condition-Dependent Folk Psychology Cognitive Traits in Humans

| Species | Scientific Name | ST | Trait | Contrast | | | | Life History | Manipulation | References |
|---|---|---|---|---|---|---|---|---|---|---|
| | | | | CD | S | Trait | Effect | | | |
| *Theory of mind and emotion recognition* | | | | | | | | | | |
| Human | *Homo sapiens* | N | Theory of mind | Y | F | Intelligence | C<T | Adult | Diet/nutrition | Tapajóz Pereira de Sampaio, Soneira, Aulicino, and Allegri (2013) |
| | | N | Theory of mind | Y | F | Nonsocial inference | C=T | Adult | Diet/nutrition | Tchanturia et al. (2004) |
| | | N | Theory of mind | Y^a | F | Nonsocial inference | C<T | Adult | Diet/nutrition | Russell, Schmidt, Doherty, Young, and Tchanturia (2009) |
| | | N | Facial emotion recognition | Y | F | Face discrimination | C<T | Adolescence | Diet/nutrition | Zonnevylle-Bender, Van Goozen, Cohen-Kettenis, van Elburg, and Van Engeland (2004) |
| | | N | Facial emotion recognition | N | F | Recovered female | C=T | Adult | Diet/nutrition | Harrison, Tchanturia, and Treasure (2010) |
| | | N | Facial emotion recognition | Y | F | Unexposed female | C<T | Adult | Diet/nutrition | Pollatos, Herbert, Schandry, and Gramann (2008) |

*Continued*

**TABLE 7.1** Condition-Dependent Folk Psychology Cognitive Traits in Humans—cont'd

| Species | Scientific Name | ST | Trait | CD | S | Contrast Trait | Effect | Life History | Manipulation | References |
|---|---|---|---|---|---|---|---|---|---|---|
| | | N | Facial emotion recognition | N | F | Unexposed female | C=T | Adult | Diet/nutrition | Mendlewicz, Linkowski, Bazelmans, and Philippot (2005) |
| | | N | Facial emotion recognition | Y | F | Affect regulation | C=T | Adult | Diet/nutrition | Harrison, Sullivan, Tchanturia, and Treasure (2009) |
| | | N | Facial emotion recognition | Y | F | Reading | C<T | Adult | Diet/nutrition | Russell et al. (2009) |
| | | N | Facial emotion recognition | N | F | Emotion recognition | C>T | Adult | Diet/nutrition | Kessler, Schwarze, Filipic, Traue, and von Wietersheim (2006) |
| | | N | Facial emotion recognition | Y | F | Face memory | C<T | Adult | Diet/nutrition | Kucharska-Pietura, Nikolaou, Masiak, and Treasure (2004) |
| | | N | Facial emotion recognition | Y | F | Face discrimination | C<T | Adult | Diet/nutrition | Zonnevylle-Bender et al. (2004) |
| | | N | Facial emotion recognition | N[b] | F | Recovered female | C=T | Adult | Diet/nutrition | Oldershaw, Hambrook, Tchanturia, Treasure, and Schmidt (2010) |
| | | N | Facial emotion recognition | N | F | Unexposed female | C=T | Adult | Diet/nutrition | Adenzato, Todisco, and Ardito (2012) |

| | | | | | | | | | | |
|---|---|---|---|---|---|---|---|---|---|---|
| | | N | Facial emotion recognition | Y | F | Intelligence | C<T | Adult | Diet/nutrition | Harrison, Sullivan, et al. (2010) |
| | | N | Facial emotion recognition | Y | F | Intelligence | C<T | Adult | Diet/nutrition | Tapajóz Pereira de Sampaio et al. (2013) |
| | | N/T | Facial emotion recognition | Yc | F | Level of exposure | C<T | Adult | Toxin | Valmas, Ruiz, Gansler, Sawyer, and Oscar-Berman (2014) |
| | | N/T | Facial memory | Yc | F | Level of exposure | C=T | Adult | Toxin | Valmas et al. (2014) |
| | | N | Vocal emotion recognition | Y | F | Recovered female | C<T | Adult | Diet/nutrition | Oldershaw et al. (2010) |
| | | N | Vocal emotion recognition | Y | F | Unexposed female | C<T | Adult | Diet/nutrition | Kucharska-Pietura et al. (2004) |
| | | N | Body emotion recognition | Y | F | Recovered female | C<T | Adult | Diet/nutrition | Oldershaw et al. (2010) |
| | | N/T | Emotion matching | Yc | F | Level of exposure | C<T | Adult | Toxin | Valmas et al. (2014) |
| **Language** | | | | | | | | | | |
| Human | *Homo sapiens* | N | Grammar understanding | Y | B | Male grammar | C<T | Prenatal | Premature birth | Largo, Molinari, Pinto, Weber, and Due (1986) |
| | | N | Language comprehension | Y | B | Male language | C=T | Prenatal | Premature birth | Taylor, Klein, Minich, and Hack (2000) |

*Continued*

**TABLE 7.1** Condition-Dependent Folk Psychology Cognitive Traits in Humans—cont'd

| Species | Scientific Name | ST | Trait | CD | S | Contrast | | Life History | Manipulation | References |
|---|---|---|---|---|---|---|---|---|---|---|
| | | | | | | Trait | Effect | | | |
| | | N | Language comprehension | N | B | Unexposed female | C=T | Prenatal | Toxin | Lewis et al. (2011) |
| | | N | Language comprehension | N | B | Male language | C=T | Prenatal | Toxin | Singer et al. (2001) |
| | | N | Sentence comprehension | Y | B | Male sentence comprehension | C<T | Prenatal | Premature birth | Largo et al. (1986) |
| | | N | Sentence comprehension | Y | B | Male sentence comprehension | C=T | Childhood | Stress/poverty | Levine, Vasilyeva, Lourenco, Newcombe, and Huttenlocher (2005) |
| | | N | Language comprehension | Y | B | Male language comprehension | C<T | Adult | Alzheimer's | Henderson, Watt, and Galen Buckwalter (1996) |
| | | N | General language | Y | B | Male language | C<T | Adult | Alzheimer's | Doraiswamy et al. (1997) |
| | | F/T | Language composite | Y | F | Unexposed female | C<T | Adult | Chemotherapy | Tchen et al. (2003) |
| | | F/T | Language composite | Y | F | Unexposed female | C<T | Adult | Chemotherapy | Brezden, Phillips, Abdolell, Bunston, and Tannock (2000) |

| | | | | | | | | |
|---|---|---|---|---|---|---|---|---|
| N | Verbal memory | Y | B | Male memory | C=T | Prenatal | Premature birth | Taylor, Klein, Minich, et al. (2000) |
| N | Verbal memory | Y | B | Male memory | C=T | Adult | Alzheimer's | Beinhoff, Tumani, Brettschneider, Bittner, and Riepe (2008) |
| N | Verbal memory | Y | B | Male memory | C<T | Adult | Alzheimer's | McPherson, Back, Buckwalter, and Cummings (1999) |
| N | Verbal memory | Y | B | Male memory | C=T | Adult | Alzheimer's | Beinhoff et al. (2008) |
| N | Verbal memory | Y | B | Male memory | C<T | Adult | Alzheimer's | Chapman et al. (2011) |
| N | Verbal memory | Y | B | Male memory | C<T | Adult | Alzheimer's | Henderson and Buckwalter (1994) |
| N | Verbal memory | Y | F | Intelligence | C<T | Adult | Stress/abuse | Bremner, Vermetten, Afzal, and Vythilingam (2004) |
| F/T | Verbal memory | N | F | Visual memory | C=T | Adult | Chemotherapy | Castellon et al. (2004) |
| F/T | Verbal memory | Y | F | Visual memory | C>T | Adult | Chemotherapy | Wieneke and Dienst (1995) |
| F/T | Verbal memory | Y | F | Pre-to-post change | C<T | Adult | Chemotherapy | Wefel, Lenzi, Theriault, Davis, and Meyers (2004) |

*Continued*

**TABLE 7.1** Condition-Dependent Folk Psychology Cognitive Traits in Humans—cont'd

| Species | Scientific Name | ST | Trait | CD | S | Contrast Trait | Effect | Life History | Manipulation | References |
|---|---|---|---|---|---|---|---|---|---|---|
| | | F/T | Verbal memory | N | F | Unexposed female | C=T | Adult | Chemotherapy | Donovan et al. (2005) |
| | | F/T | Verbal memory | Y[d] | F | Pre-to-post change | C<T | Adult | Chemotherapy | Shilling, Jenkins, Morris, Deutsch, and Bloomfield (2005) |
| | | F/T | Verbal memory | N | F | Pre-to-post change | C=T | Adult | Chemotherapy | Jenkins et al. (2006) |
| | | F/T | Verbal memory | Y[e] | F | Pre-to-post change | C<T | Adult | Chemotherapy | Bender et al. (2006) |
| | | F/T | Verbal memory | N | F | Unexposed female | C=T | Adult | Chemotherapy | Scherwath et al. (2006) |
| | | F/T | Verbal memory | Y[f] | F | Unexposed female | C<T | Adult | Chemotherapy | Schagen et al. (1999) |
| | | F/T | Verbal memory | N | F | Pre-to-post change | C<T | Adult | Chemotherapy | Hermelink et al. (2007) |
| | | N | Verbal memory | Y | B | Male memory | C<T | Adult | Toxin | Lin, Guo, Tsai, Yang, and Guo (2008) |
| | | N/T | Verbal memory | Y | F | Education level | C<T | Adult | Toxin | Weuve et al. (2009) |
| | | N/T | Verbal memory | N | F | Intelligence | C=T | Adult | Toxin | Uzzell and Oler (1986) |

| Citation | | | | | | | | |
|---|---|---|---|---|---|---|---|---|
| Zonnevylle-Bender et al. (2004) | Diet/nutrition | Adult | C=T | Unexposed female | | N | Verbal memory | N |
| Jennische and Sedin (2003) | Premature birth | Prenatal | C<T | Male fluency | B | Y | Verbal fluency | N |
| Taylor, Klein, Minich, et al. (2000) | Premature birth | Prenatal | C=T | Male fluency | B | N | Verbal fluency | N |
| de Rooij, Wouters, Yonker, Painter, and Roseboom (2010) | Diet/nutrition | Prenatal | C=T | Male fluency | B | N | Verbal fluency | N |
| Zimmermann et al. (2006) | Diet/nutrition | Childhood | C=T | Male fluency | B | Y | Verbal fluency | F |
| Marra, Ferraccioli, and Gainotti (2007) | Alzheimer's | Adult | C=T | Male fluency | B | Y | Verbal fluency | N |
| Beinhoff et al. (2008) | Alzheimer's | Adult | C=T | Male fluency | B | Y | Verbal fluency | N |
| Bayles et al. (1999) | Alzheimer's | Adult | C=T | Male fluency | B | N[g] | Verbal fluency | N |
| Moreno-Martínez, Laws, and Schulz (2008) | Alzheimer's | Adult | C<T | Male fluency | B | Y | Verbal fluency | N |
| Henderson and Buckwalter (1994) | Alzheimer's | Adult | C<T | Male fluency | B | Y | Verbal fluency | N |
| Ripich, Petrill, Whitehouse, and Ziol (1995) | Alzheimer's | Adult | C=T | Male fluency | B | N[h] | Verbal fluency | N |

*Continued*

**TABLE 7.1** Condition-Dependent Folk Psychology Cognitive Traits in Humans—cont'd

| Species | Scientific Name | ST | Trait | CD | S | Contrast Trait | Effect | Life History | Manipulation | References |
|---|---|---|---|---|---|---|---|---|---|---|
| | | N | Verbal fluency | Y[i] | B | Male fluency | C<T | Adult | Alzheimer's | Henderson et al. (1996) |
| | | N | Verbal fluency | Y | B | Male fluency | C<T | Adult | Alzheimer's | Monsch et al. (1992) |
| | | F/T | Verbal fluency | N | F | Unexposed female | C=T | Adult | Chemotherapy | Scherwath et al. (2006) |
| | | F/T | Verbal fluency | Y | F | Unexposed female | C<T | Adult | Chemotherapy | Castellon et al. (2004) |
| | | F/T | Verbal fluency | N | F | Unexposed female | C=T | Adult | Chemotherapy | van Dam et al. (1998) |
| | | F/T | Verbal fluency | Y | F | Test norms | C<T | Adult | Chemotherapy | Wieneke and Dienst (1995) |
| | | F/T | Verbal fluency | Y | F | Unexposed female | C<T | Adult | Chemotherapy | Schagen et al. (1999) |
| | | F/T | Verbal fluency | N | F | Unexposed female | C=T | Adult | Chemotherapy | Scherwath et al. (2006) |
| | | N | Verbal fluency | N | F | Unexposed female | C=T | Adult | Diet/nutrition | Zonnevylle-Bender et al. (2004) |
| | | N | Verbal fluency | N | F | Unexposed female | C=T | Adolescent | Diet/nutrition | Zonnevylle-Bender et al. (2004) |
| | | N/T | Word retrieval | Y | B | Male retrieval | C=T | Prenatal | Toxin | Grandjean et al. (1997) |

| N/T | | | | | | | | | |
| --- | --- | --- | --- | --- | --- | --- | --- | --- | --- |
| N | | Word retrieval | N | B | Unexposed female | C=T | Prenatal | Toxin | Lewis et al. (2011) |
| N | | Word retrieval | Y | B | Male retrieval | C<T | Prenatal | Premature birth | Saavalainen et al. (2006) |
| N | | Word retrieval | N | B | Male retrieval | C=T | Adult | Alzheimer's | Hebert et al. (2000) |
| N | | Word retrieval | Yi | B | Male retrieval | C<T | Adult | Alzheimer's | Henderson and Buckwalter (1994) |
| N | | Word retrieval | N | B | Male retrieval | C=T | Adult | Alzheimer's | Hebert et al. (2000) |
| N | | Word retrieval | Y | B | Male retrieval | C<T | Adult | Alzheimer's | Buckwalter et al. (1996) |
| N | | Word retrieval | Y | B | Male retrieval | C<T | Adult | Alzheimer's | Henderson et al. (1996) |
| N | | Word retrieval | Y | B | Male retrieval | C<T | Adult | Alzheimer's | Laiacona, Barbarotto, and Capitani (1998) |
| N | | Word retrieval | N | B | Male retrieval | C=T | Adult | Alzheimer's | Heun and Kockler (2002) |
| N | | Word retrieval | Y | B | Male retrieval | C<T | Adult | Alzheimer's | McPherson et al. (1999) |
| N | | Word retrieval | Y | B | Male retrieval | C<T | Adult | Vascular disease | Buckwalter et al. (1996) |
| N | | Word learning | Y | B | Male learning | C=T | Prenatal | Premature birth | Taylor, Klein, Minich, et al. (2000) |

Continued

**TABLE 7.1** Condition-Dependent Folk Psychology Cognitive Traits in Humans—cont'd

| Species | Scientific Name | ST | Trait | CD | S | Trait | Effect | Life History | Manipulation | References |
|---|---|---|---|---|---|---|---|---|---|---|
| | | | | | | | | | | |
| | | N | Word learning | Y | B | Male learning | C=T | Adult | Alzheimer's | Henderson and Buckwalter (1994) |
| | | N | Word learning | Y | B | Male learning | C=T | Adult | Alzheimer's | Beinhoff et al. (2008) |
| | | F/T | Word learning | N | F | Unexposed female | C=T | Adult | Chemotherapy | Scherwath et al. (2006) |
| | | F/T | Word learning | N | F | Pre-to-post change | C<T | Adult | Chemotherapy | Jenkins et al. (2006) |
| | | F/T | Word learning | N | F | Unexposed female | C=T | Adult | Chemotherapy | Donovan et al. (2005) |
| | | F/T | Word learning | N | F | Test norms | C=T | Adult | Chemotherapy | Wieneke and Dienst (1995) |
| | | F/T | Word learning | N | F | Unexposed female | C=T | Adult | Chemotherapy | Castellon et al. (2004) |
| | | F/T | Word learning | Y[d] | F | Pre-to-post change | C<T | Adult | Chemotherapy | Shilling et al. (2005) |
| | | F/T | Word learning | N | F | Unexposed female | C<T | Adult | Chemotherapy | Schagen et al. (1999) |
| | | F/T | Word learning | N | F | Pre-to-post change | C<T | Adult | Chemotherapy | Bender et al. (2006) |

Contrast

| N | | | | | | | | |
|---|---|---|---|---|---|---|---|---|
| N | Word learning | Y | B | Male learning | C<T | Adult | Toxin | Lin et al. (2008) |
| N | Word articulation | Y | B | Male articulation | C<T | Prenatal | Premature birth | Largo et al. (1986) |
| N | Word articulation | Y | B | Male articulation | C<T | Prenatal | Premature birth | Jennische and Sedin (2003) |
| N | Syllable articulation | Y | B | Male articulation | C=T | Prenatal | Premature birth | Largo et al. (1986) |
| N | Grammatical utterances | Y | B | Male grammar | C<T | Prenatal | Premature birth | Jennische and Sedin (2003) |
| N | Auditory discrimination | Y | B | Male discrimination | C<T | Prenatal | Premature birth | Jennische and Sedin (2003) |
| N | Phonological awareness | Y | B | Unexposed female | C<T | Prenatal | Toxin | Lewis et al. (2011) |
| N | Spontaneous speech | Y | B | Male spontaneous | C<T | Prenatal | Premature birth | Jennische and Sedin (2003) |
| N | Language development | Y[k] | B | Male language | C<T | Prenatal | Toxin | Malakoff, Mayes, Schottenfeld, and Howell (1999) |
| N | Language development | Y | B | Male language | C<T | Prenatal | Premature birth | Largo et al. (1986) |
| N | Expressive language | Y[l] | B | Unexposed female | C<T | Prenatal | Toxin | Bandstra et al. (2011) |

*Continued*

**TABLE 7.1** Condition-Dependent Folk Psychology Cognitive Traits in Humans—cont'd

| Species | Scientific Name | ST | Trait | CD | S | Contrast | | Life History | Manipulation | References |
|---------|-----------------|----|-------|----|----|----------|--|--------------|--------------|-----------|
| | | | | | | Trait | Effect | | | |
| | | N | Receptive language | N | B | Unexposed female | C<T | Prenatal | Toxin | Bandstra et al. (2011) |
| | | N | Expressive language | Y | B | Unexposed female | C<T | Prenatal | Toxin | Beeghly et al. (2006) |
| | | N | Receptive language | N | B | Unexposed female | C=T | Prenatal | Toxin | Beeghly et al. (2006) |

Note: ST, study type (F, field experiment; N, natural variation; T, toxin); CD, condition dependent (Y, yes; N, no); S, sex of participants for trait of interest (F, female; B, both sexes).

[a]There was a significant interaction between mental and physical reasoning scores across anorexic and healthy participants, whereby the latter group was better at the mental than physical reasoning task but no difference for the anorexic group.

[b]Women with current anorexia nervosa (AN) were worse than women who had recovered from AN, but the statistical result was only a trend (p=0.1), covarying IQ.

[c]Abstinent alcoholic women and men were compared to nonalcoholic women and men on a variety of social-cognition measures; the men had heavier alcohol use than the women, making a direct comparison difficult. There were no differences between alcoholic women and nonalcoholic women on any of these measures, but level of alcohol use was related. Recognizing affect in faces was negatively correlated with alcohol use in women and positively in men; matching emotions in voice and face was compromised by heavy alcohol use in both sexes; and one of two measures of face memory was correlated with alcohol use more strongly in women than men.

[d]The results were mixed. There was a reliable decline (including control group contrast) for word list memory, but no reliable decline on another verbal memory test.

[e]There were declines in word memory 1 year after chemotherapy, but no decline in visuospatial memory for the chemotherapy-only group, but there were visuospatial declines in the chemotherapy plus tamoxifen group.

[f]Chemotherapy was associated with poor word recall relative to a surgery-only group, but chemotherapy was also associated with figural memory deficits.

[g]Women with Alzheimer's disease (AD) scored lower than men with (AD), but the difference was not statistically significant.

[h]There were no differences on the word fluency test at study start but differences emerged after 18 months, with women with AD scoring lower than men with AD, but this as only a statistical trend when controlling other variables.

[i]There were differences on semantic fluency (animal naming) but not fluency-based on letter sounds; no differences in digit span.

[j]The result was found in two independent experiments.

[k]Most specific sex by cocaine exposure effects were not significant (small n), but the overall pattern showed the exposed girls were more similar to unexposed and exposed boys than unexposed girls.

[l]Exposed males were not different from unexposed males, but the sex by exposure interaction was not significant; the female-only contrast was significant.

about people's mental states than physical states, but women with anorexia did not show this mental-state advantage. Oldershaw and colleagues (2010) found a similar deficit for anorexic women's sensitivity to the emotional cues of others based on the facial expression, vocal intonation, and body movement. A nice feature of this study is the inclusion of a group of women who recovered from anorexia as well as a group of healthy women. The inclusion of a recovered group helped to address the question of whether the social-cognitive deficits associated with anorexia existed before the onset of the disease or whether the disease itself compromised these abilities. The emotion sensitivity of the groups of acute and recovered anorexics relative to the healthy women is shown in Figure 7.1. As can be seen, the recovered anorexics did not differ from their healthy peers in processing emotion cues whether signaled by body posture, vocal intonation, or facial expression (see also Cowdrey, Harmer, Park, & McCabe, 2012); Harrison, Tchanturia, and Treasure found deficits in women who had recovered from anorexia, but smaller than those with acute anorexia. Two out of three women with anorexia were less sensitive to emotions signaled through body posture and movement than was the average healthy woman, and four out of five were less sensitive to emotions signaled through vocal intonation.

The result for facial features was smaller than that found for vocal intonation and body posture and not statistically significant in this study (Oldershaw et al., 2010), but five of the six other studies that used the same facial-features test found that women with anorexia were less sensitive to emotion cues than were healthy women (Harrison et al., 2009; Harrison, Sullivan, et al., 2010;

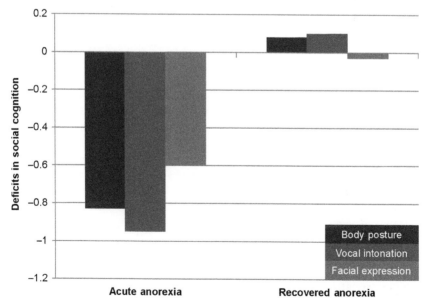

**FIGURE 7.1**    Social-cognitive deficits for women with acute anorexia and those who have recovered from anorexia relative to healthy women. *Based on data presented in Oldershaw et al. (2010).* (See the color plate section.)

Harrison, Tchanturia, et al., 2010; Russell et al., 2009; Tapajóz Pereira de Sampaio et al., 2013; the exception was Adenzato et al., 2012). One of these studies also included a group of women with bulimia (Tapajóz Pereira de Sampaio et al., 2013). These women's eating disorder involves a cycle of binge eating followed by purging (e.g., through vomiting or misuse of laxatives). Critically, for the discussion here, these women are typically of average weight but have the same issues with emotional regulation that are common with anorexia. These women's sensitivity to emotion cues did not differ from that of healthy women and was better than that of the women with anorexia (but see Kessler et al., 2006). Similarly, Jones, Harmer, Cowen, and Cooper (2008) found that women at risk for anorexia, but of normal weight were less skilled than other women at detecting happy faces, but did not differ in sensitivity to facial expressions depicting other emotions (e.g., anger, fear, sadness).

If women's social-cognitive abilities were elaborated through female-female competition, then they may be more sensitive to the mental states and emotion cues signaled by other women than those signaled by men. For groups of healthy girls and women this does appear to be the case (Rehnman & Herlitz, 2006, 2007). Most of the studies of women with anorexia did not assess whether their social-cognitive deficits were exaggerated when reading the cues of other women, and the two studies that did yielded contradictory results. Russell et al. (2009) found that women with anorexia were deficient in reading the facial expressions of other women but not those of men, whereas Tapajóz Pereira de Sampaio et al. (2013) found deficits in reading the facial cues of men but not women. It may be that any sex-specific sensitivity is limited to the signaling of hostile intent or emotions but this remains to be determined.

In all, studies of the social-cognitive deficits of women with anorexia suggest that exposure to stressors will compromise these folk psychology competencies, as I predicted (Table 5.1), but are not conclusive. Follow-up studies of exposure to other types of stressors (e.g., parasites) and using men's competence at theory of mind and recognition of emotion cues as contrast traits will provide stronger assessments of my predictions. There are, for instance, documented declines in the processing of social information, such as facial expressions, associated with Alzheimer's disease (below) but they do not typically analyze sex differences (e.g., Bediou et al., 2009).

In any case, potential variation in sensitivity to stressors across development also remains to be addressed. As with men's physical aggression and risk taking (Wilson & Daly, 1985), women's folk psychological competencies are put to full use during the years of reproductive competition and, given this, these traits may be more vulnerable to stressors during this portion of the life span (i.e., 15-35 years of age) than at earlier or later ages.

## Language

The research base on the relation between exposure to stressors and language competencies is much more comprehensive than that for theory of mind and emotion recognition. The language studies range from the effects of premature birth on natural language development (Largo et al., 1986) to the deficits (e.g., difficulty remembering common words) that emerge during the early stages of Alzheimer's disease (Henderson & Buckwalter, 1994). The other stressors assessed in this literature include poor nutrition (Zimmermann et al., 2006) and exposure to toxins (Bender et al., 2006), including chemotherapy, and the associated studies include a wide number of contrast traits. The result is a more thorough analysis of my hypothesis that exposure to stressors will more strongly affect girls' and women's language competencies than those of boys and men. Although I did not organize the tables in terms of stressors – opting instead to organize them in terms of the vulnerable traits – considering the relation between premature birth, Alzheimer's disease, and chemotherapy on girls' and women's language competencies conveys their vulnerabilities in this domain.

*Premature birth.* As with many of the domains covered in this book, most of the studies of the relation between premature birth and language development did not report sex differences or used only a single language measure. One exception is a series of follow-up assessments of very low birth weight children in early and later childhood (Hack et al., 1992; Taylor, Klein, Minich, et al., 2000). At 11 years of age, these children showed a variety of social and cognitive deficits, including language deficits. Contrary to my hypothesis, girls and boys showed similar levels of language deficit (shown in Table 7.1 for Taylor, Klein, Minich, et al. (2000)). However, the children assessed in these studies were unusually small at birth relative to most premature children. With this type of extreme stressor – as noted in Chapter 1 – broad deficits in both sexes are expected and typically found (Marlow, Wolke, Bracewell, & Samara, 2005; Wolke, Samara, Bracewell, & Marlow, 2008). A better assessment of my hypothesis is found with studies of more "typical" premature births, which will result in more subtle and varied deficits. These assessments are found in Largo et al.'s (1986) and Jennische and Sedin's (2003) large and comprehensive longitudinal studies of the natural language competencies of preterm and term children; the birth weight of the premature children in these studies was at least double that of the children in the Taylor et al. study.

Jennische and Sedin (2003) found that by 6 years of age term girls' language competencies were generally better than those of term boys, and those of preterm girls generally exceeded those of preterm boys. The subtle deficits of preterm girls became apparent when they were compared to term girls. Girls born at about 30 weeks gestation showed deficits in word articulation, word fluency, sound discrimination, and grammatical structure of utterances, among other deficits, relative to their term peers. In contrast, there were few language differences between preterm and term boys. Largo et al. (1986) followed preterm infants – born at 33 weeks gestation on average – for 5 years. Over the course of the study, the language development of these infants and a group of term peers was assessed ten times in the lab and their mothers completed multiple assessments of their word usage at home. At 5 years of age, these children were assessed on overall language competencies. Term girls had an advantage over

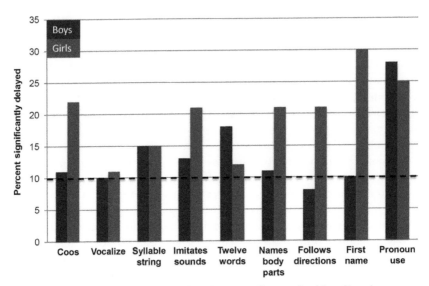

**FIGURE 7.2**    Delays in the onset of significant language milestones for girls and boys born prematurely. *Based on data presented in Largo et al. (1986).* (See the color plate section.)

term boys, as found by Jennische and Sedin. However, preterm boys' overall language competencies were better than those of preterm girls.

There were also differences between preterm girls and preterm boys in the age of achieving significant language milestones, as shown in Figure 7.2. The dashed line shows the cutoff for the slowest 10% of term children (boys and girls combined), and the bars show the percentage of preterm children that achieved the milestone later than these relatively delayed term children. As an example, 11% of the preterm boys started to coo at about the same age or a little later than the slowest 10% of term children; that is, the latest developing preterm boys were not much different than the latest developing term children. In contrast, twice as many preterm girls were delayed in the onset of cooing, and in the onset of sound imitation, learning the names of body parts, and following directions, and three times as many preterm girls as boys were delayed in the age of learning their own name. The reversal of girls' typical advantage over that of boys in language competencies is striking.

Nevertheless, in terms of day-to-day life the important differences are not between preterm boys and preterm girls, but between preterm girls and term girls. As I described in Chapter 5, the segregation of boys and girls into same-sex groups means that girls navigate childhood and much of adolescence in the midst of relationships with other girls, and language is crucial for developing and maintaining their same-sex relationships and, of course, for engaging in relational aggression.

*Alzheimer's disease.* Generally, sex differences in cognition remain the same throughout the life span for healthy adults (e.g., Ferreira, Ferreira Santos Galduróz, Ferri, & Fernandes Galduróz, 2014; Meinz & Salthouse, 1998; Willis & Schaie, 1988; Wilson et al., 1975), but differences often emerge with the onset of Alzheimer's disease. The issue is complicated, however, because Alzheimer's appears to result in greater overall cognitive declines in women than men (Irvine, Laws, Gale, & Kondel, 2012), even with similar levels of brain pathology (Barnes et al., 2005). As with very low birth weight, the cognitive deficits found toward the later stages of Alzheimer's disease are broad and extend beyond sexually and socially selected traits. The predicted sex-specific vulnerability of women's social and cognitive competences should then be most evident during the early stages of the disease.

Most of the studies of cognitive declines associated with Alzheimer's disease do not report separate results for men and women, but a meta-analysis revealed that Alzheimer-related verbal deficits were larger in studies with higher proportions of women than men, suggesting a sex-specific vulnerability (Laws, Adlington, Gale, Moreno-Martínez, & Sartori, 2007). This is indeed a consistent pattern for the studies that have reported sex differences, as shown in the Language section of Table 7.1. Compared to men with Alzheimer's disease, similarly afflicted women have more serious deficits in language comprehension (Henderson et al., 1996), verbal memory (e.g., remembering a spoken paragraph; Beinhoff et al., 2008), verbal fluency (e.g., ease of retrieving related words from long-term memory; Moreno-Martínez et al., 2008), and word learning and retrieval (Beinhoff et al., 2008; Henderson & Buckwalter, 1994).

Given the potential for more severe declines for women than men with Alzheimer's disease generally, it is also important to contrast the degree of women's language-related deficits to their deficits on nonlanguage domains. In one such comparison, Henderson and Buckwalter (1994) compared groups of men and women with Alzheimer's disease on a test that assesses ease of retrieving common words from long-term memory (i.e., naming drawings of objects) and a spatial drawing test that is sensitive to visuospatial deficits associated with some types of neurological disorders; healthy adults do not show sex differences on the latter (i.e., it is not a good measure of men's sexually selected spatial abilities). Three out of four women with Alzheimer's had more difficulties with word retrieval than did the average man with Alzheimer's, but there were no differences on the drawing test. A follow-up study using a large national registry of individuals with Alzheimer's disease (270 men, 377 women) confirmed this pattern, albeit with smaller overall effects. With control of demographic factors, such as age, education, and disease duration, women with Alzheimer's disease had larger deficits in verbal fluency and verbal memory than did men with the disease, but again there were no differences on the spatial drawing test.

Figure 7.3 shows the deficits of men and women with Alzheimer's disease relative to healthy same-sex and same-age adults for various measures of working memory (the ability to keep information in mind and mentally manipulate it) and word learning and memory (Beinhoff et al., 2008). There were no sex differences for the working memory measures, and men and women with Alzheimer's disease showed similar levels of impairment relative to healthy individuals of the same sex. For the word learning test, the participants heard a list of words that clustered in a few categories (e.g., four fruits, four spices) and

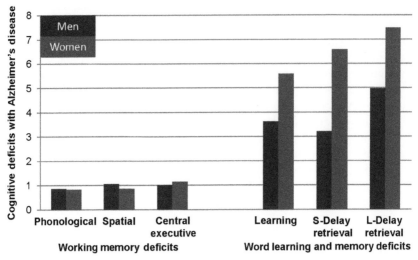

**FIGURE 7.3**  Cognitive deficits for men and women with Alzheimer's disease relative to healthy same-sex adults S, short; L, long. *Based on data presented in Beinhoff et al. (2008).* (See the color plate section.)

were asked to repeat these immediately after hearing them and after shorter (a few minutes) and longer (20 min) delays. Women typically do better than their male peers on this test and this was the case for Beinhoff et al.'s healthy adults. The women with Alzheimer's disease had lower scores than men with the disease on all three verbal measures, but the real magnitude of these deficits is found with the comparisons to same-sex healthy adults. Both men and women with Alzheimer's had larger deficits in word learning and memory than in working memory, but the magnitude of these deficits was much larger for women than men. Beinhoff et al. also administered a shape memory test with immediate and delayed recall and the women with Alzheimer's had deficits here, too, suggesting the word test results might be tapping broader memory impairments. However, the women's word learning and memory impairments were 64% higher than their shape learning and memory impairments.

This is not to say that women with Alzheimer's do not have visuospatial deficits, they do. In fact, people with this disease have difficulties learning new routes from one place to another and eventually navigating in familiar places (Lithfous, Dufour, & Després, 2013). These have been documented using experimental tests of maze and route learning and in learning real-world routes, but the associated studies do not report whether there are sex differences in the magnitude of these deficits and sometimes do not even report the number of men and women in the studies (Cushman, Stein, & Duffy, 2008; Hort et al., 2007; Monacelli, Cushman, Kavcic, & Duffy, 2003; Weniger, Ruhleder, Lange, Wolf, & Irle, 2011). For healthy adults, men have much better navigational skills than women, especially with the virtual maze tests used in some of the studies of Alzheimer's disease (Moffat, Hampson, & Hatzipantelis, 1998), and thus women with this disease would be expected to score significantly below men with the disease in this domain. The critical, unanswered question is whether language competencies show steeper declines than visuospatial competencies during the early stages of the disease and relative to healthy women.

*Chemotherapy.* Chemotherapies can of course vary in terms of dosage, specific chemicals used, length of treatment, and so forth (Wefel, Kayl, et al., 2004), and as a result can only provide broad-brush assessments of the hypothesis that women's language competencies, as well as their other folk psychological abilities (not assessed in these studies) are vulnerable traits. Nevertheless, I considered these potential effects because they may be practically useful – the development of measures to better study and thus predict the unwanted effects of chemotherapy – in ways elaborated on in the next chapter.

In reviewing this literature, I focused on breast cancer because chemotherapy studies of other types of cancer typically combined men and women. As shown in the Language section of Table 7.1, chemotherapy is not generally associated with compromised word learning (e.g., learning to associate pairs of words, such as phone-tree; Bender et al., 2006), but is often found to compromise more complex language competencies, including verbal memory (Wefel, Lenzi, et al., 2004) and verbal fluency (Schagen et al., 1999). Even in these latter cases, the overall results are mixed and nuanced (Shilling et al., 2005). Shilling and colleagues, for instance, tested women's cognitive competencies prior to the start of chemotherapy and one month after treatment ended. As found for women with Alzheimer's disease, chemotherapy was associated with significant declines in some aspects of verbal memory but no changes in shape learning and memory. At the same time, chemotherapy did not affect performance on a different type of language memory test, one that involved remembering a paragraph that was read to them; perhaps the coherence of the story helped their memory.

Bender et al. (2006) assessed women's cognitive competencies before treatment with chemotherapy or a combination of chemotherapy and tamoxifen (blocks estrogen receptors in breast tissue and can have estrogenic effects in other issues), and then again one week and one year after treatment conclusion. In this study, chemotherapy was not associated with significant deficits in word learning and memory, but was associated with substantial declines – one week and one year after chemotherapy – in memory for words under distracting conditions; that is, when they could not mentally rehearse what they were asked to remember. The latter result suggests that many of these women were able to compensate for deficits in verbal memory – which may explain why they were not deficient on the simple word learning and memory tests – and when the common compensatory strategy of mental rehearsal was disrupted the underlying deficits became apparent. In any case, chemotherapy was not associated with changes in shape learning and memory as with the Shilling et al. (2005) study, but the combination of chemotherapy and tamoxifen was. Bender et al. (2007) found that treatment with an estrogenic drug (anastrozol) that is more potent than tamoxifen was associated with broad deficits in verbal and visual memory, but not vigilance and attentional control. The latter suggests that treatments that block the actions of estrogens may have broad, dose-dependent effects on memory that are above and beyond any more specific effects of chemotherapy (see also Li & Singh, 2014; Paganini-Hill & Clark, 2000).

At this point, no conclusions can be drawn regarding whether chemotherapy has sex- and trait-specific effects on the behaviors and cognitive abilities I listed in Table 5.1. In fact, a recent meta-analysis confirmed that chemotherapy might compromise women's language competencies, but also suggested deficits in some types of visuospatial abilities; but not on a visuospatial task that is often compromised with men's exposure to stressors (Jim et al., 2012). One recent study that only included men indicated that chemotherapy did not compromise men's language abilities (visuospatial abilities were not assessed), in contrast to those of women, although there was a trend (almost statistically significant) for high doses of chemotherapy to modestly compromise men's word learning (Wefel et al., 2014). In any event, the potential for women to develop deficits in complex verbal memory following chemotherapy and the sex-specific effects of other types of toxins (e.g., on sex-typed play) suggest assessments of sex-specific vulnerabilities are possible and merit investigation. As with all toxins, any such effects are likely to be dose dependent and may be most evident with the least toxic treatments. Analogous to earlier (i.e., sex-specific vulnerabilities) and later (i.e., broad deficits) stages of Alzheimer's disease, treatments that are especially toxic will likely affect many cognitive domains whereas those with lower levels of toxicity may affect boys and men differently than girls and women.

## Folk Physics

Folk physics includes cognitive abilities that enable navigation in and the mental representation (for humans) of the physical world, visually detecting and tracking the movement of objects in space, and implicitly understanding how objects can be used as tools, among other competencies. We learned in Chapter 2 that for species in which males increase territory size during the mating season and search for females dispersed throughout the ecology, males have better spatial and navigational abilities than females (Gaulin & Fitzgerald, 1986). The studies reviewed in Chapter 4 (Table 4.8) indicated that the development of these abilities is condition dependent for males of these species but not for males of related species in which spatial abilities are not sexually selected (Jašarević et al., 2011; Williams et al., 2013). The same pattern should be found for human navigational abilities (see Chapter 5), as well as competence at tracking the velocity and trajectory of moving objects (Schiff & Oldak, 1990), detecting camouflaged objects (Linn & Petersen, 1985; Morgan, Adam, & Mollon, 1992), and throwing accuracy (Jardine & Martin, 1983), among others (Table 5.1).

With the exception of Cherrier and colleagues' research on route learning (Cherrier et al., 2005; Cherrier, Rose, & Higano, 2003) and Levine and colleagues (2005) results for map reading, none of the studies shown in Table 7.2

**TABLE 7.2** Condition-Dependent Folk Physics Cognitive Traits in Humans

| Species | Scientific Name | ST | Trait | CD | S | Contrast | | Life History | Manipulation | References |
|---|---|---|---|---|---|---|---|---|---|---|
| | | | | | | Trait | Effect | | | |
| Human | *Homo sapiens* | L | Visual memory | N | M | Untreated male | C=T | Adult | Testosterone | Janowsky, Oviatt, and Orwoll (1994) |
| | | N/T | Visual memory | N | M | Unexposed male | C=T | Adult | Toxin | Morrow, Ryan, Goldstein, and Hodgson (1989) |
| | | N/T | Visual memory | Y[a] | M | Unexposed male | C<T | Adult | Toxin | Nilson, Sällsten, Hagberg, Bäckman, and Barregård (2002) |
| | | N/T | Visual memory | Y[b] | M | Unexposed male | C<T | Adult | Toxin | Mathiesen, Ellingsen, and Kjuus (1999) |
| | | N/T | Visual memory | Y | B | Female visual | C=T | Adult | Toxin | Echeverria et al. (2005) |
| | | N/T | Visual memory | Y[c] | M | Pre-to-post change | C<T | Adult | Antiandrogen | Salminen, Portin, Koskinen, Helenius, and Nurmi (2005) |
| | | N/T | Visual memory | N | M | Pre-to-post change | C=T | Adult | Antiandrogen | Salminen, Portin, Koskinen, Helenius, and Nurmi (2004) |
| | | N/T | Visual memory | N | M | Unexposed male | C=T | Adult | Antiandrogen | Joly et al. (2006) |

*Continued*

**TABLE 7.2** Condition-Dependent Folk Physics Cognitive Traits in Humans—cont'd

| Species | Scientific Name | ST | Trait | CD | S | Contrast | | | Manipulation | References |
|---|---|---|---|---|---|---|---|---|---|---|
| | | | | | | Trait | Effect | Life History | | |
| | | N/T | Visual memory | N | M | Pre-to-post change | C=T | Adult | Antiandrogen | Almeida, Waterreus, Spry, Flicker, and Martins (2004) |
| | | L | Visual memory | N | M | Untreated male | C=T | Adult | Testosterone | Janowsky et al. (1994) |
| | | N/T | Visual memory | N | M | Unexposed male | C=T | Adult | Toxin | Haut et al. (1999) |
| | | N | Visual memory | N | M | Unexposed male | C=T | Adult | Stress/combat | Bremner et al. (1995) |
| | | N | Visual memory | N[d] | M | Unexposed male | C=T | Adult | Stress/combat | Bremner et al. (1993) |
| | | N | Visual memory | Y | M | Female visual | C>T | Adult | Alzheimer's | Beinhoff et al. (2008) |
| | | N | Visual memory | Y | M | Female visual | C>T | Adult | Alzheimer's | Beinhoff et al. (2008) |
| | | N | Visual memory | Y[d] | M | Unexposed male | C<T | Adult | Stress/combat | Bremner et al. (1993) |
| | | N/T | Visual attention | Y | B | Female visual attention | C<T | Childhood | Toxin | Rosado et al. (2007) |

| N/T | | | | | | | | |
|---|---|---|---|---|---|---|---|---|
| N/T | Visual attention | Y | M | Verbal fluency | C=T | Adult | Toxin | Haut et al. (1999) |
| N/T | Visual comparison | Y | M | Pre-to-post change | C=T | Adult | Toxin | Weisskopf et al. (2007) |
| N/T | Route Learning | Y | M | Unexposed male | C<T | Adult | Antiandrogen | Cherrier et al. (2003) |
| L | Route Learning | Y | M | Untreated male | C<T | Adult | Testosterone | Cherrier et al. (2005) |
| L | Route Learning | Y | M | Untreated male | C<T | Adult | Testosterone | Cherrier et al. (2001) |
| L | Route Learning | Y* | M | Untreated male | C<T | Adult | Testosterone | Cherrier et al. (2007) |
| N | Spatial cognition | Y | M | SES | C<T | Inbreeding | Inbreeding | Agrawal, Sinha, and Jensen (1984) |
| N | Spatial cognition | Y | M | NA | NA | Inbreeding | Inbreeding | Schreider (1969) |
| N | Spatial cognition | N | M | NA | NA | Prenatal | Diet/nutrition | Stein, Susser, Saenger, and Marolla (1972) |
| N/T | Spatial cognition | Y | M | Unexposed brother | C<T | Prenatal | Toxin | Reinisch and Sanders (1992) |
| N/T | Spatial cognition | Y | B | Girls spatial | C<T | Prenatal | Toxin | Guo, Lai, Chen, and Hsu (1995) |

*Continued*

**TABLE 7.2** Condition-Dependent Folk Physics Cognitive Traits in Humans—cont'd

| Species | Scientific Name | ST | Trait | CD | S | Contrast Trait | Effect | Life History | Manipulation | References |
|---|---|---|---|---|---|---|---|---|---|---|
| | | N/T | Spatial cognition | $Y^i$ | B | Female spatial | C<T | Prenatal | Toxin | Jacobson and Jacobson (2002) |
| | | N/T | Spatial cognition | Y | B | Female spatial | C=T | Prenatal | Toxin | Grandjean et al. (1997) |
| | | N | Spatial cognition | N | B | Female spatial | C=T | Prenatal | Toxin | Singer et al. (2004) |
| | | N | Spatial cognition | $Y^g$ | B | Female spatial | C<T | Prenatal | Toxin | Bennett, Bendersky, and Lewis (2008) |
| | | F | Spatial cognition | Y | B | Female spatial | C<T | Childhood | Diet/nutrition | Whaley et al. (2003) |
| | | F | Spatial cognition | N | B | Female spatial | C=T | Childhood | Diet/nutrition | Wachs et al. (1995) |
| | | N | Spatial cognition | Y | M | Noninfected males | C=T | Childhood | Infection/parasite | Nokes, Grantham-McGregor, Sawyer, Cooper, and Bundy (1992) |
| | | N | Spatial cognition | Y | B | Female spatial | C<T | Childhood | Infection/parasite | Venkataramani (2012) |
| | | F | Spatial cognition | Y | B | Female spatial | C=T | Childhood | Diet/nutrition | Zimmermann et al. (2006) |

| | | | | | | | | Reference |
|---|---|---|---|---|---|---|---|---|
| N | Spatial cognition | Y | B | Female spatial | C<T | Childhood | SES | Levine et al. (2005) |
| N/T | Spatial cognition | Y | B | Female spatial | C<T | Childhood | Toxin | Rosado et al. (2007) |
| N/T | Spatial cognition | Y[h] | B | Female spatial | C=T | Childhood | Toxin | Tong, McMichael, and Baghurst (2000) |
| N | Spatial cognition | Y[i] | M | Intelligence | C=T | Childhood | Stress/separation | Pesonen et al. (2011) |
| N/T | Spatial cognition | N | M | Unexposed male | C=T | Adult | Toxin | Morrow, Steinhauer, Condray, and Hodgson (1997) |
| N/T | Spatial cognition | Y | M | Unexposed male | C<T | Adult | Toxin | Nilson et al. (2002) |
| N/T | Spatial cognition | N | M | Unexposed male | C=T | Adult | Toxin | Mathiesen et al. (1999) |
| N/T | Spatial cognition | Y | M | Intelligence | C=T | Adult | Toxin | Ryan, Morrow, Parkinson, and Bromet (1987) |
| N/T | Spatial cognition | Y | M | Memory | C<T | Adult | Toxin | Haenninen, Hernberg, Mantere, Vesanto, and Jalkanen (1978) |
| N/T | Spatial cognition | Y | M | Word retrieval | C<T | Adult | Toxin | Kishi et al. (1994) |

*Continued*

**TABLE 7.2** Condition-Dependent Folk Physics Cognitive Traits in Humans—cont'd

| Species | Scientific Name | ST | Trait | CD | S | Contrast Trait | Effect | Life History | Manipulation | References |
|---|---|---|---|---|---|---|---|---|---|---|
|  |  | L | Spatial cognition | N$^j$ | M | Untreated male | C=T | Adult | Testosterone | Wolf et al. (2000) |
|  |  | L | Spatial cognition | Y | M | Untreated male | C<T | Adult | Testosterone | Cherrier et al. (2001) |
|  |  | L | Spatial cognition | Y | M | Untreated male | C<T | Adult | Testosterone | Cherrier et al. (2005) |
|  |  | L | Spatial cognition | N | M | Verbal fluency | C>T | Adult | Testosterone | Alexander et al. (1998) |
|  |  | L | Spatial cognition | Y | M | Untreated male | C<T | Adult | Testosterone | Janowsky et al. (1994) |
|  |  | N/T | Spatial cognition | Y$^k$ | M | Unexposed male | C<T | Adult | Antiandrogen | Cherrier et al. (2003) |
|  |  | N/T | Spatial cognition | N | M | Pre-to-post change | C=T | Adult | Antiandrogen | Salminen et al. (2005) |
|  |  | N/T | Spatial cognition | N | M | Pre-to-post change | C=T | Adult | Antiandrogen | Salminen et al. (2004) |
|  |  | N/T | Spatial cognition | N | M | Unexposed male | C=T | Adult | Antiandrogen | Joly et al. (2006) |

| | | | | | | | | |
|---|---|---|---|---|---|---|---|---|
| N/T | Spatial cognition | N | M | Pre-to-post change | C=T | Adult | Antiandrogen | Almeida et al. (2004) |
| N/T | Spatial cognition | Y | M | Unexposed male | C<T | Adult | Antiandrogen | Jenkins, Bloomfield, Shilling, and Edginton (2005) |
| N | Spatial cognition | Y | B | Female spatial | C=T | Adult | Alzheimer's | Heun and Kockler (2002) |
| N | Spatial cognition | Y | B | Female spatial | C=T | Adult | Alzheimer's | Buckwalter et al. (1996) |
| N | Spatial cognition | Y | B | Female spatial | C=T | Adult | Vascular disease | Buckwalter et al. (1996) |

Note: ST, study type (L, lab experiment; F, field experiment; N, natural variation; T, Toxin); CD, condition dependent (Y, yes; N, no; S, sex of participants for trait of interest (M, male; B, both sexes).

[a] Solvent exposure was not associated with memory deficits in younger men but exposed men showed steeper age-related declines in memory.

[b] Mercury exposure was related to deficits in one visual memory test but not another; there were dose-response effects for the former.

[c] Decline in estradiol was related to decline in visual memory after 6 months of treatment, whereas verbal fluency increased; no change in group means.

[d] No effects for short-term shape memory, but significant effects for delayed shape memory.

[e] This is a randomized random control study showing that moderate increases in testosterone (T) resulted in improved route learning and improved word learning, but gains were higher for route learning; no effects for large increases in T.

[f] For boys, there was a significant relation between PCB exposure and performance on a composite measure of spatial and nonverbal reasoning but no effect for speed of mentally rotating letters. There was no relation between PCB levels and girls' spatial reasoning but higher PCB levels were associated with faster mental rotation.

[g] There was a sex by cocaine exposure interaction for visuospatial reasoning, and statistical trends for the interaction for verbal reasoning and memory; exposed boys had lower IQ scores.

[h] Lead exposure was associated with lower IQ scores and generally lower performance in all areas for girls relative to boys. For boys, lead levels were associated with lower spatial scores on one test (Mazes) but not another (Block Design; Wechsler, 1974).

[i] Separation from parents during WWII was associated with lower visuospatial scores for men but only if separation for > 1 year and from 2 to 4 years of age, not earlier or later separation.

[j] The study involved a one-time injection of testosterone vs. placebo. No effect on map memory or two-dimensional mental rotation after 5 days; blocked practice gains in verbal fluency

[k] Seven out of ten men treated with antiandrogens for prostate cancer showed declines in skill at mentally rotating images; this ability rebounded 3 months after treatment ended. However, there were no treatment-related effects for a second measure of spatial cognition.

used visuospatial measures that would be particularly sensitive to disruption by exposure to stressors (e.g., Fastenau, Denburg, & Hufford, 1999). Despite the general lack of sensitivity, the available evidence suggests that boys' and men's competencies in folk physics may be disrupted by exposure to a variety of natural stressors, such as parasites (Venkataramani, 2012), as well as by exposure to toxins (Jacobson & Jacobson, 2002) and by antiandrogen treatments for prostate cancer (Cherrier et al., 2003).

## Natural Stressors

As covered in Chapter 2, ubiquitous natural stressors include exposure to parasites, poor nutrition, and social competition; inbreeding can also affect the expression of sexually selected traits (Jennions, Møller, & Petrie, 2001). There is very little research available on the relation between parasite infestation and sex differences in spatial cognition. For instance, in a study of 432 Indonesian children and adolescents, Sakti et al. (1999) found that infestation with hookworms (species not specified) was associated with poor performance on a number cognitive tests, but especially on a test of verbal fluency and a mazes test that was dependent in part on visuospatial abilities, controlling other factors including infestation with other parasites. They did not, however, test whether infected girls were relatively more affected on the verbal fluency test and infected boys on the mazes test.

In an intriguing yet indirect assessment of male vulnerability, Venkataramani (2012) examined the spatial reasoning ability (Raven's Progressive Matrices Test; Raven, Court, & Raven, 1993) of adults from regions of Mexico with high rates of infection with malaria (*Plasmodium vivax*) before and after eradication of disease-carrying mosquitos. Men born after the eradication had higher spatial reasoning abilities than those born before the eradication, and the spatial reasoning gap between men from high- and low-infestation regions declined 25-51% posteradication, controlling other factors (e.g., regional wealth). Eradication had no effect on women's spatial reasoning or men's success in school, suggesting sex- and trait-specific effects. Also keeping with heightened vulnerability is the finding that boys' and men's performance on this same spatial reasoning test is reduced by inbreeding (Agrawal et al., 1984; Schreider, 1969) and by prenatal exposure to toxins (below).

As with parasites, research on the relation between boys' and men's visuospatial competencies and poor nutrition and exposure to social stressors is sparse and inconclusive, as shown in Table 7.2. One exception is Levine et al.'s (2005) study of socioeconomic status (SES) and children's performance on a test of sentence comprehension (a proxy for intelligence) and two tests of spatial ability, map reading, and mentally rotating the images of objects (see Figure 7.4). There were no sex differences on the sentence comprehension test, but boys performed better than girls on both spatial tests, as is commonly found (e.g., Levine, Huttenlocher, Taylor, & Langrock, 1999; Linn & Petersen, 1985; Voyer, Voyer, & Bryden, 1995). As shown in Figure 7.5, there was no relation between SES and girls' spatial abilities, but the spatial abilities of boys from

**FIGURE 7.4**    Mental rotation task. (See the color plate section.)

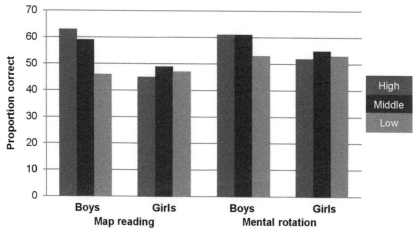

**FIGURE 7.5**    Spatial abilities of boys and girls from families of high-, middle-, and low-socioeconomic status. *Based on data presented in Levine et al. (2005).* (See the color plate section.)

lower SES families was significantly compromised relative to the abilities of their better-off peers. Levine and colleagues suggested the restricted activities of children from lower SES families might affect boys' developing spatial abilities more strongly than those of girls, and this is certainly possible; engaging in environmental exploration appears to contribute to the development of spatial abilities and boys engage in these activities more than girls (Matthews, 1992). It is also possible that toxin exposure contributed to these effects, because children living in lower SES neighborhoods have heavier exposure to many toxins than do children living in other contexts (e.g., Landrigan et al., 1999) and because toxin exposure can disrupt boys' and men's visuospatial abilities (below).

## Toxins

Compared to natural stressors, more is known about the effects of toxin exposure on boys' and men's visual memory and attention (Nilson et al., 2002; Rosado et al., 2007), as well as their more complex spatial abilities (Guo et al., 1995; Jacobson & Jacobson, 2002). The largest group of studies is based on exposure to a variety of toxins in male-dominated professions and thus comparisons to similarly exposed women are not always available, but comparisons with unexposed men and across cognitive abilities are available, as shown in Table 7.2 (e.g., Nilson et al., 2002; Ryan et al., 1987).

As an example, Nilson et al. (2002) provided two assessments, 18 years apart, of the cognitive functioning of floor layers – exposure to organic solvents in adhesives – and carpenters (unexposed) on a variety of cognitive abilities. Exposed men's largest deficit was for a measure of complex spatial abilities (block design, the ability to reproduce geometric designs using blocks; Wechsler, 2008). Over the 18-year assessment period, the exposed men's spatial reasoning deteriorated more than the typical age-related declines found in the unexposed men, but the effect was not quite significant. A dose-response assessment found that higher levels of exposure were associated with larger deficits in memory for visual images. The exposed men also had deficits in basic speed of processing visual information but had no verbal deficits. Visual memory and attention deficits or deficits in complex spatial abilities have also been found for men (and sometimes women) exposed to mercury (Echeverria et al., 2005; Mathiesen et al., 1999) and lead (Ryan et al., 1987), but Morrow and colleagues found no such effects for exposure to different types of solvents, those found in paint thinner (Morrow et al., 1997); in fact, the latter had deficits in word learning and verbal memory.

I located two studies of children's exposure to environmental toxins that reported sex differences in visuospatial abilities (Rosado et al., 2007; Tong et al., 2000). Rosado et al. examined the cognitive abilities of more than 600 6-8-year olds who lived in a region of Mexico with heavy smelting industries and as a result groundwater contaminated with arsenic. Boys with higher levels of arsenic in their urine had lower complex spatial abilities and poor visual attention, but their memory for images and word sounds was intact. The only effect for girls with similar arsenic levels was a poor memory for word sounds. Tong et al. examined the cognitive abilities of 11-13-year olds who grew up in a lead smelting region of Australia, but here the results were more mixed. Girls with higher levels of lead in their blood and especially those also living in a lower SES family had lower verbal and nonverbal intelligence scores than similarly affected, lower SES boys. Once confounding variables (e.g., parental occupation) were controlled, the only relation between lead levels and boys' cognition was for one test of spatial abilities, although this did not emerge for another spatial ability test.

As shown in Table 7.2, the results for prenatal exposure to a variety of toxins, ranging from PCBs (polychlorinated biphenyls) to cocaine appear to more consistently compromise boys' and men's later spatial abilities than does exposure during childhood (e.g., Bennett et al., 2008; Guo et al., 1995; Jacobson & Jacobson, 2002). In 1979, several thousand people in Taiwan were exposed to PCB-contaminated cooking oil, including 74 women who were pregnant at the time or became pregnant soon thereafter (Rogan et al., 1988). The children of these women were smaller at birth and at higher risk for a variety of medical and developmental problems, although the overall effects were not large in

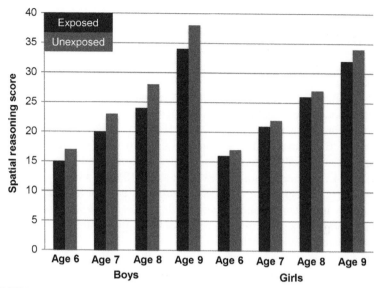

FIGURE 7.6    Boys prenatally exposed to polychlorinated biphenyls had significantly lower spatial reasoning scores than unexposed boys matched on age and demographic factors. *Based on data presented in Guo et al. (1995)*. (See the color plate section.)

most areas. Guo et al. assessed these children and a group of demographically matched peers on a test of spatial reasoning abilities – a children's version of the same test used by Venkataramani (2012) in the above described malaria eradication study – once a year from 6 to 9 years of age, inclusive. As shown in Figure 7.6, exposed boys but not exposed girls had consistently lower spatial reasoning scores relative to their same-sex unexposed peers.

A similar pattern emerged in Bennett et al.'s (2008) study of children who were prenatally exposed to cocaine. The cognitive abilities of these children were assessed when they were 4, 6, and 9 years old. Controlling other factors (e.g., maternal smoking and IQ), exposed girls did not differ from unexposed girls in overall cognitive functioning. At all three ages, prenatally exposed boys tended to score lower than other children across domains, but the largest and only statistically significant effect was that these boys had lower abstract visuo-spatial reasoning scores than did unexposed boys and lower scores than exposed and unexposed girls.

## Testosterone and Antiandrogen Therapy

As noted earlier, studies of the cognitive sequelae of chemotherapy typically combine men and women, and because of this there is no literature for men analogous to the breast cancer literature for women. Prostate cancer is of course unique to men but the treatment typically involves use of androgen blocking or suppressing drugs (Nelson, Lee, Gamboa, & Roth, 2008); these reduce circulating levels of testosterone and estradiol (converted to testosterone in the brain). In contrast, testosterone administration is sometimes used to treat Alzheimer's disease in men (Cherrier et al., 2005) and sometimes age-related cognitive decline in healthy, older men (Cherrier et al., 2007). The relation between androgens and boys' and men's spatial abilities is not fully understood, but a contribution of these hormones is clear. Prenatal and early postnatal exposure to androgens is associated with enhanced visuospatial abilities (Berenbaum, Bryk, & Beltz, 2012; Hines et al., 2003; Puts, McDaniel, Jordan, & Breedlove, 2008), and circulating testosterone is sometimes found to be related to men's spatial abilities and sometimes not (Driscoll, Hamilton, Yeo, Brooks, & Sutherland, 2005; Puts et al., 2010); the mixed results may be related in part to different types of spatial tasks used in the various studies. Even with important hormonal contributions, the full development of many spatial competencies requires exploring the environment and engaging in other spatial-related activities (Matthews, 1992).

The question for us is whether treatments that involve manipulating androgen levels influence men's spatial abilities and, as shown in Table 7.2, the pattern is mixed. The mixed results are due in part to the different tasks used to assess spatial ability, with consistent results for route learning (Cherrier et al., 2003) and variable results for visual memory (Joly et al., 2006; Salminen et al., 2004) and spatial cognition (Almeida et al., 2004; Janowsky et al., 1994). For the route-learning task, the man is brought to an otherwise empty $13.7\,m^2$ (144 square feet) room that is demarcated into a grid. The experimenter uses a ribbon to create a route that the man then walks, and is asked to retrace the route immediately after the ribbon is removed and then 20 min later. The task is much easier than navigating in novel, large-scale terrain in the real world, as is necessary for men in traditional societies (Cashdan et al., 2012; MacDonald & Hewlett, 1999), but this task is a more complex and closer to actual navigation than any of the other visuospatial tasks used in this literature.

Cherrier et al. (2003) administered the route test and a battery of spatial and verbal ability measures to men being treated for prostate cancer before the onset of treatment, after 9 months of treatment, and then 3 months later. For younger men (< 66 years), 9 months of androgen suppression was related to lower route-learning scores relative to untreated men, and 7 out of 10 of these men showed declines in skill at mentally rotating images. The latter deficits disappeared 3 months after treatment ended. There was, however, no relation between treatment and performance on a block design task and no relation to their verbal fluency. Treatment was nevertheless related to *improvement* on one measure of verbal memory, a gain they lost 3 months after treatment ended. In a similar study, antiandrogen treatment resulted in a decline in memory for images and improvement in verbal fluency (Salminen et al., 2005), but a related study did not confirm the impaired visual memory but did find improvement in word learning (Almeida et al., 2004).

The spatial cognition tasks used in these studies typically included block design or mental rotation tests. Separating these results by specific task revealed that none of the androgen suppression studies found any treatment-related effects for block design (Almeida et al., 2004; Cherrier et al., 2003; Salminen et al., 2004, 2005), but there were consistent treatment-related declines in mental rotation (Cherrier et al., 2003; Jenkins et al., 2005). In contrast, testosterone enhancement was found to improve the block design performance of men with Alzheimer's disease (Cherrier et al., 2005) and that of healthy older men in two of three studies (Cherrier et al., 2001; Janowsky et al., 1994).

## BRAIN VULNERABILITIES

In Chapter 5, I provided examples of brain regions that contribute to the normal functioning of many of the behavioral and cognitive traits described in this chapter and the last, and thus are candidates for sex-specific vulnerabilities. Identifying any such vulnerability is complicated by the fact that behavioral and cognitive traits will be dependent on an integrated system of brain regions. The vulnerability of behavioral or cognitive traits could evolve if only one of these brain regions or the connections between regions is susceptible to disruption by stressors. We covered a potential nonhuman example of this with birdsong, whereby exposure to stressors during development can disrupt the functioning of one critical underlying brain region but not another (e.g., MacDonald et al., 2006). Disruption of one of these regions is all that is needed to compromise males' song in adulthood (Garamszegi & Eens, 2004). To complicate the goal of identifying vulnerability, disruption could involve changes in the functioning of the vulnerable region (e.g., in changes in cell receptors for androgens) without creating any obvious changes in region volume or connections to other regions. In these cases, the deficits would not be as easily detectable.

As a result of these complications and the very sparse literature on human sex differences in brain vulnerability, all that I am able to do here is to illustrate the feasibility of using sexual and social selection to help to identify sex differences in vulnerability: The reader will recall that I outlined potential places to look for them in the brain in Chapter 5.

## Threat Detection and Emotion Regulation

For this illustration, we return to the argument that men's emotional composure, including lower levels of anxiety and depression than women, is an evolved trait that supports engagement in and coping with male-male competition and as a result could be vulnerable to disruption. The system that supports emotional reactions to threat and regulation of these emotions includes but is not limited to the amygdala, hippocampus, and medial prefrontal cortex, as was described in Chapter 5 (see Figure 5.5; Bremner, 2006; Sotres-Bayon, Bush, & LeDoux, 2004).

Recall, the amygdala is important for eliciting negative emotions in threatening contexts, including fear and anxiety that will motivate behavioral response to the threat (e.g., flight or fight). The hippocampus serves multiple functions including forming memories for the threatening context and contextualization of the fear or anxiety to this context, and perhaps directly influencing the emotional response itself (Oler et al., 2010). Low engagement of the medial prefrontal cortex is associated with poor regulation of emotional responses and poor elimination (extinction) of the fear when the context is no longer threatening (Etkin & Wager, 2007; Sehlmeyer et al., 2009; Sotres-Bayon et al., 2004).

Although this integrated system is found in both sexes, my argument is that male-male competition favored a muting of emotions that signal threat and an enhanced ability to regulate and compartmentalize (e.g., not overgeneralize) these emotions so that men can stay behaviorally focused when threatened, especially contexts that have implications for one's status. Critically, if evolution has resulted in these modifications and they are condition dependent, then any disruption of the system has to be signaled to other people, in the same way that stress-related disruption of one of the brain regions (HVC, Table 3.4) that support birdsong is signaled by males' song quality (Nowicki et al., 1998; Spencer & MacDougall-Shackleton, 2011).

I would also expect boys and men to attempt to elicit these signals and through this test the integrity of the system in both competitors and potential allies. On this view, it is not surprising that in societies in which warfare is frequent and deadly, boys' and men's ability to cope with extreme stressors is assessed through painful initiation rites or a series of rites, typically in adolescence; for instance, the ability to remain stoic while being publicly circumcised at the onset of puberty (Sosis, Kress, & Boster, 2007). The albeit toned-down expression of the same types of social rituals is also found in modern societies, with the hazing that is common in men's groups and as part of military training (Browne, 2012; Winslow, 1999). These rites of passage test men's ability to regulate their emotions under stress, and emotional composure in these contexts helps to build trust among the group of men.

## Amygdala, Hippocampus, and Trauma

The first question is when during development the emotion regulation system might be most vulnerable to disruption. It is known, for instance, that exposure to prenatal and postnatal stressors can compromise the development of the brain regions that support emotion regulation (Weinstock, 2008), and result in heightened sensitivity of the amygdala to threat cues (McCrory et al., 2011; Tottenham et al., 2011), but sex differences are not typically reported in these studies. Nevertheless, based on risk for later anxiety and depression discussed in Chapter 6, the system may be more sensitive in boys than girls during the prenatal period, as was discussed for the hippocampus and the spatial abilities of the males of many nonhuman species (Table 4.8). I expect that pubertal development is another period of differential risk. The increase in girl's anxiety during this time reflects, from an evolutionary perspective, an increase in risk aversion and perhaps increased sensitivity to the subtleties of relational aggression, as previously discussed (Chapter 6). For boys, vulnerability would be reflected in disruption of the normal growth of these brain regions (Bramen et al., 2011; Neufang et al., 2009), and a lower ability of testosterone to dampen the activation of the amygdala in threatening contexts (Stanton et al., 2009). The result would be heightened – relative to other males – sensitivity to threats and poor emotion regulation.

An ideal study of sex differences in the condition dependence of this brain system would require assessments of prenatal and other developmental stressors and assessments of the integrity and functioning of these interrelated brain regions in adulthood, especially in threatening contexts. Until such studies are conducted, the alternative is to examine the correlation between exposure to stressors and the integrity of these regions, and I did this for the amygdala and hippocampus – the medial prefrontal cortex and other brain regions are also important, as noted, but my goal here is only to illustrate how an evolutionary approach can be used to make inferences about sex differences in brain vulnerability, not to provide an exhaustive review. The associated studies are shown in Table 7.3 and largely focused on the relation between exposure to stressors during childhood (maltreatment) and combat-related post-traumatic stress disorder (PTSD) and the volume and sometimes the integrity (e.g., cell number) and functioning of these brain regions. As a contrast, I included these same relations for girls and women; again, exposure to stressors will increase girls' and women's sensitivity to threat (Felmingham et al., 2010), but the consequences, at least in traditional contexts, are more severe for men (Chapter 6).

As shown in Table 7.3, the available evidence suggests that childhood maltreatment – either assessed in children or retrospectively reported by adults – is not associated with lower amygdala volumes (e.g., De Bellis et al., 2002; see also Woon & Hedges, 2008). There is, however, evidence that maltreatment is associated with how the amygdala is connected to the hippocampus, prefrontal cortex, and other brain regions that support sensitivity to threat or regulation of associated emotions (Herringa et al., 2013; see also De Bellis & Keshavan, 2003). The studies of childhood maltreatment suggest the same connectivity relation for boys and men (i.e., men who reported being maltreated as children) and girls and women, and perhaps a stronger relation for girls and women (Birn et al., 2014; Herringa et al., 2013). The research on the relation between hippocampal volume and childhood maltreatment is mixed for girls and women – some studies show a relation (Bremner et al., 2003) and others do not (De Bellis et al., 2002) – and shows no relation for boys and men (De Bellis et al., 2002). But again there may be a relation to connectivity: The connectivity of the left but not the right hippocampus appears to be associated with childhood maltreatment in girls and women (Bremner et al., 2003) and the left and possibly the right with boys and men (Birn et al., 2014).

**TABLE 7.3** Condition-Dependent Brain Regions in Humans

| Species | Scientific Name | ST | Trait | CD | S | Trait | Effect | Life History | Manipulation | References |
|---|---|---|---|---|---|---|---|---|---|---|
| | | | | | | | Contrast | | | |
| *Amygdala* | | | | | | | | | | |
| Human | *Homo sapiens* | N | Whole volume | N | F | Unexposed female | C=T | Childhood | Stress/abuse | De Bellis et al. (2002) |
| | | N | Whole volume | N | F | Unexposed female | C=T | Childhood | Stress/abuse | De Bellis, Hall, Boring, Frustaci, and Moritz (2001) |
| | | N | Connectivity | Y | F | Level of exposure | C<T | Childhood | Stress/abuse | Herringa et al. (2013) |
| | | N | Whole volume | N | M | Unexposed male | C=T | Childhood | Stress/abuse | De Bellis et al. (2002) |
| | | N | Whole volume | N | M | Unexposed male | C=T | Childhood | Stress/abuse | De Bellis et al. (2001) |
| | | N | Connectivity | N | M | Level of exposure | C=T | Childhood | Stress/abuse | Herringa et al. (2013) |
| | | N | Connectivity | Y[a] | M | Level of exposure | C<T | Childhood | Stress/abuse | Birn, Patriat, Phillips, Germain, and Herringa (2014) |
| | | N | Left volume | N | F | Unexposed female | C=T | Adult | Stress/abuse | Fennema-Notestine, Stein, Kennedy, Archibald, and Jernigan (2002) |

| Reference | Stress type | Age | Comparison | Group | Sex | | Measure | |
|---|---|---|---|---|---|---|---|---|
| Fennema-Notestine et al. (2002) | Stress/abuse | Adult | C=T | Unexposed female | F | N | Right volume | N |
| Felmingham et al. (2010) | Stress/trauma | Adult | C<T | Unexposed female | F | Y | Left reactivity | N |
| Felmingham et al. (2010) | Stress/trauma | Adult | C<T | Unexposed female | F | Y | Right reactivity | N |
| Felmingham et al. (2010) | Stress/trauma | Adult | C<T | Unexposed male | M | Y | Left reactivity | N |
| Felmingham et al. (2010) | Stress/trauma | Adult | C<T | Unexposed male | M | Y | Right reactivity | N |
| Gurvits et al. (1996) | Stress/combat | Adult | C=T | No PTSD veteran | M | N | Whole volume | N |
| Hedges et al. (2007) | Stress/combat | Adult | C=T | No PTSD veteran | M | N[b] | Left volume | N |
| Gilbertson et al. (2002) | Stress/combat | Adult | C=T | Cotwin | M | N | Left volume | N |
| Hedges et al. (2007) | Stress/combat | Adult | C=T | No PTSD veteran | M | N[b] | Right volume | N |
| Gilbertson et al. (2002) | Stress/combat | Adult | C=T | Cotwin | M | N | Right volume | N |
| Sripada et al. (2012) | Stress/combat | Adult | C<T | No PTSD veteran | M | Y | Connectivity | N |
| Rabinak et al. (2011) | Stress/combat | Adult | C<T | No PTSD veteran | M | Y[c] | Connectivity | N |

Continued

**TABLE 7.3 Condition-Dependent Brain Regions in Humans—cont'd**

| Species | Scientific Name | ST | Trait | CD | S | Contrast Trait | Contrast Effect | Life History | Manipulation | References |
|---|---|---|---|---|---|---|---|---|---|---|
| **Left hippocampus** | | | | | | | | | | |
| Human | *Homo sapiens* | N | Volume | N[d] | F | Brain volume | C=T | Childhood | Stress/abuse | Buss et al. (2007) |
| | | N | Volume | Y | F | Unexposed female | C<T | Childhood | Stress/abuse | Stein, Koverola, Hanna, Torchia, and McClarty (1997) |
| | | N | Volume | Y | F | Brain volume | C<T | Childhood | Stress/abuse | Bremner et al. (2003) |
| | | N | Volume | N[e] | F | Unexposed female | C=T | Childhood | Stress/abuse | De Bellis et al. (2002) |
| | | N | Volume | N | F | Unexposed female | C=T | Childhood | Stress/abuse | De Bellis et al. (2001) |
| | | N | Functioning | Y | F | Volume | C<T | Childhood | Stress/abuse | Bremner et al. (2003) |
| | | N | Connectivity | Y | F | Level of exposure | C<T | Childhood | Stress/abuse | Herringa et al. (2013) |
| | | N | Volume | N[d] | M | Brain volume | C=T | Childhood | Stress/abuse | Buss et al. (2007) |
| | | N | Volume | N | M | Unexposed male | C=T | Childhood | Stress/abuse | De Bellis et al. (2001) |

| Reference | | | | | | | | |
|---|---|---|---|---|---|---|---|---|
| De Bellis et al. (2002) | Stress/abuse | Childhood | C=T | Unexposed male | M | N[f] | Volume | N |
| Gilbertson et al. (2002) | Stress/abuse | Childhood | C=T | Level of exposure | M | N | Volume | N |
| Herringa et al. (2013) | Stress/abuse | Childhood | C<T | Level of exposure | M | Y | Connectivity | N |
| Birn et al. (2014) | Stress/abuse | Childhood | C<T | Level of exposure | M | Y[o] | Connectivity | N |
| Fennema-Notestine et al. (2002) | Stress/abuse | Adult | C=T | Unexposed female | F | N | Volume | N |
| Felmingham et al. (2010) | Stress/trauma | Adult | C=T | Unexposed female | F | N | Reactivity | N |
| Bremner et al. (1995) | Stress/combat | Adult | C<T | Unexposed male | M | Y[g] | Volume | N |
| Gurvits et al. (1996) | Stress/combat | Adult | C<T | No PTSD veteran | M | Y[h] | Volume | N |
| Gilbertson et al. (2002) | Stress/combat | Adult | C=T | Cotwin | M | Y | Volume | N |
| Schuff et al. (2001) | Stress/combat | Adult | C=T | Unexposed male | M | N | Volume | N |
| Neylan et al. (2003) | Stress/combat | Adult | C=T | Unexposed male | M | N | Volume | N |
| Hedges et al. (2007) | Stress/combat | Adult | C=T | No PTSD veteran | M | N[b] | Volume | N |

*Continued*

**TABLE 7.3** Condition-Dependent Brain Regions in Humans—cont'd

| Species | Scientific Name | ST | Trait | CD | S | Contrast Trait | Contrast Effect | Life History | Manipulation | References |
|---|---|---|---|---|---|---|---|---|---|---|
| | | N | Volume | N | M | No PTSD veteran | C=T | Adult | Stress/combat | Pavić et al. (2007) |
| | | N | Volume | Y[t] | M | No PTSD veteran | C<T | Adult | Stress/combat | Wang et al. (2010) |
| | | N | Reactivity | Y | M | Unexposed male | C<T | Adult | Stress/trauma | Felmingham et al. (2010) |
| | | N | Neuron number | Y | M | Unexposed male | C<T | Adult | Stress/combat | Schuff et al. (2001) |
| | | N | Neuron number | Y | M | Unexposed male | C<T | Adult | Stress/combat | Neylan et al. (2003) |
| **Right hippocampus** | | | | | | | | | | |
| Human | *Homo sapiens* | N | Volume | Y[d] | F | Brain volume | C<T | Childhood | Stress/abuse | Buss et al. (2007) |
| | | N | Volume | N | F | Unexposed female | C=T | Childhood | Stress/abuse | Stein et al. (1997) |
| | | N | Volume | N | F | Unexposed female | C=T | Childhood | Stress/abuse | De Bellis et al. (2002) |
| | | N | Volume | Y[i] | F | Brain volume | C<T | Childhood | Stress/abuse | Bremner et al. (2003) |

*Continued*

| De Bellis et al. (2001) | Stress/abuse | Childhood | $C=T$ | Unexposed female | F | N | Volume | N |
|---|---|---|---|---|---|---|---|---|
| Bremner et al. (2003) | Stress/abuse | Childhood | $C=T$ | Other female | F | N | Functioning | N |
| Herringa et al. (2013) | Stress/abuse | Childhood | $C=T$ | Level of exposure | F | N | Connectivity | N |
| Buss et al. (2007) | Stress/abuse | Childhood | $C=T$ | Brain volume | M | N[d] | Volume | N |
| De Bellis et al. (2002) | Stress/abuse | Childhood | $C=T$ | Unexposed male | M | N[f] | Volume | N |
| De Bellis et al. (2001) | Stress/abuse | Childhood | $C=T$ | Unexposed male | M | N | Volume | N |
| Gilbertson et al. (2002) | Stress/abuse | Childhood | $C=T$ | Level of exposure | M | N | Volume | N |
| Herringa et al. (2013) | Stress/abuse | Childhood | $C=T$ | Level of exposure | M | N | Connectivity | N |
| Birn et al. (2014) | Stress/abuse | Childhood | $C<T$ | Level of exposure | M | Y[a] | Connectivity | N |
| Fennema-Notestine et al. (2002) | Stress/abuse | Adult | $C=T$ | Unexposed female | F | N | Volume | N |
| Felmingham et al. (2010) | Stress/trauma | Adult | $C=T$ | Unexposed female | F | N | Reactivity | N |

**TABLE 7.3** Condition-Dependent Brain Regions in Humans—cont'd

| Species | Scientific Name | ST | Trait | CD | S | Contrast | | Life History | Manipulation | References |
|---|---|---|---|---|---|---|---|---|---|---|
| | | | | | | Trait | Effect | | | |
| | | N | Volume | Y[g] | M | Unexposed male | C<T | Adult | Stress/combat | Bremner et al. (1995) |
| | | N | Volume | Y[h] | M | No PTSD veteran | C<T | Adult | Stress/combat | Gurvits et al. (1996) |
| | | N | Volume | Y | M | Cotwin | C=T | Adult | Stress/combat | Gilbertson et al. (2002) |
| | | N | Volume | N | M | Unexposed male | C=T | Adult | Stress/combat | Schuff et al. (2001) |
| | | N | Volume | N | M | Unexposed male | C=T | Adult | Stress/combat | Neylan et al. (2003) |
| | | N | Volume | N[b] | M | No PTSD veteran | C=T | Adult | Stress/combat | Hedges et al. (2007) |
| | | N | Volume | Y | M | No PTSD veteran | C<T | Adult | Stress/combat | Pavić et al. (2007) |
| | | N | Volume | Y[i] | M | No PTSD veteran | C<T | Adult | Stress/combat | Wang et al. (2010) |
| | | N | Reactivity | Y | M | Unexposed male | C<T | Adult | Stress/trauma | Felmingham et al. (2010) |

| | | | | | | | | |
|---|---|---|---|---|---|---|---|---|
| N | Neuron number | Y | M | Unexposed male | C<T | Adult | Stress/combat | Neylan et al. (2003) |
| N | Neuron number | Y | M | Unexposed male | C<T | Adult | Stress/combat | Schuff et al. (2001) |

Note: ST, study type (N, natural variation); CD, condition dependent (Y, yes; N, no); S, sex of participants for trait of interest (M, male; F, female).

[a]Retrospective report of childhood maltreatment.

[b]The study included a very small sample of six combat veterans with post-traumatic stress disorder (PTSD) and five veterans without PTSD.

[c]The right amygdala showed higher connectivity to the insula.

[d]Prenatal stress was inferred based on low (<10th percentile) birth weight for normal term babies. The combination of birth weight and parental nurturance was associated with lower right but not left hippocampal volume in young adults. Separate analyses by sex indicated the combination of low birth weight and poor parenting predicted hippocampal volume in women but not men. The latter effect appeared to be for overall volume; that is, it was not clear if this was only for the right hippocampus.

[e]There was, however, a sex by group interaction with maltreated girls having a smaller left hippocampus than maltreated boys.

[f]There were, however, other differences in brain volume with exposed boys having smaller prefrontal and temporal cortex, less white matter, and more cerebral spinal fluid.

[g]The study also included unexposed men who had a larger right hippocampus than exposed men, but there were no group differences in temporal lobe volume.

[h]The study also included combat veterans without PTSD as controls, with significant hippocampal volume differences with control of whole brain volume.

[i]The differences were significant only in the dentate gyrus and CA3 and not for other areas of the hippocampus or for total brain volume.

[j]This was a positron emission tomography (PET) study of abused women with and without PTSD, and examined blood flow during processing of a verbal paragraph for later recall.

More central to the male-male competition hypothesis is the relation between combat-related PTSD symptoms and the integrity of these same brain regions. As with childhood maltreatment, there is no evidence of smaller amygdala volumes for men with PTSD (Gilbertson et al., 2002; Gurvits et al., 1996), but two studies have found the amygdala of these men has a different pattern of connections to other brain regions than does the amygdala of combat veterans without PTSD (Rabinak et al., 2011; Sripada et al., 2012). Other studies suggest that PTSD may be associated with exaggerated responses of the amygdala and hippocampus in threatening contexts (Felmingham et al., 2010; Lebron-Milad & Milad, 2012; Shin, Rauch, & Pitman, 2006). In a brain imaging study, Felmingham et al. found that both men and women with PTSD had heightened activation of the amygdala when viewing threatening facial expressions, compared to individuals who experienced similar levels of trauma (e.g., being assaulted) but did not have PTSD. The most intriguing finding was that men with PTSD had higher activation of the hippocampus than did women with PTSD. Felmingham and colleagues suggested the normal process of fear extinction might be compromised in these men.

Most (seven of nine) of the studies that compared men with PTSD to men who had not experienced combat showed no differences in the total volumes of the left or the right hippocampus but several studies show differences in the number of neurons in the hippocampus (e.g., Neylan et al., 2003; Schuff et al., 2001). Neylan et al. suggested the latter might reflect differences in the connection between the hippocampus and the hypothalamus as related to regulation of the stress-response system. In contrast, many of the studies that compared combat veterans with and without PTSD found smaller hippocampal volumes for those with PTSD, especially in the right hippocampus (Pavić et al., 2007; Wang et al., 2010; see also Childress et al., 2013; Kitayama, Vaccarino, Kutner, Weiss, & Bremner, 2005); the one study that did not find right hippocampal differences had a very small number of participants (six men with PTSD, and five without; Hedges et al., 2007). In a finer-grain assessment of these volume differences, Wang and colleagues examined specific subregions of the hippocampus and found that about 85% of men with PTSD had smaller volumes than veterans without PTSD for the dentate gyrus – involved in generation of new neurons – and CA3 – primary site for stress hormone binding – but other areas of the hippocampus did not differ nor did total brain volume.

For all of these studies, the question of cause and effect is unclear but critical. It is certainly possible that exposure to the stress of combat can affect the volume and integrity of the brain regions we have been considering (e.g., Sapolsky, Uno, Rebert, & Finch, 1990). It is also possible that preexisting differences contribute to stress-induced PTSD or related (e.g., generalized anxiety) symptoms. Gilbertson and colleagues (2002) unique study of identical twins, one of whom was a combat veteran, suggests a preexisting vulnerability for men in the hippocampus, but not the amygdala (see also Kremen, Koenen, Afari, & Lyons, 2012). Of the combat veterans, those with PTSD had a smaller left and right hippocampus than those without PTSD, as shown in Table 7.3. The crucial finding was the twins of men with PTSD also had a smaller hippocampus than did the veterans without PTSD or these veterans' cotwins. Moreover, hippo-campal size of the cotwin predicted symptom severity of their veteran brothers with PTSD; there was no relation between reported maltreatment during child-hood and hippocampal volume for the men with or without PTSD.

The design of the study did not allow for an estimate of how much of the variation in hippocampal volume was due to genes but other studies suggest that about 70% of this volume is heritable and the rest due to unique experiences (Kremen et al., 2010). Kremen et al. suggested that their finding of no effect of shared environment suggested that exposure to prenatal stressors or post-natal stressors common to both twins is not influencing hippocampal volume (but see below). This is consistent with Gilbertson et al.'s (2002) findings for childhood maltreatment and the general results described above, but remains to be assessed for hippocampal subregions (Wang et al., 2010). The heritability of hippocampal white matter tracks – axonal connections within and between brain regions – in contrast is about half that (34%) found for volume (Kochunov et al., 2010). The implication is that connectivity of the hippocampus may be more sensitive to stressors than volume per se, again consistent with the results described above.

## Men's Condition-Dependent Hippocampus

At this point, it appears that areas of the hippocampus and connections of these areas to other brain regions involved in remembering threatening contexts and extinguishing the fears associated with these contexts are prime candidates for condition dependence in men. The amygdala is also an important component of the emotion regulation system, but the available evidence suggests it is not more vulnerable in men than women: Rather, men and women with intense fear reactions to threat and poor regulation of it appear to be more similar than dif-ferent in terms of the reactivity and connectivity of the amygdala (Birn et al., 2014; Felmingham et al., 2010). The finding that combat veterans with PTSD are more likely to have a smaller hippocampus than veterans without PTSD but often do not differ from nonveterans suggests any associated vulnerability may only be expressed under extreme conditions. In other words, assessments of whether hippocampal volume is a vulnerable trait in men are the most sensi-tive for individuals who have experienced the stressors under which condition dependence evolved; specifically, male-male competition, or combat in this ex-ample. On this view, many of the men in the nonveteran control groups used in these studies would have likely experienced PTSD symptoms had they been exposed to combat.

The finding that maltreatment in childhood does not consistently affect hip-pocampal volume (e.g., De Bellis et al., 2002) combined with Gilbertson and colleagues (2002) twin study suggests that any associated vulnerability has a strong heritable component. Although I have emphasized how environmental and social stressors affect the development and expression of condition dependent traits, heritable influences are still expected. On the basis of Pomiankowski and Møller's (1995) argument outlined in Chapter 2, the heritability of hippocampal volume and perhaps especially the subregions identified by Wang et al. (2010) should be larger for men than women if these are condition dependent in men. At the same time, I would not rule out prenatal and pubertal exposure to stressors as potentially important influences on boys' hippocampal development, including sensitivity to testosterone and connectivity to other brain regions, for reasons noted earlier. As we covered in Chapter 2, the combination of genetic risk and exposure to stressors may be particularly harmful to the development of condition-dependent traits (Fox & Reed, 2011). Indeed, in estimating genetic and environmental contributions to trait variability, any interaction between genetic risk and exposure to environmental stressors will often be estimated as a unique environmental effect (Purcell, 2002). As unique environmental effects include about 30% of the variation in hippocampal volume and as much as 65% of the variation in hippocampal connections (Kochunov et al., 2010; Kremen et al., 2010), the possibility of these effects as related to men's emotional composure should be considered.

The reader might then ask why childhood maltreatment does not appear to affect hippocampal volume, although its effect on connectivity and functioning remain unclear. I do not wish to downplay the harm that can be done to children by maltreatment, but in addition to gene-environment interactions we have to consider the full range of stressors experienced by children in natural contexts. With the possible exception of the most severe cases of maltreatment, the widespread and oftentimes chronic infestation with parasites and the poor nutrition that is common in traditional contexts has not been experienced by most of the individuals in the PTSD studies reviewed in Table 7.3; the same argument applies to many studies conducted in Western settings (Chapter 8). Even the social and emotional stress of maltreatment may not be as severe as experiencing the premature death of a sibling or parent or living in a village that might be raided at any time by warriors from a neighboring village. This is not to say that exposure to these stressors will affect hippocampal development, and more so in boys than girls, just that the study of maltreated children in Western contexts does not fully address the question.

Finally, consideration of the social and psychological predictors of risk for combat-related PTSD helps to integrate these results with discussion of some previously considered traits. First of all, the best predictor of PTSD symptoms is severity of combat exposure (Lee, Vaillant, Torrey, & Elder, 1995; McNally, 2003); even the most psychologically and physically fit men can experience PTSD symptoms with exposure to extreme stressors. The question here is whether there are other predictors of risk of PTSD above and beyond the severity of combat exposure. Most studies of differences between veterans with and without PTSD involve after-the-fact comparisons and thus suffer from the same limitations as the studies of the brain correlates of PTSD, but there have been several potentially important prospective studies (Brailey, Vasterling, Proctor, Constans, & Friedman, 2007; Schnurr, Friedman, & Rosenberg, 1993). Brailey et al. assessed the prior life stressors, such as childhood maltreatment, and cohesion within their military unit (e.g., "my unit is like family to me") of more than 1,500 soldiers prior to deployment to a combat zone (Iraq). Ten percent of these soldiers were later diagnosed with PTSD after experiencing combat. Those with a childhood history of trauma were at elevated risk and those who were well integrated within their unit had reduced risk. Moreover, strong unit cohesion reduced the risks of PTSD for those with a history of being maltreated.

Schnurr and colleagues (1993) examined the relation between young men's personality and later combat-related PTSD symptoms. In this study, Dartmouth freshmen were administered a measure of psychopathology and personality just prior to the start of the Vietnam war and their military history and psychological functioning was assessed more than 20 years later. Among the combat veterans, the best combination of predictors of PTSD symptoms is shown in Figure 7.7. Men who experienced the most violent combat (~top 15% to 20%) were nearly 4.5 times more likely to have PTSD symptoms than men with average levels of combat exposure. Men with an asocial personality or who had more feminine scores on a masculinity-femininity scale – lower male-typical interests and behaviors – were also at elevated risk, above and beyond the level of combat exposure. The measure of asocial personality assesses in part respect for authority and rules and men who score highly on this scale and men with more feminine behaviors and interests are not likely to integrate well with their military unit, potentially consistent with Brailey et al.'s (2007) findings.

The findings for the masculinity-femininity measure, if replicated, also has implications for more fully understanding the consequences of disruptions in

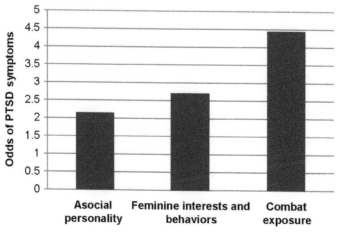

**FIGURE 7.7**   The odds of having combat-related post-traumatic stress disorder (PTSD) symptoms. *Based on data presented in Schnurr et al. (1993).* (See the color plate section.)

sex-typical behaviors described in the Chapter 6. Recall, poor nutrition and prenatal exposure to toxins disrupt boys' sex-typical play, interests, and social behaviors (Table 6.3). Boys who differ from their peers in these areas are at risk for social exclusion and ridicule (Fagot, 1977, 1984; Green, 1976) and are at heightened risk of anxiety and depression (Young & Sweeting, 2004). One possibility is that engagement in sex-atypical behaviors during development is a social signal that these boys are less likely than other boys to grow up to be reliable allies during male-male competition. This would explain why boys who engage in sex-atypical behaviors are treated more harshly than girls who engage in sex-atypical behaviors. It is also possible that social reaction to these boys alone is enough to make them more vulnerable to later stressors – through increased risk of anxiety and depression – than they might otherwise be. It is also unclear whether or not these behaviors are correlated with vulnerability of the hippocampus as related to emotion regulation and memories, but this is a testable question.

## CONCLUSION

Although none of the research reviewed in this chapter was designed to explicitly assess sex differences in brain and cognitive vulnerabilities, the results of the associated studies are consistent with sex differences for some of these traits. Difficulties during prenatal development (Largo et al., 1986) and during the early stages of Alzheimer's disease at the other end of the life span (Henderson & Buckwalter, 1994) may compromise girls' and women's natural language development and many specific language competencies, such as fluency of retrieving common words from long-term memory, more severely than those of similarly afflicted boys and men. Follow-up studies of how these language competencies are disrupted by exposure to natural stressors, such as parasite infestation, and especially during pubertal development and the intensification of relational aggression will provide important tests of the vulnerability hypothesis. For instance, the stress associated with relational aggression may be particularly disruptive of the functional language and other folk psychological competencies of girls who have other risk factors (e.g., genetic, earlier maltreatment). The poor theory of mind and deficits in reading social-emotional cues associated with anorexia is also consistent with the prediction that women's folk psychological competencies are condition-dependent cognitive traits (Oldershaw et al., 2010; Russell et al., 2009), but these too require follow-up study. It will be important to determine whether comparably malnourished men suffer the same degree of deficit as women with anorexia, and the extent to which these deficits result directly from malnutrition or are preexisting risks for the disease itself.

The studies assessing boys' and men's competencies in folk physics domains suggest, among other things, that prenatal exposure to toxins (Guo et al., 1995), infectious disease (Venkataramani, 2012), and social stressors (Levine et al., 2005) affect their spatial reasoning and related abilities more severely than girls and women exposed to the same stressors. Exposure to toxins during childhood (Rosado et al., 2007) and in adulthood (Nilson et al., 2002) may have similar effects, but questions of potential dose-response effects and identifying which environmental chemicals are potentially toxic and which are not remain to be determined (Chapter 8). In any case, the results of the studies reviewed in this domain are very likely to have underestimated the cognitive vulnerabilities of boys and men. With a few exceptions, as noted earlier (e.g., Cherrier et al., 2003), the visual and spatial tests used in this literature are not the most sensitive measures of boys' and men's folk physics abilities (see Geary, 2010), but this can be easily remedied in future studies.

Identifying and assessing sex differences in brain vulnerabilities will be a particularly difficult yet doable undertaking. Our understanding of sex differences in brain development, architecture, and functioning is expanding rapidly (Giedd et al., 1999; Ingalhalikar et al., 2014; Leonard et al., 2008) and thus provides the foundation for these studies. My argument here is that a deep understanding of human evolutionary history and especially sexual and social selection can narrow the focus of where and when in development to look for any such vulnerability. There is much that remains to be sorted out, but my analysis of men's emotional composure under stress suggests that some subregions of the hippocampus and connections of other brain regions may be one such condition-dependent trait in men.

# Chapter 8

# Implications for Human Health and Development

## Chapter Outline

There is a growing appreciation that women and men are differentially susceptible to a variety of diseases and react differently to a wide range of biomedical and other interventions (Jacquemont et al., 2014; Legato, 2004; Yoon et al., 2014). Our poor understanding of these differences stems in part from an implicit assumption of biological equality, and a heavy reliance on males in health-related research, to avoid the underappreciated effects of hormonal changes across females' menstrual cycle (Jacquemont et al., 2014; Kim, Tingen, & Woodruff, 2010; Legato, 2004; Yoon et al., 2014). Much of the current research that does deal with sex differences focuses on the molecular mechanisms, such as medication or nutrient absorption and metabolism, that act differently in men and women (e.g., Greenblatt et al., 2014; Marino et al., 2011). A more thorough understanding of these molecular mechanisms will have important implications for improving human health, but this is just the tip of the iceberg. A broader, evolutionarily informed understanding of sex differences has the potential to contribute to not only this research but also research and interventions in the many other facets of life that influence well-being (below). This broader perspective will help to develop better methods to assess and address the different ways in which women and men and girls and boys react to the stresses of life, and a better understanding of exactly what constitutes a stressor and why.

There is of course a very potent evolutionary process that makes the sexes more similar than different – natural selection (Darwin, 1859). Sexual selection and social selection more broadly will, in contrast, typically act differently on males and females. The result is that some traits – and presumably many of the

Evolution of Vulnerability. http://dx.doi.org/10.1016/B978-0-12-801562-9.00008-9

underlying metabolic pathways needed for the development and expression of these traits (Hill, 2014) – are elaborated more in one sex or the other (Darwin, 1871; West-Eberhard, 1983). As I have detailed in the previous chapters, the evolutionary and developmental elaboration of these traits provide individuals with a competitive advantage and makes them desirable mates. The cost-benefit trade-offs associated with competition and mate-choice is such that many of these same traits have evolved to be signals of the individual's exposure and ability to tolerate natural stressors, especially parasites, poor nutrition, and social competition (Zahavi & Zahavi, 1997). My proposal is that this evolved sensitivity to environmental and social stressors can be reframed and used to better understand human vulnerabilities. Below, I touch on a few practical implications of this framing by highlighting how it can be used to design assessment batteries for identifying vulnerabilities, and by providing perspective on the stressors that expose these vulnerabilities.

## DEFINING AND ASSESSING WELL-BEING AND VULNERABILITY

The World Health Organization (WHO, 1948) defines well-being in terms of physical, psychological (e.g., freedom from anxiety), and social (e.g., having satisfying relationships) health. It is difficult to argue with this definition, but if men and women and boys and girls differ in these domains then a complete understanding of well-being needs to incorporate these differences. If we want to gauge whether the growth of 16-year-old boys living in difficult circumstances is compromised, for instance, we would not use girls' height norms (which would place stunted boys in the normal range) or combine boys' and girls' norms (which would place stunted boys in the low normal range). If we did, we would incorrectly conclude that boys' with stunted growth are in the normal range, and we would incorrectly conclude that the physical growth of adolescent boys is not compromised relative to that of same-age girls by poor nutrition or disease (Table 6.1). A reasonable solution to this dilemma is to make use of sex-specific norms when assessing any trait where there are probable sex differences.

Without such norms, the same incorrect conclusions would result for any trait for which the sexes differ – including social, psychological, and cognitive traits – but are assumed not to. To be sure, if boys and girls and men and women differ on these types of traits because they are reacting to differences in parental treatment or social opportunity, as some have argued, then conflating the sexes when searching for vulnerabilities will not influence our conclusions (Hyde, 2005; Wood & Eagly, 2002). The sexes will be equally vulnerable or resilient to poor nutrition, parasites, social maltreatment, and toxins for the trait of interest. However, if the sexes differ on these traits as a result of differences in how sexual selection and social selection have operated during our evolutionary history, as I have argued here and elsewhere (Geary, 2010; Geary et al., 2014), then conflating the sexes can be problematic. It can lead to an underestimation or overestimation of risk for one sex or the other or the conclusion that there is no risk at all, when sex-specific risks do exist. I am not arguing that social or cultural factors cannot influence sex differences, but rather that an evolutionary perspective allows us to identify those traits that are the most likely to show sex-specific vulnerabilities.

As covered in previous chapters, the task of identifying vulnerabilities is further complicated because even within one sex, different traits may be vulnerable to different stressors and at different ages (below). Moreover, exposure to stressors early in development may not manifest until adulthood; in biomedical research this process is referred to as developmental origins of disease (see Gluckman & Hanson, 2004). These nuances mean that there is much to learn about the types of sex-specific vulnerabilities I have been discussing, and more practically that any one individual's deviation from sex-typical norms cannot be attributed to exposure to some type of stressor (e.g., any such effect could be due to natural, genetic variation in the trait). At the same time, the framework I have outlined can be used to design broader assessments of the consequences of exposure to parasites, poor nutrition, maltreatment, or toxins on groups of girls and boys and women and men.

To illustrate my point, let's consider Assis et al.'s (1998) field study of the effects of treatment of schistosomiasis (*Schistosoma mansoni*) on the physical development of 7–14-year-old boys and girls. The children were randomly assigned to treatment and placebo control groups and their physical growth was followed for the next year. One year after treatment, treated boys were taller, weighed more, had larger fat reserves, and more muscle mass than their untreated peers, but there were no differences in the growth of treated and untreated girls. On the basis of these results, we might conclude that infection with this particular worm is not particularly harmful for girls, and thus if medicine is in short supply, the treatment of boys should be prioritized. This however would be a premature conclusion, if schistosomiasis compromises different physical traits in girls than boys. As described in Chapter 6, these traits might include pelvic width – with implications for later birth complications (Prentice et al., 2013) – and fat reserves for adolescent girls; Assis et al. combined across age and thus the latter could not be assessed in this study. Furthermore, the study leaves unanswered the questions of whether and how schistosomiasis differentially affects the sex-typical play, behavioral and social development, and specific cognitive competencies (e.g., reading facial expressions vs. navigating a maze) of girls and boys.

A more complete understanding of how this parasite, or any other disease or stressor, affects developing girls and boys will require assessment of vulnerable physical, behavioral, and cognitive traits, such as those described in Table 5.1. Granted, it is not feasible to assess every one of these traits, but it is possible to assess a subset of them using currently available, age-appropriate measures. Until we understand better sex-specific vulnerabilities, a good place to start might be the traits that appear to be especially sensitive to stressors, based on reviews in Chapters 6 and 7. I provide some suggestions about how these findings can be used to expand assessments of sex-specific vulnerabilities of children at different ages as well as adults.

## Assessing Vulnerability in Preschool Children

The physical growth of preschool boys and girls is similar (Tanner, 1990), which means any deleterious effects of stressor exposure are likely to be more similar than different for boys and girls (e.g., for height). Even so, sex differences in physical endurance and fitness begin to emerge during this time and might be more easily compromised in boys than girls (Table 6.1). By 3 years of age boys outperform girls on the shuttle run (Thomas & French, 1985), a frequently used test of cardiovascular fitness described in Chapter 6 (e.g., Yap et al., 2012). This test could be used to gauge if exposure to a particular stressor compromises the physical fitness of boys more than girls.

I also noted in Chapter 6 that there are very large and easily assessed – using the *Pre-School Activities Inventory* (Golombok & Rust, 1993) – sex differences in the suite of early play behaviors and that these same behaviors appear to be compromised by prenatal exposure to toxins and maternal stress (e.g., Barrett et al., 2014; Swan et al., 2010). The same inventory should provide a good, broad-brush assessment of whether other stressors have sex-specific effects on preschoolers' behavioral and social development. In addition to the typically used summary measures of boy-typical and girl-typical play, differences in stressor-exposed and unexposed children for specific behaviors might provide useful information; for example, playing with "Trains, Cars, or Airplanes" and "Enjoys rough and tumble play" for boys, and "Playing taking care of babies" for girls (Golombok & Rust, 1993, pp. 135–136). If stressors are found to disrupt sex-typical play on this inventory, the next step would be direct observation of play with objects (e.g., dolls and cars) and with other children (e.g., see Berenbaum & Hines, 1992; DiPietro, 1981). The evidence is mixed at this time, but there is some indication that toxin exposure can differentially affect the internalizing (e.g., depression) and externalizing (e.g., aggressive behavior) behaviors of boys and girls (Braun et al., 2011). Preschoolers' functioning is these areas can be assessed with the preschool version of the *Child Behavior Checklist* (Achenbach & Rescorla, 2000).

Of the cognitive abilities listed in Table 5.1 and based on the reviews described in Chapter 7, measures of natural language development (not just vocabulary) would be important to include in any assessment of preschool girls' sensitivity to stressors. In their studies of the language development of children born prematurely, Largo et al. (1986) and Jennische and Sedin (2003) included the *Illinois Test of Psycholinguistic Abilities* (Hammill, Mather, & Roberts, 2004). This measure is appropriate for 5-year-olds and older children, and other measures are available for use with younger children (e.g., Zimmerman, Steiner, & Pond, 2011). It will also be important to include one or several measures of spatial abilities in any such assessment; specifically, to assess boys' sensitivity to stressors. There are standardized measures of these abilities, such as the block design subtest of the *Wechsler Preschool and Primary Scale of Intelligence* (Wechsler, 2012), but these tests will not be the most sensitive measures of vulnerability in this domain. Rather, an experimental measure developed by Levine et al. (1999) is likely to be more sensitive, at least for 4½-year-olds and older children; the task involves mentally rotating two shapes to create a single shape that is then matched to one of four possibilities.

## Assessing Vulnerability in School-Age Children and Adolescents

The growth of school-age boys and girls will be more similar than different (Tanner, 1990), although boys might be somewhat more vulnerable during this time in terms of skeletal growth and muscle development (Table 6.1). Nutritional deficits and exposure to other stressors may compromises boys' fat reserves – as can be measured by triceps skinfold – more than that of girls', particularly in late childhood (Frisancho, 1974). As described in Chapter 6, school-age boys' physical fitness is more strongly compromised by exposure to stressors than that of girls, and the shuttle run would be a good measure of this vulnerability (Yap et al., 2012). If the run is not feasible, measures of return-to-baseline heart rate after a few minutes of physical exertion or vital (lung) capacity might also be sensitive to this vulnerability (Blair et al., 1989; Stephenson et al., 1990). All of these measures can also be used to assess the vulnerability of adolescents' physical fitness, with the expectation that boys' fitness will be more severely compromised than girls' fitness by exposure to stressors (Table 6.1). In addition, height and muscle mass are useful measures of adolescent boys' physical vulnerability (Assis et al., 1998). Less common but potentially useful measures of adolescent girls' physical vulnerability would include assessment of lower-body fat reserves and pelvic width relative to height (Hautvast, 1971), but with respect to their stage of pubertal development, not simply chronological age; pubertal stage can be assessed for both sexes using Marshall and Tanner's (1969, 1970) scale.

As described in Chapter 5, sex-typed behavior and social activities continue and even intensify in childhood, relative to the preschool years (e.g., Maccoby, 1988; Pellegrini & Smith, 1998; Rose & Rudolph, 2006). Broad-based assessments of these differences and their potential sex-specific sensitivity to stressors can be assessed using the *Child Activities Inventory* (Golombok et al., 2008) and the *Child Game Participation Questionnaire* (Sandberg & Meyer-Bahlburg, 1994). In addition to the overall sex-typical scores for these measures, specific behaviors and activities might be more sensitive than others to disruption by exposure to stressors; these would include play fighting and playing with guns and tools for boys, and playing with dolls and dressing up for girls.

There are other sex differences in social behavior and friendships that might also be more easily disrupted by stressors in one sex or the other, but standardized measures are not available to assess them. Broadly, these would include boys' integration into a larger group of boys and mutual engagement in group activities (e.g., team sports), and girls' development of dyadic friendships characterized by disclosure of personal problems and mutual emotional support (Geary et al., 2003; Rose & Rudolph, 2006). The latter can be assessed using a questionnaire (Rose et al., 2012). Integration within a social network (all members know and like one another) requires a sociometric analysis (Dijkstra et al., 2013), but can probably be inferred by the amount of time boys spend playing or competing within a stable group (Parker & Seal, 1996; Savin-Williams, 1987). If stressors are found to result in sex-specific disruptions of friendships, the next step would be to focus on the specific behaviors, such as providing positive emotional support in the context of girls' dyadic friendships, that are important for the development and maintenance of these relationships (Table 5.1).

The rampant sex segregation of childhood begins to wane during adolescence with heightened interest in heterosexual relationships. But, many of the sex differences in behavioral and social activities (e.g., team sports) will continue, especially those related to same-sex friendships. In other words, the social competencies needed to develop and maintain these relationships may remain sensitive to stressors and thus an assessment of at least the maintenance of and satisfaction with same-sex friendships would be useful for adolescents (Rose et al., 2012). During this time girls' risk of depression and anxiety increases (Nolen-Hoeksema, 1987), as does boys' engagement in status-related risk taking and aggressive behaviors (Wilson & Daly, 1985). If men's emotional composure is a condition-dependent trait as I hypothesize, then exposure to stressors should result in heightened risk of anxiety and depression – potentially manifesting as *impulsive* aggression – in adolescent boys, an increase in harm avoidance behaviors, and less risk taking. For instance, exposure to stressors during early adolescence might disrupt the upward developmental trajectory of risk-taking behaviors and the muted fear that is needed to engage in these behaviors (Stanton et al., 2009). These could be inferred using the internalizing scale of the *Child Behavior Checklist* (Achenbach, 1991), and the harm avoidance subscale of the *Temperament and Character Inventory* (Cloninger, Przybeck, Svrakic, & Wetzel, 1994).

Potential sex-specific vulnerabilities in natural language competencies can continue to be assessed into early adolescence with the *Illinois Test of Psycholinguistic Abilities* (Hammill et al., 2004). However, experimental tests that assess ease of word retrieval, generation of anagrams, or language comprehension might provide more sensitive assessments (Hyde & Linn, 1988); reading comprehension would provide a good measure of the latter. Following my discussion of folk psychological competencies in Chapter 5 and the social-cognitive deficits associated with anorexia nervosa in the previous chapter, adolescent assessments might also include the Happé et al. (1999) theory of mind measure, measures of emotion recognition (e.g., *The Eyes Test*; Baron-Cohen, Wheelwright, Hill, Raste, & Plumb, 2001), and face memory (Rehnman & Herlitz, 2006).

The potential condition dependence of boys' folk physics competencies can be assessed with a variety of pencil-and-paper measures of spatial abilities. For instance, variations on Thurstone's (1938) hands tests – whether a hand with different finger patterns and orientation is the left or right hand – would be useful in childhood (Johnson & Meade, 1987) and the mental rotation test (Vandenberg & Kuse, 1978) in adolescence. Other abilities that might prove sensitive to stressors include competence at visually tracking objects, catching projectiles, and identifying objects embedded in others; all of these can be assessed with currently available measures (e.g., Law, Pellegrino, & Hunt, 1993; Raskin & Witkin, 1971).

## Assessing Vulnerability in Adults

With the exception of physical growth, the tasks used to assess sex-specific vulnerabilities of adolescents should be just as useful for the assessment of adults. There are also newly available, standardized measures of emotion recognition based on faces and voices and face memory that can be used to assess adults and older adolescents (Pearson, 2009). There are of course well developed and widely used neuropsychological test batteries used to assess adults' functioning following exposure to toxins, chemotherapy, Alzheimer's disease, and so forth (Beinhoff et al., 2008; Hermelink et al., 2007). These measures are very useful for assessing the integrity of a variety of cognitive competencies and for making inferences about the functioning of the underlying brain systems, and I am not suggesting they be replaced. Rather, inclusion of measures that are more sensitive to sex differences and thus potential sex-specific deficits, as illustrated for Alzheimer's disease (Chapter 7), would broaden these assessments and enable a more complete evaluation of how the stressor might differentially compromise the well-being of women and men.

## DEFINING STRESSORS

The natural stressors I have emphasized throughout this book – disease, poor nutrition, and social competition – represent three of the four horsemen of the apocalypse (i.e., disease, famine, and war, respectively). These are ubiquitous stressors that are incessantly nipping at the heels of all living beings until the arrival of the fourth horseman (death). The motivations that have driven advances in medicine, sanitation, and policing, among other cultural innovations are at least in part to keep these horsemen at bay, and have succeeded for most people living in the modern world. Even so, people in these societies are still exposed to social stressors, as well as a variety of potential environmental toxins and sometimes therapeutic toxins (e.g., chemotherapy) that can have unintended and poorly understood consequences. Of course, the billions of people living in the developing world are exposed to even harsher social stressors, more environmental toxins, as well as to multiple parasites and, oftentimes, chronic poor nutrition.

My general thesis is that the sensitivity of sexually selected and socially selected traits can be used to understand better the consequence of exposure to these stressors in all of these contexts. At the same time, there are questions to be resolved regarding which stressors compromise which traits and when in development. There are also unresolved questions about the potential toxic effects of environmental contaminants and chemotherapies that might be clarified if studied in the context of trait vulnerability.

## Are All Natural Stressors Equal?

One critical and yet unanswered question concerns whether all natural stressors compromise all traits in the same way or whether some traits are sensitive to some stressors and other traits to different stressors. As reviewed in Chapter 2, if the expression of sexually selected and socially selected traits is dependent on the overall health and physical condition of the individual, including perhaps Hill's (2014) cellular respiration, then exposure to any stressor that degrades the individuals' health could in theory compromise the expression of all condition-dependent traits (Rowe & Houle, 1996). In contrast, Wedekind (1992) suggested that different parasites can affect hosts' hormonal and immune systems in different ways such that one parasite will compromise one condition-dependent trait and another parasite will compromise a different trait. The pattern of compromised traits then provides information on the mix of parasites the host is coping with.

Very few of the studies reviewed in this book were designed to assess these alternatives. As the reader knows, many of the studies examined the effects of a specific stressor (e.g., poor nutrition or parasite exposure) on a condition-dependent trait and contrasted this with the effects of the same stressor on another trait (e.g., the same trait in the opposite sex). These studies provide a critical test of whether the trait of interest is in fact more easily compromised by exposure to stressors than are other traits (Cotton et al., 2004a), but not information on the range of stressors that can compromise the trait of interest. To answer the specificity question, these studies would have to compare whether different stressors compromised the same trait and to the same extent. Comparisons across studies provide a mixed picture. Some combinations of studies suggest different stressors can indeed compromise the same trait. For instance, the red plumage color of the male house finch (*Carpodacus mexicanus*) can be compromised by poor nutrition during development (Hill, 2000) and by developmental exposure to parasites (Brawner et al., 2000). Poor nutrition during development can also compromise the later spot color of the male guppy (*Poecilia reticulata*; Grether, 2000) but has less consistent effects on spot size or later courtship displays (Kodric-Brown, 1989). Courtship displays are, however, compromised by infestations with parasites in adulthood (Houde & Torio, 1992).

As with guppies, it follows from the nature of different condition-dependent traits that at least some aspects of their expression will be more sensitive to some stressors than others, and more sensitive at some points in the life span than others. As covered in Chapters 3 and 4, vigorous and energetically demanding courtship displays are reliable signals of current condition and can be compromised by exposure to a variety of natural stressors in adulthood. This has been demonstrated in species and traits as varied as the chirping of the male field cricket (*Gryllus campestris*; Holzer et al., 2003) to the scent marking of the female marmoset (*Callithrix jacchus*; Epple, 1970). In theory, traits that develop at specific points in the life span or vary seasonally would capture the individuals' condition during that time; that is, in the distant (during development) or recent (e.g., during feather molt) past. Signals from the distant past are illustrated by the finding that poor postnatal nutrition can compromise the size and integrity of the HVC (recall, supports song learning, and production) and thus compromise the song repertoire of the male song sparrow (*Melospiza melodi*; MacDonald et al., 2006; Schmidt et al., 2013) in adulthood. Signals from the recent past are illustrated by the finding that intense competition for food during the summer months can compromise the antler development of the male red deer (*Cervus elaphus*) and thus undermine breeding success during the fall mating season (Kruuk et al., 2002).

Although these types of findings are consistent with stressor- and age-specific sensitivities of at least some condition-dependent traits, there might be more basic processes that place limits on the expression of all of these traits. As I noted in Chapter 2, the efficiency of cellular respiration determines the capacity to produce the energy needed to engage in vigorous courtship displays or to build elaborate traits, and its by-product creates cell damaging oxidative stress (see Hill, 2014; von Schantz et al., 1999). Individuals that can efficiently produce energy, for instance, will be able to engage in sustained courtship displays longer than individuals with less-efficient cellular respiration, even if they both are well nourished. These differences will be even more apparent, under nutritional stress, and for any trait – whatever it might be – that requires considerable energy to build and maintain. Even with the same underlying limiting mechanisms, the traits that signal this capacity can still differ across species, sex, and age. For instance, a combination of poor cellular respiration and poor nutrition during gestation would especially compromise energy-demanding prenatal brain development, whereas the same combination might be most obvious with energy-demanding courtship displays in adulthood.

If future research confirms that cellular respiration is a limiting factor in the development and expression of condition-dependent traits, as proposed by Hill (2014) then noninvasive measures of these processes may prove useful for identifying at-risk individuals. Combining these measures with an understanding of sex- and trait-specific vulnerabilities might provide a means to more effectively target interventions. For instance, interventions to reduce nutritional stressors for at-risk boys during puberty would be more beneficial to their physical development than would similar interventions during childhood. Moreover, any such intervention may benefit at-risk boys and girls in different ways. Reduction of stressors, for example, might have a more substantive impact on the visuospatial competencies of at-risk boys relative to more resilient – defined by efficiency of cellular respiration – boys in the same circumstances, and a more substantive impact on the folk psychological competencies of at-risk girls relative to resilient girls.

## Toxins

Toxins are not natural stressors, but their ubiquity and potential to compromise the expression of traits related to competition and mate-choice means they have the potential to influence the reproduction and evolution of exposed populations and thus are now selection pressures. At the same time, we cannot assume that all man-made chemicals are toxins. In fact, many of the advances that have reduced our vulnerability to natural stressors produce many of these same chemicals, either directly or as by-products of other activities (e.g., manufacturing). My suggestion and that of several evolutionary biologists before me is that the sensitivity of sexually selected and socially selected traits can be used to better gauge the potential toxicity of environmental contaminants (Bortolotti et al., 2003; Hill, 1995) and, for instance, therapeutic drugs. The reviews presented in earlier chapters confirm the sensitivity of these traits to toxin exposure, and thus their potential utility in toxicology studies. However, to make full use of their sensitivity requires an understanding of the natural history of the species in which they are assessed, as well as an appreciation that the inbreeding and artificial selection common in laboratory mice (*Mus musculus*) and rats (*Rattus norvegicus*) might affect these same traits (O'Leary, Savoie, & Brown, 2011). One potential consequence is that the traits of interest (e.g., spatial navigation) might be less sensitive in some laboratory strains than they would be in wild animals of the same species and, therefore, results based on studies of standard laboratory animals might underestimate the consequences of toxin exposure.

In any case, to illustrate the usefulness of this approach we return to the relation between prenatal exposure to bisphenol A (BPA) and the development and expression of sexually selected traits in outbred strains of the deer (*Peromyscus maniculatus*) and California mouse (*P. californicus*; Jašarević et al., 2011, 2013; Williams et al., 2013). Recall, male deer mice expand their territory during the breeding season and search for mates dispersed throughout the ecology (Stickel, 1968). These are sexually selected cognitive traits in these males, because the competition for mates favors males with enhanced abilities (e.g., route learning and memory; Gaulin, 1992). For their cousins, the California mouse, males are monogamous and share a territory with their mate. Thus, these males do not expand their territory during the mating season and do not have enhanced spatial abilities (Jašarević et al., 2012). But, female California mice will mate promiscuously and therefore the males must mate guard and defend their territory against intrusions by other males (Ribble & Salvioni, 1990). One associated behavior is scent making (through urine) that signals social dominance; this is a sexually selected trait for males of this species (Eisenberg, 1962).

The key finding to emerge from this series of studies was that prenatal exposure to BPA compromised the spatial learning and memory and activity of male deer mice and the territorial marking of male California mice, but had no other effects. In short, exposure only compromised sexually selected traits. If we had only tested the spatial abilities of male deer mice, we might have overgeneralized the potential deleterious effects of BPA exposure. In fact, it is sometimes assumed that the male advantage in spatial abilities is universal and as a result exposure to BPA will compromise these abilities in males of every species (Peluso, Munnia, & Ceppi, 2014). This is not the case: There are such effects, but they are selective; the spatial abilities of female deer mice were not compromised nor were the spatial abilities of female or male California mice, nor for that matter were the basic sensory abilities of male deer mice (Jašarević et al., 2011). If we had only assessed the spatial learning and memory of California mice, we might have incorrectly concluded there are no deleterious cognitive effects of BPA exposure.

My point is that the ability to detect any such effects will be strongly influenced by the species, sex, and the trait chosen as the outcome of interest. Without a conceptual framework to choose these outcomes, there is abundant potential for inconsistent results across studies and thus confusion about whether or not the chemical is a potential toxin. The issue is further complicated by the inconsistent and sometimes contradictory nature of dosage effects; sometimes, lower doses can have stronger effects than intermediate doses (e.g., Palanza et al., 1999; Peluso et al., 2014). Here too, sexually selected and socially selected traits are likely to be more sensitive to dosage effects than are other traits; even the spatial abilities of male deer mice are unaffected by low-dose exposure to BPA (Jašarević et al., 2013). Moreover, contrasts of these traits with less sensitive, naturally selected traits – such as the spatial abilities of female deer mice or male California mice – might enable the identification of extremely toxic chemicals or dosages (e.g., with chemotherapy). Specifically, exposures that compromise naturally selected traits are likely to be more toxic than those that only compromise sexually selected or socially selected traits.

## CONCLUSION

Much has been learned about the evolution and expression of sex differences, since Darwin (1871) outlined his theory of sexual selection. Indeed, this is now a thriving area of scientific study that has yielded extensive, evolutionarily informed insights about sex differences in nonhuman species from behaviors to genes (Adkins-Regan, 2005; Andersson, 1994). There is, however, a general reluctance to apply these same principles to humans (Hyde, 2005; Wood & Eagly, 2002), based at least in part on an unfounded assumption of "genetic determinism" and an unmalleability of evolved traits. Given this, it is somewhat ironic that traits elaborated through sexual selection and social selection more broadly are in fact generally more sensitive to social and ecological conditions than are naturally selected traits; they have evolved to be malleable, within genetic constraints.

In any case, the overall effect of eschewing evolution has been a lost opportunity to use this wealth of knowledge to better understand, assess, and promote human well-being. To be sure, my argument here and the evidence presented herein are only the starting points for how an evolutionary framework can be used to inform our understanding of sex differences in risk and resiliency; much remains to be learned. In time, these insights might inform the development of measures to assess sex-specific vulnerabilities and interventions to reduce their expression in at-risk populations and individuals. At this time, I hope the reader is at least intrigued by my evolutionary framing of sex-specific human vulnerabilities, and will reflect on how this framing might be used to improve the well-being of women and men and girls and boys.

# References

Abaheseen, M. A. A., Harrison, G. G., & Pearson, P. B. (1981). Nutritional status of Saudi Arab preschool children in the eastern province. *Ecology of Food and Nutrition, 10*, 163–168.

Abbott, D. H. (1993). Social conflict and reproductive suppression in marmoset and tamarin monkeys. In W. A. Mason, & S. P. Mendoza (Eds.), *Primate social conflict* (pp. 331–372). Albany, NY: State University of New York Press.

Achenbach, T. M. (1991). *Integrative guide for the 1991 CBCL/4-18, YSR, and TRF profiles*. Burlington, VT: Department of Psychiatry, University of Vermont.

Achenbach, T. M., & Rescorla, L. A. (2000). *Manual for the ASEBA preschool forms & profiles*. Burlington, VT: Department of Psychiatry, University of Vermont.

Adams, E. J., Stephenson, L. S., Latham, M. C., & Kinoti, S. N. (1994). Physical activity and growth of Kenyan school children with hookworm, *Trichuris trichiura* and *Ascaris lumbricoides* infections are improved after treatment with albendazole. *Journal of Nutrition, 124*, 1199–1206.

Adenzato, M., Todisco, P., & Ardito, R. B. (2012). Social cognition in anorexia nervosa: Evidence of preserved theory of mind and impaired emotional functioning. *PLoS ONE, 7*, e44414.

Adkins-Regan, E. (2005). *Hormones and animal social behavior*. Princeton, NJ: Princeton University Press.

Adler, N. E., Boyce, T., Chesney, M. A., Cohen, S., Folkman, S., Kahn, R. L., et al. (1994). Socioeconomic status and health: The challenge of the gradient. *American Psychologist, 49*, 15–24.

Adolphs, R. (2003). Cognitive neuroscience of human social behaviour. *Nature Reviews Neuroscience, 4*, 165–178.

Adolphs, R., Gosselin, F., Buchanan, T. W., Tranel, D., Schyns, P., & Damasio, A. R. (2005). A mechanism for impaired fear recognition after amygdala damage. *Nature, 433*, 68–72.

Agrawal, N., Sinha, S. N., & Jensen, A. R. (1984). Effects of inbreeding on Raven matrices. *Behavior Genetics, 14*, 579–585.

Ahlgren, A., & Johnson, D. W. (1979). Sex differences in cooperative and competitive attitudes from the 2nd to the 12th grades. *Developmental Psychology, 15*, 45–49.

Ahtiainen, J. J., Alatalo, R. V., Kortet, R., & Rantala, M. J. (2004). Sexual advertisement and immune function in an arachnid species (*Lycosidae*). *Behavioral Ecology, 15*, 602–606.

Alatalo, R. V., Glynn, C., & Lundberg, A. (1990). Singing rate and female attraction in the pied flycatcher: An experiment. *Animal Behaviour, 39*, 601–603.

Alatalo, R. V., Höglund, J., Lundberg, A., Rintamaki, P. T., & Silverin, B. (1996). Testosterone and male mating success on the black grouse leks. *Proceedings of the Royal Society of London B, 263*, 1697–1702.

Alatalo, R. V., Höglund, J., Lundberg, A., & Sutherland, W. J. (1992). Evolution of black grouse leks: Female preferences benefit males in larger leks. *Behavioral Ecology, 3*, 53–59.

Alexander, R. D. (1989). Evolution of the human psyche. In P. Mellars, & C. Stringer (Eds.), *The human revolution: Behavioural and biological perspectives on the origins of modern humans* (pp. 455–513). Princeton, NJ: Princeton University Press.

Alexander, G. M., Swerdloff, R. S., Wang, C., Davidson, T., McDonald, V., Steiner, B., et al. (1998). Androgen-behavior correlations in hypogonadal men and eugonadal men. *Hormones and Behavior, 33*, 85–94.

Allen, L. H. (2000). Anemia and iron deficiency: Effects on pregnancy outcome. *American Journal of Clinical Nutrition, 71*, 1280s–1284s.

Allman, J., Rosin, A., Kumar, R., & Hasenstaub, A. (1998). Parenting and survival in anthropoid primates: Caretakers live longer. *Proceedings of the National Academy of Sciences of the United States of America, 95*, 6866–6869.

Almbro, M., & Simmons, L. W. (2014). Sexual selection can remove an experimentally induced mutation load. *Evolution, 68*, 295–300.

Almeida, O. P., Waterreus, A., Spry, N., Flicker, L., & Martins, R. N. (2004). One year follow-up study of the association between chemical castration, sex hormones, beta-amyloid, memory and depression in men. *Psychoneuroendocrinology, 29*, 1071–1081.

Alonso-Alvarez, C., & Galván, I. (2011). Free radical exposure creates paler carotenoid-based ornaments: A possible interaction in the expression of black and red traits. *PLoS ONE, 6*, e19403.

Álvarez, H. A., Serrano-Meneses, M. A., Reyes-Márquez, I., Jiménez-Cortés, J. G., & Córdoba-Aguilar, A. (2013). Allometry of a sexual trait in relation to diet experience and alternative mating tactics in two rubyspot damselflies (*Calopterygidae*: *Hetaerina*). *Biological Journal of the Linnean Society, 108*, 521–533.

Alvergne, A., Jokela, M., & Lummaa, V. (2010). Personality and reproductive success in a high-fertility human population. *Proceedings of the National Academy of Sciences of the United States of America, 107*, 11745–11750.

Amann, A., de Lacy Costello, B., Miekisch, W., Schubert, J., Buszewski, B., Pleil, J., et al. (2014). The human volatilome: Volatile organic compounds (VOCs) in exhaled breath, skin emanations, urine, feces and saliva. *Journal of Breath Research, 8*, 034001.

Amazigo, U. O. (1994). Detrimental effects of onchocerciasis on marriage age and breast-feeding. *Tropical and Geographical Medicine, 46*, 322–325.

American Psychiatric Association. (2013). *Diagnostic and statistical manual of psychiatric disorders* (5th ed.). Washington, DC: American Psychiatric Association.

Amey, F. K. (2005). Polygyny and child survival in West Africa. *Social Biology, 49*, 74–89.

Amundsen, T., & Forsgren, E. (2001). Male mate choice selects for female coloration in a fish. *Proceedings of the National Academy of Sciences of the United States of America, 98*, 13155–13160.

Amundsen, T., & Pärn, H. (2006). Female coloration: Review of functional and nonfunctional hypotheses. In G. E. Hill, & K. J. McGraw (Eds.), *Bird coloration: Function and evolution: Vol. 2.* (pp. 280–345). Cambridge, MA: Harvard University Press.

Amunts, K., Armstrong, E., Malikovic, A., Hömke, L., Mohlberg, H., Schleicher, A., et al. (2007). Gender-specific left–right asymmetries in human visual cortex. *Journal of Neuroscience, 27*, 1356–1364.

Anderson, J. L., Crawford, C. B., Nadeau, J., & Lindberg, T. (1992). Was the Duchess of Windsor right? A cross-cultural review of the socioecology of ideals of female body shape. *Ethology and Sociobiology, 13*, 197–227.

Anderson, K. J., & Leaper, C. (1998). Meta-analyses of gender effects on conversational interruption: Who, what, when, where, and how? *Sex Roles, 39*, 225–252.

Andersson, S. (1989). Sexual selection and cues for female choice in leks of Jackson's widowbird *Euplectes jacksoni. Behavioral Ecology and Sociobiology, 25*, 403–410.

Andersson, M. (1994). *Sexual selection.* Princeton, NJ: Princeton University Press.

Andersson, M. (2004). Social polyandry, parental investment, sexual selection, and evolution of reduced female gamete size. *Evolution, 58*, 24–34.

Apicella, C. L. (2014). Upper-body strength predicts hunting reputation and reproductive success in Hadza hunter-gatherers. *Evolution and Human Behavior, 35*, 508–518.

Apicella, C. L., Feinberg, D. R., & Marlowe, F. W. (2007). Voice pitch predicts reproductive success in male hunter-gatherers. *Biology Letters, 3*, 682–684.

Apostolou, M. (2007). Sexual selection under parental choice: The role of parents in the evolution of human mating. *Evolution and Human Behavior, 28*, 403–409.

Archer, J. (2004). Sex differences in aggression in real-world settings: A meta-analytic review. *Review of General Psychology, 8*, 291–322.

Archer, J. (2006). Testosterone and human behavior: An evaluation of the challenge hypothesis. *Neuroscience and Biobehavioral Reviews, 30*, 319–345.

Archer, J., & Coyne, S. M. (2005). An integrated review of indirect, relational, and social aggression. *Personality and Social Psychology Review, 9*, 212–230.

Argyle, M. (1994). *The psychology of social class*. New York: Routledge.

Armbruster, P., & Reed, D. H. (2005). Inbreeding depression in benign and stressful environments. *Heredity, 95*, 235–242.

Arnold, J. L., & Siviy, S. M. (2002). Effects of neonatal handling and maternal separation on rough-and-tumble play in the rat. *Developmental Psychobiology, 41*, 205–215.

Arnott, M. A., Cassella, J. P., Aitken, P. P., & Hay, J. (1990). Social interactions of mice with congenital *Toxoplasma* infection. *Annals of Tropical Medicine and Parasitology, 84*, 149–156.

Arnqvist, G., & Thornhill, R. (1998). Evolution of animal genitalia: Patterns of phenotypic and genotypic variation and condition dependence of genital and non-genital morphology in water strider (*Heteroptera: Gerridae: Insecta*). *Genetical Research, 71*, 193–212.

Ashcroft, M. T., Heneage, P., & Lovell, H. G. (1966). Heights and weights of Jamaican schoolchildren of various ethnic groups. *American Journal of Physical Anthropology, 24*, 35–44.

Aspi, J. (2000). Inbreeding and outbreeding depression in male courtship song characters in *Drosophila montana*. *Heredity, 84*, 273–282.

Assis, A. M., Barreto, M. L., Prado, M. S., Reis, M. G., Parraga, I. M., & Blanton, R. E. (1998). *Schistosoma mansoni* infection and nutritional status in schoolchildren: A randomized, double-blind trial in northeastern Brazil. *American Journal of Clinical Nutrition, 68*, 1247–1253.

Baatrup, E., & Junge, M. (2001). Antiandrogenic pesticides disrupt sexual characteristics in the adult male guppy *Poecilia reticulata*. *Environmental Health Perspectives, 109*, 1063–1070.

Backwell, P. R., Jennions, M. D., Christy, J. H., & Schober, U. (1995). Pillar building in the fiddler crab *Uca beebei*: Evidence for a condition-dependent ornament. *Behavioral Ecology and Sociobiology, 36*, 185–192.

Bailey, D. H., Walker, R. S., Blomquist, G. E., Hill, K. R., Hurtado, A. M., & Geary, D. C. (2013). Heritability and fitness correlates of personality in the Ache, a natural-fertility population in Paraguay. *PLoS ONE, 8*, e59325.

Bakker, T. C., & Mundwiler, B. (1994). Female mate choice and male red coloration in a natural three-spined stickleback (*Gasterosteus aculeatus*) population. *Behavioral Ecology, 5*, 74–80.

Ball, G. F., & Hulse, S. H. (1998). Birdsong. *American Psychologist, 53*, 37–58.

Banday, K. M., Pasikanti, K. K., Chan, E. C. Y., Singla, R., Rao, K. V. S., Chauhan, V. S., et al. (2011). Use of urine volatile organic compounds to discriminate tuberculosis patients from healthy subjects. *Analytical Chemistry, 83*, 5526–5534.

Bandstra, E. S., Morrow, C. E., Accornero, V. H., Mansoor, E., Xue, L., & Anthony, J. C. (2011). Estimated effects of *in utero* cocaine exposure on language development through early adolescence. *Neurotoxicology and Teratology, 33*, 25–35.

Banerjee, M. (1997). Hidden emotions: Preschoolers' knowledge of appearance-reality and emotion display rules. *Social Cognition, 15*, 107–132.

Banik, S. D. (2014). Menarche, nutritional status and body size in 10 to 12 year-old girls from Kashipur, Purulia, West Bengal, India. *Malaysian Journal of Nutrition, 20*, 39–49.

Barker, D. J., Osmond, C., Forsén, T. J., Kajantie, E., & Eriksson, J. G. (2005). Trajectories of growth among children who have coronary events as adults. *New England Journal of Medicine, 353*, 1802–1809.

Barker, D. J., Osmond, C., Kajantie, E., & Eriksson, J. G. (2009). Growth and chronic disease: Findings in the Helsinki Birth Cohort. *Annals of Human Biology, 36*, 445–458.

Barnes, L. L., Wilson, R. S., Bienias, J. L., Schneider, J. A., Evans, D. A., & Bennett, D. A. (2005). Sex differences in the clinical manifestations of Alzheimer disease pathology. *Archives of General Psychiatry, 62*, 685–691.

Baron-Cohen, S. (1995). *Mindblindness: An essay on autism and theory of mind*. Cambridge, MA: MIT Press/Bradford Books.

Baron-Cohen, S., Wheelwright, S., Hill, J., Raste, Y., & Plumb, I. (2001). The "Reading the Mind in the Eyes" test revised version: A study with normal adults, and adults with Asperger syndrome or high-functioning autism. *Journal of Child Psychology and Psychiatry, 42*, 241–251.

Baron-Cohen, S., Wheelwright, S., Stone, V., & Rutherford, M. (1999). A mathematician, a physicist and a computer scientist with Asperger syndrome: Performance on folk psychology and folk physics tests. *Neurocase, 5*, 475–483.

Barrett, J., Abbott, D. H., & George, L. M. (1990). Extension of reproductive suppression by pheromonal cues in subordinate female marmoset monkeys, *Callithrix jacchus*. *Journal of Reproduction and Fertility, 90*, 411–418.

Barrett, J., Abbott, D. H., & George, L. M. (1993). Sensory cues and the suppression of reproduction in subordinate female marmoset monkeys, *Callithrix jacchus*. *Journal of Reproduction and Fertility, 97*, 301–310.

Barrett, D. E., & Radke-Yarrow, M. (1985). Effects of nutritional supplementation on children's responses to novel, frustrating, and competitive situations. *American Journal of Clinical Nutrition, 42*, 102–120.

Barrett, D. E., Radke-Yarrow, M., & Klein, R. E. (1982). Chronic malnutrition and child behavior: Effects of early caloric supplementation on social and emotional functioning at school age. *Developmental Psychology, 18*, 541–556.

Barrett, E. S., Redmon, J. B., Wang, C., Sparks, A., & Swan, S. H. (2014). Exposure to prenatal life events stress is associated with masculinized play behavior in girls. *Neurotoxicology, 41*, 20–27.

Barry, H., III, Josephson, L., Lauer, E., & Marshall, C. (1976). Traits inculcated in childhood: Cross-cultural codes 5. *Ethnology, 15*, 83–106.

Bartoš, L., & Bahbouh, R. (2006). Antler size and fluctuating asymmetry in red deer (*Cervus elaphus*) stags and probability of becoming a harem holder in rut. *Biological Journal of the Linnean Society, 87*, 59–68.

Bartoš, L., & Losos, S. (1997). Response of antler growth to changing rank of fallow deer buck during the velvet period. *Canadian Journal of Zoology, 75*, 1934–1939.

Baube, C. L. (1997). Manipulations of signalling environment affect male competitive success in three-spined sticklebacks. *Animal Behaviour, 53*, 819–833.

Bayles, K. A., Azuma, T., Cruz, R. F., Tomoeda, C. K., Wood, J. A., Montgomery, E. B., Jr. (1999). Gender differences in language of Alzheimer disease patients revisited. *Alzheimer Disease & Associated Disorders, 13*, 138–146.

Bayley, M., Junge, M., & Baatrup, E. (2002). Exposure of juvenile guppies to three antiandrogens causes demasculinization and a reduced sperm count in adult males. *Aquatic Toxicology, 56,* 227–239.

Bayley, M., Larsen, P. F., Bækgaard, H., & Baatrup, E. (2003). The effects of vinclozolin, an antiandrogenic fungicide, on male guppy secondary sex characters and reproductive success. *Biology of Reproduction, 69,* 1951–1956.

Bayley, M., Nielsen, J. R., & Baatrup, E. (1999). Guppy sexual behavior as an effect biomarker of estrogen mimics. *Ecotoxicology and Environmental Safety, 43,* 68–73.

Becker, E. A., Petruno, S., & Marler, C. A. (2012). A comparison of scent marking between a monogamous and promiscuous species of *Peromyscus*: Pair bonded males do not advertise to novel females. *PLoS ONE, 7,* e32002.

Bediou, B., Ryff, I., Mercier, B., Milliery, M., He, M. A., d'Amato, T., et al. (2009). Impaired social cognition in mild Alzheimer disease. *Journal of Geriatric Psychiatry and Neurology, 22,* 130–140.

Beecher, M. D., & Brenowitz, E. A. (2005). Functional aspects of song learning in songbirds. *Trends in Ecology & Evolution, 20,* 143–149.

Beeghly, M., Martin, B., Rose-Jacobs, R., Cabral, H., Heeren, T., Augustyn, M., et al. (2006). Prenatal cocaine exposure and children's language functioning at 6 and 9.5 years: Moderating effects of child age, birthweight, and gender. *Journal of Pediatric Psychology, 31,* 98–115.

Behr, O., Von Helversen, O., Heckel, G., Nagy, M., Voigt, C. C., & Mayer, F. (2006). Territorial songs indicate male quality in the sac-winged bat *Saccopteryx bilineata* (*Chiroptera, Emballonuridae*). *Behavioral Ecology, 17,* 810–817.

Beinhoff, U., Tumani, H., Brettschneider, J., Bittner, D., & Riepe, M. W. (2008). Gender-specificities in Alzheimer's disease and mild cognitive impairment. *Journal of Neurology, 255,* 117–122.

Bekoff, M., & Byers, J. A. (Eds.), (1998). *Animal play: Evolutionary, comparative, and ecological perspectives.* Cambridge, UK: Cambridge University Press.

Bell, A. M. (2001). Effects of an endocrine disrupter on courtship and aggressive behaviour of male three-spined stickleback, *Gasterosteus aculeatus*. *Animal Behaviour, 62,* 775–780.

Bellamy, L., Chapman, N., Fowler, K., & Pomiankowski, A. (2013). Sexual traits are sensitive to genetic stress and predict extinction risk in the stalk-eyed fly, *Diasemposis meigenii*. *Evolution, 67,* 2662–2673.

Belsky, J., Steinberg, L., & Draper, P. (1991). Childhood experience, interpersonal development, and reproductive strategy: An evolutionary theory of socialization. *Child Development, 62,* 647–670.

Bender, C. M., Sereika, S. M., Berga, S. L., Vogel, V. G., Brufsky, A. M., Paraska, K. K., et al. (2006). Cognitive impairment associated with adjuvant therapy in breast cancer. *Psycho-Oncology, 15,* 422–430.

Bender, C. M., Sereika, S. M., Brufsky, A. M., Ryan, C. M., Vogel, V. G., Rastogi, P., et al. (2007). Memory impairments with adjuvant anastrozole versus tamoxifen in women with early-stage breast cancer. *Menopause, 14,* 995–998.

Bendich, A. (1991). β-Carotene and the immune response. *Proceedings of the Nutrition Society, 50,* 263–274.

Bénéfice, E., Garnier, D., Simondon, K. B., & Malina, R. M. (2001). Relationship between stunting in infancy and growth and fat distribution during adolescence in Senegalese girls. *European Journal of Clinical Nutrition, 55,* 50–58.

Benenson, J. F. (1990). Gender differences in social networks. *Journal of Early Adolescence, 10,* 472–495.

Benenson, J. F. (1993). Greater preference among females than males for dyadic interaction in early childhood. *Child Development, 64*, 544–555.

Benenson, J. F. (2014). *Warriors and worriers: The survival of the sexes.* New York: Oxford University Press.

Benenson, J. F., & Christakos, A. (2003). The greater fragility of females' versus males' closest same-sex friendships. *Child Development, 74*, 1123–1129.

Benenson, J. F., Markovits, H., Emery Thompson, M., & Wrangham, R. W. (2011). Social exclusion threatens adult females more than males. *Psychological Science, 22*, 538–544.

Benenson, J. F., Markovits, H., Hultgren, B., Nguyen, T., Bullock, G., & Wrangham, R. W. (2013). Social exclusion: More important to human females than males. *PLoS ONE, 8*, e55851.

Bennett, D. S., Bendersky, M., & Lewis, M. (2002). Children's intellectual and emotional-behavioral adjustment at 4 years as a function of cocaine exposure, maternal characteristics, and environmental risk. *Developmental Psychology, 38*, 648–658.

Bennett, D. S., Bendersky, M., & Lewis, M. (2008). Children's cognitive ability from 4 to 9 years old as a function of prenatal cocaine exposure, environmental risk, and maternal verbal intelligence. *Developmental Psychology, 44*, 919–928.

Berenbaum, S. A., Bryk, K. L. K., & Beltz, A. M. (2012). Early androgen effects on spatial and mechanical abilities: Evidence from congenital adrenal hyperplasia. *Behavioral Neuroscience, 126*, 86–96.

Berenbaum, S. A., & Hines, M. (1992). Early androgens are related to childhood sex-typed toy preferences. *Psychological Science, 3*, 203–206.

Berenbaum, S. A., Korman Bryk, K., Duck, S. C., & Resnick, S. M. (2004). Psychological adjustment in children and adults with congenital adrenal hyperplasia. *Journal of Pediatrics, 144*, 741–746.

Berg, V., Lummaa, V., Lahdenperä, M., Rotkirch, A., & Jokela, M. (2014). Personality and long-term reproductive success measured by the number of grandchildren. *Evolution and Human Behavior, 35*, 533–539.

Bergeron, P., Festa-Bianchet, M., Von Hardenberg, A., & Bassano, B. (2008). Heterogeneity in male horn growth and longevity in a highly sexually dimorphic ungulate. *Oikos, 117*, 77–82.

Berglund, A., & Rosenqvist, G. (2001). Male pipefish prefer dominant over attractive females. *Behavioral Ecology, 12*, 402–406.

Berglund, A., Rosenqvist, G., & Bernet, P. (1997). Ornamentation predicts reproductive success in female pipefish. *Behavioral Ecology and Sociobiology, 40*, 145–150.

Bergman, T. J., Ho, L., & Beehner, J. C. (2009). Chest color and social status in male geladas (*Theropithecus gelada*). *International Journal of Primatology, 30*, 791–806.

Beronius, A., Johansson, N., Rudén, C., & Hanberg, A. (2013). The influence of study design and sex-differences on results from developmental neurotoxicity studies of bisphenol A, implications for toxicity testing. *Toxicology, 311*, 13–26.

Betzig, L. L. (1986). *Despotism and differential reproduction: A Darwinian view of history.* New York: Aldine Publishing Company.

Betzig, L. (1989). Causes of conjugal dissolution: A cross-cultural study. *Current Anthropology, 30*, 654–676.

Betzig, L. (2012). Means, variances, and ranges in reproductive success: Comparative evidence. *Evolution and Human Behavior, 33*, 309–317.

Bharati, P. (1989). Variation in adult body dimensions in relation to economic condition among the Mahishyas of Howrah district, West Bengal, India. *Annals of Human Biology, 16*, 529–541.

Biard, C., Surai, P. F., & Møller, A. P. (2005). Effects of carotenoid availability during laying on reproduction in the blue tit. *Oecologia, 144*, 32–44.

Birkhead, T. R., Fletcher, F., & Pellatt, E. J. (1998). Sexual selection in the zebra finch *Taeniopygia guttata*: Condition, sex traits and immune capacity. *Behavioral Ecology and Sociobiology, 44*, 179–191.

Birkhead, T. R., Fletcher, F., & Pellatt, E. J. (1999). Nestling diet, secondary sexual traits and fitness in the zebra finch. *Proceedings of the Royal Society of London B, 266*, 385–390.

Birn, R. M., Patriat, R., Phillips, M. L., Germain, A., & Herringa, R. J. (2014). Childhood maltreatment and combat posttraumatic stress differentially predict fear-related fronto-subcortical connectivity. *Depression and Anxiety, 31*, 880–892.

Bischoff, L. L., Tschirren, B., & Richner, H. (2009). Long-term effects of early parasite exposure on song duration and singing strategy in great tits. *Behavioral Ecology, 20*, 265–270.

Björkqvist, K., Osterman, K., & Lagerspetz, K. M. J. (1994). Sex differences in covert aggression among adults. *Aggressive Behavior, 20*, 27–34.

Blair, S. N., Kannel, W. B., Kohl, H. W., Goodyear, N., & Wilson, P. W. (1989). Surrogate measures of physical activity and physical fitness evidence for sedentary traits of resting tachycardia, obesity, and low vital capacity. *American Journal of Epidemiology, 129*, 1145–1156.

Blanchard-Dallaire, C., & Hébert, M. (2014). Social relationships in sexually abused children: Self-reports and teachers' evaluation. *Journal of Child Sexual Abuse, 23*, 326–344.

Block, R. A., Arnott, D. P., Quigley, B., & Lynch, W. C. (1989). Unilateral nostril breathing influences lateralized cognitive performance. *Brain and Cognition, 9*, 181–190.

Blount, J. D., Metcalfe, N. B., Arnold, K. E., Surai, P. F., Devevey, G. L., & Monaghan, P. (2003). Neonatal nutrition, adult antioxidant defences and sexual attractiveness in the zebra finch. *Proceedings of the Royal Society of London B, 270*, 1691–1696.

Blount, J. D., Metcalfe, N. B., Birkhead, T. R., & Surai, P. F. (2003). Carotenoid modulation of immune function and sexual attractiveness in zebra finches. *Science, 300*, 125–127.

Boelsma, E., Van de Vijver, L. P., Goldbohm, R. A., Klöpping-Ketelaars, I. A., Hendriks, H. F., & Roza, L. (2003). Human skin condition and its associations with nutrient concentrations in serum and diet. *American Journal of Clinical Nutrition, 77*, 348–355.

Bogin, B. A., & MacVean, R. B. (1978). Growth in height and weight of urban Guatemalan primary school children of low and high socioeconomic class. *Human Biology, 50*, 477–487.

Boitard, C., Etchamendy, N., Sauvant, J., Aubert, A., Tronel, S., Marighetto, A., et al. (2012). Juvenile, but not adult exposure to high-fat diet impairs relational memory and hippocampal neurogenesis in mice. *Hippocampus, 22*, 2095–2100.

Boivin, M., Dodge, K. A., & Coie, J. D. (1995). Individual-group behavioral similarity and peer status in experimental play groups of boys: The social misfit revisited. *Journal of Personality and Social Psychology, 69*, 269–279.

Boivin, M. J., Giordani, B., Ndanga, K., Maky, M. M., Manzeki, K. M., Ngunu, N., et al. (1993). Effects of treatment for intestinal parasites and malaria on the cognitive abilities of schoolchildren in Zaire, Africa. *Health Psychology, 12*, 220–226.

Bolger, K. E., Patterson, C. J., & Kupersmidt, J. B. (1998). Peer relationships and self-esteem among children who have been maltreated. *Child Development, 69*, 1171–1197.

Bolund, E., Martin, K., Kempenaers, B., & Forstmeier, W. (2010). Inbreeding depression of sexually selected traits and attractiveness in the zebra finch. *Animal Behaviour, 79*, 947–955.

Bond, L., Carlin, J. B., Thomas, L., Rubin, K., & Patton, G. (2001). Does bullying cause emotional problems? A prospective study of young teenagers. *British Medical Journal, 323*, 480–484.

Bonduriansky, R. (2001). The evolution of male mate choice in insects: A synthesis of ideas and evidence. *Biological Reviews, 76*, 305–339.

Bonduriansky, R., & Rowe, L. (2003). Interactions among mechanisms of sexual selection on male body size and head shape in a sexually dimorphic fly. *Evolution, 57*, 2046–2053.

Bonduriansky, R., & Rowe, L. (2005). Sexual selection, genetic architecture, and the condition dependence of body shape in the sexually dimorphic fly *Prochyliza xanthostoma* (*Piophilidae*). *Evolution, 59*, 138–151.

Boogert, N. J., Fawcett, T. W., & Lefebvre, L. (2011). Mate choice for cognitive traits: A review of the evidence in nonhuman vertebrates. *Behavioral Ecology, 22*, 447–459.

Boogert, N. J., Giraldeau, L.-A., & Lefebvre, L. (2008). Song complexity correlates with learning ability in zebra finch males. *Animal Behaviour, 76*, 1735–1741.

Boonekamp, J. J., Ros, A. H. F., & Verhulst, S. (2008). Immune activation suppresses plasma testosterone level: A meta-analysis. *Biology Letters, 4*, 741–744.

Borgerhoff Mulder, M. (1990). Kipsigis women's preferences for wealthy men: Evidence for female choice in mammals? *Behavioral Ecology and Sociobiology, 27*, 255–264.

Borgia, G. (1985a). Bower destruction and sexual competition in the satin bower bird (*Ptilonorhynchus violaceus*). *Behavioral Ecology and Sociobiology, 18*, 91–100.

Borgia, G. (1985b). Bower quality, number of decorations and mating success of male satin bower birds (*Ptilonorhynchus violaceus*): An experimental analysis. *Animal Behaviour, 33*, 266–271.

Borgia, G. (1995a). Complex male display and female choice in the spotted bowerbird: Specialized functions for different bower decorations. *Animal Behaviour, 49*, 1291–1301.

Borgia, G. (1995b). Threat reduction as a cause of differences in bower architecture, bower decoration and male display in two closely related bowerbirds *Chlamydera nuchalis and C. maculata*. *Emu, 95*, 1–12.

Borgia, G. (2006). Preexisting male traits are important in the evolution of elaborated male sexual display. *Advances in the Study of Behavior, 36*, 249–302.

Borgia, G., & Coleman, S. W. (2000). Co-option of male courtship signals from aggressive display in bowerbirds. *Proceedings of the Royal Society of London B, 267*, 1735–1740.

Borgia, G., & Wingfield, J. C. (1991). Hormonal correlates of bower decoration and sexual display in the satin bowerbird (*Ptilonorhynchus violaceus*). *Condor, 93*, 935–942.

Bortolotti, G. R., Fernie, K. J., & Smits, J. E. (2003). Carotenoid concentration and coloration of American Kestrels (*Falco sparverius*) disrupted by experimental exposure to PCBs. *Functional Ecology, 17*, 651–657.

Bortolotti, G. R., Mougeot, F., Martinez-Padilla, J., Webster, L. M. I., & Piertney, S. B. (2009). Physiological stress mediates the honesty of social signals. *PLoS ONE, 4*, e4983.

Bosacki, S. L. (2000). Theory of mind and self-concept in preadolescents: Links with gender and language. *Journal of Educational Psychology, 92*, 709–717.

Bosacki, S. L., & Astington, J. W. (1999). Theory of mind in preadolescents: Relations between social understanding and social competence. *Social Development, 8*, 237–254.

Boulet, M., Crawford, J. C., Charpentier, M. J. E., & Drea, C. M. (2010). Honest olfactory ornamentation in a female-dominant primate. *Journal of Evolutionary Biology, 23*, 1558–1563.

Bradley, B. J., & Mundy, N. I. (2008). The primate palette: The evolution of primate coloration. *Evolutionary Anthropology, 17*, 97–111.

Brailey, K., Vasterling, J. J., Proctor, S. P., Constans, J. I., & Friedman, M. J. (2007). PTSD symptoms, life events, and unit cohesion in US soldiers: Baseline findings from the neurocognition deployment health study. *Journal of Traumatic Stress, 20*, 495–503.

Bramen, J. E., Hranilovich, J. A., Dahl, R. E., Forbes, E. E., Chen, J., Toga, A. W., et al. (2011). Puberty influences medial temporal lobe and cortical gray matter maturation differently in boys than girls matched for sexual maturity. *Cerebral Cortex, 21*, 636–646.

Braun, J. M., Kalkbrenner, A. E., Calafat, A. M., Yolton, K., Ye, X., Dietrich, K. N., et al. (2011). Impact of early-life bisphenol A exposure on behavior and executive function in children. *Pediatrics, 128*, 873–882.

Brawner, W. R., III, Hill, G. E., & Sundermann, C. A. (2000). Effects of coccidial and mycoplas-mal infections on carotenoid-based plumage pigmentation in male house finches. *Auk, 117,* 952–963.

Bremner, J. D. (2006). Traumatic stress: Effects on the brain. *Dialogues in Clinical Neuroscience, 8,* 445–461.

Bremner, J. D., Randall, P. R., Scott, T. M., Bronen, R. A., Delaney, R. C., Seibyl, J. P., et al. (1995). MRI-based measurement of hippocampal volume in posttraumatic stress disorder. *American Journal of Psychiatry, 152,* 973–981.

Bremner, J. D., Scott, T. M., Delaney, R. C., Southwick, S. M., Mason, J. W., Johnson, D. R., et al. (1993). Deficits in short-term memory in posttraumatic stress disorder. *American Journal of Psychiatry, 150,* 1015–1019.

Bremner, J. D., Vermetten, E., Afzal, N., & Vythilingam, M. (2004). Deficits in verbal declarative memory function in women with childhood sexual abuse-related posttraumatic stress disorder. *Journal of Nervous and Mental Disease, 192,* 643–649.

Bremner, J. D., Vythilingam, M., Vermetten, E., Southwick, S. M., McGlashan, T., Nazeer, A., et al. (2003). MRI and PET study of deficits in hippocampal structure and function in women with childhood sexual abuse and posttraumatic stress disorder. *American Journal of Psychiatry, 160,* 924–932.

Brezden, C. B., Phillips, K. A., Abdolell, M., Bunston, T., & Tannock, I. F. (2000). Cognitive func-tion in breast cancer patients receiving adjuvant chemotherapy. *Journal of Clinical Oncology, 18,* 2695–2701.

Brieger, W. R., Oshiname, F. O., & Ososanya, O. O. (1998). Stigma associated with onchocercal skin disease among those affected near the Ofiki and Oyan Rivers in western Nigeria. *Social Science & Medicine, 47,* 841–852.

Briere, J., & Elliott, D. M. (2003). Prevalence and psychological sequelae of self-reported child-hood physical and sexual abuse in a general population sample of men and women. *Child Abuse & Neglect, 27,* 1205–1222.

Brodmann, K. (1909). *Vergleichende Lokalisationslehre der Grosshirnrinde in ihren Prinzipien dargestellt auf Grund des Zellenbaues. [Comparative localization of the cerebral cortex based on cell composition.].* Leipzig: Barth.

Brooker, S., Hotez, P. J., & Bundy, D. A. (2008). Hookworm-related anaemia among pregnant wom-en: A systematic review. *PLoS Neglected Tropical Diseases, 2,* e291.

Brown, A. S., Susser, E. S., Lin, S. P., Neugebauer, R., & Gorman, J. M. (1995). Increased risk of affective disorders in males after second trimester prenatal exposure to the Dutch hunger winter of 1944–45. *British Journal of Psychiatry, 166,* 601–606.

Browne, J. (2001). Darwin in caricature: A study in the popularisation and dissemination of evolu-tion. *Proceedings of the American Philosophical Society, 145,* 496–509.

Browne, K. (2007). *Co-ed combat: The new evidence that women shouldn't fight the nation's wars.* New York: Penguin.

Browne, K. R. (2012). Band of brothers or band of siblings? An evolutionary perspective on sexual integration of combat forces. In T. K. Shackelford, & V. Weekes-Shackelford (Eds.), *Oxford handbook of evolutionary perspectives on violence, homicide, and war* (pp. 372–392). New York: Oxford University Press.

Brumm, H., Zollinger, S. A., & Slater, P. J. B. (2009). Developmental stress affects song learning but not song complexity and vocal amplitude in zebra finches. *Behavioral Ecology and Socio-biology, 63,* 1387–1395.

Buchanan, K. L., Catchpole, C. K., Lewis, J. W., & Lodge, A. (1999). Song as an indicator of para-sitism in the sedge warbler. *Animal Behaviour, 57,* 307–314.

Buchanan, K. L., Leitner, S., Spencer, K. A., Goldsmith, A. R., & Catchpole, C. K. (2004). Developmental stress selectively affects the song control nucleus HVC in the zebra finch. *Proceedings of the Royal Society of London B, 271*, 2381–2386.

Buchanan, K. L., Spencer, K. A., Goldsmith, A. R., & Catchpole, C. K. (2003). Song as an honest signal of past developmental stress in the European starling (*Sturnus vulgaris*). *Proceedings of the Royal Society of London B, 270*, 1149–1156.

Buchholz, R. (1995). Female choice, parasite load and male ornamentation in wild turkeys. *Animal Behaviour, 50*, 929–943.

Buck Louis, G. M., Lum, K. J., Sundaram, R., Chen, Z., Kim, S., Lynch, C. D., et al. (2011). Stress reduces conception probabilities across the fertile window: Evidence in support of relaxation. *Fertility and Sterility, 95*, 2184–2189.

Buck, R. W., Savin, V. J., Miller, R. E., & Caul, W. F. (1972). Communication of affect through facial expression in humans. *Journal of Personality and Social Psychology, 23*, 362–371.

Buckwalter, J. G., Rizzo, A. A., McCleary, R., Shankle, R., Dick, M., & Henderson, V. W. (1996). Gender comparisons of cognitive performances among vascular dementia, Alzheimer disease, and older adults without dementia. *Archives of Neurology, 53*, 436–439.

Buller, W. L., & Keulemans, J. G. (1888). *A history of the birds of New Zealand* (2nd ed.). London: Self-published.

Burghardt, G. M. (2005). *The genesis of animal play: Testing the limits.* Cambridge, MA: Bradford/MIT Press.

Burley, N. T., Price, D. K., & Zann, R. A. (1992). Bill color, reproduction and condition effects in wild and domesticated zebra finches. *Auk, 109*, 13–23.

Burt, C., & Moore, R. C. (1912). The mental differences between the sexes. *Journal of Experimental Pedagogy, 1*, 355–388.

Burton, G. W., & Ingold, K. U. (1984). Beta-carotene: An unusual type of lipid antioxidant. *Science, 224*, 569–573.

Buss, D. M. (1988). From vigilance to violence: Tactics of mate retention in American undergraduates. *Ethology and Sociobiology, 9*, 291–317.

Buss, D. M. (1989). Sex differences in human mate preferences: Evolutionary hypothesis tested in 37 cultures. *Behavioral and Brain Sciences, 12*, 1–49.

Buss, C., Lord, C., Wadiwalla, M., Hellhammer, D. H., Lupien, S. J., Meaney, M. J., et al. (2007). Maternal care modulates the relationship between prenatal risk and hippocampal volume in women but not in men. *Journal of Neuroscience, 27*, 2592–2595.

Buss, D. M., & Shackelford, T. K. (1997). From vigilance to violence: Mate retention tactics in married couples. *Journal of Personality and Social Psychology, 72*, 346–361.

Bustinduy, A. L., Thomas, C. L., Fiutem, J. J., Parraga, I. M., Mungai, P. L., Muchiri, E. M., et al. (2011). Measuring fitness of Kenyan children with polyparasitic infections using the 20-meter shuttle run test as a morbidity metric. *PLoS Neglected Tropical Diseases, 5*, e1213.

Butler, M. W., & McGraw, K. J. (2012). Differential effects of early- and late-life access to carotenoids on adult immune function and ornamentation in mallard ducks (*Anas platyrhynchos*). *PLoS ONE, 7*, e38043.

Cacioppo, J. T., Berntson, G. C., Adolphs, R., Carter, C. S., Davidson, R. J., & McClintock, M. K., et al. (Eds.). (2002). *Foundations in social neuroscience.* Cambridge, MA: MIT Press.

Cahill, L., Haier, R. J., White, N. S., Fallon, J., Kilpatrick, L., Lawrence, C., et al. (2001). Sex-related differences in amygdala activity during emotionally influenced memory storage. *Neurobiology of Learning and Memory, 75*, 1–9.

Calero, C. I., Salles, A., Semelman, M., & Sigman, M. (2013). Age and gender dependent development of theory of mind in 6-to 8-years old children. *Frontiers in Human Neuroscience, 7*, 128.

Cameron, N. (1992). The monitoring of growth and nutritional status in South Africa. *American Journal of Human Biology, 4*, 223–234.

Cameron, H. A., & Mckay, R. D. (2001). Adult neurogenesis produces a large pool of new granule cells in the dentate gyrus. *Journal of Comparative Neurology, 435*, 406–417.

Campbell, B. (Ed.). (1971). *Sexual selection and the descent of man 1871–1971*. Chicago, IL: Aldine Publishing.

Campbell, A. (1995). A few good men: Evolutionary psychology and female adolescent aggression. *Ethology and Sociobiology, 16*, 99–123.

Campbell, A. (2002). *A mind of her own: The evolutionary psychology of women*. New York: Oxford University Press.

Candolin, U. (1999). The relationship between signal quality and physical condition: Is sexual signalling honest in the three-spined stickleback? *Animal Behaviour, 58*, 1261–1267.

Candolin, U. (2000a). Increased signalling effort when survival prospects decrease: Male–male competition ensures honesty. *Animal Behaviour, 60*, 417–422.

Candolin, U. (2000b). Male–male competition ensures honest signaling of male parental ability in the three-spined stickleback (*Gasterosteus aculeatus*). *Behavioral Ecology and Sociobiology, 49*, 57–61.

Candolin, U. (2000c). Changes in expression and honesty of sexual signalling over the reproductive lifetime of sticklebacks. *Proceedings of the Royal Society of London B, 267*, 2425–2430.

Cao, J., Joyner, L., Mickens, J. A., Leyrer, S. M., & Patisaul, H. B. (2014). Sex-specific Esr2 mRNA expression in the rat hypothalamus and amygdala is altered by neonatal bisphenol A exposure. *Reproduction, 147*, 537–554.

Cao, J., Rebuli, M. E., Rogers, J., Todd, K. L., Leyrer, S. M., Ferguson, S. A., et al. (2013). Prenatal bisphenol A exposure alters sex-specific estrogen receptor expression in the neonatal rat hypothalamus and amygdala. *Toxicological Sciences, 133*, 157–173.

Caravale, B., Tozzi, C., Albino, G., & Vicari, S. (2005). Cognitive development in low risk preterm infants at 3–4 years of life. *Archives of Disease in Childhood-Fetal and Neonatal Edition, 90*, F474–F479.

Card, N. A., Stucky, B. D., Sawalani, G. M., & Little, T. D. (2008). Direct and indirect aggression during childhood and adolescence: A meta-analytic review of gender differences, intercorrelations, and relations to maladjustment. *Child Development, 79*, 1185–1229.

Carere, C., Costantini, D., Sorace, A., Santucci, D., & Alleva, E. (2010). Bird populations as sentinels of endocrine disrupting chemicals. *Annali dell'Istituto Superiore di Sanità, 46*, 81–88.

Caro, T. (2013). The colours of extant mammals. *Seminars in Cell & Developmental Biology, 24*, 542–552.

Carré, J. M., & McCormick, C. M. (2008). In your face: Facial metrics predict aggressive behaviour in the laboratory and in varsity and professional hockey players. *Proceedings of the Royal Society B, 275*, 2651–2656.

Carré, J. M., McCormick, C. M., & Mondloch, C. J. (2009). Facial structure is a reliable cue of aggressive behavior. *Psychological Science, 20*, 1194–1198.

Carter, J. P., Grivetti, L. E., Davis, J. T., Nasiff, S., Mansour, A., Mousa, W. A., et al. (1969). Growth and sexual development of adolescent Egyptian village boys effects of zinc, iron, and placebo supplementation. *American Journal of Clinical Nutrition, 22*, 59–78.

Carton, Y., & Nappi, A. J. (1997). *Drosophila* cellular immunity against parasitoids. *Parasitology Today, 13*, 218–227.

Cashdan, E. (1993). Attracting mates: Effects of paternal investment on mate attraction strategies. *Ethology and Sociobiology, 14*, 1–24.

Cashdan, E. (2008). Waist-to-hip ratio across cultures: Trade-offs between androgen- and estrogen-dependent traits. *Current Anthropology, 49*, 1099–1107.

Cashdan, E., Marlowe, F. W., Crittenden, A., Porter, C., & Wood, B. M. (2012). Sex differences in spatial cognition among Hadza foragers. *Evolution and Human Behavior, 33*, 274–284.

Caspi, A., Houts, R. M., Belsky, D. W., Goldman-Mellor, S. J., Harrington, H., Israel, S., et al. (2014). The *p* factor one general psychopathology factor in the structure of psychiatric disorders? *Clinical Psychological Science, 2*, 119–137.

Castellon, S. A., Ganz, P. A., Bower, J. E., Petersen, L., Abraham, L., & Greendale, G. A. (2004). Neurocognitive performance in breast cancer survivors exposed to adjuvant chemotherapy and tamoxifen. *Journal of Clinical and Experimental Neuropsychology, 26*, 955–969.

Castillo-Durán, C., García, H.E.R.N.A.N., Venegas, P., Torrealba, I., Panteon, E., Concha, N., et al. (1994). Zinc supplementation increases growth velocity of male children and adolescents with short stature. *Acta Paediatrica, 83*, 833–837.

Casto, J. M., Ward, O. B., & Bartke, A. (2003). Play, copulation, anatomy, and testosterone in gonadally intact male rats prenatally exposed to flutamide. *Physiology & Behavior, 79*, 633–641.

Cavalli-Sforza, L. L., & Bodmer, W. F. (1999). *The genetics of human populations*. Mineola, NY: Dover Publications.

Chagnon, N. A. (1988). Life histories, blood revenge, and warfare in a tribal population. *Science, 239*, 985–992.

Chagnon, N. A. (1997). *Yanomamö* (5th ed.). Fort Worth, TX: Harcourt.

Chagnon, N. A., & Macfarlan, S. J. (2015). Yanomamö: The sociobiology people. In J. H. Turner, R. Machalek, & A. Maryansk (Eds.), *Evolutionary analysis of the social sciences* (pp. 114–121). Boulder, CO: Paradigm Press.

Chapman, R. M., Mapstone, M., Gardner, M. N., Sandoval, T. C., McCrary, J. W., Guillily, M. D., et al. (2011). Women have farther to fall: Gender differences between normal elderly and Alzheimer's disease in verbal memory engender better detection of Alzheimer's disease in women. *Journal of the International Neuropsychological Society, 17*, 654–662.

Chargé, R., Sorci, G., Hingrat, Y., Lacroix, F., & Jalme, M. S. (2011). Immune-mediated change in the expression of a sexual trait predicts offspring survival in the wild. *PLoS ONE, 6*, e25305.

Charlesworth, D., & Charlesworth, B. (1987). Inbreeding depression and its evolutionary consequences. *Annual Review of Ecology and Systematics, 18*, 237–268.

Charman, T., & Clements, W. (2002). Is there a gender difference in false belief development? *Social Development, 11*, 1–10.

Charpentier, M. J. E., Boulet, M., & Drea, C. M. (2008). Smelling right: The scent of male lemurs advertises genetic quality and relatedness. *Molecular Ecology, 17*, 3225–3233.

Charpentier, M., Setchell, J. M., Prugnolle, F., Wickings, E. J., Peignot, P., Balloux, F., et al. (2006). Life history correlates of inbreeding depression in mandrills (*Mandrillus sphinx*). *Molecular Ecology, 15*, 21–28.

Chastel, O., Barbraud, C., Weimerskirch, H., Lormée, H., Lacroix, A., & Tostain, O. (2005). High levels of LH and testosterone in a tropical seabird with an elaborate courtship display. *General and Comparative Endocrinology, 140*, 33–40.

Chelliah, K., & Sukumar, R. (2013). The role of tusks, musth and body size in male–male competition among Asian elephants, *Elephas maximus. Animal Behaviour, 86*, 1207–1214.

Chen, L. C., Huq, E., & d'Souza, S. (1981). Sex bias in the family allocation of food and health care in rural Bangladesh. *Population and Development Review, 7*, 55–70.

Cherrier, M. M., Asthana, S., Plymate, S., Baker, L., Matsumoto, A. M., Peskind, E., et al. (2001). Testosterone supplementation improves spatial and verbal memory in healthy older men. *Neurology, 57*, 80–88.

Cherrier, M. M., Matsumoto, A. M., Amory, J. K., Asthana, S., Bremner, W., Peskind, E. R., et al. (2005). Testosterone improves spatial memory in men with Alzheimer disease and mild cognitive impairment. *Neurology, 64*, 2063–2068.

Cherrier, M. M., Matsumoto, A. M., Amory, J. K., Johnson, M., Craft, S., Peskind, E. R., et al. (2007). Characterization of verbal and spatial memory changes from moderate to supraphysiological increases in serum testosterone in healthy older men. *Psychoneuroendocrinology, 32*, 72–79.

Cherrier, M. M., Rose, A. L., & Higano, C. (2003). The effects of combined androgen blockade on cognitive function during the first cycle of intermittent androgen suppression in patients with prostate cancer. *Journal of Urology, 170*, 1808–1811.

Childress, J. E., McDowell, E. J., Dalai, V. V. K., Bogale, S. R., Ramamurthy, C., Jawaid, A., et al. (2013). Hippocampal volumes in patients with chronic combat-related posttraumatic stress disorder: A systematic review. *Journal of Neuropsychiatry and Clinical Neurosciences, 25*, 12–25.

Choi, J., & Silverman, I. (2003). Processing underlying sex differences in route-learning strategies in children and adolescents. *Personality and Individual Differences, 34*, 1153–1166.

Christy, J. H. (1983). Female choice in the resource-defense mating system of the sand fiddler crab, *Uca pugilator*. *Behavioral Ecology and Sociobiology, 12*, 169–180.

Ciuti, S., & Apollonio, M. (2011). Do antlers honestly advertise the phenotypic quality of fallow buck (*Dama dama*) in a lekking population? *Ethology, 117*, 133–144.

Clayton, D. H. (1990). Mate choice in experimentally parasitized rock doves: Lousy males lose. *American Zoologist, 30*, 251–262.

Cloninger, C., Przybeck, T., Svrakic, D., & Wetzel, R. (1994). *The temperament and character inventory (TCI): A guide to its development and use.* St. Louis, MO: Washington University, Center for Psychobiology of Personality.

Clough, D., Heistermann, M., & Kappeler, P. M. (2009). Individual facial coloration in male *Eulemur fulvus rufus*: A condition-dependent ornament? *International Journal of Primatology, 30*, 859–875.

Clutton-Brock, T. H. (1988). Reproductive success. In T. H. Clutton-Brock (Ed.), *Reproductive success: Studies of individual variation in contrasting breeding systems* (pp. 472–485). Chicago, IL: University of Chicago Press.

Clutton-Brock, T. H. (1989). Mammalian mating systems. *Proceedings of the Royal Society of London B, 236*, 339–372.

Clutton-Brock, T. H. (1991). *The evolution of parental care.* Princeton, NJ: Princeton University Press.

Clutton-Brock, T. (2007). Sexual selection in males and females. *Science, 318*, 1882–1885.

Clutton-Brock, T. (2009). Sexual selection in females. *Animal Behaviour, 77*, 3–11.

Clutton-Brock, T. H., & Albon, S. D. (1979). The roaring of red deer and the evolution of honest advertisement. *Behaviour, 69*, 145–170.

Clutton-Brock, T. H. & Pemberton, J. M. (Eds.). (2004). *Soay sheep: Dynamics and selection in an island population.* Cambridge, UK: Cambridge University Press.

Clutton-Brock, T. H., & Vincent, A. C. J. (1991). Sexual selection and the potential reproductive rates of males and females. *Nature, 351*, 58–60.

Clutton-Brock, T. H., Wilson, K., & Stevenson, I. R. (1997). Density-dependent selection on horn phenotype in Soay sheep. *Philosophical Transactions of the Royal Society of London B, 352*, 839–850.

Coe, T. S., Hamilton, P. B., Hodgson, D., Paull, G. C., Stevens, J. R., Sumner, K., et al. (2008). An environmental estrogen alters reproductive hierarchies, disrupting sexual selection in group-spawning fish. *Environmental Science & Technology, 42*, 5020–5025.

Coetzee, V., Faerber, S. J., Greeff, J. M., Lefevre, C. E., Re, D. E., & Perrett, D. I. (2012). African perceptions of female attractiveness. *PLoS ONE, 7*, e48116.

Colbert, N. K., Pelletier, N. C., Cote, J. M., Concannon, J. B., Jurdak, N. A., Minott, S. B., et al. (2005). Perinatal exposure to low levels of the environmental antiandrogen vinclozolin alters sex-differentiated social play and sexual behaviors in the rat. *Environmental Health Perspectives, 113*, 700–707.

Cole, T. J., Salem, S. I., Hafez, A. S., Galal, O. M., & Massoud, A. (1982). Plasma albumin, parasitic infection and pubertal development in Egyptian boys. *Transactions of the Royal Society of Tropical Medicine and Hygiene, 76*, 17–20.

Coleman, S. W., Patricelli, G. L., & Borgia, G. (2004). Variable female preferences drive complex male displays. *Nature, 428*, 742–745.

Collaer, M. L., & Hines, M. (1995). Human behavioral sex differences: A role for gonadal hormones during early development? *Psychological Bulletin, 118*, 55–107.

Collins, S. A. (2000). Men's voices and women's choices. *Animal Behaviour, 60*, 773–780.

Collins, S. A., & Missing, C. (2003). Vocal and visual attractiveness are related in women. *Animal Behaviour, 65*, 997–1004.

Collis, K., & Borgia, G. (1992). Age-related effects of testosterone, plumage, and experience on aggression and social dominance in juvenile male satin bowerbirds (*Ptilonorhynchus violaceus*). *Auk, 109*, 422–434.

Colom, R., Stein, J. L., Rajagopalan, P., Martínez, K., Hermel, D., Wang, Y., et al. (2013). Hippocampal structure and human cognition: Key role of spatial processing and evidence supporting the efficiency hypothesis in females. *Intelligence, 41*, 129–140.

Coltman, D. W., Festa-Bianchet, M., Jorgenson, J. T., Strobeck, C., Coltman, D. W., Festa-Bianchet, M., et al. (2002). Age-dependent sexual selection in bighorn rams. *Proceedings of the Royal Society of London B, 269*, 165–172.

Coluccia, E., Iosue, G., & Brandimonte, M. A. (2007). The relationship between map drawing and spatial orientation abilities: A study of gender differences. *Journal of Environmental Psychology, 27*, 135–144.

Condray, R., Morrow, L. A., Steinhauer, S. R., Hodgson, M., & Kelley, M. (2000). Mood and behavioral symptoms in individuals with chronic solvent exposure. *Psychiatry Research, 97*, 191–206.

Contreras-Garduño, J., Buzatto, B. A., Serrano Meneses, M. A., Nájera Cordero, K., & Córdoba Aguilar, A. (2008). The size of the red wing spot of the American rubyspot as a heightened condition-dependent ornament. *Behavioral Ecology, 19*, 724–732.

Contreras-Garduño, J., Buzatto, B. A., Abundis, L., Nájera-Cordero, K., & Córdoba-Aguilar, A. (2007). Wing colour properties do not reflect male condition in the American rubyspot (*Hetaerina americana*). *Ethology, 113*, 944–952.

Contreras-Garduño, J., Lanz-Mendoza, H., & Córdoba-Aguilar, A. (2007). The expression of a sexually selected trait correlates with different immune defense components and survival in males of the American rubyspot. *Journal of Insect Physiology, 53*, 612–621.

Córdoba-Aguilar, A. (2002). Wing pigmentation in territorial male damselflies, *Calopteryx haemorrhoid*: A possible relation to sexual selection. *Animal Behaviour, 63*, 759–766.

Cordoba-Aguilar, A., Lesher-Trevino, A. C., & Anderson, C. N. (2007). Sexual selection in *Hetaerina titia* males: A possible key species to understand the evolution of pigmentation in calopterygid damselflies (*Odonata: Zygoptera*). *Behaviour, 144*, 931–952.

Costa, P., Jr., Terracciano, A., & McCrae, R. R. (2001). Gender differences in personality traits across cultures: Robust and surprising findings. *Journal of Personality and Social Psychology, 81*, 322.

Cotton, S., Fowler, K., & Pomiankowski, A. (2004a). Do sexual ornaments demonstrate heightened condition-dependent expression as predicted by the handicap hypothesis? *Proceedings of the Royal Society of London B, 271*, 771–783.

Cotton, S., Fowler, K., & Pomiankowski, A. (2004b). Condition dependence of sexual ornament size and variation in the stalk-eyed fly *Cyrtodiopsis dalmanni* (*Diptera: Diopsidae*). *Evolution, 58*, 1038–1046.

Cowdrey, F. A., Harmer, C. J., Park, R. J., & McCabe, C. (2012). Neural responses to emotional faces in women recovered from anorexia nervosa. *Psychiatry Research: Neuroimaging, 201*, 190–195.

Crews, D., Gore, A. C., Hsu, T. S., Dangleben, N. L., Spinetta, M., Schallert, T., et al. (2007). Transgenerational epigenetic imprints on mate preference. *Proceedings of the National Academy of Sciences of the United States of America, 104*, 5942–5946.

Crick, N. R. (1997). Engagement in gender normative versus nonnormative forms of aggression: Links to social-psychological adjustment. *Developmental Psychology, 33*, 610–617.

Crick, N. R., Casas, J. F., & Mosher, M. (1997). Relational and overt aggression in preschool. *Developmental Psychology, 33*, 579–588.

Crick, N. R., & Nelson, D. A. (2002). Relational and physical victimization within friendships: Nobody told me there would be friends like these. *Journal of Abnormal Child Psychology, 30*, 599–607.

Crnic, K. A., Ragozin, A. S., Greenberg, M. T., Robinson, N. M., & Basham, R. B. (1983). Social interaction and developmental competence of preterm and full-term infants during the first year of life. *Child Development, 54*, 1199–1210.

Cronin, H. (1991). *The ant and the peacock*. New York: Cambridge University Press.

Cunningham, M. R. (1986). Measuring the physical in physical attractiveness: Quasi-experiments on the sociobiology of female beauty. *Journal of Personality and Social Psychology, 50*, 925–935.

Cunningham, M. R., Barbee, A. P., & Pike, C. L. (1990). What do women want? Facialmetric assessment of multiple motives in the perception of male facial physical attractiveness. *Journal of Personality and Social Psychology, 59*, 61–72.

Cushman, L. A., Stein, K., & Duffy, C. J. (2008). Detecting navigational deficits in cognitive aging and Alzheimer disease using virtual reality. *Neurology, 71*, 888–895.

Dabbs, J. M., Jr., & Mallinger, A. (1999). High testosterone levels predict low voice pitch among men. *Personality and Individual Differences, 27*, 801–804.

Dakin, R., & Montgomerie, R. (2013). Eye for an eyespot: How iridescent plumage ocelli influence peacock mating success. *Behavioral Ecology, 24*, 1048–1057.

Daly, M., & Wilson, M. (1988). *Homicide*. New York: Aldine de Gruyter.

Darwin, C. (1859). *On the origin of species by means of natural selection*. London: John Murray.

Darwin, C. (1871). *The descent of man, and selection in relation to sex*. London: John Murray.

Darwin, C., & Wallace, A. (1858). On the tendency of species to form varieties, and on the perpetuation of varieties and species by natural means of selection. *Journal of the Linnean Society of London, Zoology, 3*, 45–62.

Dauwe, T., & Eens, M. (2008). Melanin- and carotenoid-dependent signals of great tits (*Parus major*) relate differently to metal pollution. *Naturwissenschaften, 95*, 969–973.

Davey Smith, G., Hart, C., Upton, M., Hole, D., Gillis, C., Watt, G., et al. (2000). Height and risk of death among men and women: Aetiological implications of associations with cardiorespiratory disease and cancer mortality. *Journal of Epidemiology and Community Health, 54*, 97–103.

David, P., Bjorksten, T., Fowler, K., & Pomiankowski, A. (2000). Condition-dependent signaling of genetic variation in stalk-eyed flies. *Nature, 406*, 186–188.

David, P., Hingle, A., Greig, D., Rutherford, A., Pomiankowski, A., & Fowler, K. (1998). Male sexual ornament size but not asymmetry reflects condition in stalk-eyed flies. *Proceedings of the Royal Society of London B, 265,* 2211–2216.

Davis, L. E., Cheng, L. C., & Strube, M. J. (1996). Differential effects of racial composition on male and female groups: Implications for group work practice. *Social Work Research, 20,* 157–166.

Day, L. B., Westcott, D. A., & Olster, D. H. (2005). Evolution of bower complexity and cerebellum size in bowerbirds. *Brain, Behavior and Evolution, 66,* 62–72.

Dayan, S. H., Arkins, J. P., Sharma, V., Paterson, E., & Barnes, D. (2011). A phase 2, double-blind, randomized, placebo-controlled trial of a novel nutritional supplement product to promote healthy skin. *Journal of Drugs in Dermatology, 10,* 1106–1114.

De Bellis, M. D., Hall, J., Boring, A. M., Frustaci, K., & Moritz, G. (2001). A pilot longitudinal study of hippocampal volumes in pediatric maltreatment-related posttraumatic stress disorder. *Biological Psychiatry, 50,* 305–309.

De Bellis, M. D., & Keshavan, M. S. (2003). Sex differences in brain maturation in maltreatment-related pediatric posttraumatic stress disorder. *Neuroscience & Biobehavioral Reviews, 27,* 103–117.

De Bellis, M. D., Keshavan, M. S., Shifflett, H., Iyengar, S., Beers, S. R., Hall, J., et al. (2002). Brain structures in pediatric maltreatment-related posttraumatic stress disorder: A sociodemographi-cally matched study. *Biological Psychiatry, 52,* 1066–1078.

de Kogel, C. H. (1997). Long-term effects of brood size manipulation on morphological development and sex-specific mortality of offspring. *Journal of Animal Ecology, 66,* 167–178.

de Kogel, C. H., & Prijs, H. J. (1996). Effects of brood size manipulations on sexual attractiveness of offspring in the zebra finch. *Animal Behaviour, 51,* 699–708.

De Neve, L., Fargallo, J. A., Vergara, P., Lemus, J. A., Jarén-Galán, M., & Luaces, I. (2008). Effects of maternal carotenoid availability in relation to sex, parasite infection and health status of nestling kestrels (*Falco tinnunculus*). *Journal of Experimental Biology, 211,* 1414–1425.

de Rooij, S. R., Painter, R. C., Phillips, D. I., Raikkonen, K., Schene, A. H., & Roseboom, T. J. (2011). Self-reported depression and anxiety after prenatal famine exposure: Mediation by cardio-metabolic pathology. *Journal of Developmental Origins of Health and Disease, 2,* 136–143.

de Rooij, S. R., Veenendaal, M. V., Räikkönen, K., & Roseboom, T. J. (2012). Personality and stress appraisal in adults prenatally exposed to the Dutch famine. *Early Human Development, 88,* 321–325.

de Rooij, S. R., Wouters, H., Yonker, J. E., Painter, R. C., & Roseboom, T. J. (2010). Prenatal undernutrition and cognitive function in late adulthood. *Proceedings of the National Academy of Sciences of the United States of America, 107,* 16881–16886.

Deaner, R. O., Geary, D. C., Puts, D. A., Ham, S. A., Kruger, J., Fles, E., et al. (2012). Sex difference in the predisposition for physical competition: Males play sports much more than females even in the contemporary U.S. *PLoS ONE, 7,* e49168.

Deaner, R. O., Goetz, S. M. M., Shattuck, K., & Schnotala, T. (2012). Body weight, not facial width-to-height ratio, predicts aggression in pro hockey players. *Journal of Research in Personality, 46,* 235–238.

Deaner, R. O., & Smith, B. A. (2013). Sex differences in sports across 50 societies. *Cross-Cultural Research, 47,* 268–309.

Dechmann, D. K., Kalko, E. K., König, B., & Kerth, G. (2005). Mating system of a Neotropical roost-making bat: The white-throated, round-eared bat, *Lophostoma silvicolum* (*Chiroptera: Phyllostomidae*). *Behavioral Ecology and Sociobiology, 58,* 316–325.

Del Giudice, M. (2009). Sex, attachment, and the development of reproductive strategies. *Behavioral and Brain Sciences, 32,* 1–67.

Delcourt, M., & Rundle, H. D. (2011). Condition dependence of a multicomponent sexual display trait in *Drosophila serrata*. *American Naturalist*, *177*, 812–823.

Delhey, K., & Peters, A. (2008). Quantifying variability of avian colours: Are signalling traits more variable? *PLoS ONE*, *3*, e1689.

Delis, D. C., Kramer, J. H., Kaplan, E., & Ober, B. A. (2000). *California verbal learning test* (2nd ed.). San Antonio, TX: Psychological Corporation.

Demuth, J. P., Naidu, A., & Mydlarz, L. D. (2012). Sex, war, and disease: The role of parasite infection on weapon development and mating success in a horned beetle (*Gnatocerus cornutus*). *PLoS ONE*, *7*, e28690.

Deviche, P., & Cortez, L. (2005). Androgen control of immunocompetence in the male house finch, *Carpodacus mexicanus Müller*. *Journal of Experimental Biology*, *208*, 1287–1295.

DeVoogd, T. J. (1991). Endocrine modulation of the development and adult function of the avian song system. *Psychoneuroendocrinology*, *16*, 41–66.

DeVoogd, T. J., Krebs, J. R., Healy, S. D., & Purvis, A. (1993). Relations between song repertoire size and the volume of brain nuclei related to song: Comparative evolutionary analyses amongst oscine birds. *Proceedings of the Royal Society of London B*, *254*, 75–82.

Dewey, K. G. (1980). Part two: The impact of agricultural development on child nutrition in Tabasco, Mexico. *Medical Anthropology*, *4*, 21–54.

Dewey, K. G. (1983). Nutrition survey in Tabasco, Mexico: Nutritional status of preschool children. *American Journal of Clinical Nutrition*, *37*, 1010–1019.

Dickson, R., Awasthi, S., Williamson, P., Demellweek, C., & Garner, P. (2000). Effects of treatment for intestinal helminth infection on growth and cognitive performance in children: Systematic review of randomised trials. *British Medical Journal*, *320*, 1697–1701.

Dijkstra, J. K., Cillessen, A. H., & Borch, C. (2013). Popularity and adolescent friendship networks: Selection and influence dynamics. *Developmental Psychology*, *49*, 1242–1252.

Dimberg, U., & Öhman, A. (1996). Behold the wrath – Psychophysiological responses to facial stimuli. *Motivation & Emotion*, *20*, 149–182.

DiPietro, J. A. (1981). Rough and tumble play: A function of gender. *Developmental Psychology*, *17*, 50–58.

Ditchkoff, S. S., Lochmiller, R. L., Masters, R. E., Hoofer, S. R., & Bussche, R. A. (2001). Major-histocompatibility-complex-associated variation in secondary sexual traits of white-tailed deer (*Odocoileus virginianus*): Evidence for good-genes advertisement. *Evolution*, *55*, 616–625.

Dittrich, F., ter Maat, A., Jansen, R. F., Pieneman, A., Hertel, M., Frankl-Vilches, C., et al. (2013). Maximized song learning of juvenile male zebra finches following BDNF expression in the HVC. *European Journal of Neuroscience*, *38*, 3338–3344.

Dodge, K. A., Pettit, G. S., & Bates, J. E. (1994). Effects of physical maltreatment on the development of peer relations. *Development and Psychopathology*, *6*, 43–55.

Donnen, P., Brasseur, D., Dramaix, M., Vertongen, F., Zihindula, M., Muhamiriza, M., et al. (1998). Vitamin A supplementation but not deworming improves growth of malnourished preschool children in eastern Zaire. *Journal of Nutrition*, *128*, 1320–1327.

Donovan, K. A., Small, B. J., Andrykowski, M. A., Schmitt, F. A., Munster, P., & Jacobsen, P. B. (2005). Cognitive functioning after adjuvant chemotherapy and/or radiotherapy for early-stage breast carcinoma. *Cancer*, *104*, 2499–2507.

Doraiswamy, P. M., Bieber, F., Kaiser, L., Krishnan, K. R., Reuning-Scherer, J., & Gulanski, B. (1997). The Alzheimer's disease assessment scale: Patterns and predictors of baseline cognitive performance in multicenter Alzheimer's disease trials. *Neurology*, *48*, 1511–1517.

Doucet, S. M. (2002). Structural plumage coloration, male body size, and condition in the blue-black grassquit. *Condor*, *104*, 30–38.

Douglas, J. W., & Simpson, H. R. (1964). Height in relation to puberty family size and social class: A longitudinal study. *The Milbank Memorial Fund Quarterly, 42*, 20–34.

Doyle, C. J., & Lim, R. P. (2002). The effect of 17β-estradiol on the gonopodial development and sexual activity of *Gambusia holbrooki*. *Environmental Toxicology and Chemistry, 21*, 2719–2724.

Drayton, J. M., Hall, M. D., Hunt, J., & Jennions, M. D. (2012). Sexual signaling and immune function in the black field cricket *Teleogryllus commodus*. *PLoS ONE, 7*, e39631.

Drayton, J. M., Hunt, J., Brooks, R., & Jennions, M. D. (2007). Sounds different: Inbreeding depression in sexually selected traits in the cricket *Teleogryllus commodus*. *Journal of Evolutionary Biology, 20*, 1138–1147.

Drayton, J. M., Milner, R. N., Hunt, J., & Jennions, M. D. (2010). Inbreeding and advertisement calling in the cricket *Teleogryllus commodus*: Laboratory and field experiments. *Evolution, 64*, 3069–3083.

Dreizen, S., Currie, C., Gilley, E. J., & Spies, T. D. (1953). The effect of nutritive failure on the growth patterns of white children in Alabama. *Child Development, 24*, 189–202.

Dreyfuss, M. L., Stoltzfus, R. J., Shrestha, J. B., Pradhan, E. K., LeClerq, S. C., Khatry, S. K., et al. (2000). Hookworms, malaria and vitamin A deficiency contribute to anemia and iron deficiency among pregnant women in the plains of Nepal. *Journal of Nutrition, 130*, 2527–2536.

Drickamer, L. C. (1992). Oestrous female house mice discriminate dominant from subordinate males and sons of dominant from sons of subordinate males by odour cues. *Animal Behaviour, 43*, 868–870.

Drickamer, L. C., & Vandenbergh, J. G. (1973). Predictors of social dominance in the adult female golden hamster (*Mesocricetus auratus*). *Animal Behaviour, 21*, 564–570.

Drickamer, L. C., Vandenbergh, J. G., & Colby, D. R. (1973). Predictors of dominance in the male golden hamster (*Mesocricetus auratus*). *Animal Behaviour, 21*, 557–563.

Driscoll, I., Hamilton, D. A., Yeo, R. A., Brooks, W. M., & Sutherland, R. J. (2005). Virtual navigation in humans: The impact of age, sex, and hormones on place learning. *Hormones and Behavior, 47*, 326–335.

Droney, D. C. (1996). Environmental influences on male courtship and implications for female choice in a lekking Hawaiian Drosophila. *Animal Behaviour, 51*, 821–830.

Dubuc, C., Winters, S., Allen, W. L., Brent, L. J., Cascio, J., Maestripieri, D., et al. (2014). Sexually selected skin colour is heritable and related to fecundity in a non-human primate. *Proceedings of the Royal Society of London B, 281*, 20141602.

Duda, P., & Zrzavý, J. (2013). Evolution of life history and behavior in Hominidae: Towards phylogenetic reconstruction of the chimpanzee–human last common ancestor. *Journal of Human Evolution, 65*, 424–446.

Dufour, D. L., & Sauther, M. L. (2002). Comparative and evolutionary dimensions of the energetics of human pregnancy and lactation. *American Journal of Human Biology, 14*, 584–602.

Dunbar, R. I. M. (1998). The social brain hypothesis. *Evolutionary Anthropology, 6*, 178–190.

East, M. L., Burke, T., Wilhelm, K., Greig, C., & Hofer, H. (2003). Sexual conflicts in spotted hyenas: Male and female mating tactics and their reproductive outcome with respect to age, social status and tenure. *Proceedings of the Royal Society of London B, 270*, 1247–1254.

Echeverria, D., Woods, J. S., Heyer, N. J., Rohlman, D. S., Farin, F. M., Bittner, A. C., Jr., et al. (2005). Chronic low-level mercury exposure, BDNF polymorphism, and associations with cognitive and motor function. *Neurotoxicology and Teratology, 27*, 781–796.

Ecuyer-Dab, I., & Robert, M. (2004). Spatial ability and home-range size: Examining the relationship in Western men and women (*Homo sapiens*). *Journal of Comparative Psychology, 118*, 217–231.

Eder, D., & Hallinan, M. T. (1978). Sex differences in children's friendships. *American Sociological Review, 43,* 237–250.

Edward, D. A., & Chapman, T. (2011). The evolution and significance of male mate choice. *Trends in Ecology & Evolution, 26,* 647–654.

Eens, M., & Pinxten, R. (2000). Sex-role reversal in vertebrates: Behavioural and endocrinological accounts. *Behavioural Processes, 51,* 135–147.

Egan, S. K., & Perry, D. G. (2001). Gender identity: A multidimensional analysis with implications for psychosocial adjustment. *Developmental Psychology, 37,* 451–463.

Eibl-Eibesfeldt, I. (1989). *Human ethology.* New York: Aldine de Gruyter.

Eisenberg, J. F. (1962). Studies on the behavior of *Peromyscus maniculatus gambelii* and *Peromyscus californicus parasiticus. Behaviour, 19,* 177–207.

Ekstrom, A. D., Kahana, M. J., Caplan, J. B., Fields, T. A., Isham, E. A., Newman, E. L., et al. (2003). Cellular networks underlying human spatial navigation. *Nature, 425,* 184–187.

Elias, M. F., & Samonds, K. W. (1977). Protein and calorie malnutrition in infant cebus monkeys: Growth and behavioral development during deprivation and rehabilitation. *American Journal of Clinical Nutrition, 30,* 355–366.

Ellis, B. J. (2004). Timing of pubertal maturation in girls: An integrated life history approach. *Psychological Bulletin, 130,* 920–958.

Ellis, B. J., & Del Giudice, M. (2014). Beyond allostatic load: Rethinking the role of stress in regulating human development. *Development and Psychopathology, 26,* 1–20.

Ellis, L., Hershberger, S., Field, E., Wersinger, S., Sergio, P., Geary, D., et al. (2008). *Sex differences: Summarizing more than a century of scientific research.* New York: Francis & Taylor.

El-Mahgoub, S. (1982). Pelvic schistosomiasis and infertility. *International Journal of Gynecology & Obstetrics, 20,* 201–206.

Ember, C. R. (1978). Myths about hunter-gatherers. *Ethnology, 17,* 439–448.

Emlen, D. J. (1994). Environmental control of horn length dimorphism in the beetle *Onthophagus acuminatus* (*Coleoptera: Scarabaeidae*). *Proceedings of the Royal Society of London B, 256,* 131–136.

Emlen, D. J. (1997). Diet alters male horn allometry in the beetle *Onthophagus acuminatus* (i). *Proceedings of the Royal Society of London B, 264,* 567–574.

Emlen, D. J., Marangelo, J., Ball, B., & Cunningham, C. W. (2005). Diversity in the weapons of sexual selection: Horn evolution in the beetle genus *Onthophagus* (*Coleoptera: Scarabaeidae*). *Evolution, 59,* 1060–1084.

Emlen, S. T., & Oring, L. W. (1977). Ecology, sexual selection, and the evolution of mating systems. *Science, 197,* 215–223.

Enstrom, D. A., Ketterson, E. D., & Nolan, J. (1997). Testosterone and mate choice in the dark-eyed junco. *Animal Behaviour, 54,* 1135–1146.

Epple, G. (1970). Quantitative studies on scent marking in the marmoset (*Callithrix jacchus*). *Folia Primatologica, 13,* 48–62.

Erlinge, S., Sandell, M., & Brinck, C. (1982). Scent-marking and its territorial significance in stoats, *Mustela erminea. Animal Behaviour, 30,* 811–818.

Espinosa, M. P., Sigman, M. D., Neumann, C. G., Bwibo, N. O., & McDonald, M. A. (1992). Playground behaviors of school-age children in relation to nutrition, schooling, and family characteristics. *Developmental Psychology, 28,* 1188–1195.

Espmark, Y. (1964). Studies in dominance-subordination relationship in a group of semi-domestic reindeer (*Rangifer tarandus*). *Animal Behaviour, 12,* 420–426.

Etkin, A., & Wager, T. (2007). Functional neuroimaging of anxiety: A meta-analysis of emotional processing in PTSD, social anxiety disorder, and specific phobia. *American Journal of Psychiatry, 164*, 1476–1488.

Evans, L. (2006). Innate sex differences supported by untypical traffic fatalities. *Chance, 19*, 10–15.

Evans, S. F., Kobrosly, R. W., Barrett, E. S., Thurston, S. W., Calafat, A. M., Weiss, B., et al. (2014). Prenatal bisphenol A exposure and maternally reported behavior in boys and girls. *NeuroToxicology, 45*, 91–99.

Evans, S., Neave, N., & Wakelin, D. (2006). Relationships between vocal characteristics and body size and shape in human males: An evolutionary explanation for a deep male voice. *Biological Psychology, 72*, 160–163.

Evans, S., Neave, N., Wakelin, D., & Hamilton, C. (2008). The relationship between testosterone and vocal frequencies in human males. *Physiology & Behavior, 93*, 783–788.

Ey, E., Pfefferle, D., & Fischer, J. (2007). Do age- and sex-related variations reliably reflect body size in non-human primate vocalizations? A review. *Primates, 48*, 253–267.

Ezeamama, A. E., Friedman, J. F., Acosta, L. P., Bellinger, D. C., Langdon, G. C., Manalo, D. L., et al. (2005). Helminth infection and cognitive impairment among Filipino children. *American Journal of Tropical Medicine and Hygiene, 72*, 540–548.

Ezenwa, V. O., & Jolles, A. E. (2008). Horns honestly advertise parasite infection in male and female African buffalo. *Animal Behaviour, 75*, 2013–2021.

Fagot, B. I. (1977). Consequences of moderate cross-gender behavior in preschool children. *Child Development, 48*, 902–907.

Fagot, B. I. (1984). Teacher and peer reactions to boys' and girls' play styles. *Sex Roles, 11*, 691–702.

Faivre, B., Grégoire, A., Préault, M., Cézilly, F., & Sorci, G. (2003). Immune activation rapidly mirrored in a secondary sexual trait. *Science, 300*, 103.

Fan, Y., Ding, S., Ye, X., Manyande, A., He, D., Zhao, N., et al. (2013). Does preconception paternal exposure to a physiologically relevant level of bisphenol A alter spatial memory in an adult rat? *Hormones and Behavior, 64*, 598–604.

Farrell, T. M., Weaver, K., An, Y.-S., & MacDougall-Shackleton, S. A. (2012). Song bout length is indicative of spatial learning in European starlings. *Behavioral Ecology, 23*, 101–111.

Fastenau, P. S., Denburg, N. L., & Hufford, B. J. (1999). Adult norms for the Rey-Osterrieth complex figure test and for supplemental recognition and matching trials from the extended complex figure test. *Clinical Neuropsychologist, 13*, 30–47.

Felmingham, K., Williams, L. M., Kemp, A. H., Liddell, B., Falconer, E., Peduto, A., et al. (2010). Neural responses to masked fear faces: Sex differences and trauma exposure in posttraumatic stress disorder. *Journal of Abnormal Psychology, 119*, 241–247.

Feng, Z., Zou, X., Jia, H., Li, X., Zhu, Z., Liu, X., et al. (2012). Maternal docosahexaenoic acid feeding protects against impairment of learning and memory and oxidative stress in prenatally stressed rats: Possible role of neuronal mitochondria metabolism. *Antioxidants & Redox Signaling, 16*, 275–289.

Fennema-Notestine, C., Stein, M. B., Kennedy, C. M., Archibald, S. L., & Jernigan, T. L. (2002). Brain morphometry in female victims of intimate partner violence with and without posttraumatic stress disorder. *Biological Psychiatry, 52*, 1089–1101.

Ferguson, S. A., Flynn, K. M., Delclos, K. B., & Newbold, R. R. (2000). Maternal and offspring toxicity but few sexually dimorphic behavioral alterations result from nonylphenol exposure. *Neurotoxicology and Teratology, 22*, 583–591.

Ferreira, L., Ferreira Santos Galduróz, R., Ferri, C. P., & Fernandes Galduróz, J. C. (2014). Rate of cognitive decline in relation to sex after 60 years-of-age: A systematic review. *Geriatrics & Gerontology International, 14*, 23–31.

Feshbach, N. D. (1969). Sex differences in children's modes of aggressive responses toward outsiders. *Merrill-Palmer Quarterly, 15*, 249–258.

Festa-Bianchet, M., Jorgenson, J. T., & Réale, D. (2000). Early development, adult mass, and reproductive success in bighorn sheep. *Behavioral Ecology, 11*, 633–639.

Figueredo, A. J., Vásquez, G., Brumbach, B. H., Schneider, S. M. R., Sefcek, J. A., Tal, I. R., et al. (2006). Consilience and life history theory: From genes to brain to reproductive strategy. *Developmental Review, 26*, 243–275.

Figuerola, J., Domenech, J., & Senar, J. C. (2003). Plumage colour is related to ectosymbiont load during moult in the serin, *Serinus serinus*: An experimental study. *Animal Behaviour, 65*, 551–557.

Fink, B., Grammer, K., & Matts, P. J. (2006). Visible skin color distribution plays a role in the perception of age, attractiveness, and health in female faces. *Evolution and Human Behavior, 27*, 433–442.

Fink, B., Neave, N., & Seydel, H. (2007). Male facial appearance signals physical strength to women. *American Journal of Human Biology, 19*, 82–87.

Fischer, J., Kitchen, D. M., Seyfarth, R. M., & Cheney, D. L. (2004). Baboon loud calls advertise male quality: Acoustic features and their relation to rank, age, and exhaustion. *Behavioral Ecology and Sociobiology, 56*, 140–148.

Fisher, R. A. (1930). *The genetical theory of natural selection*. Oxford, UK: The Clarendon Press.

Fitze, P. S., & Richner, H. (2002). Differential effects of a parasite on ornamental structures based on melanins and carotenoids. *Behavioral Ecology, 13*, 401–407.

Fitze, P. S., Tschirren, B., Gasparini, J., & Richner, H. (2007). Carotenoid-based plumage colors and immune function: Is there a trade-off for rare carotenoids? *American Naturalist, 169*, S137–S144.

Fitzstephens, D. M., & Getty, T. (2000). Colour, fat and social status in male damselflies, *Calopteryx maculata*. *Animal Behaviour, 60*, 851–855.

Flegr, J., Novotná, M., Fialová, A., Kolbeková, P., & Gašová, Z. (2010). The influence of RhD phenotype on toxoplasmosis- and age-associated changes in personality profile of blood donors. *Folia Parasitologica, 57*, 143–150.

Flinn, M. V., Geary, D. C., & Ward, C. V. (2005). Ecological dominance, social competition, and coalitionary arms races: Why humans evolved extraordinary intelligence. *Evolution and Human Behavior, 26*, 10–46.

Flinn, M. V., & Low, B. S. (1986). Resource distribution, social competition, and mating patterns in human societies. In D. I. Rubenstein, & R. W. Wrangham (Eds.), *Ecological aspects of social evolution: Birds and mammals* (pp. 217–243). Princeton, NJ: Princeton University Press.

Foley, A. M., DeYoung, R. W., Lukefahr, S. D., Lewis, J. S., Hewitt, D. G., Hellickson, M. W., et al. (2012). Repeatability of antler characteristics in mature white-tailed deer in South Texas: Consequences of environmental effects. *Journal of Mammalogy, 93*, 1149–1157.

Folstad, I., & Karter, A. J. (1992). Parasites, bright males, and the immunocompetence handicap. *American Naturalist, 139*, 603–622.

Formisano, E., De Martino, F., Bonte, M., & Goebel, R. (2008). "Who" is saying "what?" Brain-based decoding of human voice and speech. *Science, 322*, 970–973.

Forsgren, E., Amundsen, T., Borg, A. A., & Bjelvenmark, J. (2004). Unusually dynamic sex roles in a fish. *Nature, 429*, 551–554.

Fox, C. W., & Reed, D. H. (2011). Inbreeding depression increases with environmental stress: An experimental study and meta-analysis. *Evolution, 65*, 246–258.

Freire-Maia, N., Chautard Freire-Maia, E. A., de Aguiar-Wolter, I. P., Azevedo-Fialho, M. D. G., de Azevedo, M. B., Krieger, H., et al. (1983). Inbreeding studies in Brasilian schoolchildren. *American Journal of Medical Genetics, 16*, 331–355.

Frisancho, A. R. (1974). Triceps skin fold and upper arm muscle size norms for assessment of nutritional status. *American Journal of Clinical Nutrition, 27*, 1052–1058.

Frisancho, A. R., & Garn, S. M. (1971a). The implications of skinfolds and muscle size to developmental and nutritional status of Central American children. 3. Guatemala. *Tropical and Geographical Medicine, 23*, 167–172.

Frisancho, A. R., & Garn, S. M. (1971b). Skin-fold thickness and muscle size: Implications for developmental status and nutritional evaluation of children from Honduras. *American Journal of Clinical Nutrition, 24*, 541–546.

Frisancho, A. R., Garn, S. M., & Ascoli, W. (1970). Childhood retardation resulting in reduction of adult body size due to lesser adolescent skeletal delay. *American Journal of Physical Anthropology, 33*, 325–336.

Frisancho, A. R., Guire, K., Babler, W., Borken, G., & Way, A. (1980). Nutritional influence on childhood development and genetic control of adolescent growth of Quechuas and Mestizos from the Peruvian lowlands. *American Journal of Physical Anthropology, 52*, 367–375.

Frisch, R. E. (1984). Body fat, puberty and fertility. *Biological Reviews, 59*, 161–188.

Frischknecht, M. (1993). The breeding colouration of male three-spined sticklebacks (*Gasterosteus aculeatus*) as an indicator of energy investment in vigour. *Evolutionary Ecology, 7*, 439–450.

Frommen, J. G., Luz, C., Mazzi, D., & Bakker, T. (2008). Inbreeding depression affects fertilization success and survival but not breeding coloration in threespine sticklebacks. *Behaviour, 145*, 425–441.

Galea, L. A. M. (2008). Gonadal hormone modulation of neurogenesis in the dentate gyrus of adult male and female rodents. *Brain Research Reviews, 57*, 332–341.

Galea, L. A. M., & Kimura, D. (1993). Sex differences in route-learning. *Personality and Individual Differences, 14*, 53–65.

Galea, L. A. M., & McEwen, B. S. (1999). Sex and seasonal changes in the rate of cell proliferation in the dentate gyrus of adult wild meadow voles. *Neuroscience, 89*, 955–964.

Galea, L. A. M., Perrot-Sinal, T. S., Kavaliers, M., & Ossenkopp, K.-P. (1999). Relations of hippocampal volume and dentate gyrus width to gonadal hormone levels in male and female meadow voles. *Brain Research, 821*, 383–391.

Gallistel, C. R. (1990). *The organization of learning.* Cambridge, MA: The MIT Press.

Gangestad, S. W., & Buss, D. M. (1993). Pathogen prevalence and human mate preferences. *Ethology and Sociobiology, 14*, 89–96.

Garamszegi, L. Z., & Eens, M. (2004). Brain space for a learned task: Strong intraspecific evidence for neural correlates of singing behavior in songbirds. *Brain Research Reviews, 44*, 187–193.

Garamszegi, L. Z., Møller, A. P., Török, J., Michl, G., Péczely, P., & Richard, M. (2004). Immune challenge mediates vocal communication in a passerine bird: An experiment. *Behavioral Ecology, 15*, 148–157.

Garn, S. M., Shaw, H. A., & McCabe, K. D. (1978). Effect of socioeconomic status on early growth as measured by three different indicators. *Ecology of Food and Nutrition, 7*, 51–55.

Garner, C. E., Smith, S., Bardhan, P. K., Ratcliffe, N. M., & Probert, C. S. J. (2009). A pilot study of faecal volatile organic compounds in faeces from cholera patients in Bangladesh to determine their utility in disease diagnosis. *Transactions of the Royal Society of Tropical Medicine and Hygiene, 103*, 1171–1173.

Gaulin, S. J. C. (1992). Evolution of sex differences in spatial ability. *Yearbook of Physical Anthropology, 35,* 125–151.

Gaulin, S. J. C., & Fitzgerald, R. W. (1986). Sex differences in spatial ability: An evolutionary hypothesis and test. *American Naturalist, 127,* 74–88.

Geary, D. C. (1995). Reflections of evolution and culture in children's cognition: Implications for mathematical development and instruction. *American Psychologist, 50,* 24–37.

Geary, D. C. (1996). Sexual selection and sex differences in mathematical abilities. *Behavioral and Brain Sciences, 19,* 229–284.

Geary, D. C. (1998). *Male, female: The evolution of human sex differences.* Washington, DC: American Psychological Association.

Geary, D. C. (2000). Evolution and proximate expression of human paternal investment. *Psychological Bulletin, 126,* 55–77.

Geary, D. C. (2005). *The origin of mind: Evolution of brain, cognition, and general intelligence.* Washington, DC: American Psychological Association.

Geary, D. C. (2010). *Male, female: The evolution of human sex differences* (2nd ed.). Washington, DC: American Psychological Association.

Geary, D. C., Bailey, D. H., & Oxford, J. (2011). Reflections on the human family. In C. Salmon, & T. Shackelford (Eds.), *The Oxford handbook of evolutionary family psychology* (pp. 365–385). New York: Oxford University Press.

Geary, D. C., Byrd-Craven, J., Hoard, M. K., Vigil, J., & Numtee, C. (2003). Evolution and development of boys' social behavior. *Developmental Review, 23,* 444–470.

Geary, D. C., & Flinn, M. V. (2002). Sex differences in behavioral and hormonal response to social threat: Commentary on Taylor et al. (2000). *Psychological Review, 109,* 745–750.

Geary, D. C., Winegard, B., & Winegard, B. (2014). Reflections on the evolution of human sex differences: Social selection and the evolution of competition among women. In V. A. Weekes-Shackelford & T. K. Shackelford (Eds.), *Evolutionary perspectives on human sexual psychology and behavior* (pp. 395–414). New York: Springer.

Geens, A., Dauwe, T., & Eens, M. (2009). Does anthropogenic metal pollution affect carotenoid colouration, antioxidative capacity and physiological condition of great tits (*Parus major*)? *Comparative Biochemistry and Physiology Part C: Toxicology & Pharmacology, 150,* 155–163.

Gelman, R. (1990). First principles organize attention to and learning about relevant data: Number and animate–inanimate distinction as examples. *Cognitive Science, 14,* 79–106.

Gerald, M. S. (2001). Primate colour predicts social status and aggressive outcome. *Animal Behaviour, 61,* 559–566.

Gerhardt, H. C., & Huber, F. (2002). *Acoustic communication in insects and anurans: Common problems and diverse solutions.* Chicago, IL: University of Chicago Press.

Geschwind, N., & Levitsky, W. (1968). Human brain: Left-right asymmetries in temporal speech region. *Science, 161,* 186–187.

Getty, T. (2002). Signal health versus parasites. *American Naturalist, 159,* 363–371.

Getty, T. (2006). Sexually selected signals are not similar to sports handicaps. *Trends in Ecology and Evolution, 21,* 83–88.

Gibson, M. A., & Mace, R. (2006). Polygyny, reproductive success and child health in rural Ethiopia: Why marry a married man? *Journal of Biosocial Science, 39,* 287–300.

Giddens, C. L., Barron, K. W., Byrd-Craven, J., Clark, K. F., & Winter, A. S. (2013). Vocal indices of stress: A review. *Journal of Voice, 27*(3), 390-e21.

Giedd, J. N., Blumenthal, J., Jeffries, N. O., Castellanos, F. X., Liu, H., Zijdenbos, A., et al. (1999). Brain development during childhood and adolescence: A longitudinal MRI study. *Nature Neuroscience, 2,* 861–863.

Gil, D., Naguib, M., Reibel, K., Rutstein, A., & Gahr, M. (2006). Early condition, song learning, and the volume of song brain nuclei in the zebra finch (*Taeniopygia guttata*). *Journal of Neurobiology, 66,* 1602–1612.

Gilbert, M. E., Mundy, W. R., & Crofton, K. M. (2000). Spatial learning and long-term potentiation in the dentate gyrus of the hippocampus in animals developmentally exposed to Aroclor 1254. *Toxicological Sciences, 57,* 102–111.

Gilbertson, M. W., Shenton, M. E., Ciszewski, A., Kasai, K., Lasko, N. B., Orr, S. P., et al. (2002). Smaller hippocampal volume predicts pathologic vulnerability to psychological trauma. *Nature Neuroscience, 5,* 1242–1247.

Gilliard, E. T. (1969). *Birds of paradise and bower birds.* London: Weidenfeld and Nicolson.

Gilman, S., Blumstein, D. T., & Foufopoulos, J. (2007). The effect of hemosporidian infections on white-crowned sparrow singing behavior. *Ethology, 113,* 437–445.

Gindhart, P. S. (1973). Growth standards for the tibia and radius in children aged one month through eighteen years. *American Journal of Physical Anthropology, 39,* 41–48.

Gladen, B. C., Ragan, N. B., & Rogan, W. J. (2000). Pubertal growth and development and prenatal and lactational exposure to polychlorinated biphenyls and dichlorodiphenyl dichloroethene. *Journal of Pediatrics, 136,* 490–496.

Gluckman, P. D., & Hanson, M. A. (2004). Developmental origins of disease paradigm: A mechanistic and evolutionary perspective. *Pediatric Research, 56,* 311–317.

Golan, O., Baron-Cohen, S., Hill, J. J., & Golan, Y. (2006). The "reading the mind in films" task: Complex emotion recognition in adults with and without autism spectrum conditions. *Social Neuroscience, 1,* 111–123.

Golan, O., Baron-Cohen, S., Hill, J. J., & Rutherford, M. D. (2007). The 'reading the mind in the voice' test-revised: A study of complex emotion recognition in adults with and without autism spectrum conditions. *Journal of Autism and Developmental Disorders, 37,* 1096–1106.

Goldstein, G., Flory, K. R., Browne, B. A., Majid, S., Ichida, J. M., Burtt, E. H., Jr. (2004). Bacterial degradation of black and white feathers. *Auk, 121,* 656–659.

Goldstein, J. M., Seidman, L. J., Horton, N. J., Makris, M., Kennedy, D. N., Caviness, V. S., Jr., et al. (2001). Normal sexual dimorphism of the adult human brain assessed by *in vivo* magnetic resonance imaging. *Cerebral Cortex, 11,* 490–497.

Golombok, S., & Rust, J. (1993). The Pre-School Activities Inventory: A standardized assessment of gender role in children. *Psychological Assessment, 5,* 131–136.

Golombok, S., Rust, J., Zervoulis, K., Croudace, T., Golding, J., & Hines, M. (2008). Developmental trajectories of sex-typed behavior in boys and girls: A longitudinal general population study of children aged 2.5–8 years. *Child Development, 79,* 1583–1593.

Gómez-Valdés, J., Hünemeier, T., Quinto-Sánchez, M., Paschetta, C., de Azevedo, S., González, M. F., et al. (2013). Lack of support for the association between facial shape and aggression: A reappraisal based on a worldwide population genetics perspective. *PLoS ONE, 8,* e52317.

González, J. (2004). Formant frequencies and body size of speaker: A weak relationship in adult humans. *Journal of Phonetics, 32,* 277–287.

Gonzalez, G., Sorci, G., Møller, A. P., Ninni, P., Haussy, C., & De Lope, F. (1999). Immunocompetence and condition-dependent sexual advertisement in male house sparrows (*Passer domesticus*). *Journal of Animal Ecology, 68,* 1225–1234.

González-Tokman, D. M., & Córdoba-Aguilar, A. (2010). Survival after experimental manipulation in the territorial damselfly *Hetaerina titia* (*Odonata: Calopterygidae*): More ornamented males are not more pathogen resistant. *Journal of Ethology, 28,* 29–33.

Good, C. D., Johnsrude, I., Ashburner, J., Henson, R. N. A., Friston, K. J., & Frackowiak, R. S. J. (2001). Cerebral asymmetry and the effects of sex and handedness on brain structure: A voxel-based morphometric analysis of 465 normal adult brains. *NeuroImage, 14*, 685–700.

Gorissen, L., Snoeijs, T., Van Duyse, E., & Eens, M. (2005). Heavy metal pollution affects dawn singing behaviour in a small passerine bird. *Oecologia, 145*, 504–509.

Gosden, T. P., & Chenoweth, S. F. (2011). On the evolution of heightened condition dependence of male sexual displays. *Journal of Evolutionary Biology, 24*, 685–692.

Graham, G. G., Adrianzen, B., Rabold, J., & Mellits, E. D. (1982). Later growth of malnourished infants and children: Comparison With 'healthy' siblings and parents. *American Journal of Diseases of Children, 136*, 348–352.

Graham, G. G., Creed, H. M., MacLean, W. C., Kallman, C. H., Rabold, J., & Mellits, E. D. (1981). Determinants of growth among poor children: Nutrient intake-achieved growth relationships. *American Journal of Clinical Nutrition, 34*, 539–554.

Grandjean, P., Weihe, P., White, R. F., Debes, F., Araki, S., Yokoyama, K., et al. (1997). Cognitive deficit in 7-year-old children with prenatal exposure to methylmercury. *Neurotoxicology and Teratology, 19*, 417–428.

Gray, D. A., & Eckhardt, G. (2001). Is cricket courtship song condition dependent? *Animal Behaviour, 62*, 871–877.

Green, R. (1976). One-hundred ten feminine and masculine boys: Behavioral contrasts and demographic similarities. *Archives of Sexual Behavior, 5*, 425–446.

Greenblatt, D. J., Harmatz, J. S., Singh, N. N., Steinberg, F., Roth, T., Moline, M. L., et al. (2014). Gender differences in pharmacokinetics and pharmacodynamics of zolpidem following sublingual administration. *Journal of Clinical Pharmacology, 54*, 282–290.

Grether, G. F. (1996). Sexual selection and survival selection on wing coloration and body size in the rubyspot damselfly *Hetaerina americana. Evolution, 50*, 1939–1948.

Grether, G. F. (2000). Carotenoid limitation and mate preference evolution: A test of the indicator hypothesis in guppies (*Poecilia reticulata*). *Evolution, 54*, 1712–1724.

Greulic, W. W., & Thoms, H. (1938). The dimensions of the pelvic inlet of 789 white females. *Anatomical Record, 72*, 45–51.

Greulich, W. W. (1951). The growth and developmental status of Guamanian school children in 1947. *American Journal of Physical Anthropology, 9*, 55–70.

Griffith, S. C. (2000). A trade-off between reproduction and a condition-dependent sexually selected ornament in the house sparrow *Passer domesticus. Proceedings of the Royal Society of London B, 267*, 1115–1119.

Griffith, S. C., Owens, I. P., & Burke, T. (1999). Environmental determination of a sexually selected trait. *Nature, 400*, 358–360.

Griffith, S. C., Parker, T. H., & Olson, V. A. (2006). Melanin- versus carotenoid-based sexual signals: Is the difference really so black and red? *Animal Behaviour, 71*, 749–763.

Grigorenko, E. L., Sternberg, R. J., Jukes, M., Alcock, K., Lambo, J., Ngorosho, D., et al. (2006). Effects of antiparasitic treatment on dynamically and statically tested cognitive skills over time. *Journal of Applied Developmental Psychology, 27*, 499–526.

Grillenberger, M., Neumann, C. G., Murphy, S. P., Bwibo, N. O., Weiss, R. E., Jiang, L., et al. (2006). Intake of micronutrients high in animal-source foods is associated with better growth in rural Kenyan school children. *British Journal of Nutrition, 95*, 379–390.

Gross, J. J., & John, O. P. (1998). Mapping the domain of expressivity: Multimethod evidence for a hierarchical model. *Journal of Personality and Social Psychology, 74*, 170–191.

Grossman, C. J. (1985). Interactions between the gonadal steroids and the immune system. *Science, 227*, 257–261.

Grotpeter, J. K., & Crick, N. R. (1996). Relational aggression, overt aggression and friendship. *Child Development, 67*, 2328–2338.

Guerin, M., Huntley, M. E., & Olaizola, M. (2003). *Haematococcus* astaxanthin: Applications for human health and nutrition. *Trends in Biotechnology, 21*, 210–216.

Guigueno, M. F., Snow, D. A., MacDougall-Shackleton, S. A., & Sherry, D. F. (2014). Female cowbirds have more accurate spatial memory than males. *Biology Letters, 10*, 20140026.

Guo, Y. L., Lai, T. J., Chen, S. J., & Hsu, C. C. (1995). Gender-related decrease in Raven's progressive matrices scores in children prenatally exposed to polychlorinated biphenyls and related contaminants. *Bulletin of Environmental Contamination and Toxicology, 55*, 8–13.

Gur, R. C., Gunning-Dixon, F., Bilker, W. B., & Gur, R. E. (2002). Sex differences in temporo limbic and frontal brain volumes of healthy adults. *Cerebral Cortex, 12*, 998–1003.

Gur, R. C., Turetsky, B. I., Matsui, M., Yan, M., Bilker, W., Hughett, P., et al. (1999). Sex differences in brain gray and white matter in healthy young adults: Correlations with cognitive performance. *Journal of Neuroscience, 19*, 4065–4072.

Gurven, M., von Rueden, C., Stieglitz, J., Kaplan, H., & Rodriguez, D. E. (2014). The evolutionary fitness of personality traits in a small-scale subsistence society. *Evolution and Human Behavior, 35*, 17–25.

Gurvits, T. V., Shenton, M. E., Hokama, H., Ohta, H., Lasko, N. B., Gilbertson, M. W., et al. (1996). Magnetic resonance imaging study of hippocampal volume in chronic, combat-related posttraumatic stress disorder. *Biological Psychiatry, 40*, 1091–1099.

Gustafsson, L., Qvarnström, A., & Sheldon, B. C. (1995). Trade-offs between life-history traits and a secondary sexual character in male collared flycatchers. *Nature, 375*, 311–313.

Guttentag, M., & Secord, P. (1983). *Too many women?*. Beverly Hills, CA: Sage.

Hack, M., Breslau, N., Aram, D., Weissman, B., Klein, N., & Borawski-Clark, E. (1992). The effect of very low birth weight and social risk on neurocognitive abilities at school age. *Journal of Developmental & Behavioral Pediatrics, 13*, 412–420.

Haenninen, H., Hernberg, S., Mantere, P., Vesanto, R., & Jalkanen, M. (1978). Psychological performance of subjects with low exposure to lead. *Journal of Occupational and Environmental Medicine, 20*, 683–689.

Hagen, E. H., Hames, R. B., Craig, N. M., Lauer, M. T., & Price, M. E. (2001). Parental investment and child health in a Yanomamö village suffering short-term food stress. *Journal of Biosocial Science, 33*, 503–528.

Hale, M. L., Verduijn, M. H., Møller, A. P., Wolff, K., & Petrie, M. (2009). Is the peacock's train an honest signal of genetic quality at the major histocompatibility complex? *Journal of Evolutionary Biology, 22*, 1284–1294.

Haley, M. P., Deutsch, C. J., & Le Boeuf, B. J. (1994). Size, dominance and copulatory success in male northern elephant seals, *Mirounga angustirostris*. *Animal Behaviour, 48*, 1249–1260.

Hall, J. A. (1978). Gender effects in decoding nonverbal cues. *Psychological Bulletin, 85*, 845–857.

Hall, J. A. (1984). *Nonverbal sex differences: Communication accuracy and expressive style.* Baltimore, MD: The Johns Hopkins University Press.

Hall, J. A., & Matsumoto, D. (2004). Gender differences in judgments of multiple emotions from facial expressions. *Emotion, 4*, 201–206.

Hallsson, L. R., Chenoweth, S. F., & Bonduriansky, R. (2012). The relative importance of genetic and nongenetic inheritance in relation to trait plasticity in *Callosobruchus maculatus. Journal of Evolutionary Biology, 25*, 2422–2431.

Halpern, D. F. (2000). *Sex differences in cognitive abilities* (3rd ed.). Mahwah, NJ: Erlbaum.

Halsted, J. A., Ronaghy, H. A., Abadi, P., Haghshenass, M., Amirhakemi, G. H., Barakat, R. M., et al. (1972). Zinc deficiency in man: The Shiraz experiment. *American Journal of Medicine, 53*, 277–284.

Hamilton, W. D. (1980). Sex versus non-sex versus parasite. *Oikos, 35*, 282–290.

Hamilton, W. D. (1990). Mate choice near or far. *American Zoologist, 30*, 341–352.

Hamilton, W. D., Axelrod, R., & Tanese, R. (1990). Sexual reproduction as an adaptation to resist parasites (A review). *Proceedings of the National Academy of Sciences of the United States of America, 87*, 3566–3573.

Hamilton, W. D., & Zuk, M. (1982). Heritable true fitness and bright birds: A role for parasites? *Science, 218*, 384–387.

Hammill, D. D., Mather, N., & Roberts, R. (2004). *Illinois Test of Psycholinguistic Abilities (ITPA-3)*. Austin, TX: Pro-Ed.

Hampson, E. (1990). Estrogen-related variations in human spatial and articulatory-motor skills. *Psychoneuroendocrinology, 15*, 97–111.

Happé, F., Brownell, H., & Winner, E. (1999). Acquired theory of mind impairments following stroke. *Cognition, 70*, 211–240.

Harley, K. G., Gunier, R. B., Kogut, K., Johnson, C., Bradman, A., Calafat, A. M., et al. (2013). Prenatal and early childhood bisphenol A concentrations and behavior in school-aged children. *Environmental Research, 126*, 43–50.

Harris, T. R., Fitch, W. T., Goldstein, L. M., & Fashing, P. J. (2006). Black and white colobus monkey (*Colobus guereza*) roars as a source of both honest and exaggerated information about body mass. *Ethology, 112*, 911–920.

Harrison, A., Sullivan, S., Tchanturia, K., & Treasure, J. (2009). Emotion recognition and regulation in anorexia nervosa. *Clinical Psychology & Psychotherapy, 16*, 348–356.

Harrison, A., Sullivan, S., Tchanturia, K., & Treasure, J. (2010). Emotional functioning in eating disorders: Attentional bias, emotion recognition and emotion regulation. *Psychological Medicine, 40*, 1887–1897.

Harrison, A., Tchanturia, K., & Treasure, J. (2010). Attentional bias, emotion recognition, and emotion regulation in anorexia: State or trait? *Biological Psychiatry, 68*, 755–761.

Harrison, S. J., Thomson, I. R., Grant, C. M., & Bertram, S. M. (2013). Calling, courtship, and condition in the fall field cricket, *Gryllus pennsylvanicus. PLoS ONE, 8*, e60356.

Hata, T. R., Scholz, T. A., Ermakov, I. V., McClane, R. W., Khachik, F., Gellermann, W., et al. (2000). Non-invasive Raman spectroscopic detection of carotenoids in human skin. *Journal of Investigative Dermatology, 115*, 441–448.

Haut, M. W., Morrow, L. A., Pool, D., Callahan, T. S., Haut, J. S., & Franzen, M. D. (1999). Neurobehavioral effects of acute exposure to inorganic mercury vapor. *Applied Neuropsychology, 6*, 193–200.

Hautvast, J. (1971). Physical growth and menarcheal age in Tanzanian schoolchildren and adults. *Human Biology, 43*, 421–444.

Hebert, P. R., Rich-Edwards, J. W., Manson, J. E., Ridker, P. M., Cook, N. R., O'Connor, G. T., et al. (1993). Height and incidence of cardiovascular disease in male physicians. *Circulation, 88*, 1437–1443.

Hebert, L. E., Wilson, R. S., Gilley, D. W., Beckett, L. A., Scherr, P. A., Bennett, D. A., et al. (2000). Decline of language among women and men with Alzheimer's disease. *Journals of Gerontology Series B, Psychological Sciences and Social Sciences, 55*, P354–P361.

Hedges, D. W., Thatcher, G. W., Bennett, P. J., Sood, S., Paulson, D., Creem-Regehr, S., et al. (2007). Brain integrity and cerebral atrophy in Vietnam combat veterans with and without posttraumatic stress disorder. *Neurocase, 13*, 402–410.

Heinrich, U., Neukam, K., Tronnier, H., Sies, H., & Stahl, W. (2006). Long-term ingestion of high flavanol cocoa provides photoprotection against UV-induced erythema and improves skin condition in women. *Journal of Nutrition, 136*, 1565–1569.

Heinsohn, R. (2008). The ecological basis of unusual sex roles in reverse-dichromatic Eclectus parrots. *Animal Behaviour, 76,* 97–103.

Heistermann, M., Kleis, E., Pröve, E., & Wolters, H. J. (1989). Fertility status, dominance, and scent marking behavior of family-housed female cotton-top tamarins (*Saguinus oedipus*) in absence of their mothers. *American Journal of Primatology, 18,* 177–189.

Henderson, V. W., & Buckwalter, J. G. (1994). Cognitive deficits of men and women with Alzheimer's disease. *Neurology, 44,* 90–96.

Henderson, L. J., Heidinger, B. J., Evans, N. P., & Arnold, K. E. (2013). Ultraviolet crown coloration in female blue tits predicts reproductive success and baseline corticosterone. *Behavioral Ecology, 24,* 1299–1305.

Henderson, V. W., Watt, L., & Galen Buckwalter, J. (1996). Cognitive skills associated with estrogen replacement in women with Alzheimer's disease. *Psychoneuroendocrinology, 21,* 421–430.

Henrich, J., Boyd, R., & Richerson, P. J. (2012). The puzzle of monogamous marriage. *Philosophical Transactions of the Royal Society B, 367,* 657–669.

Henzi, S. P. (1985). Genital signalling and the coexistence of male vervet monkeys (*Cercopithecus aethiops pygerythrus*). *Folia Primatologica, 45,* 129–147.

Herlitz, A., Nilsson, L.-G., & Bäckman, L. (1997). Gender differences in episodic memory. *Memory & Cognition, 25,* 801–811.

Herlitz, A., & Rehnman, J. (2008). Sex differences in episodic memory. *Current Directions in Psychological Science, 17,* 52–56.

Hermelink, K., Untch, M., Lux, M. P., Kreienberg, R., Beck, T., Bauerfeind, I., et al. (2007). Cognitive function during neoadjuvant chemotherapy for breast cancer. *Cancer, 109,* 1905–1913.

Herringa, R. J., Birn, R. M., Ruttle, P. L., Burghy, C. A., Stodola, D. E., Davidson, R. J., et al. (2013). Childhood maltreatment is associated with altered fear circuitry and increased internalizing symptoms by late adolescence. *Proceedings of the National Academy of Sciences of the United States of America, 110,* 19119–19124.

Herz, R. S., & Inzlicht, M. (2002). Sex differences in response to physical and social factors involved in human mate selection: The importance of smell for women. *Evolution and Human Behavior, 23,* 359–364.

Heun, R., & Kockler, M. (2002). Gender differences in the cognitive impairment in Alzheimer's disease. *Archives of Women's Mental Health, 4,* 129–137.

Hewitt, D., Westropp, C. K., & Acheson, R. M. (1955). Oxford Child Health Survey: Effect of childish ailments on skeletal development. *British Journal of Preventive & Social Medicine, 9,* 179–186.

Hill, G. E. (1990). Female house finches prefer colourful males: Sexual selection for a condition-dependent trait. *Animal Behaviour, 40,* 563–572.

Hill, G. E. (1991). Plumage coloration is a sexually selected indicator of male quality. *Nature, 350,* 337–339.

Hill, G. E. (1992). Proximate basis of variation in carotenoid pigmentation in male house finches. *Auk, 109,* 1–12.

Hill, G. E. (1993). Geographic variation in the carotenoid plumage pigmentation of male house finches (*Carpodacus mexicanus*). *Biological Journal of the Linnean Society, 49,* 63–86.

Hill, G. E. (1995). Ornamental traits as indicators of environmental quality. *Bioscience, 45,* 25–31.

Hill, G. E. (2000). Energetic constraints on expression of carotenoid-based plumage coloration. *Journal of Avian Biology, 31,* 559–566.

Hill, G. E. (2006). Female male choice for ornamental coloration. In G. E. Hill, & K. McGraw (Eds.), *Bird coloration: Function and evolution: Vol. 2.* (pp. 137–200). Cambridge, MA: Harvard University Press.

Hill, G. E. (2014). Cellular respiration: The nexus of stress, condition, and ornamentation. *Integrative and Comparative Biology*, *54*, 645–657, icu029.

Hill, G. E., & Brawner, W. R. (1998). Melanin-based plumage coloration in the house finch is unaffected by coccidial infection. *Proceedings of the Royal Society of London B*, *265*, 1105–1109.

Hill, G. E., Doucet, S. M., & Buchholz, R. (2005). The effect of coccidial infection on iridescent plumage coloration in wild turkeys. *Animal Behaviour*, *69*, 387–394.

Hill, G. E., & McGraw, K. J. (Eds.), (2006). *Bird coloration: Function and evolution: Vol. 2*. Cambridge, MA: Harvard University Press.

Hill, G. E., & Montgomerie, R. (1994). Plumage colour signals nutritional condition in the house finch. *Proceedings of the Royal Society of London B*, *258*, 47–52.

Hines, M., Allen, L. S., & Gorski, R. A. (1992). Sex differences in subregions of the medial nucleus of the amygdala and the bed nucleus of the stria terminalis of the rat. *Brain Research*, *579*, 321–326.

Hines, M., Fane, B. A., Pasterski, V. L., Mathews, G. A., Conway, G. S., & Brook, C. (2003). Spatial abilities following prenatal androgen abnormality: Targeting and mental rotations performance in individuals with congenital adrenal hyperplasia. *Psychoneuroendocrinology*, *28*, 1010–1026.

Hines, M., Johnston, K. J., Golombok, S., Rust, J., Stevens, M., & Golding, J. (2002). Prenatal stress and gender role behavior in girls and boys: A longitudinal, population study. *Hormones and Behavior*, *42*, 126–134.

Hjollund, N. H. I., Jensen, T. K., Bonde, J. P. E., Henriksen, T. B., Andersson, A.-M., & Olsen, J. (1999). Distress and reduced fertility: A follow-up study of first-pregnancy planners. *Fertility and Sterility*, *72*, 47–53.

Hoelzel, A. R., Le Boeuf, B. J., Reiter, J., & Campagna, C. (1999). Alpha-male paternity in elephant seals. *Behavioral Ecology and Sociobiology*, *46*, 298–306.

Hoffmeyer, I. (1982). Responses of female bank voles (*Clethrionomys glareolus*) to dominant vs subordinate conspecific males and to urine odors from dominant vs subordinate males. *Behavioral and Neural Biology*, *36*, 178–188.

Höglund, J., & Alatalo, R. V. (1995). *Leks*. Princeton, NJ: Princeton University Press.

Höglund, J., Johansson, T., & Pelabon, C. (1997). Behaviourally mediated sexual selection: Characteristics of successful male black grouse. *Animal Behaviour*, *54*, 255–264.

Holding, C. S., & Holding, D. H. (1989). Acquisition of route network knowledge by males and females. *Journal of Genetic Psychology*, *116*, 29–41.

Hollister-Smith, J. A., Alberts, S. C., & Rasmussen, L. E. L. (2008). Do male African elephants, *Loxodonta africana*, signal musth via urine dribbling? *Animal Behaviour*, *76*, 1829–1841.

Hollister-Smith, J. A., Poole, J. H., Archie, E. A., Vance, E. A., Georgiadis, N. J., Moss, C. J., et al. (2007). Age, musth and paternity success in wild male African elephants, *Loxodonta africana*. *Animal Behaviour*, *74*, 287–296.

Holloway, W. R., JR., & Thor, D. H. (1987). Low level lead exposure during lactation increases rough and tumble play fighting of juvenile rats. *Neurotoxicology and Teratology*, *9*, 51–57.

Holm, E. A., Esmann, S., & Jemec, G. B. (2004). Does visible atopic dermatitis affect quality of life more in women than in men? *Gender Medicine*, *1*, 125–130.

Holmberg, K., Edsman, L., & Klint, T. (1989). Female mate preferences and male attributes in mallard ducks *Anas platyrhynchos*. *Animal Behaviour*, *38*, 1–7.

Holveck, M.-J., Vieira de Castro, A. C., Lachlan, R. F., Carel ten Cate, C., & Riebel, K. (2008). Accuracy of song syntax learning and singing consistency signal early condition in zebra finches. *Behavioral Ecology*, *19*, 267–1281.

Holzer, B., Jacot, A., & Brinkhof, M. W. (2003). Condition-dependent signaling affects male sexual attractiveness in field crickets, *Gryllus campestris*. *Behavioral Ecology*, *14*, 353–359.

Hönekopp, J., Rudolph, U., Beier, L., Liebert, A., & Müller, C. (2007). Physical attractiveness of face and body as indicators of physical fitness in men. *Evolution and Human Behavior, 28,* 106–111.

Hong, S. B., Hong, Y. C., Kim, J. W., Park, E. J., Shin, M. S., Kim, B. N., et al. (2013). Bisphenol A in relation to behavior and learning of school-age children. *Journal of Child Psychology and Psychiatry, 54,* 890–899.

Honig, P. J., Frieden, I. J., Kim, H. J., & Yan, A. C. (2003). Streptococcal intertrigo: An underrecognized condition in children. *Pediatrics, 112,* 1427–1429.

Hooper, R. E., Tsubaki, Y., & Siva Jothy, M. T. (1999). Expression of a costly, plastic secondary sexual trait is correlated with age and condition in a damselfly with two male morphs. *Physiological Entomology, 24,* 364–369.

Hõrak, P., Saks, L., Karu, U., Ots, I., Surai, P. F., & McGraw, K. J. (2004). How coccidian parasites affect health and appearance of greenfinches. *Journal of Animal Ecology, 73,* 935–947.

Hort, J., Laczó, J., Vyhnálek, M., Bojar, M., Bureš, J., & Vlček, K. (2007). Spatial navigation deficit in amnestic mild cognitive impairment. *Proceedings of the National Academy of Sciences of the United States of America, 104,* 4042–4047.

Hotchkiss, A. K., Ostby, J. S., Vandenbergh, J. G., & Gray, L. E., Jr. (2003). An environmental antiandrogen, vinclozolin, alters the organization of play behavior. *Physiology & Behavior, 79,* 151–156.

Hotez, P. J., Brindley, P. J., Bethony, J. M., King, C. H., Pearce, E. J., & Jacobson, J. (2008). Helminth infections: The great neglected tropical diseases. *Journal of Clinical Investigation, 118,* 1311–1321.

Houde, A. E., & Endler, J. A. (1990). Correlated evolution of female mating preferences and male color patterns in the guppy *Poecilia reticulata. Science, 248,* 1405–1408.

Houde, A. E., & Torio, A. J. (1992). Effect of parasitic infection on male color pattern and female choice in guppies. *Behavioral Ecology, 3,* 346–351.

Howard, R. W., & Blomquist, G. J. (2005). Ecological, behavioral, and biochemical aspects of insect hydrocarbons. *Annual Review of Entomology, 50,* 371–393.

Howe, T. R., & Parke, R. D. (2001). Friendship quality and sociometric status: Between-group differences and links to loneliness in severely abused and nonabused children. *Child Abuse & Neglect, 25,* 585–606.

Huck, U. W., & Banks, E. M. (1982). Differential attraction of females to dominant males: Olfactory discrimination and mating preference in the brown lemming (*Lemmus trimucronatus*). *Behavioral Ecology and Sociobiology, 11,* 217–222.

Huck, W. U., Banks, E. M., & Wang, S. C. (1981). Olfactory discrimination of social status in the brown lemming. *Behavioral and Neural Biology, 33,* 364–371.

Huck, W. U., Lisk, R. D., & Gore, A. C. (1985). Scent marking and mate choice in the golden hamster. *Physiology & Behavior, 35,* 389–393.

Hughes, S. M., Dispenza, F., & Gallup, G. G., Jr. (2004). Ratings of voice attractiveness predict sexual behavior and body configuration. *Evolution and Human Behavior, 25,* 295–304.

Hume, D. K., & Montgomerie, R. (2001). Facial attractiveness signals different aspects of "quality" in women and men. *Evolution and Human Behavior, 22,* 93–112.

Hunt, J., & Simmons, L. W. (1997). Patterns of fluctuating asymmetry in beetle horns: An experimental examination of the honest signalling hypothesis. *Behavioral Ecology and Sociobiology, 41,* 109–114.

Hürlimann, E., Houngbedji, C. A., Prisca, B. N., Bänninger, D., Coulibaly, J. T., Yap, P., et al. (2014). Effect of deworming on school-aged children's physical fitness, cognition and clinical parameters in a malaria–helminth co-endemic area of Cote d'Ivoire. *BMC Infectious Diseases, 14,* e411.

Huxley, T. H. (1863). *Evidence as to man's place in nature*. New York: Appleton and Company.

Hwang, L. L., Wang, C. H., Li, T. L., Chang, S. D., Lin, L. C., Chen, C. P., et al. (2010). Sex differences in high-fat diet-induced obesity, metabolic alterations and learning, and synaptic plasticity deficits in mice. *Obesity, 8*, 463–469.

Hyde, J. S. (2005). The gender similarities hypothesis. *American Psychologist, 60*, 581–592.

Hyde, J. S., & Linn, M. C. (1988). Gender differences in verbal ability: A meta-analysis. *Psychological Bulletin, 104*, 53–69.

Ibanez, A., Huepe, D., Gempp, R., Gutiérrez, V., Rivera-Rei, A., & Toledo, M. I. (2013). Empathy, sex and fluid intelligence as predictors of theory of mind. *Personality and Individual Differences, 54*, 616–621.

Ibáñez, A., Marzal, A., López, P., & Martín, J. (2013). Sexually dichromatic coloration reflects size and immunocompetence in female Spanish terrapins, *Mauremys leprosa. Naturwissenschaften, 100*, 1137–1147.

Ibrahim, I. I., Barakat, R. M. R., Bassiouny, H. K., Hanna, L. S., Aboul-Atta, A. M., Bayad, M. A., et al. (1983). Effect of urinary bilharzial infection on male pubertal development and endocrine functions. *Systems Biology in Reproductive Medicine, 11*, 59–64.

Ingalhalikar, M., Smith, A., Parker, D., Satterthwaite, T. D., Elliott, M. A., Ruparel, K., et al. (2014). Sex differences in the structural connectome of the human brain. *Proceedings of the National Academy of Sciences of the United States of America, 111*, 823–828.

Ingleby, F. C., Hosken, D. J., Flowers, K., Hawkes, M. F., Lane, S. M., Rapkin, J., et al. (2013). Genotype-by-environment interactions for cuticular hydrocarbon expression in *Drosophila simulans. Journal of Evolutionary Biology, 26*, 94–107.

Insley, S. J., Holt, M. M., Southall, B., & Atwood, E. C. (2011). Vocal recognition of individuals versus relative dominance rank among breeding male northern elephant seals (*Mirounga angustirostris*). *Proceedings of Meetings on Acoustics, 12*, 1–5.

Irons, W. (1979). Cultural and biological success. In N. A. Chagnon, & W. Irons (Eds.), *Natural selection and social behavior* (pp. 257–272). North Scituate, MA: Duxbury Press.

Irvine, K., Laws, K. R., Gale, T. M., & Kondel, T. K. (2012). Greater cognitive deterioration in women than men with Alzheimer's disease: A meta analysis. *Journal of Clinical and Experimental Neuropsychology, 34*, 989–998.

Isbell, L. A. (1995). Seasonal and social correlates of changes in hair, skin, and scrotal condition in vervet monkeys (*Cercopithecus aethiops*) of Amboseli National Park, Kenya. *American Journal of Primatology, 36*, 61–70.

Jacob, J. A., & Nair, M. K. C. (2012). Protein and micronutrient supplementation in complementing pubertal growth. *Indian Journal of Pediatrics, 79*, 84–91.

Jacobs, L. F., Gaulin, S. J. C., Sherry, D. F., & Hoffman, G. E. (1990). Evolution of spatial cognition: Sex-specific patterns of spatial behavior predict hippocampal size. *Proceedings of the National Academy of Sciences of the United States of America, 87*, 6349–6352.

Jacobs, A. C., & Zuk, M. (2012). Sexual selection and parasites: Do mechanisms matter? In G. E. Demas, & R. J. Nelson (Eds.), *Ecoimmunology* (pp. 468–496). New York: Oxford University Press.

Jacobson, J. L., & Jacobson, S. W. (2002). Breast-feeding and gender as moderators of teratogenic effects on cognitive development. *Neurotoxicology and Teratology, 24*, 349–358.

Jacobziner, H., Rich, H., Bleiberg, N., & Merchant, R. (1963). How well are well children? *American Journal of Public Health, 53*, 1937–1952.

Jacquemont, S., Coe, B. P., Hersch, M., Duyzend, M. H., Krumm, N., Bergmann, S., et al. (2014). A higher mutational burden in females supports a "female protective model" in neurodevelopmental disorders. *American Journal of Human Genetics, 94*, 415–425.

Jaeger, J. J., Lockwood, A. H., Van Valin, R. D., Jr., Kemmerer, D. L., Murphy, B. W., & Wack, D. S. (1998). Sex differences in brain regions activated by grammatical and reading tasks. *NeuroReport*, *9*, 2803–2807.

Jaenike, J. (1978). An hypothesis to account for the maintenance of sex within populations. *Evolutionary Theory*, *3*, 191–194.

Jainudeen, M. R., Katongole, C. B., & Short, R. V. (1972). Plasma testosterone levels in relation to musth and sexual activity in the male Asiatic elephant, *Elephas maximus*. *Journal of Reproduction and Fertility*, *29*, 99–103.

Jainudeen, M. R., McKay, G. M., & Eisenberg, J. F. (1972). Observations on musth in the domesticated Asiatic elephant (*Elephas maximus*). *Mammalia*, *36*, 247–261.

Jankowiak, W., Sudakov, M., & Wilreker, B. C. (2005). Co-wife conflict and co-operation. *Ethnology*, *44*, 81–98.

Janowsky, J. S., Oviatt, S. K., & Orwoll, E. S. (1994). Testosterone influences spatial cognition in older men. *Behavioral Neuroscience*, *108*, 325–332.

Jardim-Botelho, A., Brooker, S., Geiger, S. M., Fleming, F., Souza Lopes, A. C., Diemert, D. J., et al. (2008). Age patterns in undernutrition and helminth infection in a rural area of Brazil: Associations with ascariasis and hookworm. *Tropical Medicine & International Health*, *13*, 458–467.

Jardine, R., & Martin, N. G. (1983). Spatial ability and throwing accuracy. *Behavior Genetics*, *13*, 331–340.

Jarosz, W., Mizgajska-Wiktor, H., Kirwan, P., Konarski, J., Rychlicki, W., & Wawrzyniak, G. (2010). Developmental age, physical fitness and *Toxocara* seroprevalence amongst lower-secondary students living in rural areas contaminated with *Toxocara* eggs. *Parasitology*, *137*, 53–63.

Jašarević, E., Hecht, P. M., Fritsche, K. L., Beversdorf, D. Q., & Geary, D. C. (2014). Dissociable effects of dorsal and ventral hippocampal DHA levels on spatial learning and fear-related behavior. *Neurobiology of Learning and Memory*, *116*, 59–68.

Jašarević, E., Sieli, P. T., Twellman, E. E., Welsh, T.H. Jr, Schachtman, T. R., Roberts, R. M., et al. (2011). Disruption of adult expression of sexually selected traits by early exposure to bisphenol A. *Proceedings of the National Academy of Sciences of the United States of America*, *108*, 11715–11720.

Jašarević, E., Williams, S. A., Roberts, R. M., Geary, D. C., & Rosenfeld, C. S. (2012). Spatial navigation strategies in *Peromyscus*: A comparative study. *Animal Behaviour*, *84*, 1141–1149.

Jašarević, E., Williams, S. A., Vandas, G., Ellersieck, M. R., Liao, C., Kannan, K., et al. (2013). Sex and dose-dependent effects of developmental exposure to bisphenol A on anxiety and spatial learning in deer mice (*Peromyscus maniculatus bairdii*) offspring. *Hormones and Behavior*, *63*, 180–189.

Jasieńska, G., Ziomkiewicz, A., Ellison, P. T., Lipson, S. F., & Thune, I. (2004). Large breasts and narrow waists indicate high reproductive potential in women. *Proceedings of the Royal Society of London B*, *271*, 1213–1217.

Jeannerod, M. (2003). Simulation of action as a unifying concept for motor cognition. In S. H. Johnson-Frey (Ed.), *Taking action: Cognitive neuroscience perspectives on intentional acts* (pp. 139–163). Cambridge, MA: MIT Press.

Jenkins, V. A., Bloomfield, D. J., Shilling, V. M., & Edginton, T. L. (2005). Does neoadjuvant hormone therapy for early prostate cancer affect cognition? Results from a pilot study. *BJU International*, *96*, 48–53.

Jenkins, V., Shilling, V., Deutsch, G., Bloomfield, D., Morris, R., Allan, S., et al. (2006). A 3-year prospective study of the effects of adjuvant treatments on cognition in women with early stage breast cancer. *British Journal of Cancer*, *94*, 828–834.

Jennions, M. D., & Backwell, P. R. (1998). Variation in courtship rate in the fiddler crab *Uca annulipes*: Is it related to male attractiveness? *Behavioral Ecology, 9*, 605–611.

Jennions, M. D., Kahn, A. T., Kelly, C. D., & Kokko, H. (2012). Meta-analysis and sexual selection: Past studies and future possibilities. *Evolutionary Ecology, 26*, 1119–1151.

Jennions, M. D., Møller, A. P., & Petrie, M. (2001). Sexually selected traits and adult survival: A meta-analysis. *Quarterly Review of Biology, 76*, 3–36.

Jennische, M., & Sedin, G. (2003). Gender differences in outcome after neonatal intensive care: Speech and language skills are less influenced in boys than in girls at 6.5 years. *Acta Paediatrica, 92*, 364–378.

Jim, H. S., Phillips, K. M., Chait, S., Faul, L. A., Popa, M. A., Lee, Y. H., et al. (2012). Meta-analysis of cognitive functioning in breast cancer survivors previously treated with standard-dose chemotherapy. *Journal of Clinical Oncology, 30*, 3578–3587.

Johnson, E. S., & Meade, A. C. (1987). Developmental patterns of spatial ability: An early sex difference. *Child Development, 58*, 725–740.

Johnson, K., Rosetta, D., & Burley, D. N. (1993). Preferences of female American goldfinches (*Carduelis tristis*) for natural and artificial male traits. *Behavioral Ecology, 4*, 138–143.

Johnston, R. E. (1977). The causation of two scent-marking behaviour patterns in female hamsters (*Mesocricetus auratus*). *Animal Behaviour, 25*, 317–327.

Johnston, R. E., Sorokin, E. S., & Ferkin, M. H. (1997a). Scent counter-marking by male meadow voles: Females prefer the top-scent male. *Ethology, 103*, 443–453.

Johnston, R. E., Sorokin, E. S., & Ferkin, M. H. (1997b). Female voles discriminate males' overmarks and prefer top-scent males. *Animal Behaviour, 54*, 679–690.

Johnstone, R. A. (1995). Sexual selection, honest advertisement and the handicap principle: Reviewing the evidence. *Biological Reviews, 70*, 1–65.

Jokela, M., Alvergne, A., Pollet, T. V., & Lummaa, V. (2011). Reproductive behavior and personality traits of the Five Factor Model. *European Journal of Personality, 25*, 487–500.

Joly, F., Alibhai, S. M. H., Galica, J., Park, A., Yi, Q. L., Wagner, L., et al. (2006). Impact of androgen deprivation therapy on physical and cognitive function, as well as quality of life of patients with nonmetastatic prostate cancer. *Journal of Urology, 176*, 2443–2447.

Jonason, P. K. (2007). An evolutionary psychology perspective on sex differences in exercise behaviors and motivations. *Journal of Social Psychology, 147*, 5–14.

Jones, L., Harmer, C., Cowen, P., & Cooper, M. (2008). Emotional face processing in women with high and low levels of eating disorder related symptoms. *Eating Behaviors, 9*, 389–397.

Jones, A. G., Moore, G. I., Kvarnemo, C., Walker, D., & Avise, J. C. (2003). Sympatric speciation as a consequence of male pregnancy in seahorses. *Proceedings of the National Academy of Sciences of the United States of America, 100*, 6598–6603.

Joron, M., & Brakefield, P. M. (2003). Captivity masks inbreeding effects on male mating success in butterflies. *Nature, 424*, 191–194.

Josephson, S. C. (2002). Does polygyny reduce fertility? *American Journal of Human Biology, 14*, 222–232.

Kao, M. H., Doupe, A. J., & Brainard, M. S. (2005). Contributions of an avian basal ganglia–forebrain circuit to real-time modulation of song. *Nature, 433*, 638–643.

Kasprian, G., Langs, G., Brugger, P. C., Bittner, M., Weber, M., Arantes, M., et al. (2011). The prenatal origin of hemispheric asymmetry: An in utero neuroimaging study. *Cerebral Cortex, 21*, 1076–1083.

Katsuki, M., Okada, Y., & Okada, K. (2012). Impacts of diet quality on life-history and reproductive traits in male and female armed beetle, *Gnatocerus cornutus*. *Ecological Entomology, 37*, 463–470.

Kavaliers, M., & Colwell, D. D. (1995a). Odours of parasitized males induce aversive responses in female mice. *Animal Behaviour, 50,* 1161–1169.

Kavaliers, M., & Colwell, D. D. (1995b). Discrimination by female mice between the odours of parasitized and non-parasitized males. *Proceedings of the Royal Society of London B, 261,* 31–35.

Kavaliers, M., & Colwell, D. D. (1995c). Reduced spatial learning in mice infected with the nematode, *Heligmosomoides polygyrus. Parasitology, 110,* 591–597.

Kavaliers, M., & Colwell, D. D. (1995d). Exposure to stable flies reduces spatial learning in mice: Involvement of endogenous opioid systems. *Medical and Veterinary Entomology, 9,* 300–306.

Kavaliers, M., Colwell, D. D., & Galea, L. A. (1995). Parasitic infection impairs spatial learning in mice. *Animal Behaviour, 50,* 223–229.

Keagy, J., Savard, J. F., & Borgia, G. (2012). Cognitive ability and the evolution of multiple behavioral display traits. *Behavioral Ecology, 23,* 448–456.

Kee, N., Teixeira, C. M., Wang, A. H., & Frankland, P. W. (2007). Preferential incorporation of adult-generated granule cells into spatial memory networks in the dentate gyrus. *Nature Neuroscience, 10,* 355–362.

Keeley, L. H. (1996). *War before civilization: The myth of the peaceful savage.* New York: Oxford University Press.

Kelly, R. J., Murphy, T. G., Tarvin, K. A., & Burness, G. (2012). Carotenoid-based ornaments of female and male American goldfinches (*Spinus tristis*) show sex-specific correlations with immune function and metabolic rate. *Physiological and Biochemical Zoology, 85,* 348–363.

Kemp, D. J. (2008). Resource-mediated condition dependence in sexually dichromatic butterfly wing coloration. *Evolution, 62,* 2346–2358.

Kemp, D. J., & Rutowski, R. L. (2007). Condition dependence, quantitative genetics, and the potential signal content of iridescent ultraviolet butterfly coloration. *Evolution, 61,* 168–183.

Kendler, K. S., Bulik, C. M., Silberg, J., Hettema, J. M., Myers, J., & Prescott, C. A. (2000). Childhood sexual abuse and adult psychiatric and substance use disorders in women: An epidemiological and cotwin control analysis. *Archives of General Psychiatry, 57,* 953–959.

Kendler, K. S., Myers, J., & Prescott, C. A. (2005). Sex differences in the relationship between social support and risk for major depression: A longitudinal study of opposite-sex twin pairs. *American Journal of Psychiatry, 162,* 250–256.

Kenrick, D. T., & Keefe, R. C. (1992). Age preferences in mates reflect sex differences in human reproductive strategies. *Behavioral and Brain Sciences, 15,* 75–133.

Kessler, R. C., Berglund, P., Demler, O., Jin, R., Merikangas, K. R., & Walters, E. E. (2005). Lifetime prevalence and age-of-onset distributions of DSM-IV disorders in the National Comorbidity Survey Replication. *Archives of General Psychiatry, 62,* 593–602.

Kessler, H., Schwarze, M., Filipic, S., Traue, H. C., & von Wietersheim, J. (2006). Alexithymia and facial emotion recognition in patients with eating disorders. *International Journal of Eating Disorders, 39,* 245–251.

Keyser, A. J., & Hill, G. E. (1999). Condition-dependent variation in the blue–ultraviolet coloration of a structurally based plumage ornament. *Proceedings of the Royal Society of London B, 266,* 771–777.

Keyser, A. J., & Hill, G. E. (2000). Structurally based plumage coloration is an honest signal of quality in male blue grosbeaks. *Behavioral Ecology, 11,* 202–209.

Khan, M. R., & Ahmed, F. (2005). Physical status, nutrient intake and dietary pattern of adolescent female factory workers in urban Bangladesh. *Asia Pacific Journal of Clinical Nutrition, 14,* 19–26.

Khandaker, G. M., Zimbron, J., Lewis, G., & Jones, P. B. (2013). Prenatal maternal infection, neurodevelopment and adult schizophrenia: A systematic review of population-based studies. *Psychological Medicine, 43,* 239–257.

Kilpatrick, L. A., Zald, D. H., Pardo, J. V., & Cahill, L. F. (2006). Sex-related differences in amygdala functional connectivity during resting conditions. *NeuroImage, 30*, 452–461.

Kim, T. W., & Choe, J. C. (2003). The effect of food availability on the semilunar courtship rhythm in the fiddler crab *Uca lactea* (*de Haan*) (*Brachyura: Ocypodidae*). *Behavioral Ecology and Sociobiology, 54*, 210–217.

Kim, J., & Cicchetti, D. (2003). Social self-efficacy and behavior problems in maltreated and nonmaltreated children. *Journal of Clinical Child and Adolescent Psychology, 32*, 106–117.

Kim, J., Shen, W., Gallagher, D., Jones, A., Jr., Wang, Z., Wang, J., et al. (2006). Total-body skeletal muscle mass: Estimation by dual-energy X-ray absorptiometry in children and adolescents. *American Journal of Clinical Nutrition, 84*, 1014–1020.

Kim, A. M., Tingen, C. M., & Woodruff, T. K. (2010). Sex bias in trials and treatment must end. *Nature, 465*, 688–689.

Kimura, D. (1999). *Sex and cognition*. Cambridge, MA: Bradford/MIT Press.

Kishi, R., Doi, R., Fukuchi, Y., Satoh, H., Satoh, T., Ono, A., et al. (1994). Residual neurobehavioural effects associated with chronic exposure to mercury vapour. *Occupational and Environmental Medicine, 51*, 35–41.

Kitayama, N., Vaccarino, V., Kutner, M., Weiss, P., & Bremner, J. D. (2005). Magnetic resonance imaging (MRI) measurement of hippocampal volume in posttraumatic stress disorder: A meta-analysis. *Journal of Affective Disorders, 88*, 79–86.

Kjetland, E. F., Kurewa, E. N., Mduluza, T., Midzi, N., Gomo, E., Friis, H., et al. (2010). The first community-based report on the effect of genital *Schistosoma haematobium* infection on female fertility. *Fertility and Sterility, 94*, 1551–1553.

Klein, S. L. (2003). Parasite manipulation of the proximate mechanisms that mediate social behavior in vertebrates. *Physiology & Behavior, 79*, 441–449.

Knell, R. J., Fruhauf, N., & Norris, K. A. (1999). Conditional expression of a sexually selected trait in the stalk-eyed fly *Diasemopsis aethiopica*. *Ecological Entomology, 24*, 323–328.

Knight, G. P., Guthrie, I. K., Page, M. C., & Fabes, R. A. (2002). Emotional arousal and gender differences in aggression: A meta-analysis. *Aggressive Behavior, 28*, 366–393.

Kochunov, P., Glahn, D. C., Lancaster, J. L., Winkler, A. M., Smith, S., Thompson, P. M., et al. (2010). Genetics of microstructure of cerebral white matter using diffusion tensor imaging. *NeuroImage, 53*, 1109–1116.

Kodric Brown, A., Sibly, R. M., & Brown, J. H. (2006). The allometry of ornaments and weapons. *Proceedings of the National Academy of Sciences of the United States of America, 103*, 8733–8738.

Kodric-Brown, A. (1985). Female preference and sexual selection for male coloration in the guppy (*Poecilia reticulata*). *Behavioral Ecology and Sociobiology, 17*, 199–205.

Kodric-Brown, A. (1989). Dietary carotenoids and male mating success in the guppy: An environmental component to female choice. *Behavioral Ecology and Sociobiology, 25*, 393–401.

Kokko, H., & Jennions, M. D. (2008). Parental investment, sexual selection and sex ratios. *Journal of Evolutionary Biology, 21*, 919–948.

Kokko, H., Klug, H., & Jennions, M. D. (2012). Unifying cornerstones of sexual selection: Operational sex ratio, Bateman gradient and the scope for competitive investment. *Ecology Letters, 15*, 1340–1351.

Kokko, H., Rintamaki, P. T., Alatalo, R. V., Hoglund, J., Karvonen, E., & Lundberg, A. (1999). Female choice selects for lifetime lekking performance in black grouse males. *Proceedings of the Royal Society of London B, 266*, 2109–2115.

Koskimäki, J., Rantala, M. J., Taskinen, J., Tynkkynen, K., & Suhonen, J. (2004). Immunocompetence and resource holding potential in the damselfly, *Calopteryx virgo* L. *Behavioral Ecology, 15*, 169–173.

Kotiaho, J. S. (2002). Sexual selection and condition dependence of courtship display in three species of horned dung beetles. *Behavioral Ecology, 13,* 791–799.

Kotiaho, J., Alatalo, R. V., Mappes, J., & Parri, S. (1996). Sexual selection in a wolf spider: Male drumming activity, body size, and viability. *Evolution, 50,* 1977–1981.

Kotiaho, J. S., Simmons, L. W., & Tomkins, J. L. (2001). Towards a resolution of the lek paradox. *Nature, 410,* 684–686.

Koutsos, E. A., Clifford, A. J., Calvert, C. C., & Klasing, K. C. (2003). Maternal carotenoid status modifies the incorporation of dietary carotenoids into immune tissues of growing chickens (*Gallus gallus domesticus*). *Journal of Nutrition, 133,* 1132–1138.

Kraaijeveld, K., Kraaijeveld-Smit, F. J. L., & Komdeur, J. (2007). The evolution of mutual ornament. *Animal Behaviour, 74,* 657–677.

Krebs, N. F., Hambidge, K. M., & Walravens, P. A. (1984). Increased food intake of young children receiving a zinc supplement. *American Journal of Diseases of Children, 138,* 270–273.

Kremen, W. S., Koenen, K. C., Afari, N., & Lyons, M. J. (2012). Twin studies of posttraumatic stress disorder: Differentiating vulnerability factors from sequelae. *Neuropharmacology, 62,* 647–653.

Kremen, W. S., Prom-Wormley, E., Panizzon, M. S., Eyler, L. T., Fischl, B., Neale, M. C., et al. (2010). Genetic and environmental influences on the size of specific brain regions in midlife: The VETSA MRI study. *NeuroImage, 49,* 1213–1223.

Kristensen, T., Baatrup, E., & Bayley, M. (2005). 17α-Ethinylestradiol reduces the competitive reproductive fitness of the male guppy (*Poecilia reticulata*). *Biology of Reproduction, 72,* 150–156.

Kruczek, M. (1997). Male rank and female choice in the bank vole, *Clethrionomys glareolus. Behavioural Processes, 40,* 171–176.

Kruuk, L. E., Slate, J., Pemberton, J. M., Brotherstone, S., Guinness, F., & Clutton Brock, T. (2002). Antler size in red deer: Heritability and selection but no evolution. *Evolution, 56,* 1683–1695.

Kucharska-Pietura, K., Nikolaou, V., Masiak, M., & Treasure, J. (2004). The recognition of emotion in the faces and voice of anorexia nervosa. *International Journal of Eating Disorders, 35,* 42–47.

Kulin, H. E., Bwibo, N., Mutie, D., & Santner, S. J. (1982). The effect of chronic childhood malnutrition on pubertal growth and development. *American Journal of Clinical Nutrition, 36,* 527–536.

Kvalsvig, J. D. (1986). The effects of *Schistosomiasis haematobium* on the activity of school children. *Journal of Tropical Medicine and Hygiene, 89,* 85–90.

LaFontana, K. M., & Cillessen, A. H. N. (2002). Children's perceptions of popular and unpopular peers: A multimethod assessment. *Developmental Psychology, 38,* 635–647.

Laiacona, M., Barbarotto, R., & Capitani, E. (1998). Semantic category dissociations in naming: Is there a gender effect in Alzheimer's disease? *Neuropsychologia, 36,* 407–419.

Lamminmäki, A., Hines, M., Kuiri-Hänninen, T., Kilpeläinen, L., Dunkel, L., & Sankilampi, U. (2012). Testosterone measured in infancy predicts subsequent sex-typed behavior in boys and in girls. *Hormones and Behavior, 61,* 611–616.

Lande, R. (1980). Sexual dimorphism, sexual selection, and adaptation in polygenic characteristics. *Evolution, 34,* 292–305.

Landrigan, P. J., Claudio, L., Markowitz, S. B., Berkowitz, G. S., Brenner, B. L., Romero, H., et al. (1999). Pesticides and inner-city children: Exposures, risks, and prevention. *Environmental Health Perspectives, 107*(Suppl. 3), 431–437.

Largo, R. H., Molinari, L., Pinto, L. C., Weber, M., & Due, G. (1986). Language development of term and preterm children during the first five years of life. *Developmental Medicine & Child Neurology, 28,* 333–350.

Lassek, W. D., & Gaulin, S. J. C. (2008). Waist-to-hip ratio and cognitive ability: Is gluteofemoral fat a privileged store of neurodevelopmental resources? *Evolution and Human Behavior, 29,* 26–34.

Lassek, W. D., & Gaulin, S. J. (2009). Costs and benefits of fat-free muscle mass in men: Relationship to mating success, dietary requirements, and native immunity. *Evolution and Human Behavior, 30*, 322–328.

Latham, M. C., Stephenson, L. S., Kurz, K. M., & Kinoti, S. N. (1990). Metrifonate or praziquantel treatment improves physical fitness and appetite of Kenyan schoolboys with *Schistosoma haematobium* and hookworm infections. *American Journal of Tropical Medicine and Hygiene, 43*, 170–179.

Law, D. J., Pellegrino, J. W., & Hunt, E. B. (1993). Comparing the tortoise and the hare: Gender differences and experience in dynamic spatial reasoning tasks. *Psychological Science, 4*, 35–40.

Laws, K. R., Adlington, R. L., Gale, T. M., Moreno-Martínez, F. J., & Sartori, G. (2007). A meta-analytic review of category naming in Alzheimer's disease. *Neuropsychologia, 45*, 2674–2682.

Lazaro-Perea, C., Snowdon, C. T., & de Fátima Arruda, M. (1999). Scent-marking behavior in wild groups of common marmosets (*Callithrix jacchus*). *Behavioral Ecology and Sociobiology, 46*, 313–324.

Le Boeuf, B. J. (1974). Male–male competition and reproductive success in elephant seals. *American Zoologist, 14*, 163–176.

Le Boeuf, B. J., & Peterson, R. S. (1969). Social status and mating activity in elephant seals. *Science, 163*, 91–93.

Le Boeuf, B. J., & Reiter, J. (1988). Lifetime reproductive success in northern elephant seals. In T. H. Clutton-Brock (Ed.), *Reproductive success: Studies of individual variation in contrasting breeding systems* (pp. 344–362). Chicago, IL: University of Chicago Press.

Leadbeater, B. J., Blatt, S. J., & Quinlan, D. M. (1995). Gender-linked vulnerabilities to depressive symptoms, stress, and problem behaviors in adolescents. *Journal of Research on Adolescence, 5*, 1–29.

Leakey, M. G., Feibel, C. S., McDougall, I., Ward, C., & Walker, A. (1998). New specimens and confirmation of an early age for *Australopithecus anamensis*. *Nature, 393*, 62–66.

Leaper, C., & Smith, T. E. (2004). A meta-analytic review of gender variations in children's language use: Talkativeness, affiliative speech, and assertive speech. *Developmental Psychology, 40*, 993–1027.

Leary, C. J., & Knapp, R. (2014). The stress of elaborate male traits: Integrating glucocorticoids with androgen-based models of sexual selection. *Animal Behaviour, 89*, 85–92.

LeBas, N. R., Hockham, L. R., & Ritchie, M. G. (2003). Nonlinear and correlational sexual selection on 'honest' female ornamentation. *Proceedings of the Royal Society of London B, 270*, 2159–2165.

Lebron-Milad, K., & Milad, M. R. (2012). Sex differences, gonadal hormones and the fear extinction network: Implications for anxiety disorders. *Biology of Mood & Anxiety Disorders, 2*, 3.

Lee, K. A., Vaillant, G. E., Torrey, W. C., & Elder, G. H. (1995). A 50-year prospective study of the psychological sequelae of World War II combat. *American Journal of Psychiatry, 152*, 516–522.

Leenaars, L. S., Dane, A. V., & Marini, Z. A. (2008). Evolutionary perspective on indirect victimization in adolescence: The role of attractiveness, dating and sexual behavior. *Aggressive Behavior, 34*, 404–415.

Lefevre, C. E., Ewbank, M. P., Calder, A. J., von dem Hagen, E., & Perrett, D. I. (2013). It is all in the face: Carotenoid skin coloration loses attractiveness outside the face. *Biology Letters, 9*, 20130633.

Lefevre, C. E., Lewis, G. J., Perrett, D. I., & Penke, L. (2013). Telling facial metrics: Facial width is associated with testosterone levels in men. *Evolution and Human Behavior, 34*, 273–279.

Legato, M. J. (Ed.), (2004). *Principles of gender-specific medicine: Vol. 2.* San Diego, CA: Elsevier Academic Press.

Leggio, M. G., Molinari, M., Neri, P., Graziano, A., Mandolesi, L., & Petrosini, L. (2000). Representation of action in rats: The role of cerebellum in learning spatial performance by observation. *Proceedings of the National Academy of Sciences of the United States of America, 97,* 2320–2325.

Leigh, S. R. (1995). Socioecology and the ontogeny of sexual size dimorphism in anthropoid primates. *American Journal of Physical Anthropology, 97,* 339–356.

Leigh, S. R. (1996). Evolution of human growth spurts. *American Journal of Physical Anthropology, 101,* 455–474.

Lemaire, V., Koehl, M., Le Moal, M., & Abrous, D. N. (2000). Prenatal stress produces learning deficits associated with an inhibition of neurogenesis in the hippocampus. *Proceedings of the National Academy of Sciences of the United States of America, 97,* 11032–11037.

Lenington, S. (1983). Social preferences for partners carrying 'good genes' in wild house mice. *Animal Behaviour, 31,* 325–333.

Leonard, C. M., Towler, S., Welcome, S., Halderman, L. K., Otto, R., Eckert, M. A., et al. (2008). Size matters: Cerebral volume influences sex differences in neuroanatomy. *Cerebral Cortex, 18,* 2920–2931.

Leslie, A. M., Friedman, O., & German, T. P. (2004). Core mechanisms in 'theory of mind'. *Trends in Cognitive Sciences, 8,* 528–533.

Lever, J. (1978). Sex differences in the complexity of children's play and games. *American Sociological Review, 43,* 471–483.

Levine, S. C., Huttenlocher, J., Taylor, A., & Langrock, A. (1999). Early sex differences in spatial skill. *Developmental Psychology, 35,* 940–949.

Levine, S. C., Vasilyeva, M., Lourenco, S. F., Newcombe, N., & Huttenlocher, J. (2005). Socioeconomic status modifies the sex differences in spatial skill. *Psychological Science, 16,* 841–845.

Lewin, C., Wolgers, G., & Herlitz, A. (2001). Sex differences favoring women in verbal but not in visuospatial episodic memory. *Neuropsychology, 15,* 165–173.

Lewis, K. P., & Barton, R. A. (2006). Amygdala size and hypothalamus size predict social play frequency in nonhuman primates: A comparative analysis using independent contrasts. *Journal of Comparative Psychology, 120,* 31–37.

Lewis, B. A., Minnes, S., Short, E. J., Weishampel, P., Satayathum, S., Min, M. O., et al. (2011). The effects of prenatal cocaine on language development at 10 years of age. *Neurotoxicology and Teratology, 33,* 17–24.

Li, N. P. (2007). Mate preference necessities in long- and short-term mating: People prioritize in themselves what their mates prioritize in them. *Acta Psychologica Sinica, 39,* 528–535.

Li, R., & Singh, M. (2014). Sex differences in cognitive impairment and Alzheimer's disease. *Frontiers in Neuroendocrinology, 35,* 385–403.

Ligon, J. D., Thornhill, R., Zuk, M., & Johnson, K. (1990). Male-male competition, ornamentation and the role of testosterone in sexual selection in red jungle fowl. *Animal Behaviour, 40,* 367–373.

Lim, M. L., & Li, D. (2013). UV-green iridescence predicts male quality during jumping spider contests. *PLoS ONE, 8,* e59774.

Lin, K. C., Guo, N. W., Tsai, P. C., Yang, C. Y., & Guo, Y. L. (2008). Neurocognitive changes among elderly exposed to PCBs/PCDFs in Taiwan. *Environmental Health Perspectives, 116,* 184–189.

Lindová, J., Příplatová, L., & Flegr, J. (2012). Higher extraversion and lower conscientiousness in humans infected with Toxoplasma. *European Journal of Personality, 26,* 285–291.

Lindqvist, A., Mohapel, P., Bouter, B., Frielingsdorf, H., Pizzo, D., Brundin, P., et al. (2006). High-fat diet impairs hippocampal neurogenesis in male rats. *European Journal of Neurology, 13,* 1385–1388.

Linn, M. C., & Petersen, A. C. (1985). Emergence and characterization of sex differences in spatial abilities: A meta-analysis. *Child Development*, *56*, 1479–1498.

Lippa, R. A. (2007). The preferred traits of mates in a cross-national study of heterosexual and homosexual men and women: An examination of biological and cultural influences. *Archives of Sexual Behavior*, *36*, 193–208.

Lithfous, S., Dufour, A., & Després, O. (2013). Spatial navigation in normal aging and the prodromal stage of Alzheimer's disease: Insights from imaging and behavioral studies. *Ageing Research Reviews*, *12*, 201–213.

Litt, E., Baker, M. C., & Molyneux, D. (2012). Neglected tropical diseases and mental health: A perspective on comorbidity. *Trends in Parasitology*, *28*, 195–201.

Locatello, L., Rasotto, M. B., Evans, J. P., & Pilastro, A. (2006). Colourful male guppies produce faster and more viable sperm. *Journal of Evolutionary Biology*, *19*, 1595–1602.

Loehr, J., & O'Hara, R. B. (2013). Facial morphology predicts male fitness and rank but not survival in Second World War Finnish soldiers. *Biology Letters*, *9*, 20130049.

Loyau, A., Saint Jalme, M., Cagniant, C., & Sorci, G. (2005). Multiple sexual advertisements honestly reflect health status in peacocks (*Pavo cristatus*). *Behavioral Ecology and Sociobiology*, *58*, 552–557.

Loyau, A., Saint Jalme, M., & Sorci, G. (2005). Intra-and intersexual selection for multiple traits in the Peacock (*Pavo cristatus*). *Ethology*, *111*, 810–820.

Lucariello, J. M., Durand, T. M., & Yarnell, L. (2007). Social versus intrapersonal ToM: Social ToM is a cognitive strength for low- and middle-SES children. *Journal of Applied Developmental Psychology*, *28*, 285–297.

Lyon, B. E., & Montgomerie, R. (2012). Sexual selection is a form of social selection. *Philosophical Transactions of the Royal Society, B*, *367*, 2266–2273.

Maccoby, E. E. (1988). Gender as a social category. *Developmental Psychology*, *24*, 755–765.

Maccoby, E. E. (1990). Gender and relationships: A developmental account. *American Psychologist*, *45*, 513–520.

Maccoby, E. E. (1998). *The two sexes: Growing up apart, coming together*. Cambridge, MA: Belknap Press.

MacDonald, D. H., & Hewlett, B. S. (1999). Reproductive interests and forager mobility. *Current Anthropology*, *40*, 501–523.

MacDonald, I. F., Kempster, B., Zanette, L., & MacDougall Shackleton, S. A. (2006). Early nutritional stress impairs development of a song control brain region in both male and female juvenile song sparrows (*Melospiza melodia*) at the onset of song learning. *Proceedings of the Royal Society of London B*, *273*, 2559–2564.

MacFarlan, S. J., Walker, R. S., Flinn, M. V., & Chagnon, N. A. (2014). Lethal coalitionary aggression and long-term alliances among Yanomamö men. *Proceedings of the National Academy of Sciences of the United States of America*, *111*, 16662–16669.

Machón, R. A., Mednick, S. A., & Huttunen, M. O. (1997). Adult major affective disorder after prenatal exposure to an influenza epidemic. *Archives of General Psychiatry*, *54*, 322–328.

Madden, J. (2001). Sex, bowers and brains. *Proceedings of the Royal Society of London B*, *268*, 833–838.

Maguire, E. A., Burgess, N., Donnett, J. G., Frackowiak, R. S. J., Frith, C. D., & O'Keefe, J. (1998). Knowing where and getting there: A human navigational network. *Science*, *280*, 921–924.

Maia, R., Brasileiro, L., Lacava, R. V., & Macedo, R. H. (2012). Social environment affects acquisition and color of structural nuptial plumage in a sexually dimorphic tropical passerine. *PLoS ONE*, *7*, e47501.

Majeres, R. L. (2007). Sex differences in phonological coding: Alphabet transformation speed. *Intelligence, 35,* 335–346.

Malakoff, M. E., Mayes, L. C., Schottenfeld, R., & Howell, S. (1999). Language production in 24-month-old inner-city children of cocaine-and-other-drug-using mothers. *Journal of Applied Developmental Psychology, 20,* 159–180.

Malina, R. M., Himes, J. H., Stepick, C. D., Lopez, F. G., & Buschang, P. H. (1981). Growth of rural and urban children in the Valley of Oaxaca, Mexico. *American Journal of Physical Anthropology, 54,* 327–336.

Malo, A. F., Roldan, E. R., Garde, J., Soler, A. J., & Gomendio, M. (2005). Antlers honestly advertise sperm production and quality. *Proceedings of the Royal Society of London B, 272,* 149–157.

Mandyam, C. D., Crawford, E. F., Eisch, A. J., Rivier, C. L., & Richardson, H. N. (2008). Stress experienced in utero reduces sexual dichotomies in neurogenesis, microenvironment, and cell death in the adult rat hippocampus. *Developmental Neurobiology, 68,* 575–589.

Maner, J. K., Richey, J. A., Cromer, K., Mallott, M., Lejuez, C. W., Joiner, T. E., et al. (2007). Dispositional anxiety and risk-avoidant decision-making. *Personality and Individual Differences, 42,* 665–675.

Mappes, J., Alatalo, R. V., Kotiaho, J., & Parri, S. (1996). Viability costs of condition-dependent sexual male display in a drumming wolf spider. *Proceedings of the Royal Society of London B, 263,* 785–789.

Mariette, M., Kelley, J. L., Brooks, R., & Evans, J. P. (2006). The effects of inbreeding on male courtship behaviour and coloration in guppies. *Ethology, 112,* 807–814.

Marino, M., Masella, R., Bulzomi, P., Campesi, I., Malorni, W., & Franconi, F. (2011). Nutrition and human health from a sex–gender perspective. *Molecular Aspects of Medicine, 32,* 1–70.

Markovits, H., Benenson, J., & Dolenszky, E. (2001). Evidence that children and adolescents have internal models of peers interactions that are gender differentiated. *Child Development, 72,* 879–886.

Marler, P. (1991). The instinct to learn. In S. Carey, & R. Gelman (Eds.), *The epigenesis of mind: Essays on biology and cognition* (pp. 37–66). Hillsdale, NJ: Erlbaum.

Marler, P., & Peters, S. (1987). A sensitive period for song acquisition in the song sparrow, *Melospiza melodia*: A case of age-limited learning. *Ethology, 76,* 89–100.

Marler, P., & Peters, S. (1988). Sensitive periods for song acquisition from tape recordings and live tutors in the swamp sparrow, *Melospiza georgiana. Ethology, 77,* 76–84.

Marlow, N., Wolke, D., Bracewell, M. A., & Samara, M. (2005). Neurologic and developmental disability at six years of age after extremely preterm birth. *New England Journal of Medicine, 352,* 9–19.

Marra, C., Ferraccioli, M., & Gainotti, G. (2007). Gender-related dissociations of categorical fluency in normal subjects and in subjects with Alzheimer's disease. *Neuropsychology, 21,* 207.

Marshall, W. A., & Tanner, J. M. (1969). Variations in pattern of pubertal changes in girls. *Archives of Disease in Childhood, 44,* 291–303.

Marshall, W. A., & Tanner, J. M. (1970). Variations in the pattern of pubertal changes in boys. *Archives of Disease in Childhood, 45,* 13–23.

Martin, W. J. (1949). Infant mortality. *British Medical Journal, 1,* 438–441.

Martin, C. L., DiDonato, M. D., Clary, L., Fabes, R. A., Kreiger, T., Palermo, F., et al. (2012). Preschool children with gender normative and gender non-normative peer preferences: Psychosocial and environmental correlates. *Archives of Sexual Behavior, 41,* 831–847.

Martin, C. L., & Fabes, R. A. (2001). The stability and consequences of young children's same-sex peer interactions. *Developmental Psychology, 37,* 431–446.

Martinez-Padilla, J., Vergara, P., Perez-Rodriguez, L., Mougeot, F., Casas, F., Ludwig, S. C., et al. (2011). Condition- and parasite-dependent expression of a male-like trait in a female bird. *Biology Letters*, *7*, 364–367.

Martorell, R., Leslie, J., & Moock, P. R. (1984). Characteristics and determinants of child nutritional status in Nepal. *American Journal of Clinical Nutrition*, *39*, 74–86.

Martorell, R., Yarbrough, C., Lechtig, A., Habicht, J. P., & Klein, R. E. (1975). Diarrheal diseases and growth retardation in preschool Guatemalan children. *American Journal of Physical Anthropology*, *43*, 341–346.

Marty, J. S., Higham, J. P., Gadsby, E. L., & Ross, C. (2009). Dominance, coloration, and social and sexual behavior in male drills *Mandrillus leucophaeus*. *International Journal of Primatology*, *30*, 807–823.

Mathiesen, T., Ellingsen, D. G., & Kjuus, H. (1999). Neuropsychological effects associated with exposure to mercury vapor among former chloralkali workers. *Scandinavian Journal of Work, Environment & Health*, *25*, 342–350.

Matthews, M. H. (1992). *Making sense of place: Children's understanding of large-scale environments*. Savage, MD: Barnes & Noble Books.

Maynard Smith, J., & Price, G. R. (1973). The logic of animal conflict. *Nature*, *246*, 15–18.

McCarron, P., Okasha, M., McEwen, J., & Smith, G. D. (2002). Height in young adulthood and risk of death from cardiorespiratory disease: A prospective study of male former students of Glasgow University, Scotland. *American Journal of Epidemiology*, *155*, 683–687.

McCarty, J. P., & Secord, A. L. (2000). Possible effects of PCB contamination on female plumage color and reproductive success in Hudson River Tree Swallows. *Auk*, *117*, 987–995.

McClure, E. B. (2000). A meta-analytic review of sex differences in facial expression processing and their development in infants, children, and adolescents. *Psychological Bulletin*, *126*, 424–453.

McCrory, E. J., De Brito, S. A., Sebastian, C. L., Mechelli, A., Bird, G., Kelly, P. A., et al. (2011). Heightened neural reactivity to threat in child victims of family violence. *Current Biology*, *21*, R947–R948.

McGarvey, S. T., Aligui, G., Daniel, B. L., Peters, P., Olveda, R., & Olds, G. R. (1992). Child growth and schistosomiasis japonica in northeastern Leyte, The Philippines: Cross sectional results. *American Journal of Tropical Medicine and Hygiene*, *46*, 571–581.

McGlone, J. (1980). Sex differences in human brain asymmetry: A critical survey. *Behavioral and Brain Sciences*, *3*, 215–263.

McGlothlin, J. W., Duffy, D. L., Henry-Freeman, J. L., & Ketterson, E. D. (2007). Diet quality affects an attractive white plumage pattern in dark-eyed juncos (*Junco hyemalis*). *Behavioral Ecology and Sociobiology*, *61*, 1391–1399.

McGraw, K. (2006a). Mechanics of carotenoid-based coloration. In G. E. Hill & K. McGraw (Eds.), *Bird coloration: Mechanisms and measurements: Vol. 1.* (pp. 177–242). Cambridge, MA: Harvard University Press.

McGraw, K. (2006b). Mechanics of melanin-based coloration. In G. E. Hill, & K. McGraw (Eds.), *Bird coloration: Mechanisms and measurements: Vol. 1.* (pp. 243–294). Cambridge, MA: Harvard University Press.

McGraw, K. J., & Hill, G. E. (2000). Differential effects of endoparasitism on the expression of carotenoid- and melanin-based ornamental coloration. *Proceedings of the Royal Society of London B*, *267*, 1525–1531.

McGraw, K. J., Hill, G. E., & Parker, R. S. (2005). The physiological costs of being colourful: Nutritional control of carotenoid utilization in the American goldfinch, *Carduelis tristis*. *Animal Behaviour*, *69*, 653–660.

McGraw, K. J., Mackillop, E. A., Dale, J., & Hauber, M. E. (2002). Different colors reveal different information: How nutritional stress affects the expression of melanin- and structurally based ornamental plumage. *Journal of Experimental Biology, 205,* 3747–3755.

McGregor, P. K., & Krebs, J. R. (1989). Song learning in adult great tits (*Parus major*): Effects of neighbours. *Behaviour, 108,* 139–159.

McGuigan, K. (2009). Condition dependence varies with mating success in male *Drosophila bunnanda. Journal of Evolutionary Biology, 22,* 1813–1825.

McHenry, H. M. (1992). Body size and proportions in early hominids. *American Journal of Physical Anthropology, 87,* 407–431.

McHenry, H. M. (1994). Behavioral ecological implications of early hominid body size. *Journal of Human Evolution, 27,* 77–87.

McHenry, H. M., & Coffing, K. (2000). *Australopithecus* to *Homo*: Transformations in body and mind. *Annual Review of Anthropology, 29,* 125–146.

McLean, M. J., Bishop, P. J., & Nakagawa, S. (2012). Male quality, signal reliability and female choice: Assessing the expectations of inter-sexual selection. *Journal of Evolutionary Biology, 25,* 1513–1520.

McNally, R. J. (2003). Progress and controversy in the study of posttraumatic stress disorder. *Annual Review of Psychology, 54,* 229–252.

McPherson, S., Back, C., Buckwalter, J. G., & Cummings, J. L. (1999). Gender-related cognitive deficits in Alzheimer's disease. *International Psychogeriatrics, 11,* 117–122.

Meadows, M. G., Roudybush, T. E., & McGraw, K. J. (2012). Dietary protein level affects iridescent coloration in Anna's hummingbirds, *Calypte anna. Journal of Experimental Biology, 215,* 2742–2750.

Meaney, M. J., Dodge, A. M., & Beatty, W. W. (1981). Sex-dependent effects of amygdaloid lesions on the social play of prepubertal rats. *Physiology & Behavior, 26,* 467–472.

Medin, D. L. & Atran, S. (Eds.). (1999). *Folkbiology*. Cambridge, MA: MIT Press/Bradford.

Mehta, C. M., & Strough, J.-N. (2009). Sex segregation in friendships and normative contexts across the life span. *Developmental Review, 29,* 201–220.

Meinz, E. J., & Salthouse, T. A. (1998). Is age kinder to females than to males? *Psychonomic Bulletin & Review, 5,* 56–70.

Mendlewicz, L., Linkowski, P., Bazelmans, C., & Philippot, P. (2005). Decoding emotional facial expressions in depressed and anorexic patients. *Journal of Affective Disorders, 89,* 195–199.

Menken, J., Trussell, J., & Larsen, U. (1986). Age and infertility. *Science, 233,* 1389–1394.

Meunier, J., Gué, M., Récasens, M., & Maurice, T. (2004). Attenuation by a sigma1 ($\sigma$1) receptor agonist of the learning and memory deficits induced by a prenatal restraint stress in juvenile rats. *British Journal of Pharmacology, 142,* 689–700.

Meyer, L. S., & Riley, E. P. (1986). Social play in juvenile rats prenatally exposed to alcohol. *Teratology, 34,* 1–7.

Miettunen, J., Veijola, J., Lauronen, E., Kantojärvi, L., & Joukamaa, M. (2007). Sex differences in Cloninger's temperament dimensions—A meta-analysis. *Comprehensive Psychiatry, 48,* 161–169.

Milinski, M., & Bakker, T. C. (1990). Female sticklebacks use male coloration in mate choice and hence avoid parasitized males. *Nature, 344,* 330–333.

Mills, S. C., Grapputo, A., Jokinen, I., Koskela, E., Mappes, T., & Poikonen, T. (2010). Fitness trade-offs mediated by immunosuppression costs in a small mammal. *Evolution, 64,* 166–179.

Milner, A. D., & Goodale, M. A. (1995). *The visual brain in action.* New York: Oxford University Press.

Milnes, M. R., Bermudez, D. S., Bryan, T. A., Edwards, T. M., Gunderson, M. P., Larkin, I. L., et al. (2006). Contaminant-induced feminization and demasculinization of nonmammalian vertebrate males in aquatic environments. *Environmental Research, 100*, 3–17.

Miodovnik, A., Engel, S. M., Zhu, C., Ye, X., Soorya, L. V., Silva, M. J., et al. (2011). Endocrine disruptors and childhood social impairment. *Neurotoxicology, 32*, 261–267.

Moffat, S. D., Hampson, E., & Hatzipantelis, M. (1998). Navigation in a "virtual" maze: Sex differences and correlation with psychometric measures of spatial ability in humans. *Evolution and Human Behavior, 19*, 73–87.

Møller, A. P. (1991). Sexual selection in the monogamous barn swallow (*Hirundo rustica*). I. Determinants of tail ornament size. *Evolution, 45*, 1823–1836.

Møller, A. P., & Alatalo, R. V. (1999). Good-genes effects in sexual selection. *Proceedings of the Royal Society of London B, 266*, 85–91.

Møller, A. P., Soler, M., & Thornhill, R. (1995). Breast asymmetry, sexual selection, and human reproductive success. *Ethology and Sociobiology, 16*, 207–219.

Monacelli, A. M., Cushman, L. A., Kavcic, V., & Duffy, C. J. (2003). Spatial disorientation in Alzheimer's disease: The remembrance of things passed. *Neurology, 61*, 1491–1497.

Monsch, A. U., Bondi, M. W., Butters, N., Salmon, D. P., Katzman, R., & Thal, L. J. (1992). Comparisons of verbal fluency tasks in the detection of dementia of the Alzheimer type. *Archives of Neurology, 49*, 1253–1258.

Monteith, K. L., Schmitz, L. E., Jenks, J. A., Delger, J. A., & Bowyer, R. T. (2009). Growth of male white-tailed deer: Consequences of maternal effects. *Journal of Mammalogy, 90*, 651–660.

Moreno-Martínez, F. J., Laws, K. R., & Schulz, J. (2008). The impact of dementia, age and sex on category fluency: Greater deficits in women with Alzheimer's disease. *Cortex, 44*, 1256–1264.

Morgan, M. J., Adam, A., & Mollon, J. D. (1992). Dichromats detect colour-camouflaged objects that are not detected by trichromats. *Proceedings of the Royal Society of London B, 248*, 291–295.

Morley Fletcher, S., Rea, M., Maccari, S., & Laviola, G. (2003). Environmental enrichment during adolescence reverses the effects of prenatal stress on play behaviour and HPA axis reactivity in rats. *European Journal of Neuroscience, 18*, 3367–3374.

Morrow, L. A., Ryan, C. M., Goldstein, G., & Hodgson, M. J. (1989). A distinct pattern of personality disturbance following exposure to mixtures of organic solvents. *Journal of Occupational and Environmental Medicine, 31*, 743–746.

Morrow, L. A., Steinhauer, S. R., Condray, R., & Hodgson, M. (1997). Neuropsychological performance of journeymen painters under acute solvent exposure and exposure-free conditions. *Journal of the International Neuropsychological Society, 3*, 269–275.

Moshkin, M., Litvinova, N., Litvinova, E. A., Bedareva, A., Lutsyuk, A., & Gerlinskaya, L. (2012). Scent recognition of infected status in humans. *Journal of Sexual Medicine, 9*, 3211–3218.

Mougeot, F., Irvine, J. R., Seivwright, L., Redpath, S. M., & Piertney, S. (2004). Testosterone, immunocompetence, and honest sexual signaling in male red grouse. *Behavioral Ecology, 15*, 930–937.

Mougeot, F., Redpath, S. M., & Piertney, S. B. (2006). Elevated spring testosterone increases parasite intensity in male red grouse. *Behavioral Ecology, 17*, 117–125.

Mougeot, F., Redpath, S. M., Piertney, S. B., & Hudson, P. J. (2005). Separating behavioral and physiological mechanisms in testosterone-mediated trade-offs. *American Naturalist, 166*, 158–168.

Mountjoy, J. D., & Lemon, R. E. (1995). Extended song learning in wild European starlings. *Animal Behaviour, 49*, 357–366.

Mueller, U., & Mazur, A. (1997). Facial dominance in *Homo sapiens* as honest signaling of male quality. *Behavioral Ecology, 8*, 569–579.

Muller, H. J. (1950). Our load of mutations. *American Journal of Human Genetics, 2*, 111–176.

Müller, I., Coulibaly, J. T., Fürst, T., Knopp, S., Hattendorf, J., Krauth, S. J., et al. (2011). Effect of schistosomiasis and soil-transmitted helminth infections on physical fitness of school children in Côte d'Ivoire. *PLoS Neglected Tropical Diseases, 5*, e1239.

Muller, M. N., Thompson, M. E., & Wrangham, R. W. (2006). Male chimpanzees prefer mating with old females. *Current Biology, 16*, 2234–2238.

Müller, W., Vergauwen, J., & Eens, M. (2010). Testing the developmental stress hypothesis in canaries: Consequences of nutritional stress on adult song phenotype and mate attractiveness. *Behavioral Ecology and Sociobiology, 64*, 1767–1777.

Mupfasoni, D., Karibushi, B., Koukounari, A., Ruberanziza, E., Kaberuka, T., Kramer, M. H., et al. (2009). Polyparasite helminth infections and their association to anaemia and undernutrition in Northern Rwanda. *PLoS Neglected Tropical Diseases, 3*, e517.

Murdock, G. P. (1981). *Atlas of world cultures*. Pittsburgh, PA: University of Pittsburgh Press.

Murphy, T. G., Rosenthal, M. F., Montgomerie, R., & Tarvin, K. A. (2009). Female American goldfinches use carotenoid-based bill coloration to signal status. *Behavioral Ecology, 20*, 1348–1355.

Mykytowycz, R. (1965). Further observations on the territorial function and histology of the submandibular cutaneous (chin) glands in the rabbit, *Oryctolagus cuniculus*. *Animal Behaviour, 13*, 400–412.

Naguib, M., & Nemitz, A. (2007). Living with the past: Nutritional stress in juvenile males has immediate effects on their plumage ornaments and on adult attractiveness in zebra finches. *PLoS ONE, 2*, e901.

Neel, J. V., Schull, W. J., Yamamoto, M.A.N.A.B.U., Uchida, S., Yanase, T., & Fujiki, N. (1970). The effects of parental consanguinity and inbreeding in Hirado, Japan. II. Physical development, tapping rate, blood pressure, intelligence quotient, and school performance. *American Journal of Human Genetics, 22*, 263–286.

Nelson, E. C., Heath, A. C., Madden, P. A., Cooper, M. L., Dinwiddie, S. H., Bucholz, K. K., et al. (2002). Association between self-reported childhood sexual abuse and adverse psychosocial outcomes: Results from a twin study. *Archives of General Psychiatry, 59*, 139–145.

Nelson, C. J., Lee, J. S., Gamboa, M. C., & Roth, A. J. (2008). Cognitive effects of hormone therapy in men with prostate cancer. *Cancer, 113*, 1097–1106.

Nesse, R. M., & Williams, G. C. (1996). *Why we get sick: The new science of Darwinian medicine*. New York: Random House.

Nettle, D. (2002). Height and reproductive success in a cohort of British men. *Human Nature, 13*, 473–491.

Neufang, S., Specht, K., Hausmann, M., Güntürkün, O., Herpertz-Dahlmann, R., Fink, G. R., et al. (2009). Sex differences in the impact of steroid hormones on the developing human brain. *Cerebral Cortex, 19*, 463–473.

Neylan, T. C., Schuff, N., Lenoci, M., Yehuda, R., Weiner, M. W., & Marmar, C. R. (2003). Cortisol levels are positively correlated with hippocampal $N$-acetylaspartate. *Biological Psychiatry, 54*, 1118–1121.

Nicholson, J. S., Buchanan, K. L., Marshall, R. C., & Catchpole, C. K. (2007). Song sharing and repertoire size in the sedge warbler, *Acrocephalus schoenobaenus*: Changes within and between years. *Animal Behaviour, 74*, 1585–1592.

Nicoletto, P. F. (1991). The relationship between male ornamentation and swimming performance in the guppy, *Poecilia reticulata*. *Behavioral Ecology and Sociobiology, 28*, 365–370.

Nicoletto, P. F. (1993). Female sexual response to condition-dependent ornaments in the guppy, *Poecilia reticulata*. *Animal Behaviour, 46*, 441–450.

Nicoletto, P. F. (1995). Offspring quality and female choice in the guppy, *Poecilia reticulata*. *Animal Behaviour*, *49*, 377–387.

Nicoletto, P. F., & Kodric-Brown, A. (1999). The relationship among swimming performance, courtship behavior, and carotenoid pigmentation of guppies in four rivers of Trinidad. *Environmental Biology of Fishes*, *55*, 227–235.

Nilson, L. N., Sällsten, G., Hagberg, S., Bäckman, L., & Barregård, L. (2002). Influence of solvent exposure and aging on cognitive functioning: An 18 year follow up of formerly exposed floor layers and their controls. *Occupational and Environmental Medicine*, *59*, 49–57.

Nishio, H., Kasuga, S., Ushijima, M., & Harada, Y. (2001). Prenatal stress and postnatal development of neonatal rats—Sex-dependent effects on emotional behavior and learning ability of neonatal rats. *International Journal of Developmental Neuroscience*, *19*, 37–45.

Nishizuka, M., & Arai, Y. (1981). Sexual dimorphism in synaptic organization in the amygdala and its dependence on neonatal hormone environment. *Brain Research*, *212*, 31–38.

Nokes, C., Grantham-McGregor, S. M., Sawyer, A. W., Cooper, E. S., & Bundy, D. A. P. (1992). Parasitic helminth infection and cognitive function in school children. *Proceedings of the Royal Society of London B*, *247*, 77–81.

Nolen-Hoeksema, S. (1987). Sex differences in unipolar depression: Evidence and theory. *Psychological Bulletin*, *101*, 259–282.

Nottebohm, F. (1970). Ontogeny of bird song. *Science*, *167*, 950–956.

Nottebohm, F. (1971). Neural lateralization of vocal control in a passerine bird. I. Song. *Journal of Experimental Zoology*, *177*, 229–261.

Nottebohm, F. (1972). Neural lateralization of vocal control in a passerine bird. II. Subsong, calls, and a theory of vocal learning. *Journal of Experimental Zoology*, *179*, 35–49.

Nottebohm, F. (1980). Testosterone triggers growth of brain vocal control nuclei in adult female canaries. *Brain Research*, *189*, 429–436.

Nottebohm, F. (1981). A brain for all seasons: Cyclical anatomical changes in song-control nuclei of the canary brain. *Science*, *214*, 1368–1370.

Nottebohm, F. (2005). The neural basis of birdsong. *PLoS Biology*, *3*, e164.

Nottebohm, F., & Arnold, A. P. (1976). Sexual dimorphism in vocal control areas of the songbird brain. *Science*, *194*, 211–213.

Nottebohm, F., Nottebohm, M. E., Crane, L. A., & Wingfield, J. C. (1987). Seasonal changes in gonadal hormone levels of adult male canaries and their relation to song. *Behavioral and Neural Biology*, *47*, 197–211.

Nowicki, S., Peters, S., & Podos, J. (1998). Song learning, early nutrition and sexual selection in songbirds. *American Zoologist*, *38*, 179–190.

Nowicki, S., Searcy, W. A., & Peters, S. (2002). Brain development, song learning and mate choice in birds: A review and experimental test of the "nutritional stress hypothesis". *Journal of Comparative Physiology A*, *188*, 1003–1014.

O'Keefe, J., & Nadel, L. (1978). *The hippocampus as a cognitive map*. New York: Oxford University Press.

O'Leary, T. P., Savoie, V., & Brown, R. E. (2011). Learning, memory and search strategies of inbred mouse strains with different visual abilities in the Barnes maze. *Behavioural Brain Research*, *216*, 531–542.

Obert, P., Fellmann, N., Falgairette, G., Bedu, M., Van Praagh, E., Kemper, H., et al. (1994). The importance of socioeconomic and nutritional conditions rather than altitude on the physical growth of prepubertal Andean highland boys. *Annals of Human Biology*, *21*, 145–154.

Ohlsson, T., Smith, H. G., Råberg, L., & Hasselquist, D. (2002). Pheasant sexual ornaments reflect nutritional conditions during early growth. *Proceedings of the Royal Society of London B*, *269*, 21–27.

Öhman, A. (2002). Automaticity and the amygdala: Nonconscious responses to emotional faces. *Current Directions in Psychological Science, 11,* 62–66.

Oldershaw, A., Hambrook, D., Tchanturia, K., Treasure, J., & Schmidt, U. (2010). Emotional theory of mind and emotional awareness in recovered anorexia nervosa patients. *Psychosomatic Medicine, 72,* 73–79.

Oler, J. A., Fox, A. S., Shelton, S. E., Rogers, J., Dyer, T. D., Davidson, R. J., et al. (2010). Amygdalar and hippocampal substrates of anxious temperament differ in their heritability. *Nature, 466,* 864–868.

Olsson, M. J., Lundström, J. N., Kimball, B. A., Gordon, A. R., Karshikoff, B., Hosseini, N., et al. (2014). The scent of disease human body odor contains an early chemosensory cue of sickness. *Psychological Science, 25,* 817–823.

Ölveczky, B. P., Andalman, A. S., & Fee, M. S. (2005). Vocal experimentation in the juvenile songbird requires a basal ganglia circuit. *PLoS Biology, 3,* e153.

Olveda, R. M., Daniel, B. L., Ramirez, B. D., Aligui, G. D., Acosta, L. P., Fevidal, P., et al. (1996). *Schistosomiasis japonica* in the Philippines: The long-term impact of population-based chemotherapy on infection, transmission, and morbidity. *Journal of Infectious Diseases, 174,* 163–172.

Omariba, D., & Boyle, M. H. (2007). Family structure and child mortality in sub-Saharan Africa: Cross-national effects of polygyny. *Journal of Marriage and Family, 69,* 528–543.

Orledge, J. M., Blount, J. D., Hoodless, A. N., & Royle, N. J. (2012). Antioxidant supplementation during early development reduces parasite load but does not affect sexual ornament expression in adult ring-necked pheasants. *Functional Ecology, 26,* 688–700.

Ormerod, B. K., & Galea, L. A. M. (2001). Reproductive status influences cell proliferation and cell survival in the dentate gyrus of adult female meadow voles: A possible regulatory role for estradiol. *Neuroscience, 102,* 369–379.

Ormerod, B. K., & Galea, L. A. M. (2003). Reproductive status influences the survival of new cells in the dentate gyrus of adult male meadow voles. *Neuroscience Letters, 346,* 25–28.

Ormerod, B. K., Lee, T. Y., & Galea, L. A. M. (2004). Estradiol enhances neurogenesis in the dentate gyri of adult male meadow voles by increasing the survival of young granule neurons. *Neuroscience, 128,* 645–654.

Owens, I. P., & Short, R. V. (1995). Hormonal basis of sexual dimorphism in birds: Implications for new theories of sexual selection. *Trends in Ecology & Evolution, 10,* 44–47.

Özener, B. (2010). Effect of inbreeding depression on growth and fluctuating asymmetry in Turkish young males. *American Journal of Human Biology, 22,* 557–562.

Paczolt, K. A., & Jones, A. G. (2010). Post-copulatory sexual selection and sexual conflict in the evolution of male pregnancy. *Nature, 464,* 401–404.

Padgett, D. A., & Glaser, R. (2003). How stress influences the immune response. *Trends in Immunology, 24,* 444–448.

Paganini-Hill, A., & Clark, L. J. (2000). Preliminary assessment of cognitive function in breast cancer patients treated with tamoxifen. *Breast Cancer Research and Treatment, 64,* 165–176.

Palanza, P., Gioiosa, L., vom Saal, F. S., & Parmigiani, S. (2008). Effects of developmental exposure to bisphenol A on brain and behavior in mice. *Environmental Research, 108,* 150–157.

Palanza, P., Morellini, F., Parmigiani, S., & vom Saal, F. S. (1999). Prenatal exposure to endocrine disrupting chemicals: Effects on behavioral development. *Neuroscience & Biobehavioral Reviews, 23,* 1011–1027.

Panhuis, T. M., & Wilkinson, G. S. (1999). Exaggerated male eye span influences contest outcome in stalk-eyed flies (*Diopsidae*). *Behavioral Ecology and Sociobiology, 46,* 221–227.

Parker, J. G., & Asher, S. R. (1993). Friendship and friendship quality in middle childhood: Links with peer group acceptance and feelings of loneliness and social dissatisfaction. *Developmental Psychology, 29,* 611–621.

Parker, J. G., & Herrera, C. (1996). Interpersonal processes in friendship: A comparison of abused and nonabused children's experiences. *Developmental Psychology, 32,* 1025–1038.

Parker, J. G., Low, C. M., Walker, A. R., & Gamm, B. K. (2005). Friendship jealousy in young adolescents: Individual differences and links to sex, self-esteem, aggression, and social adjustment. *Developmental Psychology, 41,* 235–250.

Parker, J. G., & Seal, J. (1996). Forming, losing, renewing, and replacing friendships: Applying temporal parameters to the assessment of children's friendship experiences. *Child Development, 67,* 2248–2268.

Parker, G. A., & Simmons, L. W. (1996). Parental investment and the control of selection: Predicting the direction of sexual competition. *Proceedings of the Royal Society of London B, 263,* 315–321.

Parraga, I. M., Assis, A. M. O., Prado, M. S., Barreto, M. L., Reis, M. G., King, C. H., et al. (1996). Gender differences in growth of school-aged children with schistosomiasis and geohelminth infection. *American Journal of Tropical Medicine and Hygiene, 55,* 150–156.

Pasterski, V., Geffner, M. E., Brain, C., Hindmarsh, P., Brook, C., & Hines, M. (2011). Prenatal hormones and childhood sex segregation: Playmate and play style preferences in girls with congenital adrenal hyperplasia. *Hormones and Behavior, 59,* 549–555.

Pavić, L., Gregurek, R., Radoš, M., Brkljačić, B., Brajković, L., Šimetin-Pavić, I., et al. (2007). Smaller right hippocampus in war veterans with posttraumatic stress disorder. *Psychiatry Research: Neuroimaging, 154,* 191–198.

Pawlowski, B., & Dunbar, R. I. M. (2005). Waist-to-hip ratio versus body mass index as predictors of fitness in women. *Human Nature, 16,* 164–177.

Pearson, N. C. S. (2009). *Advanced clinical solutions for WAIS-IV and WMS-IV: Administration and scoring manual.* San Antonio: The Psychological Corporation.

Pedersen, J. M., Glickman, S. E., Frank, L. G., & Beach, F. A. (1990). Sex differences in the play behavior of immature spotted hyenas, *Crocuta crocuta. Hormones and Behavior, 24,* 403–420.

Pellegrini, A. D. (1995). Boys' rough-and-tumble play and social competence: Contemporaneous and longitudinal relations. In A. D. Pellegrini (Ed.), *The future of play theory: A multidisciplinary inquiry into the contributions of Brian Sutton-Smith* (pp. 107–126). Albany: State University of New York Press.

Pellegrini, A. D., & Bartini, M. (2001). Dominance in early adolescent boys: Affiliative and aggressive dimensions and possible functions. *Merrill-Palmer Quarterly, 47,* 142–163.

Pellegrini, A. D., & Smith, P. K. (1998). Physical activity play: The nature and function of a neglected aspect of play. *Child Development, 69,* 577–598.

Peluso, M. E., Munnia, A., & Ceppi, M. (2014). Bisphenol-A exposures and behavioural aberrations: Median and linear spline and meta-regression analyses of 12 toxicity studies in rodents. *Toxicology, 325,* 200–208.

Peng, G., Hakim, M., Broza, Y. Y., Billan, S., Abdah-Bortnyak, R., Kuten, A., et al. (2010). Detection of lung, breast, colorectal, and prostate cancers from exhaled breath using a single array of nanosensors. *British Journal of Cancer, 103,* 542–551.

Penn, D. J., Oberzaucher, E., Grammer, K., Fischer, G., Soini, H. A., Wiesler, D., et al. (2007). Individual and gender fingerprints in human body odour. *Journal of the Royal Society Interface, 4,* 331–340.

Penton-Voak, I. S., & Chen, J. Y. (2004). High salivary testosterone is linked to masculine male facial appearance in humans. *Evolution and Human Behavior, 25,* 229–241.

Perdue, B. M., Snyder, R. J., Zhihe, Z., Marr, M. J., & Maple, T. L. (2011). Sex differences in spatial ability: A test of the range size hypothesis in the order Carnivora. *Biology Letters, 7,* 380–383.

Perera, F., Vishnevetsky, J., Herbstman, J. B., Calafat, A. M., Xiong, W., Rauh, V., et al. (2012). Prenatal bisphenol A exposure and child behavior in an inner-city cohort. *Environmental Health Perspectives, 120*, 1190–1194.

Pérez, C., Lores, M., & Velando, A. (2010). Oil pollution increases plasma antioxidants but reduces coloration in a seabird. *Oecologia, 163*, 875–884.

Pesonen, A. K., Räikkönen, K., Heinonen, K., Kajantie, E., Forsén, T., & Eriksson, J. G. (2007). Depressive symptoms in adults separated from their parents as children: A natural experiment during World War II. *American Journal of Epidemiology, 166*, 1126–1133.

Pesonen, A. K., Räikkönen, K., Kajantie, E., Heinonen, K., Henriksson, M., Leskinen, J., et al. (2011). Intellectual ability in young men separated temporarily from their parents in childhood. *Intelligence, 39*, 335–341.

Peters, M. (1997). Gender differences in intercepting a moving target. *Journal of Motor Behavior, 29*, 290–296.

Peters, A., Delhey, K., Andersson, S., Van Noordwijk, H., & Förschler, M. I. (2008). Condition-dependence of multiple carotenoid-based plumage traits: An experimental study. *Functional Ecology, 22*, 831–839.

Peters, A., Kurvers, R.H.J.M., Roberts, M. L., & Delhey, K. (2011). No evidence for general condition-dependence of structural plumage colour in blue tits: An experiment. *Journal of Evolutionary Biology, 24*, 976–987.

Peters, M., Laeng, B., Latham, K., Jackson, M., Zaiyouna, R., & Richardson, C. (1995). A redrawn Vandenberg and Kuse mental rotations test-different versions and factors that affect performance. *Brain and Cognition, 28*, 39–58.

Peters, M., Lehmann, W., Takahira, S., Takeuchi, Y., & Jordan, K. (2006). Mental rotation test performance in four cross-cultural samples ($n = 3367$): Overall sex differences and the role of academic program in performance. *Cortex, 42*, 1005–1014.

Peters, S., Searcy, W. A., & Nowicki, S. (2014). Developmental stress, song-learning, and cognition. *Integrative and Comparative Biology, 54*, 555–567, icu020.

Petrie, M. (1994). Improved growth and survival of offspring of peacocks with more elaborate trains. *Nature, 371*, 598–599.

Petrie, M., Halliday, T., & Sanders, C. (1991). Peahens prefer peacocks with elaborate trains. *Animal Behavior, 41*, 323–331.

Petrinovich, L., & Baptista, L. F. (1987). Song development in the white crowned sparrow: Modification of learned song. *Animal Behaviour, 35*, 961–974.

Pfefferle, D., West, P. M., Grinnell, J., Packer, C., & Fischer, J. (2007). Do acoustic features of lion, *Panthera leo*, roars reflect sex and male condition? *Journal of the Acoustical Society of America, 121*, 3947–3953.

Pheasant, S. T. (1983). Sex differences in strength – Some observations on their variability. *Applied Ergonomics, 14*, 205–211.

Phillips, M., Gleeson, K., Hughes, J. M. B., Greenberg, J., Cataneo, R. N., Baker, L., et al. (1999). Volatile organic compounds in breath as markers of lung cancer: A cross-sectional study. *Lancet, 353*, 1930–1933.

Pinker, S. (1994). *The language instinct*. New York: William Morrow.

Pinker, S. (2011). *The better angels of our nature: The decline of violence in history and its causes*. UK: Penguin.

Pitcher, E. G., & Schultz, L. H. (1983). *Boys and girls at play: The development of sex roles*. South Hadley, MA: Bergin & Garvey Publishers.

Pizzari, T., Cornwallis, C. K., Løvlie, H., Jakobsson, S., & Birkhead, T. R. (2003). Sophisticated sperm allocation in male fowl. *Nature, 426*, 70–74.

Plavcan, J. M., & van Schaik, C. P. (1997). Intrasexual competition and body weight dimorphism in anthropoid primates. *American Journal of Physical Anthropology, 103*, 37–68.

Plavcan, J. M., van Schaik, C. P., & Kappeler, P. M. (1995). Competition, coalitions and canine size in primates. *Journal of Human Evolution, 28*, 245–276.

Pölkki, M., Krams, I., Kangassalo, K., & Rantala, M. J. (2012). Inbreeding affects sexual signalling in males but not females of *Tenebrio molitor*. *Biology Letters, 8*, 423–425.

Pollatos, O., Herbert, B. M., Schandry, R., & Gramann, K. (2008). Impaired central processing of emotional faces in anorexia nervosa. *Psychosomatic Medicine, 70*, 701–708.

Pomiankowski, A., & Møller, A. P. (1995). A resolution of the lek paradox. *Proceedings of the Royal Society of London B, 260*, 21–29.

Poole, J. H. (1987). Rutting behavior in African elephants: The phenomenon of musth. *Behaviour, 102*, 283–316.

Poole, J. H. (1989). Announcing intent: The aggressive state of musth in African elephants. *Animal Behaviour, 37*, 140–152.

Poole, J. H., & Moss, C. J. (1981). Musth in the African elephant, *Loxodonta africana*. *Nature, 292*, 830–831.

Posner, M. I. (1994). Attention: The mechanisms of consciousness. *Proceedings of the National Academy of Sciences of the United States of America, 91*, 7398–7403.

Power, T. G. (2000). *Play and exploration in children and animals*. Mahwah, NJ: Erlbaum.

Prasad, A. S. (1985). Clinical manifestations of zinc deficiency. *Annual Review of Nutrition, 5*, 341–363.

Prasad, A. S., & Cossack, Z. T. (1984). Zinc supplementation and growth in sickle cell disease. *Annals of Internal Medicine, 100*, 367–371.

Pravosudov, V. V., Lavenex, P., & Omanska, A. (2005). Nutritional deficits during early development affect hippocampal structure and spatial memory later in life. *Behavioral Neuroscience, 119*, 1368–1374.

Prentice, A. M., Ward, K. A., Goldberg, G. R., Jarjou, L. M., Moore, S. E., Fulford, A. J., et al. (2013). Critical windows for nutritional interventions against stunting. *American Journal of Clinical Nutrition, 97*, 911–918.

Preston, B. T., Stevenson, I. R., Pemberton, J. M., Coltman, D. W., & Wilson, K. (2003). Overt and covert competition in a promiscuous mammal: The importance of weaponry and testes size to male reproductive success. *Proceedings of the Royal Society of London B, 270*, 633–640.

Preston, B. T., Stevenson, I. R., Pemberton, J. M., & Wilson, K. (2001). Dominant rams lose out by sperm depletion. *Nature, 409*, 681–682.

Price, P. H. (1979). Developmental determinants of structure in zebra finch song. *Journal of Comparative and Physiological Psychology, 93*, 260–277.

Price, M. E., Dunn, J., Hopkins, S., & Kang, J. (2012). Anthropometric correlates of human anger. *Evolution and Human Behavior, 33*, 174–181.

Price, J., Sloman, L., Gardner, R., Gilbert, P., & Rohde, P. (1994). The social competition hypothesis of depression. *British Journal of Psychiatry, 164*, 309–315.

Price, A. C., Weadick, C. J., Shim, J., & Rodd, F. H. (2008). Pigments, patterns, and fish behavior. *Zebrafish, 5*, 297–307.

Prista, A., Maia, J. A. R., Damasceno, A., & Beunen, G. (2003). Anthropometric indicators of nutritional status: Implications for fitness, activity, and health in school-age children and adolescents from Maputo, Mozambique. *American Journal of Clinical Nutrition, 77*, 952–959.

Prokop, Z. M., Leś, J. E., Banaś, P. K., Koteja, P., & Radwan, J. (2010). Low inbreeding depression in a sexual trait in the stalk-eyed fly *Teleopsis dalmanni*. *Evolutionary Ecology, 24*, 827–837.

Pruett-Jones, S., & Pruett-Jones, M. (1994). Sexual competition and courtship disruptions: Why do male bowerbirds destroy each other's bowers? *Animal Behaviour, 47*, 607–620.

Prum, R. O. (2006). Anatomy, physics, and evolution of structural colors. In G. E. Hill, & K. Mc-Graw (Eds.), *Bird coloration: Mechanisms and measurements: Vol. 1.* (pp. 295–353). Cambridge: Harvard University Press.

Prum, R. O., & Torres, R. H. (2004). Structural colouration of mammalian skin: Convergent evolution of coherently scattering dermal collagen arrays. *Journal of Experimental Biology, 207*, 2157–2172.

Pryce, C. R. (1993). The regulation of maternal behaviour in marmosets and tamarins. *Behavioural Processes, 30*, 201–224.

Punzalan, D., Cooray, M., Helen Rodd, F., & Rowe, L. (2008). Condition dependence of sexually dimorphic colouration and longevity in the ambush bug *Phymata americana. Journal of Evolutionary Biology, 21*, 1297–1306.

Purcell, S. (2002). Variance components models for gene–environment interaction in twin analysis. *Twin Research, 5*, 554–571.

Puts, D. A., Apicella, C. L., & Cárdenas, R. A. (2012). Masculine voices signal men's threat potential in forager and industrial societies. *Proceedings of the Royal Society of London B, 279*, 601–609.

Puts, D. A., Cárdenas, R. A., Bailey, D. H., Burriss, R. P., Jordan, C. L., & Breedlove, S. M. (2010). Salivary testosterone does not predict mental rotation performance in men or women. *Hormones and Behavior, 58*, 282–289.

Puts, D. A., Jones, B. C., & DeBruine, L. M. (2012). Sexual selection on human faces and voices. *Journal of Sex Research, 49*, 227–243.

Puts, D. A., McDaniel, M. A., Jordan, C. L., & Breedlove, S. M. (2008). Spatial ability and prenatal androgens: Meta-analyses of congenital adrenal hyperplasia and digit ratio (2D:4D) studies. *Archives of Sexual Behavior, 37*, 100–111.

Queller, D. C. (1997). Why do females care more than males? *Proceedings of the Royal Society of London B, 264*, 1555–1557.

Qvarnstrom, A. (1999). Genotype-by-environment interactions in the determination of the size of a secondary sexual character in the collared flycatcher (*Ficedula albicollis*). *Evolution, 53*, 1564–1572.

Rabinak, C. A., Angstadt, M., Welsh, R. C., Kenndy, A. E., Lyubkin, M., Martis, B., et al. (2011). Altered amygdala resting-state functional connectivity in post-traumatic stress disorder. *Frontiers in Psychiatry, 2*, 62.

Räikkönen, K., Pesonen, A. K., Roseboom, T. J., & Eriksson, J. G. (2012). Early determinants of mental health. *Best Practice & Research Clinical Endocrinology & Metabolism, 26*, 599–611.

Raisman, G., & Field, P. M. (1973). Sexual dimorphism in the neurophil of the preoptic area of the rat and its dependence on neonatal androgen. *Brain Research, 54*, 1–29.

Ralls, K. (1971). Mammalian scent marking. *Science, 171*, 443–449.

Ralls, K., Ballou, J. D., & Templeton, A. (1988). Estimates of lethal equivalents and the cost of inbreeding in mammals. *Conservation Biology, 2*, 185–193.

Rantala, M. J., Honkavaara, J., Dunn, D. W., & Suhonen, J. (2011). Predation selects for increased immune function in male damselflies, *Calopteryx splendens. Proceedings of the Royal Society of London B, 278*, 1231–1238.

Rantala, M. J., Jokinen, I., Kortet, R., Vainikka, A., & Suhonen, J. (2002). Do pheromones reveal male immunocompetence? *Proceedings of the Royal Society of London B, 269*, 1681–1685.

Rantala, M. J., Kortet, R., Kotiaho, J. S., Vainikka, A., & Suhonen, J. (2003). Condition dependence of pheromones and immune function in the grain beetle *Tenebrio molitor. Functional Ecology, 17*, 534–540.

Rantala, M. J., Koskimïki, J., Taskinen, J., Tynkkynen, K., & Suhonen, J. (2000). Immunocompetence, developmental stability and wingspot size in the damselfly *Calopteryx splendens* L. *Proceedings of the Royal Society of London B, 267*, 2453–2457.

Raskin, E., & Witkin, H. A. (1971). *Group embedded figures test*. Palo Alto, CA: Consulting Psychologists Press.

Raveh, S., Sutalo, S., Thonhauser, K. E., Thoß, M., Hettyey, A., Winkelser, F., et al. (2014). Female partner preferences enhance offspring ability to survive an infection. *BMC Evolutionary Biology, 14*, e14.

Raven, J. C., Court, J. H., & Raven, J. (1993). *Manual for Raven's Progressive Matrices and Vocabulary Scales*. London: H. K. Lewis & Co.

Read, J. S., Troendle, J. F., & Klebanoff, M. A. (1997). Infectious disease mortality among infants in the United States, 1983 through 1987. *American Journal of Public Health, 87*, 192–198.

Reby, D., & McComb, K. (2003). Anatomical constraints generate honesty: Acoustic cues to age and weight in the roars of red deer stags. *Animal Behaviour, 65*, 519–530.

Reed, L. I., DeScioli, P., & Pinker, S. A. (2014). The commitment function of angry facial expressions. *Psychological Science, 25*, 1511–1517.

Rehnman, J., & Herlitz, A. (2006). Higher face recognition ability in girls: Magnified by own-sex and own-ethnicity bias. *Memory, 14*, 289–296.

Rehnman, J., & Herlitz, A. (2007). Women remember more faces than men do. *Acta Psychologica, 124*, 344–355.

Reiches, M. W., Moore, S. E., Prentice, A. M., Prentice, A., Sawo, Y., & Ellison, P. T. (2013). The adolescent transition under energetic stress: Body composition tradeoffs among adolescent women in The Gambia. *Evolution, Medicine, and Public Health, 2013*, 75–85.

Reid, J., Arcese, P., Cassidy, A. E., Marr, A., Smith, J. M., & Keller, L. (2005). Hamilton and Zuk meet heterozygosity? Song repertoire size indicates inbreeding and immunity in song sparrows (*Melospiza melodia*). *Proceedings of the Royal Society of London B, 272*, 481–487.

Reinisch, J. M., & Sanders, S. A. (1992). Effects of prenatal exposure to diethylstilbestrol (DES) on hemispheric laterality and spatial ability in human males. *Hormones and Behavior, 26*, 62–75.

Reis, O., Dörnte, M., & von der Lippe, H. (2011). Neuroticism, social support, and the timing of first parenthood: A prospective study. *Personality and Individual Differences, 50*, 381–386.

Rendall, D., Kollias, S., Ney, C., & Lloyd, P. (2005). Pitch (F) and formant profiles of human vowels and vowel-like baboon grunts: The role of vocalizer body size and voice-acoustic allometry. *Journal of the Acoustical Society of America, 117*, 944–955.

Reynolds, J. D. (1987). Mating system and nesting biology of the Red-necked Phalarope *Phalaropus lobatus*: What constrains polyandry? *Isis, 129*, 225–242.

Reynolds, S. M., Dryer, K., Bollback, J., Uy, J. A. C., Patricelli, G. L., Robson, T., et al. (2007). Behavioral paternity predicts genetic paternity in satin bowerbirds (*Ptilonorhynchus violaceus*), a species with a non-resource-based mating system. *Auk, 124*, 857–867.

Reznick, D. N., Shaw, F. H., Rodd, F. H., & Shaw, R. G. (1997). Evaluation of the rate of evolution in natural populations of guppies (*Poecilia reticulata*). *Science, 275*, 1934–1937.

Rhodes, M., Akohoue, S. A., Shankar, S. M., Fleming, I., Qi An, A., Yu, C., et al. (2009). Growth patterns in children with sickle cell anemia during puberty. *Pediatric Blood & Cancer, 53*, 635–641.

Ribble, D. O. (1992). Lifetime reproductive success and its correlates in the monogamous rodent, *Peromyscus californicus*. *Journal of Animal Ecology, 61*, 457–468.

Ribble, D. O., & Salvioni, M. (1990). Social organization and nest co-occupancy in *Peromyscus californicus*, a monogamous rodent. *Behavioral Ecology and Sociobiology, 26*, 9–15.

Rich, T. J., & Hurst, J. L. (1998). Scent marks as reliable signals of the competitive ability of mates. *Animal Behaviour, 56,* 727–735.

Rich, T. J., & Hurst, J. L. (1999). The competing countermarks hypothesis: Reliable assessment of competitive ability by potential mates. *Animal Behaviour, 58,* 1027–1037.

Rilling, J. K., Kaufman, T. L., Smith, E. O., Patel, R., & Worthman, C. M. (2009). Abdominal depth and waist circumference as influential determinants of human female attractiveness. *Evolution and Human Behavior, 30,* 21–31.

Ripich, D. N., Petrill, S. A., Whitehouse, P. J., & Ziol, E. W. (1995). Gender differences in language of AD patients: A longitudinal study. *Neurology, 45,* 299–302.

Roberts, M. L., Buchanan, K. L., & Evans, M. R. (2004). Testing the immunocompetence handicap hypothesis: A review of the evidence. *Animal Behaviour, 68,* 227–239.

Roberts, S. C., Little, A. C., Gosling, L. M., Perrett, D. I., Carter, V., Jones, B. C., et al. (2005). MHC-heterozygosity and human facial attractiveness. *Evolution and Human Behavior, 26,* 213–226.

Robinson, M. R., & Kruuk, L. E. (2007). Function of weaponry in females: The use of horns in intrasexual competition for resources in female Soay sheep. *Biology Letters, 3,* 651–654.

Roegge, C. S., Seo, B. W., Crofton, K. M., & Schantz, S. L. (2000). Gestational-lactational exposure to Aroclor 1254 impairs radial-arm maze performance in male rats. *Toxicological Sciences, 57,* 121–130.

Rogan, W. J., Gladen, B. C., Hung, K. L., Koong, S. L., Shih, L. Y., Taylor, J. S., et al. (1988). Congenital poisoning by polychlorinated biphenyls and their contaminants in Taiwan. *Science, 241,* 334–336.

Rohwer, S. (1977). Status signaling in the Harris' sparrow: Some experiments in deception. *Behaviour, 61,* 107–129.

Rosado, J. L., Ronquillo, D., Kordas, K., Rojas, O., Alatorre, J., Lopez, P., et al. (2007). Arsenic exposure and cognitive performance in Mexican schoolchildren. *Environmental Health Perspectives, 115,* 1371–1375.

Rose, A. J., & Asher, S. R. (1999). Children's goals and strategies in response to conflicts within a friendship. *Developmental Psychology, 35,* 69–79.

Rose, A. J., & Rudolph, K. D. (2006). A review of sex differences in peer relationship processes: Potential trade-offs for the emotional and behavioral development of girls and boys. *Psychological Bulletin, 132,* 98–131.

Rose, A. J., Schwartz-Mette, R. A., Glick, G. C., Smith, R. L., & Luebbe, A. M. (2014). An observational study of co-rumination in adolescent friendships. *Developmental Psychology, 50,* 2199–2209.

Rose, A. J., Schwartz-Mette, R. A., Smith, R. L., Asher, S. R., Swenson, L. P., Carlson, W., et al. (2012). How girls and boys expect disclosure about problems will make them feel: Implications for friendships. *Child Development, 83,* 844–863.

Rosenthal, R., Hall, J. A., DiMatteo, M. R., Rogers, P. L., & Archer, D. (1979). *Sensitivity to nonverbal communication: The PONS test.* Baltimore, MD: The Johns Hopkins University Press.

Rosenthal, M. F., Murphy, T. G., Darling, N., & Tarvin, K. A. (2012). Ornamental bill color rapidly signals changing condition. *Journal of Avian Biology, 43,* 553–564.

Ross, R., Rissanen, J., Pedwell, H., Clifford, J., & Shragge, P. (1996). Influence of diet and exercise on skeletal muscle and visceral adipose tissue in men. *Journal of Applied Physiology, 81,* 2445–2455.

Rotter, N. G., & Rotter, G. S. (1988). Sex differences in the encoding and decoding of negative facial emotions. *Journal of Nonverbal Behavior, 12,* 139–148.

Roulin, A., Ducrest, A.-L., Balloux, F., Dijkstra, C., & Riols, C. (2003). A female melanin ornament signals offspring fluctuating asymmetry in the barn owl. *Proceedings of the Royal Society of London B*, *270*, 167–171.

Roulin, A., Jungi, T. W., Pfister, H., & Dijkstra, C. (2000). Female bard owls (*Tyto alba*) advertise good genes. *Proceedings of the Royal Society of London B*, *267*, 937–941.

Rowe, L., & Houle, D. (1996). The lek paradox and the capture of genetic variance by condition dependent traits. *Proceedings of the Royal Society of London B*, *263*, 1415–1421.

Rubinow, D. R., Roca, C. A., Schmidt, P. J., Danaceau, M. A., Putnam, K., Cizza, G., et al. (2005). Testosterone suppression of CRH-stimulated cortisol in men. *Neuropsychopharmacology*, *30*, 1906–1912.

Russell, T. A., Schmidt, U., Doherty, L., Young, V., & Tchanturia, K. (2009). Aspects of social cognition in anorexia nervosa: Affective and cognitive theory of mind. *Psychiatry Research*, *168*, 181–185.

Ryan, M. J., & Keddy-Hector, A. (1992). Directional patterns of female mate choice and the role of sensory biases. *American Naturalist*, *139*, S4–S35.

Ryan, C. M., Morrow, L., Parkinson, D., & Bromet, E. (1987). Low level lead exposure and neuropsychological functioning in blue collar males. *International Journal of Neuroscience*, *36*, 29–39.

Ryder, J. J. (2000). Male calling song provides a reliable signal of immune function in a cricket. *Proceedings of the Royal Society of London B*, *267*, 1171–1175.

Saavalainen, P., Luoma, L., Bowler, D., Timonen, T., Määttä, S., Laukkanen, E., et al. (2006). Naming skills of children born preterm in comparison with their term peers at the ages of 9 and 16 years. *Developmental Medicine & Child Neurology*, *48*, 28–32.

Sakiani, S., Olsen, N. J., & Kovacs, W. J. (2013). Gonadal steroids and humoral immunity. *Nature Reviews Endocrinology*, *9*, 56–62.

Sakti, H., Nokes, C., Hertanto, W., Hendratno, S., Hall, A., & Bundy, D. A. (1999). Evidence for an association between hookworm infection and cognitive function in Indonesian school children. *Tropical Medicine & International Health*, *4*, 322–334.

Salminen, E. K., Portin, R. I., Koskinen, A., Helenius, H., & Nurmi, M. (2004). Associations between serum testosterone fall and cognitive function in prostate cancer patients. *Clinical Cancer Research*, *10*, 7575–7582.

Salminen, E. K., Portin, R. I., Koskinen, A. I., Helenius, H. Y. M., & Nurmi, M. J. (2005). Estradiol and cognition during androgen deprivation in men with prostate carcinoma. *Cancer*, *103*, 1381–1387.

Salzinger, S., Feldman, R. S., Hammer, M., & Rosario, M. (1993). The effects of physical abuse on children's social relationships. *Child Development*, *64*, 169–187.

Sandberg, D. E., & Meyer-Bahlburg, H. F. L. (1994). Variability in middle childhood play behavior: Effects of gender, age, and family background. *Archives of Sexual Behavior*, *23*, 645–663.

San-Jose, L. M., & Fitze, P. S. (2013). Corticosterone regulates multiple colour traits in *Lacerta* [*Zootoca*] *vivipara* males. *Journal of Evolutionary Biology*, *26*, 2681–2690.

Sanvito, S., Galimberti, F., & Miller, E. H. (2007). Vocal signalling of male southern elephant seals is honest but imprecise. *Animal Behaviour*, *73*, 287–299.

Sapolsky, R. M. (2005). The influence of social hierarchy on primate health. *Science*, *308*, 648–652.

Sapolsky, R. M., Uno, H., Rebert, C. S., & Finch, C. E. (1990). Hippocampal damage associated with prolonged glucocorticoid exposure in primates. *Journal of Neuroscience*, *10*, 2897–2902.

Savalli, U. M., & Fox, C. W. (1999). The effect of male size, age, and mating behavior on sexual selection in the seed beetle *Callosobruchus maculatus*. *Ethology Ecology & Evolution*, *11*, 49–60.

Savin-Williams, R. C. (1987). *Adolescence: An ethological perspective*. New York: Springer-Verlag.

Scelza, B. A. (2011). Female choice and extra-pair paternity in a traditional human population. *Biology Letters, 7,* 889–891.

Schagen, S. B., van Dam, F. S., Muller, M. J., Boogerd, W., Lindeboom, J., & Bruning, P. F. (1999). Cognitive deficits after postoperative adjuvant chemotherapy for breast carcinoma. *Cancer, 85,* 640–650.

Scherwath, A., Mehnert, A., Schleimer, B., Schirmer, L., Fehlauer, F., Kreienberg, R., et al. (2006). Neuropsychological function in high-risk breast cancer survivors after stem-cell supported high-dose therapy versus standard-dose chemotherapy: Evaluation of long-term treatment effects. *Annals of Oncology, 17,* 415–423.

Scheuber, H., Jacot, A., & Brinkhof, M. W. (2003a). Condition dependence of a multicomponent sexual signal in the field cricket *Gryllus campestris. Animal Behaviour, 65,* 721–727.

Scheuber, H., Jacot, A., & Brinkhof, M. W. (2003b). The effect of past condition on a multicomponent sexual signal. *Proceedings of the Royal Society of London B, 270,* 1779–1784.

Schiff, W., & Oldak, R. (1990). Accuracy of judging time to arrival: Effects of modality, trajectory, and gender. *Journal of Experimental Psychology: Human Perception and Performance, 16,* 303–316.

Schirmer, A., Kotz, S. A., & Friederici, A. D. (2002). Sex differentiates the role of emotional prosody during word processing. *Cognitive Brain Research, 14,* 228–233.

Schirmer, A., Kotz, S. A., & Friederici, A. D. (2005). On the role of attention for the processing of emotions in speech: Sex differences revisited. *Cognitive Brain Research, 24,* 442–452.

Schmidt, K. L., Moore, S. D., MacDougall-Shackleton, E. A., & MacDougall-Shackleton, S. A. (2013). Early-life stress affects song complexity, song learning and volume of the brain nucleus RA in adult male song sparrows. *Animal Behaviour, 86,* 25–35.

Schnurr, P. P., Friedman, M. J., & Rosenberg, S. D. (1993). Preliminary MMPI scores as predictors of combat-related PTSD symptoms. *American Journal of Psychiatry, 150,* 479–483.

Schreider, E. (1967). Body-height and inbreeding in France. *American Journal of Physical Anthropology, 26,* 1–3.

Schreider, E. (1969). Inbreeding, biological and mental variations in France. *American Journal of Physical Anthropology, 30,* 215–219.

Schuff, N., Neylan, T. C., Lenoci, M. A., Du, A. T., Weiss, D. S., Marmar, C. R., et al. (2001). Decreased hippocampal *N*-acetylaspartate in the absence of atrophy in posttraumatic stress disorder. *Biological Psychiatry, 50,* 952–959.

Scott, S. H. (2004). Optimal feedback control and the neural basis of volitional motor control. *Nature Reviews Neuroscience, 5,* 534–546.

Scribner, K. T., Smith, M. H., & Johns, P. E. (1989). Environmental and genetic components of antler growth in white-tailed deer. *Journal of Mammalogy, 70,* 284–291.

Searcy, W. A., Peters, S., Kipper, S., & Nowicki, S. (2010). Female response to song reflects male developmental history in swamp sparrows. *Behavioral Ecology and Sociobiology, 64,* 1343–1349.

Sebire, M., Allen, Y., Bersuder, P., & Katsiadaki, I. (2008). The model anti-androgen flutamide suppresses the expression of typical male stickleback reproductive behaviour. *Aquatic Toxicology, 90,* 37–47.

Segger, D., & Schönlau, F. (2004). Supplementation with Evelle® improves skin smoothness and elasticity in a double-blind, placebo-controlled study with 62 women. *Journal of Dermatological Treatment, 15,* 222–226.

Sehlmeyer, C., Schöning, S., Zwitserlood, P., Pfleiderer, B., Kircher, T., Arolt, V., et al. (2009). Human fear conditioning and extinction in neuroimaging: A systematic review. *PLoS ONE, 4,* e5865.

Sell, A., Cosmides, L., Tooby, J., Sznycer, D., von Rueden, C., & Gurven, M. (2009). Human adaptations for the visual assessment of strength and fighting ability from the body and face. *Proceedings of the Royal Society of London B, 276*, 575–584.

Semple, S., & McComb, K. (2000). Perception of female reproductive state from vocal cues in a mammal species. *Proceedings of the Royal Society of London B, 267*, 707–712.

Senar, J. C. (2006). Color displays as intrasexual signals of aggression and dominance. In G. E. Hill, & K. McGraw (Eds.), *Bird coloration: Function and evolution: Vol. 2*. (pp. 87–136). Cambridge, MA: Harvard University Press.

Serrano-Meneses, M. A., Córdoba-Aguilar, A., Méndez, V., Layen, S. J., & Székely, T. (2007). Sexual size dimorphism in the American rubyspot: Male body size predicts male competition and mating success. *Animal Behaviour, 73*, 987–997.

Setchell, J. M., Charpentier, M. J., Abbott, K. M., Wickings, E. J., & Knapp, L. A. (2009). Is brightest best? Testing the Hamilton-Zuk hypothesis in mandrills. *International Journal of Primatology, 30*, 825–844.

Setchell, J. M., & Dixson, A. F. (2001a). Arrested development of secondary sexual adornments in subordinate adult male mandrills (*Mandrillus sphinx*). *American Journal of Physical Anthropology, 115*, 245–252.

Setchell, J. M., & Dixson, A. F. (2001b). Changes in the secondary sexual adornments of male mandrills (*Mandrillus sphinx*) are associated with gain and loss of alpha status. *Hormones and Behavior, 39*, 177–184.

Setchell, J. M., Smith, T., Wickings, E. J., & Knapp, L. A. (2008). Social correlates of testosterone and ornamentation in male mandrills. *Hormones and Behavior, 54*, 365–372.

Setchell, J. M., Smith, T., Wickings, E. J., & Knapp, L. A. (2010). Stress, social behaviour, and secondary sexual traits in a male primate. *Hormones and Behavior, 58*, 720–728.

Setchell, J. M., & Wickings, E. J. (2005). Dominance, status signals and coloration in mandrills (*Mandrillus sphinx*). *Ethology, 111*, 25–50.

Setchell, J. M., Wickings, E. J., & Knapp, L. A. (2006). Signal content of red facial coloration in female mandrills (*Mandrillus sphinx*). *Proceedings of the Royal Society of London B, 273*, 2395–2400.

Sewall, K. B., Soha, J. A., Peters, S., & Nowicki, S. (2013). Potential trade-off between vocal ornamentation and spatial ability in a songbird. *Biology Letters, 9*, 20130344.

Shaywitz, B. A., Shaywitz, S. E., Pugh, K. R., Constable, R. T., Skudlarski, P., Fulbright, R. K., et al. (1995). Sex differences in the functional organization of the brain for language. *Nature, 373*, 607–609.

Sheldon, B. C., Merilä, J., Qvarnström, A., Gustafsson, L., & Ellegren, H. (1997). Paternal genetic contribution to offspring condition predicted by size of male secondary sexual character. *Proceedings of the Royal Society of London B, 264*, 297–302.

Shenoy, K. (2012). Environmentally realistic exposure to the herbicide atrazine alters some sexually selected traits in male guppies. *PLoS ONE, 7*, e30611.

Shepard, L. D. (2012). The impact of polygamy on women's mental health: A systematic review. *Epidemiology and Psychiatric Sciences, 1*, 1–16.

Sheridan, L., & Pomiankowski, A. (1997). Fluctuating asymmetry, spot asymmetry and inbreeding depression in the sexual coloration of male guppy fish. *Heredity, 79*, 515–523.

Sheridan, M., & Tamarin, R. H. (1988). Space use, longevity, and reproductive success in meadow voles. *Behavioral Ecology and Sociobiology, 22*, 85–90.

Sherif, M., Harvey, O. J., White, B. J., Hood, W. R., & Sherif, C. W. (1961). *Intergroup conflict and cooperation: The Robbers Cave experiment*. Normal, OK: Institute of Group Relations, University of Oklahoma.

Sherry, D. F., Forbes, M. R., Khurgel, M., & Ivy, G. O. (1993). Females have a larger hippocampus than males in the brood-parasitic brown-headed cowbird. *Proceedings of the National Academy of Sciences of the United States of America, 90*, 7839–7843.

Shetler, K., Marcus, R., Froelicher, V. F., Vora, S., Kalisetti, D., Prakash, M., et al. (2001). Heart rate recovery: Validation and methodologic issues. *Journal of the American College of Cardiology, 38*, 1980–1987.

Shilling, V., Jenkins, V., Morris, R., Deutsch, G., & Bloomfield, D. (2005). The effects of adjuvant chemotherapy on cognition in women with breast cancer—Preliminary results of an observational longitudinal study. *Breast, 14*, 142–150.

Shimozuru, M., Kodama, Y., Iwasa, T., Kikusui, T., Takeuchi, Y., & Mori, Y. (2007). Early weaning decreases play-fighting behavior during the postweaning developmental period of Wistar rats. *Developmental Psychobiology, 49*, 343–350.

Shin, L. M., Rauch, S. L., & Pitman, R. K. (2006). Amygdala, medial prefrontal cortex, and hippocampal function in PTSD. *Annals of the New York Academy of Sciences, 1071*, 67–79.

Shirasu, M., Nagai, S., Hayashi, R., Ochiai, A., & Touhara, K. (2009). Dimethyl trisulfide as a characteristic odor associated with fungating cancer wounds. *Bioscience, Biotechnology, and Biochemistry, 73*, 2117–2120.

Shirasu, M., & Touhara, K. (2011). The scent of disease: Volatile organic compounds of the human body related to disease and disorder. *Journal of Biochemistry, 150*, 257–266.

Sidanius, J., & Ekehammar, B. (1983). Sex, political party preference, and higher-order dimensions of sociopolitical ideology. *Journal of Psychology, 115*, 233–239.

Sidanius, J., Pratto, F., & Bobo, L. (1994). Social dominance orientation and the political psychology of gender: A case of invariance? *Journal of Personality and Social Psychology, 67*, 998–1011.

Sidanius, J., Pratto, F., & Mitchell, M. (2001). In-group identification, social dominance orientation, and differential intergroup social allocation. *Journal of Social Psychology, 134*, 151–167.

Siitari, H., Alatalo, R. V., Halme, P., Buchanan, K. L., & Kilpimaa, J. (2007). Color signals in the black grouse (*Tetrao tetrix*): Signal properties and their condition dependency. *American Naturalist, 169*, S81–S92.

Silverman, I., Choi, J., Mackewn, A., Fisher, M., Moro, J., & Ohshansky, E. (2000). Evolved mechanisms underlying wayfinding: Further studies on the hunter-gatherer theory of spatial sex differences. *Evolution and Human Behavior, 21*, 201–213.

Silverman, A. B., Reinherz, H. Z., & Giaconia, R. M. (1996). The long-term sequelae of child and adolescent abuse: A longitudinal community study. *Child Abuse & Neglect, 20*, 709–723.

Simmons, R. (1988). Honest advertising, sexual selection, courtship displays, and body condition of polygynous male harriers. *Auk, 105*, 303–307.

Simmons, L. W., Zuk, M., & Rotenberry, J. T. (2005). Immune function reflected in calling song characteristics in a natural population of the cricket *Teleogryllus commodus*. *Animal Behaviour, 69*, 1235–1241.

Simons, M. J., Cohen, A. A., & Verhulst, S. (2012). What does carotenoid-dependent coloration tell? Plasma carotenoid level signals immunocompetence and oxidative stress state in birds—A meta-analysis. *PLoS ONE, 7*, e43088.

Singer, L. T., Arendt, R., Minnes, S., Salvator, A., Siegel, A. C., & Lewis, B. A. (2001). Developing language skills of cocaine-exposed infants. *Pediatrics, 107*, 1057–1064.

Singer, L. T., Minnes, S., Short, E., Arendt, R., Farkas, K., Lewis, B., et al. (2004). Cognitive outcomes of preschool children with prenatal cocaine exposure. *JAMA, 291*, 2448–2456.

Singh, D. (1993a). Adaptive significance of female physical attractiveness: Role of waist-to-hip ratio. *Journal of Personality and Social Psychology, 65*, 293–307.

Singh, D. (1993b). Body shape and women's attractiveness: The critical role of waist-to-hip ratio. *Human Nature, 4*, 297–321.

Singh, D., & Bronstad, P. M. (2001). Female body odour is a potential cue to ovulation. *Proceedings of the Royal Society of London B, 268*, 797–801.

Siva Jothy, M. T. (2000). A mechanistic link between parasite resistance and expression of a sexually selected trait in a damselfly. *Proceedings of the Royal Society of London B, 267*, 2523–2527.

Smith, M. L., Perrett, D. I., Jones, B. C., Cornwell, R. E., Moore, F. R., Feinberg, D. R., et al. (2006). Facial appearance is a cue to oestrogen levels in women. *Proceedings of the Royal Society of London B, 273*, 135–140.

Smith, R. L., Rose, A. J., & Schwartz-Mette, R. A. (2010). Relational and overt aggression in childhood and adolescence: Clarifying mean-level gender differences and associations with peer acceptance. *Social Development, 19*, 243–269.

Söffker, M., & Tyler, C. R. (2012). Endocrine disrupting chemicals and sexual behaviors in fish—A critical review on effects and possible consequences. *Critical Reviews in Toxicology, 42*, 653–668.

Song, Y. M., Smith, G. D., & Sung, J. (2003). Adult height and cause-specific mortality: A large prospective study of South Korean men. *American Journal of Epidemiology, 158*, 479–485.

Sosis, R., Kress, H. C., & Boster, J. S. (2007). Scars for war: Evaluating alternative signaling explanations for cross-cultural variance in ritual costs. *Evolution and Human Behavior, 28*, 234–247.

Sotres-Bayon, F., Bush, D. E., & LeDoux, J. E. (2004). Emotional perseveration: An update on prefrontal-amygdala interactions in fear extinction. *Learning & Memory, 11*, 525–535.

Sowell, E. R., Peterson, B. S., Kan, E., Woods, R. P., Yoshii, J., Bansal, R., et al. (2007). Sex differences in cortical thickness mapped in 176 healthy individuals between 7 and 87 years of age. *Cerebral Cortex, 17*, 1550–1560.

Spelke, E. S., Breinlinger, K., Macomber, J., & Jacobson, K. (1992). Origins of knowledge. *Psychological Review, 99*, 605–632.

Spencer, K. A., Buchanan, K. L., Goldsmith, A. R., & Catchpole, C. K. (2003). Song as an honest signal of developmental stress in the zebra finch (*Taeniopygia guttata*). *Hormones and Behavior, 44*, 132–139.

Spencer, K. A., Buchanan, K. L., Goldsmith, A. R., & Catchpole, C. K. (2004). Developmental stress, social rank and song complexity in the European starling (*Sturnus vulgaris*). *Proceedings of the Royal Society of London B, 271*, S121–S123.

Spencer, K. A., Buchanan, K. L., Leitner, S., Goldsmith, A. R., & Catchpole, C. K. (2005). Parasites affect song complexity and neural development in a songbird. *Proceedings of the Royal Society of London B, 272*, 2037–2043.

Spencer, K. A., & MacDougall-Shackleton, S. A. (2011). Indicators of development as sexually selected traits: The developmental stress hypothesis in context. *Behavioral Ecology, 22*, 1–9.

Spiers, H. J., Burgess, N., Maguire, E. A., Baxendale, S. A., Hartley, T., Thompson, P. J., et al. (2001). Unilateral temporal lobectomy patients show lateralized topographical and episodic deficits in a virtual town. *Brain, 124*, 2476–2489.

Spritzer, M. D., Solomon, N. G., & Meikle, D. B. (2005). Influence of scramble competition for mates upon the spatial ability of male meadow voles. *Animal Behaviour, 69*, 375–386.

Sripada, R. K., King, A. P., Garfinkel, S. N., Wang, X., Sripada, C. S., Welsh, R. C., et al. (2012). Altered resting-state amygdala functional connectivity in men with posttraumatic stress disorder. *Journal of Psychiatry and Neuroscience, 37*, 241–249.

Stanton, S. J., Wirth, M. M., Waugh, C. E., & Schultheiss, O. C. (2009). Endogenous testosterone levels are associated with amygdala and ventromedial prefrontal cortex responses to anger faces in men but not women. *Biological Psychology*, *81*, 118–122.

Stein, M. B., Koverola, C., Hanna, C., Torchia, M. G., & McClarty, B. (1997). Hippocampal volume in women victimized by childhood sexual abuse. *Psychological Medicine*, *27*, 951–959.

Stein, Z., Susser, M., Saenger, G., & Marolla, F. (1972). Nutrition and mental performance. *Science*, *178*, 708–713.

Stephen, I. D., Coetzee, V., & Perrett, D. I. (2011). Carotenoid and melanin pigment coloration affect perceived human health. *Evolution and Human Behavior*, *32*, 216–227.

Stephenson, L. S., Latham, M. C., Adams, E. J., Kinoti, S. N., & Pertet, A. (1993). Physical fitness, growth and appetite of Kenyan school boys with hookworm, *Trichuris trichiura* and *Ascaris lumbricoides* infections are improved four months after a single dose of albendazole. *Journal of Nutrition*, *123*, 1036–1046.

Stephenson, L. S., Latham, M. C., Kinoti, S. N., Kurz, K. M., & Brigham, H. (1990). Improvements in physical fitness of Kenyan schoolboys infected with hookworm, *Trichuris trichiura* and *Ascaris lumbricoides* following a single dose of albendazole. *Transactions of the Royal Society of Tropical Medicine and Hygiene*, *84*, 277–282.

Stickel, L. F. (1968). Home range and travels. In J. A. King (Ed.), *Biology of peromyscus* (pp. 373–411). Stillwater, OK: American Society of Mammalogists.

Stini, W. A. (1969). Nutritional stress and growth: Sex difference in adaptive response. *American Journal of Physical Anthropology*, *31*, 417–426.

Stinson, S. (1985). Sex differences in environmental sensitivity during growth and development. *American Journal of Physical Anthropology*, *28*, 123–147.

Stirrat, M., Stulp, G., & Pollet, T. V. (2012). Male facial width is associated with death by contact violence: Narrow-faced males are more likely to die from contact violence. *Evolution and Human Behavior*, *33*, 551–556.

Stockley, P., & Bro-Jørgensen, J. (2011). Female competition and its evolutionary consequences in mammals. *Biological Reviews*, *86*, 341–366.

Stoehr, A. M. (2006). Costly melanin ornaments: The importance of taxon? *Functional Ecology*, *20*, 276–281.

Stoltzfus, R. J., Albonico, M., Tielsch, J. M., Chwaya, H. M., & Savioli, L. (1997). Linear growth retardation in Zanzibari school children. *Journal of Nutrition*, *127*, 1099–1105.

Strassmann, B. I. (1997). Polygyny as a risk factor for child mortality among the Dogon. *Current Anthropology*, *38*, 688–695.

Strassmann, B. I. (2011). Cooperation and competition in a cliff-dwelling people. *Proceedings of the National Academy of Sciences of the United States of America*, *108*, 10894–10901.

Strassmann, B. I., & Gillespie, B. (2002). Life-history theory, fertility and reproductive success in humans. *Proceedings of the Royal Society of London B*, *269*, 553–562.

Sullivan, M. S. (1994). Mate choice as an information gathering process under time constraint: Implications for behaviour and signal design. *Animal Behaviour*, *47*, 141–151.

Sumner, P., & Mollon, J. D. (2003). Colors of primate pelage and skin: Objective assessment of conspicuousness. *American Journal of Primatology*, *59*, 67–91.

Surridge, A. K., Osorio, D., & Mundy, N. I. (2003). Evolution and selection of trichromatic vision in primates. *Trends in Ecology & Evolution*, *18*, 198–205.

Svensson, P. A., & Wong, B. B. M. (2011). Carotenoid-based signals in behavioural ecology: A review. *Behaviour*, *148*, 131–189.

Swan, S. H., Liu, F., Hines, M., Kruse, R. L., Wang, C., Redmon, J. B., et al. (2010). Prenatal phthalate exposure and reduced masculine play in boys. *International Journal of Andrology*, *33*, 259–269.

Swenson, L. P., & Rose, A. J. (2003). Friends as reporters of children's and adolescents' depressive symptoms. *Journal of Abnormal Child Psychology, 31*, 619–631.

Syhre, M., Manning, L., Phuanukoonnon, S., Harino, P., & Chambers, S. T. (2009). The scent of *Mycobacterium tuberculosis* – Part II breath. *Tuberculosis, 89*, 263–266.

Számadó, S. (2011). The cost of honest and the fallacy of the handicap hypothesis. *Animal Behaviour, 81*, 3–10.

Szuran, T. F., Pliška, V., Pokorny, J., & Welzl, H. (2000). Prenatal stress in rats: Effects on plasma corticosterone, hippocampal glucocorticoid receptors, and maze performance. *Physiology & Behavior, 71*, 353–362.

Szykman, M., Engh, A. L., Van Horn, R. C., Funk, S. M., Scribner, K. T., & Holekamp, K. E. (2001). Association patterns among male and female spotted hyenas (*Crocuta crocuta*) reflect male mate choice. *Behavioral Ecology and Sociobiology, 50*, 231–238.

Takahashi, H. (2004). Do males have a better chance of mating when the number of estrous females is equal to or greater than the males' ordinal rank? Testing the hypothesis in Japanese macaques. *American Journal of Primatology, 63*, 95–102.

Tanner, J. M. (1990). *Foetus into man: Physical growth from conception to maturity*. Cambridge, MA: Harvard University Press.

Tanner, S., Leonard, W. R., & Reyes-García, V. (2014). The consequences of linear growth stunting: Influence on body composition among youth in the Bolivian amazon. *American Journal of Physical Anthropology, 153*, 92–102.

Tapajóz Pereira de Sampaio, F., Soneira, S., Aulicino, A., & Allegri, R. F. (2013). Theory of mind in eating disorders and their relationship to clinical profile. *European Eating Disorders Review, 21*, 479–487.

Taylor, S. E., Klein, L. C., Lewis, B. P., Gruenewald, T. L., Gurung, R. A. R., & Updegraff, J. A. (2000). Biobehavioral responses to stress in females: Tend-and-befriend, not fight-or-flight. *Psychological Review, 107*, 411–429.

Taylor, H. G., Klein, N., Minich, N. M., & Hack, M. (2000). Middle-school-age outcomes in children with very low birthweight. *Child Development, 71*, 1495–1511.

Tchanturia, K., Happé, F., Godley, J., Treasure, J., Bara-Carril, N., & Schmidt, U. (2004). Theory of mind in anorexia nervosa. *European Eating Disorders Review, 12*, 361–366.

Tchen, N., Juffs, H. G., Downie, F. P., Yi, Q. L., Hu, H., Chemerynsky, I., et al. (2003). Cognitive function, fatigue, and menopausal symptoms in women receiving adjuvant chemotherapy for breast cancer. *Journal of Clinical Oncology, 21*, 4175–4183.

Teicher, M. H., Anderson, C. M., & Polcari, A. (2012). Childhood maltreatment is associated with reduced volume in the hippocampal subfields CA3, dentate gyrus, and subiculum. *Proceedings of the National Academy of Sciences of the United States of America, 109*, E563–E572.

Teichroeb, J. A., & Sicotte, P. (2010). The function of male agonistic displays in ursine colobus monkeys (*Colobus vellerosus*): Male competition, female mate choice or sexual coercion? *Ethology, 116*, 366–380.

Thiessen, D. D., Owen, K., & Lindzey, G. (1971). Mechanisms of territorial marking in the male and female Mongolian gerbil (*Meriones unguiculatus*). *Journal of Comparative and Physiological Psychology, 77*, 38–47.

Thiessen, D., & Rice, M. (1976). Mammalian scent gland marking and social behavior. *Psychological Bulletin, 83*, 505–539.

Thomas, J. R., & French, K. E. (1985). Gender differences across age in motor performance: A meta-analysis. *Psychological Bulletin, 98*, 260–282.

Thornhill, R., & Gangestad, S. W. (1999). The scent of symmetry: A human sex pheromone that signals fitness? *Evolution and Human Behavior, 20*, 175–201.

Thornhill, R., Gangestad, S. W., Miller, R., Scheyd, G., McCollough, J. K., & Franklin, M. (2003). Major histocompatibility complex genes, symmetry, and body scent attractiveness in men and women. *Behavioral Ecology, 14*, 668–678.

Thurstone, L. L. (1938). Primary mental abilities. *Psychometric Monographs: Vol. 1*. Chicago, IL: University of Chicago Press.

Tibbetts, E. A. (2010). The condition dependence and heritability of signaling and nonsignaling color traits in paper wasps. *American Naturalist, 175*, 495–503.

Tibbetts, E. A., & Banan, M. (2010). Advertised quality, caste and food availability influence: The survival cost of juvenile hormone in paper wasps. *Proceedings of the Royal Society of London B, 277*, 3461–3467.

Tibbetts, E. A., & Izzo, A. (2010). Social punishment of dishonest signalers caused by mismatch between signal and behavior. *Current Biology, 20*, 1637–1640.

Tibbetts, E. A., & Sheehan, M. J. (2011). Facial patterns are a conventional signal of agonistic ability in *Polistes exclamans* paper wasps. *Ethology, 117*, 1138–1146.

Tobias, J. A., Montgomerie, R., & Lyon, B. E. (2012). The evolution of female ornaments and weaponry: Social selection, sexual selection and ecological competition. *Philosophical Transactions of the Royal Society B, 367*, 2274–2293.

Toft, G., & Baatrup, E. (2001). Sexual characteristics are altered by 4-*tert*-octylphenol and 17 β-estradiol in the adult male guppy (*Poecilia reticulata*). *Ecotoxicology and Environmental Safety, 48*, 76–84.

Toïgo, C., Gaillard, J. M., & Michallet, J. (1999). Cohort affects growth of males but not females in alpine ibex (*Capra ibex ibex*). *Journal of Mammalogy, 80*, 1021–1027.

Tolin, D. F., & Foa, E. B. (2006). Sex differences in trauma and posttraumatic stress disorder: A quantitative review of 25 years of research. *Psychological Bulletin, 132*, 959–992.

Tolle, A. E., & Wagner, W. E., Jr. (2011). Costly signals in a field cricket can indicate high- or low-quality direct benefits depending upon the environment. *Evolution, 65*, 283–294.

Tomkins, J. L., Radwan, J., Kotiaho, J. S., & Tregenza, T. (2004). Genic capture and resolving the lek paradox. *Trends in Ecology & Evolution, 19*, 323–328.

Tong, S., McMichael, A. J., & Baghurst, P. A. (2000). Interactions between environmental lead exposure and sociodemographic factors on cognitive development. *Archives of Environmental Health: An International Journal, 55*, 330–335.

Tottenham, N., Hare, T. A., Millner, A., Gilhooly, T., Zevin, J. D., & Casey, B. J. (2011). Elevated amygdala response to faces following early deprivation. *Developmental Science, 14*, 190–204.

Towson, S. M. J., Lerner, M. J., & de Carufel, A. (1981). Justice rules or ingroup loyalties: The effects of competition on children's allocation behavior. *Personality and Social Psychology Bulletin, 7*, 696–700.

Tranel, D., Damasio, H., Denburg, J. L., & Bechara, A. (2005). Does gender play a role in functional asymmetry of the ventromedial prefrontal cortex? *Brain, 128*, 2872–2881.

Trivers, R. L. (1972). Parental investment and sexual selection. In B. Campbell (Ed.), *Sexual selection and the descent of man 1871–1971* (pp. 136–179). Chicago, IL: Aldine Publishing.

Tschirren, B., Fitze, P. S., & Richner, H. (2003). Proximate mechanisms of variation in the carotenoid-based plumage coloration of nestling great tits (*Parus major* L.). *Journal of Evolutionary Biology, 16*, 91–100.

Udompataikul, M., Sripiroj, P., & Palungwachira, P. (2009). An oral nutraceutical containing antioxidants, minerals and glycosaminoglycans improves skin roughness and fine wrinkles. *International Journal of Cosmetic Science, 31*, 427–435.

Ulukanligil, M., & Seyrek, A. (2004). Anthropometric status, anaemia and intestinal helminthic infections in shantytown and apartment schoolchildren in the Sanliurfa province of Turkey. *European Journal of Clinical Nutrition, 58*, 1056–1061.

Uzzell, B. P., & Oler, J. (1986). Chronic low-level mercury exposure and neuropsychological functioning. *Journal of Clinical and Experimental Neuropsychology, 8*, 581–593.

Valmas, M. M., Ruiz, S. M., Gansler, D. A., Sawyer, K. S., & Oscar-Berman, M. (2014). Social cognition deficits and associations with drinking history and alcoholic men and women. *Alcoholism: Clinical and Experimental Research, 38*, 2998–3007.

van Beek, Y., & Dubas, J. S. (2008). Age and gender differences in decoding basic and non-basic facial expressions in late childhood and early adolescence. *Journal of Nonverbal Behavior, 32*, 37–52.

van Bergen, E., Brakefield, P. M., Heuskin, S., Zwaan, B. J., & Nieberding, C. M. (2013). The scent of inbreeding: A male sex pheromone betrays inbred males. *Proceedings of the Royal Society of London B, 280*, 20130102.

van Dam, F. S., Boogerd, W., Schagen, S. B., Muller, M. J., Fortuyn, M. E. D., v.d. Wall, E., et al. (1998). Impairment of cognitive function in women receiving adjuvant treatment for high-risk breast cancer: High-dose versus standard-dose chemotherapy. *Journal of the National Cancer Institute, 90*, 210–218.

van der Linden, D., te Nijenhuis, J., & Bakker, A. B. (2010). The general factor of personality: A meta-analysis of Big Five intercorrelations and a criterion-related validity study. *Journal of Research in Personality, 44*, 315–327.

Van Hout, A. J. M., Eens, M., & Pinxten, R. (2011). Carotenoid supplementation positively affects the expression of a non-visual sexual signal. *PLoS ONE, 6*, e16326.

Van Iersel, J. J. A. (1953). An analysis of the parental behaviour of the male three-spined stickleback (*Gasterosteus aculeatus* L.). *Behaviour*, (Suppl. III), 1–159.

Van Oosterhout, C., Trigg, R. E., Carvalho, G. R., Magurran, A. E., Hauser, L., & Shaw, P. W. (2003). Inbreeding depression and genetic load of sexually selected traits: How the guppy lost its spots. *Journal of Evolutionary Biology, 16*, 273–281.

Van Vugt, M., De Cremer, D., & Janssen, D. P. (2007). Gender differences in cooperation and competition: The male-warrior hypothesis. *Psychological Science, 18*, 19–23.

Van Vugt, M., & Spisak, B. R. (2008). Sex differences in the emergence of leadership during competitions within and between groups. *Psychological Sciences, 19*, 854–858.

Vandenberg, S. G., & Kuse, A. R. (1978). Mental rotations, a group test of three-dimensional spatial visualization. *Perceptual and Motor Skills, 47*, 599–604.

Vannoni, E., & McElligott, A. G. (2008). Low frequency groans indicate larger and more dominant fallow deer (*Dama dama*) males. *PLoS ONE, 3*, e3113.

Vanpé, C., Gaillard, J. M., Kjellander, P., Liberg, O., Delorme, D., & Hewison, A. J. (2010). Assessing the intensity of sexual selection on male body mass and antler length in roe deer *Capreolus capreolus*: Is bigger better in a weakly dimorphic species? *Oikos, 119*, 1484–1492.

Vanpé, C., Gaillard, J. M., Kjellander, P., Mysterud, A., Magnien, P., Delorme, D., et al. (2007). Antler size provides an honest signal of male phenotypic quality in roe deer. *American Naturalist, 169*, 481–493.

Vardy, J., Rourke, S., & Tannock, I. F. (2007). Evaluation of cognitive function associated with chemotherapy: A review of published studies and recommendations for future research. *Journal of Clinical Oncology, 25*, 2455–2463.

Veiga, J. P., & Puerta, M. (1996). Nutritional constraints determine the expression of a sexual trait in the house sparrow, *Passer domesticus*. *Proceedings of the Royal Society of London B, 263*, 229–234.

Venkataramani, A. S. (2012). Early life exposure to malaria and cognition in adulthood: Evidence from Mexico. *Journal of Health Economics, 31*, 767–780.

Vergara, P., Martinez-Padilla, J., Mougeot, F., Leckie, F., & Redpath, S. M. (2012). Environmental heterogeneity influences the reliability of secondary sexual traits as condition indicators. *Journal of Evolutionary Biology, 25*, 20–28.

Vergara, P., Mougeot, F., Martinez-Padilla, J., Leckie, F., & Redpath, S. M. (2012). The condition dependence of a secondary sexual trait is stronger under high parasite infection level. *Behavioral Ecology, 23*, 502–511.

Vergara, P., Redpath, S. M., Martinez-Padilla, J., & Mougeot, F. (2012). Environmental conditions influence red grouse ornamentation at a population level. *Biological Journal of the Linnean Society, 107*, 788–798.

Verhulst, S., Dieleman, S. J., & Parmentier, H. K. (1999). A tradeoff between immunocompetence and sexual ornamentation in domestic fowl. *Proceedings of the National Academy of Sciences of the United States of America, 96*, 4478–4481.

Vigil, J. M. (2009). A socio-relational framework of sex differences in the expression of emotion. *Behavioral and Brain Sciences, 32*, 375–390.

Voigt, C. C., & von Helversen, O. (1999). Storage and display of odour by male *Saccopteryx bilineata* (*Chiroptera, Emballonuridae*). *Behavioral Ecology and Sociobiology, 47*, 29–40.

von Hardenberg, A., Bassano, B., Festa-Bianchet, M., Luikart, G., Lanfranchi, P., & Coltman, D. (2007). Age-dependent genetic effects on a secondary sexual trait in male Alpine ibex, *Capra ibex*. *Molecular Ecology, 16*, 1969–1980.

von Rueden, C., Gurven, M., & Kaplan, H. (2011). Why do men seek status? Fitness payoffs to dominance and prestige. *Proceedings of the Royal Society of London B, 278*, 2223–2232.

von Schantz, T., Bensch, S. B., Grahn, M., Hasselquist, D., & Wittzell, H. (1999). Good genes, oxidative stress and condition dependent sexual signals. *Proceedings of the Royal Society of London B, 266*, 1–12.

von Schantz, T., Göransson, G., Andersson, G., Fröberg, I., Grahn, M., Helgée, A., et al. (1989). Female choice selects for a viability-based male trait in pheasants. *Nature, 337*, 166–169.

Voyer, D., Voyer, S., & Bryden, M. P. (1995). Magnitude of sex differences in spatial abilities: A meta-analysis and consideration and consideration of critical variables. *Psychological Bulletin, 117*, 250–270.

Vreugdenhil, H. J., Slijper, F. M., Mulder, P. G., & Weisglas-Kuperus, N. (2002). Effects of perinatal exposure to PCBs and dioxins on play behavior in Dutch children at school age. *Environmental Health Perspectives, 110*, A593–A598.

Wachs, T. D., Bishry, Z., Moussa, W., Yunis, F., McCabe, G., Harrison, G., et al. (1995). Nutritional intake and context as predictors of cognition and adaptive behaviour of Egyptian school-age children. *International Journal of Behavioral Development, 18*, 425–450.

Wada, J., Clark, R., & Hamm, A. (1975). Cerebral hemisphere asymmetry in humans: Cortical speech zones in 100 adults and 100 infant brains. *Archives of Neurology, 32*, 239–246.

Wagner, H. L., Buck, R., & Winterbotham, M. (1993). Communication of specific emotions: Gender differences in sending accuracy and communication measures. *Journal of Nonverbal Behavior, 17*, 29–53.

Wagner, W. E., Jr., & Hoback, W. W. (1999). Nutritional effects on male calling behaviour in the variable field cricket. *Animal Behaviour, 57*, 89–95.

Wagner, W. E., Jr., & Reiser, M. G. (2000). The importance of calling song and courtship song in female mate choice in the variable field cricket. *Animal Behaviour, 59*, 1219–1226.

Walker, R. S., & Bailey, D. H. (2013). Body counts in lowland South American violence. *Evolution and Human Behavior, 34*, 29–34.

Walker, S. P., Chang, S. M., & Powell, C. A. (2006). The association between early childhood stunting and weight status in late adolescence. *International Journal of Obesity, 31*, 347–352.

Walker, R. S., Hill, K. R., Flinn, M. V., & Ellsworth, R. M. (2011). Evolutionary history of hunter–gatherer marriage practices. *PLoS ONE, 6*, e19066.

Walker, L. K., Stevens, M., Karadaş, F., Kilner, R. M., & Ewen, J. G. (2013). A window on the past: Male ornamental plumage reveals the quality of their early-life environment. *Proceedings of the Royal Society of London B, 280*, 20122852.

Wallace, A. R. (1869). Geological climate and origin of species. *London Quarterly Review, 126*, 187–205.

Wallace, A. R. (1892). Note on sexual selection. *Natural Science, 1*, 749–750.

Walravens, P. A., Krebs, N. F., & Hambidge, K. M. (1983). Linear growth of low income preschool children receiving a zinc supplement. *American Journal of Clinical Nutrition, 38*, 195–201.

Wang, Z., Neylan, T. C., Mueller, S. G., Lenoci, M., Truran, D., Marmar, C. R., et al. (2010). Magnetic resonance imaging of hippocampal subfields in posttraumatic stress disorder. *Archives of General Psychiatry, 67*, 296–303.

Waterflow, J. C. (1974). Some aspects of childhood malnutrition as a public health problem. *British Medical Journal, 4*, 88–90.

Watkins, W. E., & Pollitt, E. (1997). "Stupidity or worms": Do intestinal worms impair mental performance? *Psychological Bulletin, 121*, 171–191.

Watson, N. V., & Kimura, D. (1991). Nontrivial sex differences in throwing and intercepting: Relation to psychometrically-defined spatial functions. *Personality and Individual Differences, 12*, 375–385.

Watson, J. B., Mednick, S. A., Huttunen, M., & Wang, X. (1999). Prenatal teratogens and the development of adult mental illness. *Development and Psychopathology, 11*, 457–466.

Watson, N. L., & Simmons, L. W. (2010a). Mate choice in the dung beetle *Onthophagus sagittarius*: Are female horns ornaments? *Behavioral Ecology, 21*, 424–430.

Watson, N. L., & Simmons, L. W. (2010b). Reproductive competition promotes the evolution of female weaponry. *Proceedings of the Royal Society on London B, 277*, 2035–2040.

Wechsler, D. (1974). *Manual for the Wechsler intelligence scale for children, revised.* New York: Psychological Corporation.

Wechsler, D. (2008). *Wechsler adult intelligence scale – Fourth edition (WAIS–IV).* San Antonio, TX: NCS Pearson.

Wechsler, D. (2012). *Wechsler preschool and primary scale of intelligence – Fourth edition (WPPSI-IV).* San Antonio, TX: NCS Pearson.

Weddle, C. B., Mitchell, D., Bay, S. K., Sakaluk, S. K., & Hunt, J. (2012). Sex-specific genotype-by-environment interactions for cuticular hydrocarbon expression in decorated crickets, *Gryllodes sigillatus*: Implications for the evolution of signal reliability. *Journal of Evolutionary Biology, 25*, 2112–2125.

Wedekind, C. (1992). Detailed information about parasites revealed by sexual ornamentation. *Proceedings of the Royal Society of London B, 247*, 169–174.

Wedekind, C., Seebeck, T., Bettens, F., & Paepke, A. J. (1995). MHC-dependent mate preferences in humans. *Proceedings of the Royal Society of London B, 260*, 245–249.

Wefel, J. S., Kayl, A. E., & Meyers, C. A. (2004). Neuropsychological dysfunction associated with cancer and cancer therapies: A conceptual review of an emerging target. *British Journal of Cancer, 90*, 1691–1696.

Wefel, J. S., Lenzi, R., Theriault, R. L., Davis, R. N., & Meyers, C. A. (2004). The cognitive sequelae of standard-dose adjuvant chemotherapy in women with breast carcinoma. *Cancer, 100*, 2292–2299.

Wefel, J. S., Vidrine, D. J., Marani, S. K., Swartz, R. J., Veramonti, T. L., Meyers, C. A., et al. (2014). A prospective study of cognitive function in men with non-seminomatous germ cell tumors. *Psycho-Oncology, 23*, 626–633.

Weinstock, M. (2007). Gender differences in the effects of prenatal stress on brain development and behaviour. *Neurochemical Research, 32*, 1730–1740.

Weinstock, M. (2008). The long-term behavioural consequences of prenatal stress. *Neuroscience & Biobehavioral Reviews, 32,* 1073–1086.

Weiss, S. L., Mulligan, E. E., Wilson, D., & Kabelik, D. (2013). Effect of stress on female specific ornamentation. *Journal of Experimental Biology, 216,* 2641–2647.

Weisskopf, M. G., Proctor, S. P., Wright, R. O., Schwartz, J., Spiro, A., III, Sparrow, D., et al. (2007). Cumulative lead exposure and cognitive performance among elderly men. *Epidemiology, 18,* 59–66.

Welch, A. M., Semlitsch, R. D., & Gerhardt, H. C. (1998). Call duration as an indicator of genetic quality in male gray tree frogs. *Science, 280,* 1928–1930.

Welch, A. M., Smith, M. J., & Gerhardt, C. H. (2014). A multivariate analysis of genetic variation in the advertisement call of the gray treefrog, *Hyla versicolor. Evolution, 68,* 1629–1639.

Weniger, G., Ruhleder, M., Lange, C., Wolf, S., & Irle, E. (2011). Egocentric and allocentric memory as assessed by virtual reality in individuals with amnestic mild cognitive impairment. *Neuropsychologia, 49,* 518–527.

West, K. P., Djunaedi, E., Pandji, A., Tarwotjo, I., & Sommer, A. (1988). Vitamin A supplementation and growth: A randomized community trial. *American Journal of Clinical Nutrition, 48,* 1257–1264.

West, P. M., & Packer, C. (2002). Sexual selection, temperature, and the lion's mane. *Science, 297,* 1339–1343.

West-Eberhard, M. J. (1979). Sexual selection, social competition, and evolution. *Proceedings of the American Philosophical Society, 123,* 222–234.

West-Eberhard, M. J. (1983). Sexual selection, social competition, and speciation. *Quarterly Review of Biology, 58,* 155–183.

Weuve, J., Korrick, S. A., Weisskopf, M. A., Ryan, L. M., Schwartz, J., Nie, H., et al. (2009). Cumulative exposure to lead in relation to cognitive function in older women. *Environmental Health Perspectives, 117,* 574–580.

Whaley, S. E., Sigman, M., Neumann, C., Bwibo, N., Guthrie, D., Weiss, R. E., et al. (2003). The impact of dietary intervention on the cognitive development of Kenyan school children. *Journal of Nutrition, 133,* 3965S–3971S.

Wheatley, J. R., Apicella, C. A., Burriss, R. P., Cárdenas, R. A., Bailey, D. H., Welling, L. L., et al. (2014). Women's faces and voices are cues to reproductive potential in industrial and forager societies. *Evolution and Human Behavior, 35,* 264–271.

White, D. R. (1988). Rethinking polygyny: Co-wives, codes, and cultural systems. *Current Anthropology, 29,* 529–572.

White, D. R., & Burton, M. L. (1988). Causes of polygyny: Ecology, economy, kinship, and warfare. *American Anthropologist, 90,* 871–887.

White, P. J., Fischer, R. B., & Meunier, G. F. (1984). The ability of females to predict male status via urinary odors. *Hormones and Behavior, 18,* 491–494.

White, P. J., Fischer, R. B., & Meunier, G. F. (1986). Female discrimination of male dominance by urine odor cues in hamsters. *Physiology & Behavior, 37,* 273–277.

White, C. L., Pistell, P. J., Purpera, M. N., Gupta, S., Fernandez-Kim, S. O., Hise, T. L., et al. (2009). Effects of high fat diet on Morris maze performance, oxidative stress, and inflammation in rats: Contributions of maternal diet. *Neurobiology of Disease, 35,* 3–13.

Whitesell, N. R., & Harter, S. (1996). The interpersonal context of emotion: Anger with close friends and classmates. *Child Development, 67,* 1345–1359.

Whiting, B. B., & Edwards, C. P. (1973). A cross-cultural analysis of sex differences in the behavior of children aged three through 11. *Journal of Social Psychology, 91,* 171–188.

Whiting, B. B., & Edwards, C. P. (1988). *Children of different worlds: The formation of social behavior*. Cambridge, MA: Harvard University Press.

Wickings, E. J., & Dixson, A. F. (1992). Testicular function, secondary sexual development, and social status in male mandrills (*Mandrillus sphinx*). *Physiology & Behavior*, *52*, 909–916.

Wieneke, M. H., & Dienst, E. R. (1995). Neuropsychological assessment of cognitive functioning following chemotherapy for, breast cancer. *Psycho-Oncology*, *4*, 61–66.

Wilkinson, G. S., Kahler, H., & Baker, R. H. (1998). Evolution of female mating preferences in stalk-eyed flies. *Behavioral Ecology*, *9*, 525–533.

Wilkinson, G. S., & Taper, M. (1999). Evolution of genetic variation for condition-dependent traits in stalk-eyed flies. *Proceedings of the Royal Society of London B*, *266*, 1685–1690.

Williams, G. C. (1966). *Adaptation and natural selection: A critique of some current evolutionary thought*. Princeton, NJ: Princeton University Press.

Williams, S. A., Jasarevic, E., Vandas, G. M., Warzak, D. A., Geary, D. C., Ellersieck, M. R., et al. (2013). Effects of developmental bisphenol A exposure on reproductive-related behaviors in California mice (*Peromyscus californicus*): A monogamous animal model. *PLoS ONE*, *8*, e55698.

Williams, M. A., & Mattingley, J. B. (2006). Do angry men get noticed? *Current Biology*, *16*, R402–R404.

Williams, C. L., & Meck, W. H. (1991). The organizational effects of gonadal steroids on sexually dimorphic spatial ability. *Psychoneuroendocrinology*, *16*, 155–176.

Willis, S. L., & Schaie, K. W. (1988). Gender differences in spatial ability in old age: Longitudinal and intervention findings. *Sex Roles*, *18*, 189–203.

Wilson, K. J. (2004). *Flight of the Huia: Ecology and conservation of New Zealand's frogs, reptiles, birds and mammals*. Christchurch, New Zealand: Canterbury University Press.

Wilson, A. B., Ahnesjö, I., Vincent, A. C. J., & Meyer, A. (2003). The dynamics of male brooding, mating patterns, and sex roles in pipefishes and seahorses (family *Syngnathidae*). *Evolution*, *57*, 1374–1386.

Wilson, M., & Daly, M. (1985). Competitiveness, risk taking, and violence: The young male syndrome. *Ethology and Sociobiology*, *6*, 59–73.

Wilson, J. R., De Fries, J. C., McClearn, G. E., Van Denberg, S. G., Johnson, R. C., & Rashad, M. N. (1975). Cognitive abilities: Use of family data as a control to assess sex and age differences in two ethnic groups. *International Journal of Aging and Human Development*, *6*, 261–276.

Winegard, B., Winegard, B., & Geary, D. C. (2014). Eastwood's brawn and Einstein's brain: An evolutionary account of dominance, prestige, and precarious manhood. *Review of General Psychology*, *18*, 34–48.

Winneke, G., Ranft, U., Wittsiepe, J., Kasper-Sonnenberg, M., Fürst, P., Krämer, U., et al. (2014). Behavioral sexual dimorphism in school-age children and early developmental exposure to dioxins and PCBs: A follow-up study of the Duisburg Cohort. *Environmental Health Perspectives*, *122*, 292–298.

Winslow, D. (1999). Rites of passage and group bonding in the Canadian airborne. *Armed Forces & Society*, *25*, 429–457.

Winstead, B. A. (1986). Sex differences in same-sex friendships. In V. J. Derlaga & B. A. Winstead (Eds.), *Friendship and social interaction* (pp. 81–99). New York: Springer-Verlag.

Witelson, S. F., Glezer, I. I., & Kigar, D. L. (1995). Women have greater density of neurons in posterior temporal cortex. *Journal of Neuroscience*, *15*, 3418–3428.

Wojcieszek, J. M., Nicholls, J. A., Marshall, N. J., & Goldizen, A. W. (2006). Theft of bower decorations among male satin bowerbirds (*Ptilonorhynchus violaceus*): Why are some decorations more popular than others? *Emu*, *106*, 175–180.

Wolf, O. T., Preut, R., Hellhammer, D. H., Kudielka, B. M., Schürmeyer, T. H., & Kirschbaum, C. (2000). Testosterone and cognition in elderly men: A single testosterone injection blocks the practice effect in verbal fluency, but has no effect on spatial or verbal memory. *Biological Psychiatry, 47*, 650–654.

Wolke, D., Samara, M., Bracewell, M., & Marlow, N. (2008). Specific language difficulties and school achievement in children born at 25 weeks of gestation or less. *Journal of Pediatrics, 152*, 256–262.

Wood, W., & Eagly, A. H. (2002). A cross-cultural analysis of the behavior of women and men: Implications for the origins of sex differences. *Psychological Bulletin, 128*, 699–727.

Wood, J. L., Heitmiller, D., Andreasen, N. C., & Nopoulos, P. (2008). Morphology of the ventral frontal cortex: Relationship to femininity and social cognition. *Cerebral Cortex, 18*, 534–540.

Woodgate, J. L., Buchanan, K. L., Bennett, A. T., Catchpole, C. K., Brighton, R., & Leitner, S. (2014). Environmental and genetic control of brain and song structure in the zebra finch. *Evolution, 68*, 230–240.

Woodgate, J. L., Leitner, S., Catchpole, C. K., Berg, M. L., Bennett, A. T. D., & Buchanan, K. L. (2011). Developmental stressors that impair song learning in males do not appear to affect female preferences for song complexity in the zebra finch. *Behavioral Ecology, 22*, 566–573.

Woolley, H. T. (1914). The psychology of sex. *Psychological Bulletin, 11*, 353–379.

Woon, F. L., & Hedges, D. W. (2008). Hippocampal and amygdala volumes in children and adults with childhood maltreatment-related posttraumatic stress disorder: A meta-analysis. *Hippocampus, 18*, 729–736.

Worden, B. D., & Parker, P. G. (2005). Females prefer noninfected males as mates in the grain beetle *Tenebrio molitor*: Evidence in pre- and postcopulatory behaviours. *Animal Behaviour, 70*, 1047–1053.

Worden, B. D., Parker, P. G., & Pappas, P. W. (2000). Parasites reduce attractiveness and reproductive success in male grain beetles. *Animal Behaviour, 59*, 543–550.

World Health Organization. (1948). *WHO definition of health*. New York: World Health Organization.

Wyatt, T. D. (2009). Fifty years of pheromones. *Nature, 457*, 262–263.

Wyman, M. T., Mooring, M. S., McCowan, B., Penedo, M. C. T., & Hart, L. A. (2008). Amplitude of bison bellows reflects male quality, physical condition and motivation. *Animal Behaviour, 76*, 1625–1639.

Wyman, M. T., Mooring, M. S., McCowan, B., Penedo, M. C. T., Reby, D., & Hart, L. A. (2012). Acoustic cues to size and quality in the vocalizations of male North American bison, *Bison bison*. *Animal Behaviour, 84*, 1381–1391.

Xu, X., Liu, X., Zhang, Q., Zhang, G., Lu, Y., Ruan, Q., et al. (2013). Sex-specific effects of bisphenol-A on memory and synaptic structural modification in hippocampus of adult mice. *Hormones and Behavior, 63*, 766–775.

Xu, X., Tian, D., Hong, X., Chen, L., & Xie, L. (2011). Sex-specific influence of exposure to bisphenol-A between adolescence and young adulthood on mouse behaviors. *Neuropharmacology, 61*, 565–573.

Xu, X. H., Zhang, J., Wang, Y. M., Ye, Y. P., & Luo, Q. Q. (2010). Perinatal exposure to bisphenol-A impairs learning-memory by concomitant down-regulation of N-methyl-D-aspartate receptors of hippocampus in male offspring mice. *Hormones and Behavior, 58*, 326–333.

Yang, J., Han, H., Cao, J., Li, L., & Xu, L. (2006). Prenatal stress modifies hippocampal synaptic plasticity and spatial learning in young rat offspring. *Hippocampus, 16*, 431–436.

Yap, P., Du, Z. W., Chen, R., Zhang, L. P., Wu, F. W., Wang, J., et al. (2012). Soil-transmitted helminth infections and physical fitness in school-aged Bulang children in southwest China: Results from a cross-sectional survey. *Parasites & Vectors, 5*, e50.

Yarbrough, C., Habicht, J. P., Malina, R. M., Lechtig, A., & Klein, R. E. (1975). Length and weight in rural Guatemalan Ladino children: Birth to seven years of age. *American Journal of Physical Anthropology, 42*, 439–447.

Yee, M. D., & Brown, R. (1992). Self-evaluations and intergroup attitudes in children aged three to nine. *Child Development, 63*, 619–629.

Yoon, D. Y., Mansukhani, N. A., Stubbs, V. C., Helenowski, I. B., Woodruff, T. K., & Kibbe, M. R. (2014). Sex bias exists in basic science and translational surgical research. *Surgery, 156*, 508–516.

Young, R., & Sweeting, H. (2004). Adolescent bullying, relationships, psychological well-being, and gender-atypical behavior: A gender diagnosticity approach. *Sex Roles, 50*, 525–537.

Yusuf, S., Hawken, S., Ôunpuu, S., Bautista, L., Franzosi, M. G., Commerford, P., et al. (2005). Obesity and risk of myocardial infarction in 27000 participants from 52 countries: A case–control study. *Lancet, 366*, 1640–1649.

Zaadstra, B. M., Seidell, J. C., Van Noord, P. A. H., Te Velde, E. R., Habbema, J. D. F., Vrieswijk, B., et al. (1993). Fat and female fecundity: Prospective study of effect of body fat distribution on conceptions rates. *British Medical Journal, 306*, 484–487.

Zagron, G., & Weinstock, M. (2006). Maternal adrenal hormone secretion mediates behavioural alterations induced by prenatal stress in male and female rats. *Behavioural Brain Research, 175*, 323–328.

Zahavi, A. (1975). Mate selection – A selection for a handicap. *Journal of Theoretical Biology, 53*, 205–214.

Zahavi, A., & Zahavi, A. (1997). *The handicap principle: A missing piece of Darwin's puzzle*. Oxford, UK: Oxford University Press.

Zala, S. M., Potts, W. K., & Penn, D. J. (2004). Scent-marking displays provide honest signals of health and infection. *Behavioral Ecology, 15*, 338–344.

Zann, R., & Cash, E. (2008). Developmental stress impairs song complexity but not learning accuracy in non-domesticated zebra finches (*Taeniopygia guttata*). *Behavioral Ecology and Sociobiology, 62*, 391–400.

Zanollo, V., Griggio, M., Robertson, J., & Kleindorfer, S. (2012). The number and coloration of white flank spots predict the strength of a cutaneous immune response in female Diamond Firetails, *Stagonopleura guttata*. *Journal of Ornithology, 153*, 1233–1244.

Zemel, B. S., Kawchak, D. A., Ohene-Frempong, K., Schall, J. I., & Stallings, V. A. (2007). Effects of delayed pubertal development, nutritional status, and disease severity on longitudinal patterns of growth failure in children with sickle cell disease. *Pediatric Research, 61*, 607–613.

Zhang, J. X., Zhang, Z. B., & Wang, Z. W. (2001). Scent, social status, and reproductive condition in rat-like hamsters (*Cricetulus triton*). *Physiology & Behavior, 74*, 415–420.

Zhou, H., Ohtsuka, R., He, Y., Yuan, L., Yamauchi, T., & Sleigh, A. C. (2005). Impact of parasitic infections and dietary intake on child growth in the schistosomiasis-endemic Dongting Lake Region, China. *American Journal of Tropical Medicine and Hygiene, 72*, 534–539.

Zimmerman, I. L., Steiner, V. G., & Pond, R. E. (2011). *Preschool language scale* (5th ed.). San Antonio, TX: Psychological Corporation.

Zimmermann, M. B., Connolly, K., Bozo, M., Bridson, J., Rohner, F., & Grimci, L. (2006). Iodine supplementation improves cognition in iodine-deficient schoolchildren in Albania: A randomized, controlled, double-blind study. *American Journal of Clinical Nutrition, 83*, 108–114.

Zimmermann, R. R., Geist, C. R., & Ackles, P. K. (1975). Changes in the social behavior of rhesus monkeys during rehabilitation from prolonged protein-calorie malnutrition. *Behavioral Biology, 14*, 325–333.

Zimmermann, R. R., Steere, P. L., Strobel, D. A., & Hom, H. L. (1972). Abnormal social development of protein-malnourished rhesus monkeys. *Journal of Abnormal Psychology, 80*, 125–131.

Zonnevijlle-Bendek, M. J. S., Van Goozen, S. H. M., Cohen-Kettenis, P. T., Van Elburg, A., & Van Engeland, H. (2002). Do adolescent anorexia nervosa patients have deficits in emotional functioning? *European Child & Adolescent Psychiatry, 11*, 38–42.

Zonnevylle-Bender, M. J., Van Goozen, S. H., Cohen-Kettenis, P. T., van Elburg, T. A., & Van Engeland, H. (2004). Emotional functioning in adolescent anorexia nervosa patients. *European Child & Adolescent Psychiatry, 13*, 28–34.

Zucker, K. J. (2005). Gender identity disorder in children and adolescents. *Annual Review of Clinical Psychology, 1*, 467–492.

Zuckerman, M., & Kuhlman, D. M. (2000). Personality and risk-taking: Common biosocial factors. *Journal of Personality, 68*, 999–1029.

Zuena, A. R., Mairesse, J., Casolini, P., Cinque, C., Alemà, G. S., Morley-Fletcher, S., et al. (2008). Prenatal restraint stress generates two distinct behavioral and neurochemical profiles in male and female rats. *PLoS ONE, 3*, e2170.

Zuk, M., & Johnsen, T. S. (1998). Seasonal changes in the relationship between ornamentation and immune response in red jungle fowl. *Proceedings of the Royal Society of London B, 265*, 1631–1635.

Zuk, M., Johnsen, T. S., & Maclarty, T. (1995). Endocrine-immune interactions, ornaments and mate choice in red jungle fowl. *Proceedings of the Royal Society of London B, 260*, 205–210.

Zuk, M., Popma, S. L., & Johnsen, T. S. (1995). Male courtship displays, ornaments and female mate choice in captive red jungle fowl. *Behaviour, 132*, 821–836.

Zuk, M., Thornhill, R., & Ligon, J. D. (1990). Parasites and mate choice in red jungle fowl. *American Zoologist, 30*, 235–244.

# Species Index for Tables

| Common Name | Scientific Name | Table |
|---|---|---|
| African buffalo | *Syncerus caffer* | 4.5 |
| African butterfly | *Bicyclus anynana* | 4.2, 4.3 |
| African elephant | *Loxodonta africana* | 4.6 |
| Alpine ibex | *Capra ibex* | 4.5 |
| Ambush bug | *Phymata americana* | 4.1 |
| American goldfinch | *Spinus tristis* | 3.1, 3.2 |
| American kestrels | *Falco sparverius* | 3.1 |
| Anna's hummingbird | *Calypte anna* | 3.1 |
| Armed Beetle | *Gnatocerus cornutus* | 4.2 |
| Asian elephant | *Elephas maximus* | 4.6 |
| Atlantic canary | *Serinus canaria* | 3.3, 3.4 |
| Australian rabbit | *Oryctolagus cuniculus* | 4.7 |
| Bank vole | *Myodes glareolus* | 4.6 |
| Barn swallow | *Hirundo rustica* | 3.2 |
| Bighorn sheep | *Ovis canadensis* | 4.5 |
| Black field cricket | *Teleogryllus commodus* | 4.3 |
| Black grouse | *Tetrao tetrix* | 3.1, 3.2 |
| Black-and-white colobus | *Colobus guereza* | 4.7 |
| Blackbirds | *Turdus merula* | 3.1 |
| Blue grosbeaks | *Guiraca caerulea* | 3.1 |
| Blue tit | *Parus caeruleus* | 3.1 |
| Blue-black grassquits | *Volatinia jacarina* | 3.1 |
| Brown lemming | *Lemmus trimucronatus* | 4.6 |

*Continued*

| Common Name | Scientific Name | Table |
|---|---|---|
| Gelada baboon | *Theropithecus gelada* | 4.4 |
| Golden hamster | *Mesocricetus auratus* | 4.6, 4.7 |
| Grain beetle | *Tenebrio molitor* | 4.2 |
| Grass butterfly | *Eurema hecabe* | 4.1 |
| Great tit | *Parus major* | 3.1, 3.2, 3.3, 3.4 |
| Greenfinch | *Carduelis chloris* | 3.1 |
| Guppy | *Poecilia reticulata* | 3.5, 3.6, 3.7 |
| Hihi | *Notiomystis cincta* | 3.1 |
| Houbara bustard | *Chlamydotis undulata* | 3.3 |
| House finch | *Carpodacus mexicanus* | 3.1 |
| House sparrow | *Passer domesticus* | 3.1, 3.2 |
| Human | *Homo sapiens* | 6.1, 6.2, 6.3, 7.1, 7.2, 7.3 |
| Jackson's widowbird | *Euplectes jacksoni* | 3.2, 3.3 |
| Jumping spider | *Cosmophasis umbratica* | 4.1 |
| Junco | *Junco hyemalis* | 3.1, 3.2, 3.3 |
| Lion | *Panthera leo* | 4.4, 4.5, 4.7 |
| Long-tailed hamster | *Tscherskia triton* | 4.7 |
| Macaque | *Macaca sylvanus* | 4.7 |
| | *Macaca mulatta* | 4.4 |
| Mallard duck | *Anas platyrhynchos* | 3.1 |
| Mandrill | *Mandrillus sphinx* | 4.4, 4.5 |
| Marmoset | *Callithrix jacchus* | 4.6, 4.7 |
| Meadow vole | *Microtus pennsylvanicus* | 4.7 |
| Mouse | *Mus musculus* | 4.6, 4.7. 4.8 |
| | *Peromyscus maniculatus* | 4.7, 4.8 |
| | *Peromyscus californicus* | 4.7 |
| North American bison | *Bison bison* | 4.7 |
| Northern elephant seal | *Mirounga angustirostris* | 4.7 |
| Northern harrier | *Circus cyaneus* | 3.3 |

*Continued*

| Common Name | Scientific Name | Table |
|---|---|---|
| Ursine colobus | *Colobus vellerosus* | 4.7 |
| Vervet | *Cercopithecus aethiop* | 4.4 |
| Waltzing fly | *Prochyliza xanthostoma* | 4.2 |
| Water strider | *Gerris incognitus* | 4.2 |
| White throated bat | *Lophostoma silvicolum* | 4.7 |
| White-crowned sparrow | *Zonotrichia leucophrys* | 3.3 |
| White-tailed deer | *Odocoileus virginianus* | 4.5 |
| Wild turkeys | *Meleagris gallopavo* | 3.1, 3.2 |
| Wolf spider | *Hygrolycosa rubrofasciata* | 4.3 |
| Yellow baboon | *Papio cynocephalus* | 4.7 |
| Yellow-legged gull | *Larus michahellis* | 3.1, 3.2 |
| Zebra finch | *Taeniopygia guttata* | 3.1, 3.2, 3.3, 3.4 |

# Author Index

Note: Page numbers followed by *f* indicate figures and *t* indicate tables.

# Subject Index

Note: Page numbers followed by *f* indicate figures and *t* indicate tables.

**FIGURE 2.1**    The male (front) and female (back) huia (*Heteralocha acutirostris*) from Buller and Keulemans (1888, Vol. 1, p. Plate II). The differences in bill shape were (the species is now extinct) thought to reflect differences in foraging strategy (Wilson, 2004).

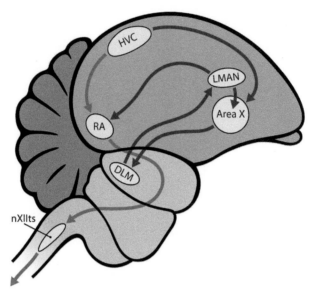

**FIGURE 2.4** Brain systems that support bird song. HVC is not an acronym but is sometimes termed higher (or high) vocal center; RA, robust nucleus of the arcopallium; nXIIts, tracheosyringeal half of the hypoglossal nucleus; LMAN, lateral magnocellular nucleus of the nidopallium; DLM, dorsolateral anterior thalamic nucleus; area X, portion of the basal ganglia. *From Nottebohm (2005). Creative commons license. http://www.plosbiology.org/article/info%3Adoi%2F10.1371%2Fjournal.pbio.0030164.*

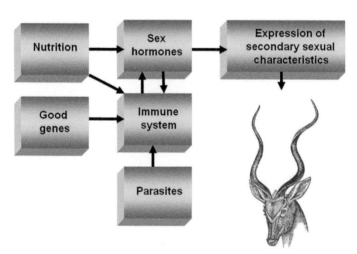

**FIGURE 2.5** Hypothesized relations among sex hormones, immune functioning, parasites, and the expression of secondary sexual characteristics. From Geary (2010, p. 99). Male kudu (*Strepsiceros kudu*) from Darwin (1871, p. 255).

**PHOTO 2.1** Two male northern elephant seals (*Mirounga angustirostris*) fighting for control of a harem. *Photo credit: Dawn Endio, 2004. Creative Commons License. http://commons.wikimedia. org/wiki/File:Elephant_seal_fight_Part-1.jpg.*

**PHOTO 2.2** Lekking black grouse (*Tetrao tetrix*) males during mating season. Males compete for location at the center of the lek. Females visit multiple males, especially central males, and choose a mate based on plumage and red comb color as well as the vigor of the courtship display.

**PHOTO 2.3** Male satin bowerbirds (*Ptilonorhynchus violaceus*) build bowers to attract females. *Photo credit: Gary Curtis, 2005. Creative commons license. http://commons.wikimedia.org/wiki/ File:BowerOfSatinBowerbird.jpg.*

**PHOTO 2.4** The male peafowl (*Pavo cristatus*) displays feathers to would-be mates, and females choose mates based on the number, density, and blue-green color of the males' eyespots.

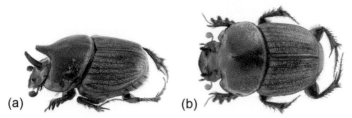

**PHOTO 2.5** Female (a) and male (b) dung beetle (*Onthophagus sagittarius*). Females with larger horns outcompete females with smaller horns for control of burrows and dung. *Photo credit: Schmidt (2009). Creative commons license. http://commons.wikimedia.org/wiki/File:Onthophagus_ sagittarius_Fabricius,_1775_female_(4140682509).jpg.*

**PHOTO 2.6** The red beak of the male zebra finch (*Taeniopygia guttata*) is an indicator of the quantity of carotenoids in the diet and the ability to efficiently process them. When exposed to stressors or pathogens carotenoids are diverted to the associated physiological reactions, resulting in a bleaching of beak color.

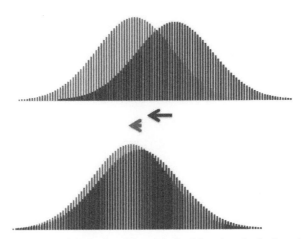

**FIGURE 3.1** Sexual or social selection will result in the elaboration of traits that enhance or signal competitive abilities or influence mate choices. The top distributions show how these processes result in larger traits (darker color) in one sex versus the other; or larger sexually selected than naturally selected traits in the same individual. Exposure to stressors has stronger effects on the elaborated than the contrast trait (bottom).

**PHOTO 3.1**    The yellow plumage of the male American goldfinch (*Spinus tristis*) is dependent on adequate dietary carotenoids and signals health of their immune system.

**PHOTO 3.2**    The red color of the comb on the top of the head of the male red jungle fowl (*Gallus gallus*) is dependent in part on adequate dietary carotenoids and exposure to male hormones. Females prefer males with larger and brighter combs as mates.

**PHOTO 3.3** The blue plumage of the male grosbeak (*Guiraca caerulea*) illustrates a structural color that signals male condition during the time when new feathers are developing.

**PHOTO 3.4** Anna's hummingbird (*Calypte anna*) males erect the magenta throat and crown feathers in dominance displays to other males and to attract females.

**PHOTO 3.5**   The size of the black head cap and the breast stripe of the great tit (*Parus major*) signal the males' ability to withstand infections and exposure to man-made toxins.

**PHOTO 3.6**   The size of the white spots of the female diamond firetail (*Stagonopleura guttata*) indicates the health of their immune system.

**PHOTO 3.7** To attract mates, males of the magnificent frigatebird (*Fregata magnificens*) inflate their red gular pouch, spread their wings, and point their beak upwards. Males with higher testosterone levels and in better physical condition engage in this courtship display more frequently than do other males. *Photo credit: Andrew Turner, 2011. Creative Commons license: http://commons. wikimedia.org/wiki/File:Fregata_magnificens_-Galapagos,_Ecuador_-male-8.jpg.*

**PHOTO 3.8** For the male guppy (*Poecilia reticulata*), color of the fins, especially the orange, makes them attractive to females and is a good indicator of their ability to cope with dietary stressors, infections, and exposure to man-made toxins.

**PHOTO 4.1** Males of the thick-legged fiddler crab (*Uca crassipes*) attempt to attract females by waving their enlarged claw, and fight for possession of burrows in which mating occurs and females lay and incubate their eggs. *Photo credit: Thomas Brown, 2011. Creative Commons license: http://commons.wikimedia.org/wiki/File:Fiddler_Crab_(Uca_crassipes%3F)_(6262758647).jpg.*

**PHOTO 4.2** The dark, melanin-based color of the male wings of the damselfly species *Mnais costalis* is a good indicator of physical condition. *Photo credit: Alpsdake, 2012. Creative Commons license: http://commons.wikimedia.org/wiki/File:Mnais_costalis_male_on_Iris_japonica.JPG#filelinks.*

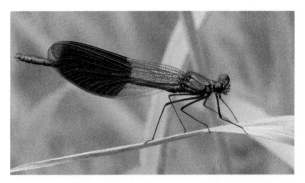

**PHOTO 4.3**   The dark, melanin-based color of the male wings of the damselfly species *Calopteryx splendens* is a good indicator of immune system health. *Photo credit: Andreas Eichler, 2013. Creative Commons license: http://commons.wikimedia.org/wiki/File:2013.08.04.-12-Ladenburg-Gebaenderte_Prachtlibelle-Maennchen.jpg.*

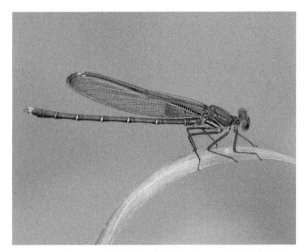

**PHOTO 4.4**   For males of the American rubyspot (*Hetaerina americana*), the size of the red wing spot signals social dominance to other males and to females, and is an indicator of the males' current resistance to parasites and quality of their developmental diet.

**PHOTO 4.5**   The pattern of the melanin patch (within the yellow) on the face of the female paper wasp (*Polistes dominulus*) is an indicator of social dominance and is influenced by quality of the developmental diet. *Photo by Zurab Tabatadze (© MzePhotos.com), used with permission.*

**PHOTO 4.6**   The length of males' eye span in most species of stalk-eyed fly (*Diopsidae*) varies with their physical condition, quality of their developmental diet, and inbreeding. *Photo credit: Hauke Koch, 2006. Creative Commons license: http://commons.wikimedia.org/wiki/File:Diopsid2.jpg.*

**PHOTO 4.7** Mature and socially dominant male mandrills (*Mandrillus sphinx*) sport blue (structural color) and red (likely related to oxygenated blood) facial signals. The red coloration is related to testosterone levels and social dominance; the blue may also correlate with dominance in some groups.

**PHOTO 4.8** The blue scrotal color of the male vervet (*Cercopithecus aethiop*) signals social dominance. *Photo credit: Stig Nygaard, 2007. Creative Commons license: http://commons.wikimedia. org/wiki/File:Black_faced_vervet_monkey.*

**PHOTO 4.9** The red chest patch of the male gelada baboon (*Theropithecus gelada*) is a signal of social dominance.

**PHOTO 4.10** Antler size of the male red deer (*Cervus elaphus*) is an indicator of social dominance and sperm quality.

**PHOTO 4.11**   Horn size of the male alpine ibex (*Capra ibex*) is an indicator of genetic diversity and nutritional condition during development.

**PHOTO 4.12**   The scent of a dominant female marmoset (*Callithrix jacchus*) can suppress the reproduction of subordinate females. *Photo credit: Leszek Leszczynski, 2012. Creative Commons license: http://commons.wikimedia.org/wiki/File:Common_marmoset_(Callithrix_jacchus).jpg.*

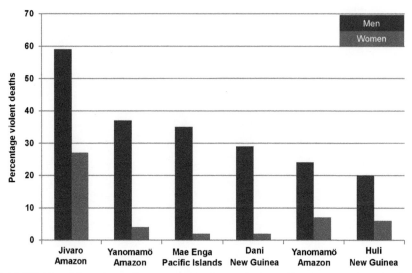

**FIGURE 5.3** Estimated mortality rates resulting from ambushes, raids, or larger-scale warfare for six traditional societies. The two estimates for the Yanomamö are for different groups. *Based on data presented in Keeley (1996).*

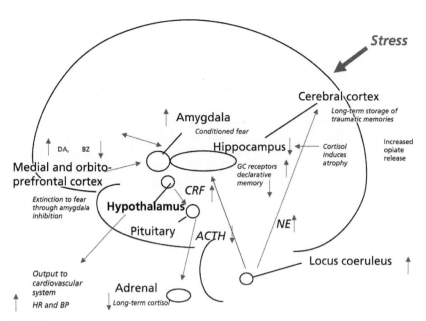

**FIGURE 5.5** The key integrated brain regions involved in stress regulation. *From Traumatic stress: Effects on the brain.* Dialogues in Clinical Neuroscience, *by J. D. Bremner, p. 447, Copyright 2006. Reprinted with permission of the author.*

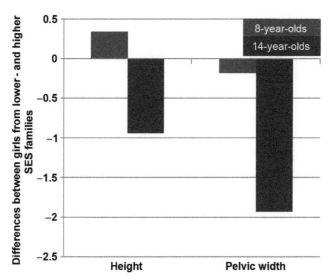

**FIGURE 6.1** The figure shows standard deviation differences (lower SES–higher SES) in height and pelvic width for 8- and 14-year-olds from lower SES and higher SES families. Eight-year-olds from lower SES families were somewhat taller than their higher-SES peers, but this reversed for 14-year-olds. Critically, the SES gap for pelvic width was larger than that for height and was nearly twice as large in adolescence as in childhood. *Based on data presented in Hautvast (1971).*

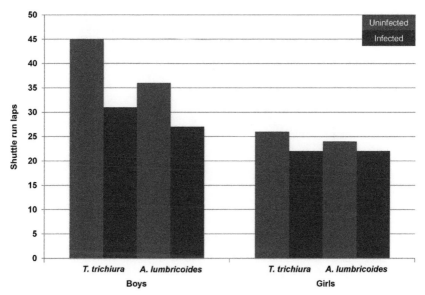

**FIGURE 6.2** Relative to healthy same-sex peers, boys infected with one or two common parasitic worms showed larger decrements in fitness than did infected girls, based on the commonly used shuttle run measure, whereby fitness is determined by the number of 20-m back-and-forth laps that can be completed in a fixed amount of time. *Based on data (combined across children and adolescents) presented in Yap et al. (2012).*

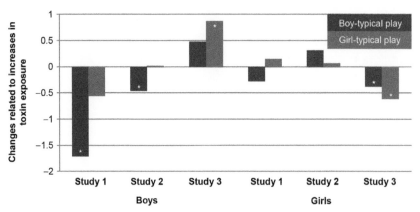

**FIGURE 6.3** Estimated changes in standard deviation units resulting from a doubling of toxin exposure. *Statistically significant effect. Different mixtures of toxins were assessed across studies, and thus general conclusions about toxin exposure and the nature of changes in children's play cannot be drawn. The critical point is exposure to toxins consistently changes sex-typical play in boys and sometimes in girls. *Based on data presented in Swan et al. (2010, Study 1), Vreugdenhil et al. (2002, Study 2), and Winneke et al. (2014, Study 3).*

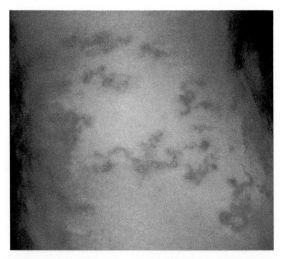

**PHOTO 6.1** Skin lesions due to infection with parasitic worms are common in the developing world. The photo shows the migration of the larva of one species of hookworm (*Ancylostoma braziliense*). *Photo credit, Weis Sagung, 2009. Creative Commons license: http://commons.wikimedia. org/wiki/File:Larva_Migrans_Cutanea.jpg.*

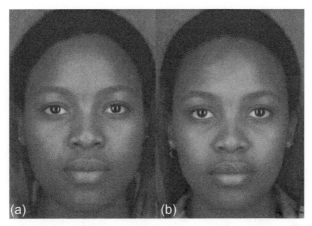

**PHOTO 6.2** Composite images of low (a) and high attractive (b) women. Several factors influence rated attractiveness, including homogeneity of skin color and a slight yellow coloration. The latter is correlated with skin carotenoid levels. *From African perceptions of female attractiveness, by Coetzee et al., 2012. Creative commons license, http://www.plosone.org/article/info%3Adoi%2F10.1371%2Fjournal.pone.0048116.*

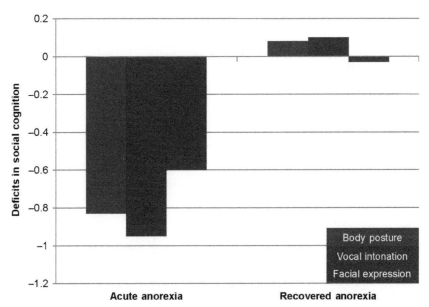

**FIGURE 7.1** Social-cognitive deficits for women with acute anorexia and those who have recovered from anorexia relative to healthy women. *Based on data presented in Oldershaw et al. (2010).*

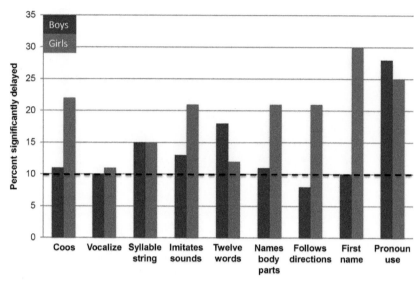

**FIGURE 7.2** Delays in the onset of significant language milestones for girls and boys born prematurely. *Based on data presented in Largo et al. (1986).*

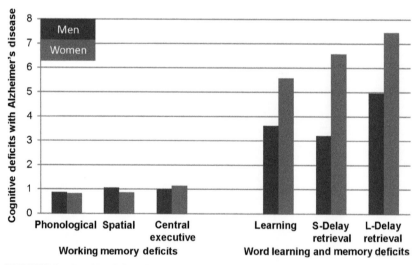

**FIGURE 7.3** Cognitive deficits for men and women with Alzheimer's disease relative to healthy same-sex adults S, short; L, long. *Based on data presented in Beinhoff et al. (2008).*

**FIGURE 7.4**  Mental rotation task.

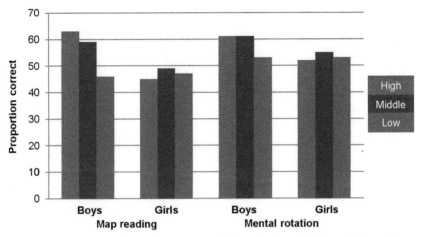

**FIGURE 7.5**  Spatial abilities of boys and girls from families of high-, middle-, and low-socioeconomic status. *Based on data presented in Levine et al. (2005).*

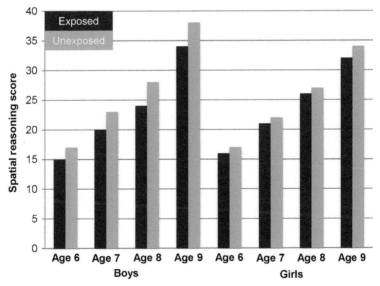

**FIGURE 7.6**  Boys prenatally exposed to polychlorinated biphenyls had significantly lower spatial reasoning scores than unexposed boys matched on age and demographic factors. *Based on data presented in Guo et al. (1995).*

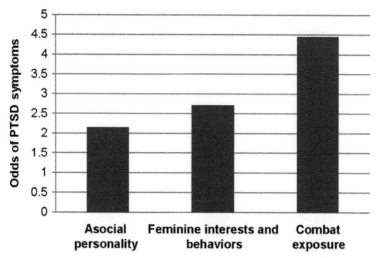

**FIGURE 7.7** The odds of having combat-related post-traumatic stress disorder (PTSD) symptoms. *Based on data presented in Schnurr et al. (1993).*